Office 97 Annoyances

Office 97 Annoyances

Woody Leonhard, Lee Hudspeth,
and T.J. Lee

O'REILLY™

Cambridge · Köln · Paris · Sebastopol · Tokyo

Office 97 Annoyances
by Woody Leonhard, Lee Hudspeth, and T.J. Lee

Copyright © 1997 PRIME Consulting Group, Inc. All rights reserved.
Portions of Chapters 3 and 4 Copyright © 1997 by Pinecliffe International.
Printed in the United States of America.

Published by O'Reilly & Associates, Inc., 101 Morris Street, Sebastopol, CA 95472.

Editor: Ron Petrusha

Production Editor: Clairemarie Fisher O'Leary

Printing History:

October 1997:   First Edition

This book is printed on acid-free paper with 85% recycled content, 15% post-consumer waste. O'Reilly & Associates is committed to using paper with the highest recycled content available consistent with high quality.

ISBN: 1-56592-310-3   [2/98]*

Four years ago, Linda and I started a non-profit organization called the Tibetan Children's Fund. As of this writing TCF sponsors more than 150 refugee children in northern India and Nepal. These children are chosen on the basis of financial need and scholastic performance—particularly in English, math, and science. Most of them come from families that can only be described as destitute; many have been orphaned. Few of the refugee families have more than one room to call their own, many live in shanties, and none can afford medical care on even the most basic level.

TCF exists because of people like you. A significant portion of the proceeds from the sale of this book go to the TCF. Donations from people like you make TCF possible. Yes, computer geeks *do* care. And the donations are deductible.

The Tibetan Children's Fund is a unique organization. Nobody draws a salary. There's no "overhead." Volunteers who travel to India pay their own way. They don't solicit donations by phone, or hire companies to mount advertising campaigns. When they need to put something together—say, a new brochure, or a newsletter, or a web page—volunteers do the work, and companies donate the supplies. The net result: every single penny donated by individuals goes directly to the children. I know. I keep a close eye on it. My money's in there, too.

TCF isn't a religious organization. It isn't a political organization. It isn't a welfare organization, either. Sponsored kids must maintain good grades or they're put on probation. If they still can't keep their grades up, we remove them, to make way for kids who can. TCF has no particular axe to grind or point of view to impose: they just want to give the kids a chance to succeed in the world at large. Heaven knows the Tibetans have had a terrible time just surviving.

I could write about TCF's successes, and its failures, but the tales would fill a book. Suffice it to say that TCF has been very fortunate to find and support a handful of really brilliant refugee kids—and it's been unfortunate enough to see more than a few children die, when good medical care at the right time would've made all the difference.

If you would like to know more about TCF, please write to:

Tibetan's Children Fund
Post Office Box 473
Pinecliffe, Colorado USA 80471
Phone: (303) 642-0492
Email: *woody@wopr.com*

Thanks for your help.

— Woody Leonhard
Coal Creek Canyon, Colorado

Table of Contents

Preface

Microsoft keeps asking us all, "Where do you want to go today?" Are they kidding? You know where you want to go today, we know where you want to go today; the only group that seems to be unclear on this issue is Microsoft. You want to get your work done and go home! Microsoft and its PR spin-meisters have lost track of the fact that you have a real life and you'd like to spend some time living it. What you want is to have your software help you get your work done so you can flip your PC's power switch to that lovely OFF position and call it a day. Your software should help you achieve this goal, and therein lies the rub.

Too often, the software gets in the way. Enter Microsoft Office. A tour-de-force of programming power. Access, Excel, Outlook, PowerPoint, and Word, all standing by to let you whip through your workday. But there's a fly in the virtual ointment. If Office is the be-all and end-all of application suites, why does it feel that sometimes Office is more part of the problem than the solution? Why doesn't each application in the Office suite work precisely the same way? Word does something one way, Excel does the same thing only slightly differently, PowerPoint does it very differently, and Access won't do it at all—it's enough to make you scream. Don't believe it? Try moving your names and addresses from Access to Outlook and see if you don't hit a high C.

Face it, Office is amazing when it's not being so blasted annoying.

Office occupies over 200 megabytes on your hard disk, yet with all the cool code hiding behind the curtain, all too often logic seems to have been thrown to the winds—some aspects of Office simply do not work the way a rational person (that's you) would expect them to. This (a) makes you crazy, which (b) keeps you from getting your work done, which in turn causes (c) see item (a). A vicious circle if there ever was one.

Now for the good news. What you need is for someone (that's us) to show you the ropes so you can turn Office into a superb surgical tool instead of a millstone around your cyberneck. This book will do just that. We'll show you how to change default settings, where to find the feature you so desperately need but that has been hidden three levels deep in some obscure dialog box, how to remove the protect-you-from-yourself-at-all-costs cotton batting that Microsoft insists on sticking into the Office machinery, how to actually employ some of this Internet hype for useful purposes, and more. We're here for you.

The Book's Audience

Despite what certain marketeers want you to think, you are not stupid. Nor are you a dummy, although many a beginner has drawn this erroneous conclusion. After all, Microsoft is an immense mega-buck software powerhouse; Office comes on a high-tech CD-ROM; it runs on a high-speed, techno-marvel computer that rivals the supercomputers of just a few years ago; so when things don't work right, you must be the dummy, right? It can't be the software, can it?

Take it from us. *It's the software.*

Whether you are a novice with a creepy feeling that maybe it's not you but Office that's crazy, or an experienced software guru who has been around long enough to know when to get ticked at a program's annoying inconsistencies and misbehaviors, relief is at hand. Literally, *in* your hands.

This book will jump-start you; help you get more out of Microsoft Office and avoid the time-wasting sinkholes that are scattered liberally throughout. If you only use one of the big five applications in Office and would like to start using the others applications that make up the suite, we'll get you started. If you are already familiar with the various applications but want to dig a bit deeper into the hot new features in this suite, we can help you too. And if you've ever gotten annoyed with the behavior of an Office application, been driven right up the wall by some inane problem, this book is for you.

Organization of This Book

The book contains eight chapters.

Chapter 1, *Initial Inanities*, discusses the causes and nature of annoyances in Office. An annoyance can arise from the complexity of the base problem itself—for example, trying to move information from a relational database (Access) to a flat-file database (Outlook). It could be a shift in the underlying paradigm, as in Word, where you have to make a conceptual leap from the typewriter era to the desktop publishing era. Annoyances can also arise from the way an application was designed, as in the case of Outlook's non-standard and non-customizable user interface. Then there's the fascinating category of annoyances arising from some truly bone-headed decision-making back in the development lab; a case in point is the maddeningly awkward process for installing Microsoft's very cool sounds.

Chapter 2, *Vital Changes and Settings*, shows you how to optimize Windows 95 as well as how to set up Microsoft Office to get the most bang for your buck. Deal with your StartUp folder, disable components that cause more problems than they solve, customize your Office Shortcut Bar, find all the pan-Office user-changeable settings—this chapter covers them all. Also included in this chapter are the top customizing tips for turning your Office applications into fine-tuned custom workhorses.

Chapter 3, *Introduction to Office Macros*, is a tutorial on the macro language Visual Basic for Applications (VBA). This chapter discusses working within the VB Editor and walks you through creating several complete VBA programs. We show you how to use VBA to control Office applications; find out just what the heck an object model is; and assign macros to toolbars, menus, and keyboard shortcuts.

Chapter 4, *VBA Fights Office Annoyances*, continues your sojourn into the world of Office macros. Use VBA to fix a plethora of specific annoyances in Excel, PowerPoint, and Word. Tackle common problems and see how easy it is to correct errant behavior with VBA.

Chapter 5, Hard-Core Office, covers the hottest new features and annoyances to be found in each of the various Office applications. In Access, Excel, Outlook, PowerPoint, and Word, we'll point you toward lots of hidden gems you might not be aware of and help you avoid some of the lurking bogs and pitfalls, with workarounds and fixes wherever possible.

Chapter 6, *More Hard-Core Office*, covers the pan-Office features, the Binder, the new semi-intelligent Office Assistant, Office Art, and the secret treasures of the ValuPack. We'll also look at the biggest common problem to all Office applications—the growing macro virus threat and what you'd better be doing about it.

Chapter 7, *Strategies*, shifts into high gear and shows you step by step how to utilize some of the coolest features in Office, from getting the latest help online to developing real Internet/intranet (or no-Net-at-all) solutions with the new hyperlink feature. We'll also deal with moving your names and addresses from the Exchange PAB into Outlook. Carpe diem!

Chapter 8, *Where and How to Get Help*, is a discussion of your best sources for additional help and information on Office. Magazines, newsletters, listservers, and Web sites—we point you in the right direction for the latest and greatest sources of news and knowledge on Office.

Conventions in This Book

Throughout this book we've used the following typographic conventions:

`Constant width`
> indicates a language construct such as in VBA. Code fragments and code examples appear exclusively in constant-width text. In syntax statements, text in constant width indicates such language elements as the function's or procedure's name and any invariable elements required by the syntax. Key combinations are also shown in constant width, as are VBA language statements (like `FOR...NEXT`) and constants.

Italic
> in command syntax indicates parameter names. Italicized words in the text also represent the names of procedures and functions, as well as variable and parameter names. System elements like filenames and path names also are italicized.

➤
> is used to indicate a drop-down or pop-up menu command. For instance, the Tools menu pops down, revealing Macro, which in turn has a submenu. To indicate the selection Macros from this submenu, we would write Tools ➤ Macro ➤ Macros.

How to Contact Us

We have tested and verified all the information in this book to the best of our ability, but you may find that features have changed (or even that we have made mistakes!). Please let us know about any errors you find, as well as your suggestions for future editions, by writing to:

O'Reilly & Associates, Inc.
101 Morris Street
Sebastopol, CA 95472
1-800-998-9938 (in the U.S. or Canada)
1-707-829-0515 (international/local)
1-707-829-0104 (FAX)

You can also send messages electronically. To be put on our mailing list or to request a catalog, send email to:

nuts@oreilly.com

To ask technical questions or comment on the book, send email to:

bookquestions@oreilly.com

Obtaining Updated Information

The VBA code listings in *Office 97 Annoyances* can be found on our web site at *ftp://ftp.oreilly.com/published/oreilly/windows/office.annoy.* These code listings, updates to the material contained in this book, plus information on the other books in the *Annoyances* series are also available on our web sites *http://www.wopr.com* and *http://www.primeconsulting.com.*

Acknowledgments

Our heartfelt thanks to Ron Petrusha, without whose help and guidance this series would not exist. Troy Mott also played an important part in getting this book in print. Claudette Moore was the linchpin that held everything together. Many thanks to M. David Stone, not only for his technical help but for his counseling and guidance; he is a true mentor. Thanks also to Don Buchanan, the emir of Excel comedy; the amazing Ronald Beekelaar, who is never at a loss for a new Word tip; Dan Butler, general Internet genius; and Al Gordon, a daring Outlook pioneer.

We'd also like to thank Helen Feddema for her insight into Access and all things database, and for her quintessential writing contribution of the Access section in Chapter 5.

Thanks to everyone who worked on production of this book. Clairemarie Fisher O'Leary was the project manager and production editor; John Files was the copyeditor; Seth Maislin created the index; Robert Romano created the screenshots; Elissa Haney provided production assistance; and Jane Ellin and Sheryl Avruch provided quality control.

Woody would like to personally thank his loving wife Linda, who's been putting up with him for 20 years, and his nine-year-old son Justin, who already describes himself as a computer nerd. Their considerable accomplishments have made him very proud. Woody would also like to mention Jud and Linda Schroeder, and all the folks at Lancer Corporation in Texas, for their help with Tibetan refugee children. You've made a big difference for those kids—given them chances they never would have had—and saved more than a few lives in the process. I appreciate your help from the bottom of my heart. And Jim Vanderford, who taught me how to say, uh, things in one syllable.

T. J. Lee thanks his wife to whom all good things in his life are directly attributable, his four kids who are just generally wonderful, and Matthew T. Smith, who always wanted to see his name mentioned in a computer book.

From Lee Hudspeth, heartfelt thanks all around to my endearing wife Liz, our son Aaron, my parents Eloise and George, and my second mom Gloria.

And from all of us to all of you out there who use Microsoft Office in the trenches, fighting annoyances day in and day out while trying to retain your sanity. We salute you!

1

Initial Inanities

Back in the olden days, each computer program you used had a completely different interface. This made them difficult to learn and to work with. So some upstart thought that it would be great if you could buy a spreadsheet, word processor, graphics, and communications package all rolled into a single, tightly integrated piece of software. Several attempts were made at doing this, and some of them were actually pretty good. But the big players (who did not have such a product) pooh-poohed the effort and initiated a media blitz about how you needed to purchase the "best of breed" in each major software category. And so the first attempts at integrated software suites died a gruesome death on the retail shelves.

Of course now that the software industry has, shall we say, *consolidated* a bit, the new media blitz tells us that a suite of products all from the same manufacturer is just the ticket for computing nirvana. You've absolutely got to get a product like Microsoft Office with a fully developed user interface that works the same way in each application in the suite. Each product is tightly integrated with all the others, easy to learn, easy to use, so chock full of IntelliSense wonderment, why, it'll get you wherever you want to go today.

Bunk!

Office goes a long way towards the ideal that the Redmond Rangers would have you believe it is, and you can actually get some real work done with Office. But unless you know where the reality falls short— sometimes very short—of the hyperbole, you'll be wheel spinning instead of getting productive work done. That's where this book comes in.

1

Just Plain Annoying

Does Office bug the living daylights out of you? Us too. Why, for the love of a 40-hour work week, does Word tackle Feature X one way, Excel another way, and heck, PowerPoint not do it at all?! If it's all supposed to look and feel the same, then why doesn't it? You'd think that the various Office development teams would at least slip the occasional note under the door to each other.

Over 200 megabytes of *stuff* makes up the Office suite, and it is truly a marvelous piece of modern engineering. It is an incredibly useful piece of software, and we all use it all day, every day. Now, if it just wasn't so blasted . . . annoying! Honestly, you could just scream. Not that it helps— we've tried it. Sure it feels good for the moment, but it's not really a long-term solution. What's needed is a way to get a handle on the many annoy-ances that are lurking in this vast software behemoth.

A lot of Office just doesn't behave the way any marginally sane program would behave. Lots of built-in features that are supposed to help novice users just get in their way—and it's devilishly difficult turning many of those features off. Some of the most usable stuff is buried three levels deep in obscure dialog boxes. Default settings—the options that control Office if you do nothing to change them—are meant to make Office more accessible to new users, but all too frequently they make things so inscru-table that new users waste hours in limbo, trading one blind alley for another. For experienced Office users, the training wheels and the protect-you-from-yourself-at-all-costs cotton batting constantly interfere with your productivity. It's all just downright depressing.

To make matters worse, many of the various Office components seem as if they were developed in a vacuum. Consider this: just how many mutu-ally inaccessible address books do you need? Arrghhh! The evolution of Office has left us with names and addresses in Access databases, Excel lists, various Schedule+ and Exchange address books, the Personal Address Book, and now the new Outlook Contacts module. Try moving your names and addresses between any of these and your annoyance level will hit the red line and beyond.

It gets worse if you try to work with products outside the Office suite. Crank out material in Word that will ultimately wind up in Quark or Page-Maker or Frame—and Word is notorious for throwing those programs into a literal loop. If you publish your own material with, say, Microsoft Publisher, you'll hit the same problems, albeit on a smaller scale. If you exchange documents with other folks, you've undoubtedly encountered occasions where they can't read your *.doc* file, or you can't read theirs. Formatting gets lost in the translation. If you're lucky. If you aren't lucky, either their machine or your machine simply locks. The Reset button emerges as your only resort.

And if you need help . . . well, don't get us started. Assuming you can get through on Microsoft's long distance toll phone line, and you don't have to hold for half an hour or more, quite often nobody there will even understand your question, much less have an answer. (Among the more stellar comments heard from Microsoft tech support: "What's a macro?" and "Tell me again how you create a new template?") When you get an answer, it may not be right; Microsoft's record is no better than the U.S. Internal Revenue Service's, and the IRS gives bad answers at least 25% of the time. On very, very simple questions. If you venture online for tech support, you'll find a bunch of well-meaning users, just like you, helping other users. But you'll rarely if ever find an official Microsoft representative, a definitive position, or a full solution from Microsoft itself. Microsoft is nowhere to be seen.

It's just plain annoying. Somebody should write a book.

Well, that's what we've tried to do. We've taken the most annoying things that we've encountered over the years, and searched for the best solutions. We've added to our personal hate lists hundreds of problems sent in to us by readers, friends, family members—anybody we've encountered who was searching for enlightenment. That's a big pool. We've tried to boil the best solutions down and stick them in a book that won't put you to sleep. What you see is what we got.

On the Nature of Annoyances

Some things that appear, at first blush, to be annoyances aren't annoying at all, once you learn how to use them. Let's take a look at some of Office's features that seem annoying, but end up being important capabilities.

One Man's Bloat Is Another Man's Feature

People love to gripe about the way Office has become "bloated"; how it seethes with useless features that nobody ever wants; how it's grown to consume every square inch of hard-drive real estate; how it hogs memory and processor power. Then in the next sentence those same people love to explain how they wrote a book, or put together a fancy form, or cooked up a mail merge, or a web page, org chart, roster, newsletter, sign, poster, sticker, equation, report, memo, phone book, template, or who-knows-what-all, that would absolutely knock your socks off. Using the features others would consider "bloat," of course.

There's a lot of cognitive dissonance at work here.

The truth is that your indispensable feature may be another's useless bloat, and as long as the indispensable, er, useless feature doesn't get in the way, it doesn't hurt anybody. Hard disk space is cheap and getting cheaper. There's been a lot of talk about the future of software programs becoming dozens of little components—"gimme a word processor, hold the grammar checker, a side of native HTML support, a spreadsheet, oh, and how do the presentation modules look today?"

"Ah, yessir . . . would that be with or without pivot tables?" We'll believe it when we see it. Yes, yes, Corel has implemented pieces of its suite as Java thingys, but are you conducting your day-to-day work using them? Thought not.

So Office has a lot of features. This is a bad thing? If you don't use a feature, it hardly takes up any processor cycles or main memory. You can buy 200 MB of hard drive space—more than enough to hold all of Office—for less than $20. What's the beef?

Nope. "Bloat" isn't an annoyance. It's a red herring.

Hyper

Some people think that Office's new-found web capabilities amount to nothing but annoyances. Sorry, but that isn't true either. Even if you never use the Internet, and you or your company never implement an intranet, the so-called "web" features in Office go much, much farther than the Information Super sLowWay. Microsoft may advertise hypertext linking as being a wonderful way to put "hot" web links into web pages. But you can use the same technology to put "hot" jumps inside your Office files. For example, somebody reading your *magnum opus* in Word can click on an index entry and be propelled directly to the associated text, or the supporting spreadsheet, or read an interesting tidbit and jump to a full-blown animated PowerPoint presentation. That's an enormously valuable feature.

Yes, the marketing hacks have decreed that 'Softies can't say 20 words without mentioning the World Wide Web, but don't let that prevent you from using these "web features" for real day-to-day Office work. Keep an open mind. Office's "web" features aren't annoyances. They're opportunities. Even if you never use the Web.

Virus Protection

Many people hate the new annoying "Warning" dialog, the one that pops up whenever you try to open an Excel workbook, PowerPoint presentation, or Word document that contains macros, as shown in Figure 1-1.

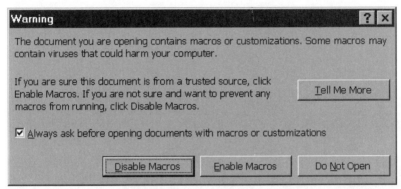

Figure 1-1: The Office last line of viral defense (shown here from Word)

The protection that you'll find in the various Office applications billed as "macro virus protection" isn't a virus checker at all. Office doesn't look for viruses, it doesn't identify viruses, it doesn't eliminate viruses, and it doesn't do a whole lot to protect you from virus infection. Still, when you get the Warning message, you need to sit up and pay attention. Nine times out of ten, whatever file you're trying to open won't be infected. But that other one time out of ten can ruin your whole day. And week, and month.

This Warning message is not an annoyance. It's a last line of defense. When we encounter the message unexpectedly, we (almost) always click on Do Not Open, then carefully check that puppy for nasty creepy crawlies. The one time you find that a file you almost opened was actually infected with WM.Concept or XM.Laroux will make up for all the false alarms. Even if you think the Warnings are annoying, they could save your tail some day. Trust us.

We'll go into greater detail on Excel and Word macro viruses in Chapter 6, *More Hard-Core Office*, but for now learn to think of the Warning dialogs as a necessary evil, not an annoyance. Disabuse yourself of any notion that Office's rather feeble virus-protection methodology is the only virus defense you'll need. Unless you have a very intimate knowledge of VBA programming and various virus propagation methods, you must buy, use, and frequently update a good third-party anti-virus software package that's specifically designed for the Office applications you use.

The Annoying Triumvirate

So much for bloat, file hyperlinking disguised as the Web fad of the week, and Office's nascent macro virus protection. Much as we might dislike each of these phenomena, they aren't true annoyances.

You're probably wondering, at this point, what parts of Office amount to real annoyances—and why you need to read the next 360 pages. That's pretty easy. Annoyances, like bugs, are in the eye of the beholder: if you find something that doesn't work the way you think it should, it's a bug. If you find that you can fix or work around the bug, it's an annoyance. From our point of view, annoyances with fairly easy workarounds are simply galling.

You're almost sure to consider at least a handful of the annoyances discussed here essential features whose demise from Office would be a disaster. But despite the room for disagreement, you're sure to find a long list of features that you consider annoying, even though the individual items in the list may vary.

We arrange Office annoyances into three distinct categories:

- Annoyances can arise from the complexity of the problem itself. These are annoyances that Microsoft really couldn't avoid. They have more to do with the conceptual leap from creating reports and documents manually (the "pen and pencil with a green eye shade" era) to creating work products using electronic software. This type of annoyance we'll fight with enlightenment and education.

- Annoyances attributable to the way Office was designed or implemented. Microsoft could've worked around these problems, but they didn't. Often these annoyances are perpetuated with the excuse that they're needed "for backward compatibility." You're the one left holding the compatibility bag. This was the excuse they used for DOS having diminutive 8.3 character filenames—it had to be backward compatible with CP/M. A lot of Office's demoware features also fall into this category. What's demoware, you ask? Demoware refers to the ambience an application acquires when it's designed by the Marketing Department in Redmond to demonstrate well to an audience full of journalists, Wall Street analysts, Fortune 500 CIOs, or just plain ordinary folk sitting through a Microsoft dog-and-pony show. Demoware puts an emphasis on hype, sex, and sizzle rather than features that are actually useful for getting real work done. We can show you how to work around or fix a number of these annoyances.

- Annoyances that are just plain stupid. This annoyance category encompasses procedures that should be a darn sight easier than they are. This includes the hidden jewels that seem to have been buried in this incredibly powerful suite, or that could certainly be more intuitive or obvious; the inter-Office anomalies—features that should work (or at least look) the same in each application but don't; and option settings that are "sticky" Office-wide (i.e., you set an option in Excel and it changes how something works in Word) but that you'd like to be different in every application. These comprise the most common types of Office annoyances. We'll point out the hidden gems as we come across them and try to show you all the various shortcuts and obscure tricks for getting the maximum use out of Office while keeping your annoyance level to a minimum.

There are general ways of attacking each of these types of annoyances. Let us step you quickly through the high points. Some day, knowing how to approach these kinds of problems may save your hide.

You Know It Ain't Easy

Much of the pain imposed by Office comes, gratis, from the nature of the underlying problem—either the problem's complexity or the paradigm shift that occurred when the job moved from the previous technology used to tackle it to the personal computer.

For example, proportionally spaced type alone has led more Word users to cry, to swear, to drink than any other modern office contrivance except, arguably, the fax machine and force-ranked employee evaluations. Back in the days when you could type out a form on a Selectric typewriter, the lousy characters stayed in place. Every letter occupied the same width: a space was as wide as an "m"; an underscore as wide as an "I". You lined things up by hitting the space bar, and marked off fill-in-the-blank spaces by counting the number of underscores. But in the brave new world of proportional type—where an "I" may only be half as wide as an "m", and a space might occupy no room at all—the whole nature of the game changes.

In the case of Excel, what was once manually and painstakingly transcribed in 14 column by 40 line ledger sheets and calculated with a trusty old 10-key adding machine is now dumped into a 256 column by 65,536 row electronic über-workpaper. Zap! Faster than you can say, "I am Pentium of Borg, division is useless, you will be approximated!" You now have more computational power than NASA had in the 60s. Trade in the green eye shades for a plastic pocket protector because you don't really build spreadsheets any more, you *program* them.

Storing your addresses and phone numbers used to be easy. You had your address book or Rolodex card wheel and that was that. You didn't have to understand anything about normalized relational database tables to find Sid's phone number. In Office, should you keep your stuff in an Access database, Outlook's Contacts facility, Outlook's Personal Address Book, the old Schedule+, or in a third party Personal Information Manager?

Caught in the Legacy Lurch with a Big Dash of Demoware

The design and implementation annoyances in Office abound, the most blatant being the demoware factor. The user interface, as presented in each of the applications that make up the Office suite, was designed first and foremost so that a Microsoft field representative could do a 20-minute presentation and dazzle the audience with the newest, most sexy, flashy features the application has to offer. Not the features that we—the everyday users—will pound on day in and day out, but the hot sizzle stuff. The toolbars in Office are teeming with this crap. For example, the person who keeps the Find button off Word's Standard toolbar is simply out to lunch (even if it's you, Bill). For years Word users have been complaining about Find's strange non-appearance. Imagine. Somebody at Microsoft decided the Find button—which in a word processor probably gets used a dozen times a day—should be left off the main toolbar, whereas the "Adjust the number of newspaper-like snaking columns" icon—which we use, oh, about once a decade—should remain. But zapping a document of text into a snazzy three column format makes for a whiz-bang demo no matter how little it has to do with reality.

Fortunately, toolbars are easily modified once you know how. But most users don't know that you can change the interface, and instead endure ungodly annoyances while wrestling with cumbersome features and drilling down through menus for things that should be a one-click no-brainer button on a toolbar.

Would that all Office annoyances were so easily resolved. The congenital defects that have come down the hereditary chain from prior versions of Office applications are quite vexing. Some of these idiosyncrasies may have once had a legitimate reason (or excuse) for existing. But no one ever went back in and eradicated them. It could be that the programmers who build and maintain Office may just be scared to go in and change the original program code, for fear of screwing up something else. This is not a totally unwarranted fear. Office represents millions of lines of source code and each of the major applications was originally developed as a separate software package without much regard to "getting along well with others." Microsoft has been pounding, re-engineering, and welding on these pieces trying to get a cohesive suite of applications for some while now, with plenty of work yet to be done. It's tough sledding because whenever they tweak *this*, they may wind up breaking *that*.

The Master Document feature in Word, where it automatically keeps track of parts of long documents, is an example of this phenomenon. For years, it simply didn't work, and the people who best understood Word (including Microsoft employees working on books in Redmond) avoided the feature like the plague. The jury's still out on Master Documents. We personally haven't hit any problems with them in Word 97, but we've heard from two experienced Word users who claim to still be having difficulties. Word's notorious font problems (what old Word hacks called the "phont phunnies") is another. Took years for Microsoft to find and eradicate them.

Other congenital defects abound. For example, when you save a file for the first time, Office applications append an application-specific extension to the filename (like *.doc* or *.xls* or *.ppt*). Why can't the applications be smart enough to ferret out their own documents and let you use whatever extension you want? Try to add your own extension and the Office application gleefully tacks on its extension after yours. In PowerPoint, *Bott Presentation.tjl* becomes *Bott Presentation.tjl.ppt*. Microsoft says its applications work that way because many other Win95 programs do, too. Right. And if everyone else jumped off the roof . . . ? Fortunately there's a simple way to work around this double extension "feature." Just enclose the entire filename in double quotation marks. Use `"Bott Presentation.tjl"` and the Office application in question will leave well enough alone.

Your best defense against congenital annoyances is to keep this book handy. Unfortunately, in most cases, logic does not pertain.

The Dummies

Then there's a huge crop of annoying aspects of Office that are just plain dumb or that fly in the face of reality. At least, reality as we understand it. Here's a simple example. Whenever you insert a picture in a Word document, Word 97 sets it up to "float over text." To see just how bizarre this "float over text" thing is, try a little experiment. Start with a new document. Click Insert ➤ Picture ➤ Clip Art and put a piece of clip art in the document. See where your cursor is? It's sitting down at the bottom of the document, just below the clip art.

Now, what would you expect to happen if you hit Enter a few times? Your cursor should move down, farther and farther away from the clip art, right? (If you've used any version of Word prior to Word 97, that's precisely how all the Words work.) Hit Enter once or twice. You'll notice that the clip art moves down, and the cursor stays directly beneath it, as Figure 1-2 illustrates. That's what "float over text" does, and for most Word users it's a downright dumb way to put pictures in text. What's even worse, if you click on the clip art and move it just a smidgen, all of a sudden the clip art starts tracking with the text, just as it did in Word 95 and all earlier versions. Just as the WordGods intended.

Figure 1-2: The "float over text" follies

No wonder people get confused by Word's behavior. If Microsoft can't get it straight, how can you?

There are numerous other stupid annoyances that are just waiting to trip you up.

Since Outlook is the long anticipated Redmond Personal Information Manager (PIM) killer, you'd think there'd be a bit of integration with Microsoft's own long-time database program, Access, no? No. Trying to move data between these two programs is a study in stupid annoyances.

Speaking of Outlook, your new and improved Universal Inbox and all things email: say you have Bob Smith at Company A in your email address book. You get a piece of email from Bob Smith at Company B, open the message and click on Reply. Type in your message and hit Send. Guess who gets the message? Bob over at Company A. Or if you have Joe Doe's CompuServe address listed in your address book but you reply to Joe's email that he sent you from his Internet ISP account, you'd better hope Joe is checking his CIS account regularly. How's that for intuitive?

In Excel, you can make numbers appear as text by either formatting the cell containing the value as text (Format ➤ Cells ➤ Number ➤ Text) or by using the value in the text function =TEXT(2,"0"). What's annoying is that the number formatted as text is treated as a number when sorted or if included in a function such as =SUM(). The result of the =TEXT function, however, is sorted as text and is ignored by the =SUM() function. But it is treated as a value if you do something simple like include the cell in a formula like =A1+A2. A simple formula ignores the number formatted as text. How's that for consistency? Oy!

Just Where Did You Want to Go Today?

Microsoft seems to have missed the fact that most people simply want to go home to their real life at the end of the work day, and that in order to do so they have to use Office to get their work done. If Office has started to seem more like part of the problem than part of the solution, take a few deep breaths and realize that Office's annoyances aren't all in your head. In fact, Office contains hundreds of annoying idiosyncrasies like these, but you *can* eliminate or work around the vast majority of them. That's what the rest of this book is all about.

The Augean Stables* weren't cleaned in a day—well, okay, they were cleaned in a day, but Hercules had the advantage of being the son of Zeus, and as far as anyone knows he did not have to contend with General Protection Faults. For mere mortals like us, you need to keep a sense of perspective and realize you aren't going to conquer Office's manifest shortcomings in a day or even a week, for that matter. But if you hang in there, your efforts to understand, defeat, and even mangle Office so it works with you instead of against you will be repaid many times. We honestly believe you'll pay for this book (and the time you took to read it) by simply following the steps in Chapter 2, *Vital Changes and Settings*, which covers the very simple changes every Office user should

---

* One of the Twelve Labors of Hercules.

make. Beyond that, your efforts with this book are simply money in the bank. Chapter 2 details modifications every single Office user should implement, as soon as he or she installs the product. They're the easy ones—primarily "dumb" annoyances—that can be contravened by a few clicks here and there. You can do these in your sleep.

Chapter 3, *Introduction to Office Macros*, gently eases you into the world of macros and Visual Basic for Applications. Even if you're genetically indisposed to programming, you'll find macros to be a godsend, and learning about them by simply typing them into the PC couldn't be easier. We'll need those first simple macros to conquer a few additional "dumb" annoyances.

From there we head into the dark, uncharted interior of Office. We'll tackle the "big five" applications—Word, Excel, Outlook, Access, and PowerPoint—and try to squash as many annoyances as we can. Where possible, we'll show you how to change your Office applications from a wimpy marketeer's foil into striking, powerful tools customized for the way you work. To accomplish all that, you have to do more than click once or twice, but the basic method is fairly simple.

All of the programs you'll find listed here are available for download at the O'Reilly & Associates web site, *www.oreilly.com/publishing/windows*. There's no charge, and you may distribute the programs freely, anywhere you like, any way you like. In return, we only ask that you encourage folks to get this book, so they can follow along and make Office work right for them, too.

If you have a question, a tip, or an observation, the best way to reach the authors is by sending email to *ask.woody@wopr.com*. If we can figure out an answer to your question, or if your tip really hits the spot, we'll publish it in our free email newsletter, called WOW—"Woody's Office Watch." No promises, of course, as the volume of mail sometimes gets overwhelming. No, Microsoft doesn't pay us a penny for our tech support services. But thanks for asking.

NOTE   You can subscribe to Woody's Office Watch, our *free* elec-
                 tronic   weekly   newsletter,   by   sending   email   to
                 ohwow@wopr.com. We think you'll find WOW an excellent
                 source of up-to-the-nanosecond news on Microsoft Office.
                 And the price sure is right.

Roger, Red Leader, we're going in . . .

2

Vital Changes and Settings

Office is comprised of five base components: Word, Excel, Outlook, Access, and PowerPoint. In order to optimize how the pieces fit and work together you have to not only deal with each individual piece, but you have to look at Office as a whole and then at how all of Office fits into Windows itself.

This chapter covers a host of changes that every single Office user should make, not only to the individual applications, but to Office as a whole, and to Windows itself. By and large they're easy, quick changes designed to rectify annoyances in the "stupid annoyance" category we discussed in Chapter 1, *Initial Inanities.*

Make these changes the minute you install Office. If you already have Office installed, make these changes immediately. Even if you've been using Office for months or years, go through this list carefully and make any changes you haven't already encountered in your copious and hard-earned experience.

It should take you between one to two hours to go through this chapter, modifying Office as you read. We guarantee you'll save at least an hour the first month you put these changes to use. By the end of the second month, you should've paid for this book—just using the tips in this chapter. And from then on it's gravy.

Office 97 Version Vertigo

Microsoft Office is now in its third major left-of-decimal release. There was the first crack at an office suite, version 4 (which was really version 1—don't you just love creative marketing?), which went through a couple of right-of-decimal revisions ending at version 4.3. "Not ready for prime time" is the phrase that comes to mind when we think back on Microsoft's early attempts at an integrated suite.

But with Office 95 (which, if we were living in a sane, reasonable world, would be called Office 2.0, but we aren't, so it isn't) the suite became a fairly stable, reliable operating environment. The whole really became greater than the sum of Office pieces with Office 95. While bashed as a simple "glitter grade," it was chock full of internal improvements that made it an order of magnitude more reliable that its predecessor. Office 97 cranks reliability up another order of magnitude. Well, half an order perhaps, but a substantial improvement nevertheless.

That's not to say there aren't some really annoying aspects, either.

System Resource Requirements

The first annoyance is the plethora of various incarnations of Office that awaits you, the wary customer. There's the basic Standard Edition (Word, Excel, PowerPoint, and Outlook), and the Professional Edition (add Access, Bookshelf Basics—a watered-down version of Microsoft Bookshelf—and Internet Explorer, which is actually free, so go figure). Then there are the hybrids: the Office 97 Small Business Edition (Word, Excel, Outlook, Publisher, Automap Streets Plus, and a financial manager) and the Office 97 Developer Edition. The Developer Edition is the Professional Edition with a runtime license for developing your own Office applications, integration tools, replication manager, a Setup Wizard, and actual printed documentation (now there's something you don't see every day, Chauncy!).

About the only general business applications not included in some flavor of Office are Project (for doing project management), FrontPage (Redmond's popular web site creation and management program), and Publisher (Microsoft's low-end desktop publishing package). Unless you're a heavy-duty developer, you should decide if you need Access for database work or not and then go with the Standard or Professional Edition. Buy Publisher, Project, and/or FrontPage separately if needed.

Once you weigh all the options and actually pick a version, you still have to deal with the hardware requirements. Office is gonna eat up anywhere from just over 100 megabytes for the Standard Edition with a typical installation, to just under 200 megabytes for the complete version of the Professional Edition (the version that includes Access). Since disk space is relatively cheap, we suggest going the Complete install route so that everything is ready to go should you need it.

If you've fallen for the marketing propaganda that you can run Office on a 486 with 8 megabytes of memory, you can eliminate a number of the annoyances you've been experiencing by taking your memory up to 32 megabytes. The expense is worth it, trust us! But in reality, productivity may still elude you until you move up to a Pentium.

Installation Odds and Ends

If you are a long-time Office user, you probably installed each new version right on top of the previous version. After all, that's just what you were supposed to do. But after a while, your disk starts to resemble an archaeological dig. You have layer upon layer of Office versions, and each layer leaves behind a glut of orphaned files. Shared applications are big offenders. Old versions of MS Chart, Equation Editor, and Text Converters all can wind up lost and alone on your disk. Installing Office 95 over the previous 4.x version of Office could leave as much as 20 megabytes of this unsightly waxy software buildup.

The solution is one that you've probably been putting off. Backup your data (twice if you're paranoid like us), prepare a fully loaded boot diskette—or two—complete with CD-ROM drive real-mode drivers, say your prayers, and reformat your drive. Like spring cleaning your garage and visiting your dentist, it's just something you should do every so often.

CD-ROM, the Only Way to Spin

Unless you're a glutton for punishment, you have a CD-ROM as your original media for your copy of Office 97. This is good, because flipping floppies can get old, real fast!

The CD requires you to enter a *key number* when you install the software. This key is a 10-digit number that you'll find on a sticker on the back of the CD-ROM plastic case. If you're like us, you probably get the cases and the CDs mixed up on a regular basis, so we recommend you write the number on the front of the CD itself. Yep, right across the printed side of the disk, using a permanent marker. It won't hurt the CD—unless you write it on the wrong, non-printed side—and now you always have the disk and the number in the same place.

You can also pop open the Help ➤ About dialog to see the Product ID number. Click on the Office Shortcut Bar's control menu (the tiny icon in the upper-left corner of the OSB) then on About Microsoft Office (see Figure 2-1). The middle two groups of numbers (making 10 digits) are the same as your key number. You can also find this number in the Help ➤ About dialog box for each Office application you installed from your Office CD. If you've already misplaced your key number, find it here and get it recorded on your actual CD. Consider doing this right now, as in right this very minute. You may not be able to read the ID number when you need it most, because a frequent reason for re-installing (and thus the need for the number) is that something catastrophic has happened and you can't get the number from any of the About boxes.

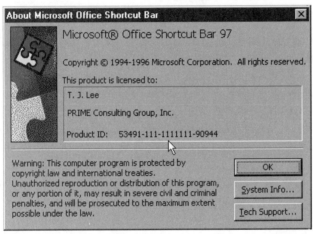

Figure 2-1: About Microsoft Office from the Office Shortcut Bar's control menu

Get the Latest Version

Microsoft has a bad habit of releasing bug fixes without notifying the "registered user base" (read: you). Fortunately, though, Microsoft has always clearly identified new versions as they are released. In spite of rumors you may have heard, we've never caught Microsoft "slip-streaming" releases of Office applications—selling two different versions with the same version number—and we watch closely. That's an important point, because many confounding problems crop up in the interstitial edges between version releases.

So the very first thing you should do with your Office installation is ensure that you're running the latest version of each major component. That's easy. Start Word (then Excel, Access, Outlook, and PowerPoint). Click Help ➤ About *application name*. The top line of the dialog box that you'll see contains the version number. The initial release of Word 97 is identified on this top line as "Microsoft® Word 97." Notice that the next line is blank. But in Internet Explorer, for example, Help ➤ About shows "Microsoft Internet Explorer" and the next line says "Version 3.02 (4.70.1300)," showing the version and even a "build" number. If Microsoft issues an interim release of an Office application (i.e., something before the next major Office release), a version number will appear on the second line of the Help ➤ About dialog box. With that information in front of you, call Microsoft: in the U.S.A. at 800-360-7561; outside the U.S.A., call your local Microsoft office. Tell the clerk who answers the phone that you want to verify that you're properly registered for each application. The clerk will want your Product ID, which we discussed in the previous section. Verify that Microsoft has your correct name and address on file. Then ask whether you have the latest version of each application.

Sometimes Microsoft will try to charge you shipping and handling charges for minor version upgrades—that's what they did in the transition from Word version 6.0a to 6.0c. We think that's a crock: Microsoft should swallow the bill for bug fixes; charging good customers to correct Microsoft's mistakes is unconscionable. So if the clerk asks you for a credit card number, just say that you've been having trouble with your current version (who hasn't, eh?), and that your personal Office gurus (that's us) told you that you needed the upgrade to "reduce the number of GPFs." Unless the clerk is having a very bad day, you'll probably get shipping and handling charges waived, and receive the update free.

Download All the Freebies

Microsoft frequently posts new Office material on their Web site. Sometimes all you'll find are cheesy gimmicks that don't work very well. Sometimes you'll find really good add-ins, or white papers that give a thorough review of a topic that's important to you. Check *http:// www.microsoft.com/office* and *http://www.microsoft.com/officefreestuff* every month or so to see the latest and greatest postings.

Converters and Viewers

All of the applications in Office 97 use a completely different "file format" from earlier versions. Generally, you can open files created with previous versions of Office with some caveats. Oftentimes, a previous-version document is opened as a read-only document. Should you want to save the file in the newer version of Office, you are reminded that this file is from a previous version of the application you are using and nudged to save it in the latest format. The logical reason for this is that if you have edited the file using any of the features in the new version, those edits may be lost if you save the file in the older format. That's assuming you can even save it in the older format. Access 97 has no provision for saving a database as an Access 2.0 file, for example.

Going upstream, from the newer version to the older, it gets worse. Word 95 won't recognize a document created with Word 97. Ditto for Access, Excel, and PowerPoint. If you exchange documents with people who are still running older versions of Office, there are several options you should be aware of.

With Access you have to start exporting pieces of the database created with the 97 version and try to reassemble them in the earlier version of Access. Not a project for the novice or faint of heart. Then again, getting a moderately complex Access 2 database to work properly in Access 97 involves considerable cleanup work, as any of you who have tried doubtless are aware.

Word 97's original converter for saving Word 97 files in a Word 95 format really did no such thing. It spun out plain RTF (rich text format) files—which are quite large, especially if they contain graphics. Since the release of Office 97, Microsoft has developed a real Word 97 to Word 95 binary converter that you can download from *http://www.microsoft.com/word*. Word 95 actually has a converter that lets Word 6 and Word 95 read the newer Word 97 format. This converter is located on your Office 97 CD. Look for the program *wrdcnv97.exe* in the CD folder called *\Valupack\Wrdcnv97*. (The same file is also available on *http://www.microsoft.com/word*.) Have each of your Word correspondents run the program on their machines. It should install itself, and suddenly allow them to view and edit new Word *.doc* files even though they're running earlier versions of Word. They won't be able to use any of the cool new Word 97 features, though.

There's a whole bunch of file converters that weren't quite ready in time for the initial release of Word 97. If you don't have converters to:

- Open or save files in RFT-DCA format
- Open or save files in IBM/Lotus Ami Pro/Word Pro 3.x format
- Open or save files in WordStar/DOS 3.3 to 7.0 format
- Open files in WordStar/Win 1.0 or 2.0 format
- Save files in WordStar/DOS 4.0 or 7.0 format
- Open or save files in DOS Word 4.x, 5.x, or 6.x format

and you want the capability, download the file *Wdsupccnv.exe* from *www.microsoft.com/kb/softlib*.

According to Microsoft, a converter that PowerPoint 95 can use to read the newer PowerPoint 97 format is slated for release in the fall of 1997 (keep your eyes on *www.microsoft.com/powerpoint*). Until then you'll have to save your PowerPoint 97 presentations in the dual file format "PowerPoint 95 & 97 Presentation (*.ppt)." We discuss this dual file format option in more detail shortly in the next paragraph.

Excel is much less malleable. There is no converter that will let prior versions read in the newer Excel 97 format. In fact, to quote Microsoft, "Microsoft Excel 5.0 and Microsoft Excel 95 *do not have an installable converter architecture*" (emphasis ours). But you can explicitly save an Excel 97 file in the "Microsoft Excel 97 & 5.0/95 Workbook (*.xls)" dual file format. This type of file can be opened in Excel 5, Excel 95, or Excel 97. However, if a user of Excel 5 or 95 makes changes and saves the file, all Excel 97-specific features and attributes are lost, and the file format is now in that version's native format.

Microsoft also has viewers for Word, PowerPoint, and Excel that you can send to anyone. A viewer allows people running Windows 95 or later who don't have Office installed on their systems to view your Office files and print them. They won't be able to edit them, though. The viewers are available at *http://www.microsoft.com/OfficeFreeStuff*. Full up-to-the-minute details on converters and viewers are at *http://www.microsoft.com/ Office/Office97/documents/o97cvert*. As of this writing, all three viewers— for Word, PowerPoint, and Excel—have been posted on Microsoft's web site.

For transferring data from Outlook or Access, you are going to have to resort to the export features provided in each of these programs.

Get Some Third-Party Anti-Virus Software

Excel, PowerPoint, and Word now sport some kind of macro virus protection. The effectiveness of this built-in protection scheme is open to discussion, and we do that in detail in Chapter 6, *More Hard-Core Office*, (especially for Word, which is, by an order of magnitude, the most common target of virus writers). But none of the built-in protection does much to help you fend off or remove viruses. Therefore, it would behoove you to find and install a decent anti-virus (AV) software package.

There are a number of major AV software packages, from companies such as Symantec (Norton), McAfee, IBM, and the like. Since they change constantly, we won't try influencing your choice, but instead point you to any of the major PC magazines, including *PC Computing* (*http://www.pccomputing.com*) and *Office Computing* (*http://www.officecomputing.com*), for the latest news and reviews. You really need to have a good AV package installed, so stop stalling and get it done.

To stay on top of Microsoft's spin on macro viruses and Office, check *http://www.microsoft.com/office/antivirus* regularly.

Custom Settings for Everyman

The sheer mass of features found in Office can be an annoyance all by itself, especially if you don't particularly favor the default choices foisted upon you by Office as it comes out of the shrink-wrap. Just figuring out where all the possible customizable settings are located, not to mention what their values should be, is a daunting task.

A major Office annoyance is that there is no one, centrally located utility you can go to that controls all the "across Office" settings. Some settings are actually pan-Office utilities like the Office Shortcut Bar. But other pan-Office settings have to be accessed from within an Office application. For example, you can set several options inside Word that will affect what happens in Excel.

Multimedia sound effects, toolbar icon size, menu animations, custom dictionaries, and more all can be tweaked to work the way you want them to instead of the way they work by default. In this section we'll look at the myriad of options you can control (and a few you can't) to make Office jump through your hoops, instead of the other way around. First, however, let's cover three fundamental issues that you must grapple with before dealing with any Office-wide settings:

* How Office modifies your StartUp folder, and how you can fight back

* How to disable Find Fast, and fast

* How to unwind Office's arrogant updates to your Start Menu

Office Components in Your StartUp Folder

You can cause Windows to launch any of your Office components (or, for that matter, any other application) when you first start your computer. Just put the executable file, or a shortcut that points to it, in the folder called *StartUp*. Finding this folder can be a bit annoying; we know where it is and still occasionally forget. On a single-user system look for:

```
C:\Windows\Start Menu\Programs\StartUp
```

If you are using a system configured to support multiple users, the most common location of the user's Start Menu folder is *C:\Windows\Profiles\<user name>\Start Menu.* But even that isn't invariable; on network installations, all user settings can be stored on a remote computer. The precise location of the user's information, including the Start Menu information, is stored in a Registry value entry named `ProfileImagePath`. If you are in this situation and can't locate your Start Menu folder, and are familiar with the Registry, you can look at

```
HKEY_LOCAL_MACHINE\Software\Microsoft\Windows\CurrentVersion\
ProfileList\<user name>
```

(where *<user name>* is your user name) to see where it's located. This presupposes that your system administrator has not locked down your system to the point where no customizations are allowed.

NOTE   To quickly open an Explorer window on your StartUp folder just right-click on the Start button on the Taskbar. From the pop-up menu choose Explore, and a Windows Explorer window will open with the StartUp folder selected.

We'll assume that you have free reign to customize the *StartUp* folder to your heart's content in the rest of this section.

By default you'll probably find the goodies shown in Table 2-1 in your *StartUp* folder after you've installed Office. Add to this anything you want started up automatically. This need not be a "set it up once and forget it" kind of thing. If you're working on a big Excel project, drop a shortcut to Excel in the *StartUp* folder. As your needs change, just add or delete items from *StartUp.*

Table 2-1: Typical Contents of the StartUp Folder

Filename	File Type	Description
Microsoft Fast Find	Shortcut to *C:\Program Files\Microsoft Office\Office\Findfast.exe*	Fast Find builds an index to speed up finding documents from the Open dialog box. (We'll discuss this utility, and why you probably want to disable it, in detail in the next section.)
Microsoft Office Shortcut Bar	Shortcut to *C:\Program Files\Microsoft Office\Office\ MSOffice.exe*	This starts your Office Shortcut Bar (OSB), a most handy advancement to the Office interface.

Table 2-1: Typical Contents of the StartUp Folder (continued)

Filename	File Type	Description
Office Startup	Shortcut to *C:\Program Files\Microsoft Office\Office\Osa.exe*	Runs the Office Startup Application, which initializes the shared code that is used by the Microsoft Office 97 programs and allows those programs to start faster.

Working with the StartUp Folder

The *StartUp* folder can be a handy resource, providing you can remember where Microsoft has buried it (it's in *C:\Windows\Start Menu\Programs\StartUp* by default). To make working with this folder easier, create a shortcut to the folder itself. Right-click the folder in Windows Explorer, click on Create Shortcut, and then put the shortcut *.lnk* file into your *C:\Windows\SendTo* folder. Now, when you right-click on a file and choose the Send To option, a shortcut to *StartUp* appears on the cascading menu.

To quickly add a shortcut to *StartUp*, right-click on the shortcut file, choose Send To on the pop-up menu and click on the StartUp option. That shortcut is automatically put in the *StartUp* folder.

Disable Find Fast

Although Microsoft touts Find Fast as one of Office's greatest features, we've had nothing but troubles with it. The concept is pretty simple: Windows waits until you aren't doing anything, and then scans and indexes the contents of all the files on your hard drives. Then, when you're searching for a particular word or phrase in an Office document, Windows' Start ➤ Find ➤ Files or Folders (or Explorer's Tools ➤ Find ➤ Files or Folders) can simply look at the index, instead of having to scan the innards of all the files. Great theory.

In practice, though, Find Fast has caused us nothing but grief. Every couple of hours it takes over the machine—the PC starts acting as if it's gone berserk, with disk lights flashing and the keyboard freezing. In Word, typing suddenly becomes an exercise in herky-jerky futility. We've also hit General Protection Faults caused by Find Fast. Some of the "cascading" GPFs get very humorous: leave your machine on overnight, and at least ten GPF boxes, delicately interleaved, may appear on your screen. We have no idea what caused the GPFs, and we couldn't replicate them, but they were very real.

Besides, we don't look for data inside documents all that often. We'd rather take the performance "hit" when we're searching for that data than withstand a "hit" every couple of hours during a busy Office working day. So the simple answer is: shut it off. Your situation may be different; if so, you have our sympathies.

To turn off Find Fast on all your drives, click Start ➤ Settings ➤ Control Panel. Double-click on the Find Fast icon. Click each drive in turn, then click Index ➤ Delete Index, OK. (See Figure 2-2.) If you ever want to start Find Fast again on a specific drive, reverse the procedure, clicking Index ➤ Create Index.

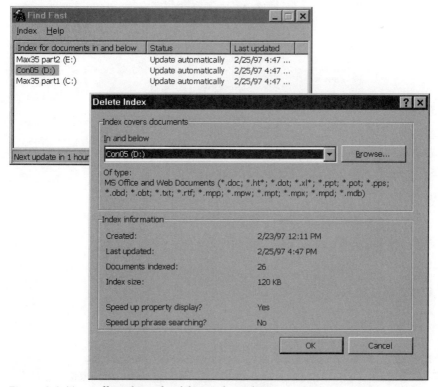

Figure 2-2: Turn off Find Fast by deleting the indexes

If you want to get rid of Find Fast entirely—and never expect to use it again—you should also remove it from the Startup program group. To do so, just delete the Microsoft Find Fast shortcut icon from your PC's *Startup* folder.

Maybe Microsoft will get it right some day.

Start Menu Hubris

Of all the software companies in all the world, only Microsoft would have the chutzpah to plant two new items on your Start Menu and nine new items on your Programs Menu, including a fly-out menu called Microsoft Reference with just one entry (see Figure 2-3). Many people find that their Programs Menu, in particular, flips to two or even three columns when bogged down with all the Office folderol. This exorbitant waste of your screen real estate warrants immediate retaliation.

Figure 2-3: Office scatters a dozen disorganized and ill-conceived entries on your Start menu

You could use the "official" Start Menu modification routines available through Start ➤ Settings ➤ Taskbar on the Start menu. But it's much simpler, and more enlightening, to attack the problem directly, using Windows Explorer.

In Windows Explorer, scroll down to your Windows folder (probably *c:\Windows*), and the *Start Menu* folder underneath it. If you take a close look at the contents of the *Start Menu* folder, you'll see rather readily how Windows turns entries in this folder into entries on the Start Menu: subfolders give rise to fly-out menus, shortcuts appear on their folders' menus, and so on. Figure 2-4 shows where the New Office Document entry on the Start Menu comes from.

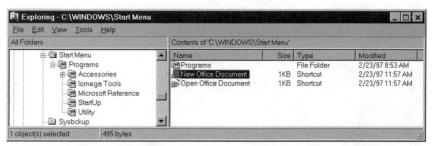

Figure 2-4: Structure of \Windows\Start Menu folder that corresponds to Figure 2-3

You can rearrange the folders any way you like, and get rid of any entries you find offensive. Rename any folders or shortcuts you like (in particular, consider getting rid of that grating "Microsoft" prefix on all the shortcuts). Since the items appear on the menus in alphabetical order, with folders all appearing before shortcuts, you can force folders or shortcuts to the top of their respective parts of the menu by preceding their names with an underscore character (_)—the underscore sorts before any alphabetic letters. (See Figure 2-5.)

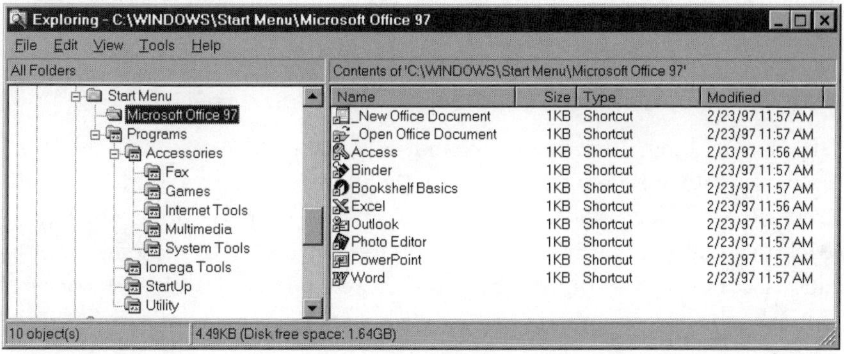

Figure 2-5: One possible way to rearrange Start Menu folders and shortcuts to streamline the Start Menu

We tend to like a very minimalist arrangement, with Microsoft Office 97 appearing on the Start Menu, and all Office-related programs hanging directly off that entry, as shown in Figure 2-6. You should modify the Start Menu until the Office entries are fast, logical, and unobtrusive, from your point of view.

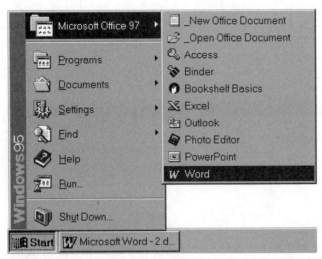

Figure 2-6: Start Menu contents corresponding to the folders and shortcuts in Figure 2-5

Now that you've got those fundamental tasks handled, on to the Office-wide settings you'll love to change . . .

Some Common Pan-Office Settings

You'd think that with a suite of applications like Office you'd have a single, central administrative tool to deal with all Office-wide settings, wouldn't you? Well, you think like we do, but annoyingly enough, we all seem to be wrong.

Icons, ScreenTips, and menu animations

The closest thing there is to a central command center is the Customize dialog box (Tools ➤ Customize, Options) that you can find in Word, Excel, PowerPoint, and Access (but not in Outlook). The quickest way to reach this dialog is to right-click on any toolbar in any of these four applications. Choose Customize from the pop-up menu, and click on the Options tab.

The dialog shown in Figure 2-7 is from Word. Access, PowerPoint, and Word all share the "Show shortcut keys in ScreenTips" option. Only Excel is missing this option. Oops. It's annoying that Excel doesn't offer this setting, and even more annoying that Excel doesn't display shortcut keys in ScreenTips—when ScreenTips are turned on—at all.

When checked, "Large icons" enlarges the buttons on the various toolbars *within* the Office applications. It doesn't do squat for the Office Shortcut

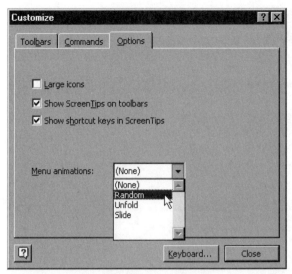

Figure 2-7: Setting pan-Office options

Bar (OSB), which you have to tweak separately. We'll discuss the OSB in some depth in just a bit. "Large icons" works as advertised. You set it in any application, and the change affects all the others.

The "Show ScreenTips on toolbars" setting controls the display of the ScreenTips—the little text labels that appear when you put the mouse over a toolbar button. It's supposed to control this across all the Office applications, and it does, sorta. This is a weird one, so follow closely. Open Excel and make sure the Show ScreenTips box is checked (Tools ➤ Customize, Options). Now, close all your applications. Start Word. Turn off "Show ScreenTips on toolbars" by unchecking the box. Put the mouse over a button in Word and there's no ScreenTip. So far so good. Open Access, PowerPoint, or Outlook, and no ScreenTips. But then open Excel. Surprise! Excel did not get the word from Word and thinks that Screen-Tips are supposed to be displayed. What's more, now that you have opened Excel, ScreenTips are suddenly displayed in all the other Office applications as well. A bug for sure.

Since Excel insists on having the last word as regards this setting, if you want to turn ScreenTips on or off, change it in Excel.

Outlook needs some special mention regarding these options. If you want to adjust the icon size from within Outlook, you have to go to Tools ➤ Options and click on the General tab. (See Figure 2-8.) Here you'll find a check box for "Large toolbar icons." You'll just have to set the other options (ScreenTips and menu animations) from within another Office application, since they cannot be configured from within Outlook.

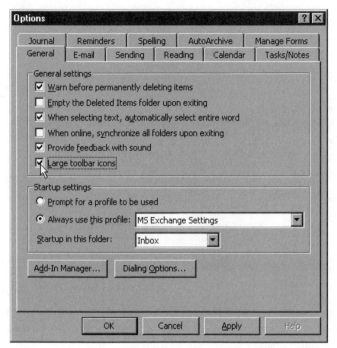

Figure 2-8: "Large toolbar icons" setting found in Tools ➤ Options in Outlook

Menu animations are a neat demoware feature. Looks good, marginal utility. We set ours to "none" to cut down on motion sickness.

Make Office go brrrrrring, whoosssssssh, and ding

This being the age of multimedia and special effects, the Office 97 developers added subtle but important auditory cues to befriend you while working with Office. Unfortunately, if you want to hear Office's remarkably cool sound effects, you're going to have to jump through some hoops. This entire process should be much smoother and seamlessly integrated into Office; one click should do it all. Maybe next time. Let's take this from the top. (This discussion assumes you have an installed and functional sound board.)

1. If all the stars are aligned properly, you might hear Office sounds out of the box. Let's find out. Start Excel (or any Office application), select Tools ➤ Options, select the General tab, check the "Provide feedback with sound" box, click OK. Do a quick sound check—open any existing file, and, if you're lucky, you'll hear a high-end strumming sound (officially, it's *Complete.wav*; more on how to find this out in a moment). If so, you're all done. If all you hear is the silent stirring of dust motes in the air, move on to the next step. (You may

also be so lucky as to see a message box that reads, "Microsoft Office Sounds are not installed on your system.")

2. Next make sure you've got Windows 95's Audio Compression component installed. We won't go through the detailed steps here, presuming by now you've had some practice at using the Control Panel's Add/Remove Programs dialog. Select the Multimedia component on the Windows Setup tab, click Details, then examine the Audio Compression check box. (See Figure 2-9.) If it's already checked, then move on to the next step; otherwise, check it, click OK twice, and now it should be installed. If a sound check by opening any existing Office file now plays *Complete.wav*— brrrrrring!—then you're all done. Otherwise, move on to the next step.

Figure 2-9: Adding Audio Compression via Add/Remove Programs, Windows Setup

3. Unfortunately, Office sounds are not—repeat, not—installed by the Office setup procedure. You have to do this manually. You can obtain *Sounds.exe* from the \ *Valupack*\ *Sounds* folder on your Office CD, or on the Web at *http://www.microsoft.com/officefreestuff/*. Install Office sounds by double-clicking *Sounds.exe* and following the simple instructions. Time for yet another sound check. If you hear *Complete.wav* now, congratulations. Otherwise, you may have a sound card or multimedia player problem that's beyond the scope of this book. (Hint: is your audio volume control applet set to Mute, or perhaps are one or more of the applet's volume potentiometers set to

zero? We've had this happen to us, so it's worth a look before you
open up your PC's chassis and start fiddling with DIP switches.)

At this point you presumably have Office sounds playing. Did you know
that Office sounds can be on (or off) independently of the Office Assistant's sounds feature? To activate the Office Assistant's sounds, right-click
on the Office Assistant, choose Options, select the Options tab, select the
"Make sounds" check box, then click OK.

If you want to see what files are being played for which actions, fire up
Control Panel, start Sounds, scroll down the Events list box until you get
to the Microsoft Office node, and select the desired action. For example,
Figure 2-10 shows what the Clear action's filename is; click the Play
button (the right pointing triangle on the right of the Preview box) to
hear the sound.

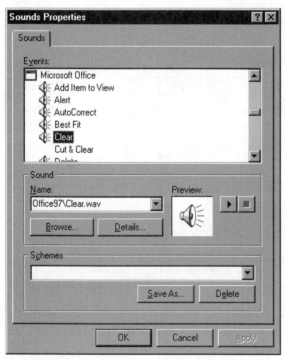

*Figure 2-10: Using the Sound Properties dialog box to reveal an Office action's
sound*

Max Your Most Recently Used File List

All the file-based Office applications except Access and Outlook (the
latter doesn't need this feature) provide a way for you to dictate how
many of your most recently used (MRU) files the application remembers.

You've probably seen this many times before: when you click the File menu, just above the Exit command at the bottom there's a list of the files you've recently had open. We suggest you crank this number all the way up to its maximum value of 9. Click Tools ➤ Options, General, then check the "Recently used file" check box and set the spin control to 9. Annoyingly, in Access, you're stuck with a fixed MRU list of 4.

User Information

Oh, and while you're in the General tab (the User Information tab in Word) of the ubiquitous Options dialog, make sure Office has your user name right. Oddly, in Access there's no user interface feature to see or change your user name.

Office Shortcut Bar

Office ships with one of the finest program launchers ever created, the so-called Office Shortcut Bar, or OSB. Its standard toolbar is shown in Figure 2-11. Unfortunately, the standard OSB contains all sorts of entries few people ever use, except for a few Outlook addicts living in Redmond. Worse, in slavish adherence to the fashionable "document-centric" point of view, the standard OSB gives no direct access to the main Office programs you've come to know and love. Fortunately, you can change these annoyances easily, too.

Figure 2-11: The standard Office Shortcut Bar

To take the OSB into your own hands, start by right-clicking on the tiny Office logo on the bar, and choosing Customize. Click the Toolbars tab and pick each of the offered Folders, one at a time, to see if any of them include entries you'll want on your OSB. Since we use Bookshelf with Word all the time, we've found the QuickShelf Toolbar (see Figure 2-12) to be a useful starting point—it contains icons for all the Bookshelf components found on the Office Pro CD. If you find a usable toolbar, choose it, and it alone. There's nothing worse than an overcrowded toolbar. If you don't find anything that suits your fancy, click Add Toolbar, give your new custom OSB toolbar a name, click OK, and choose it.

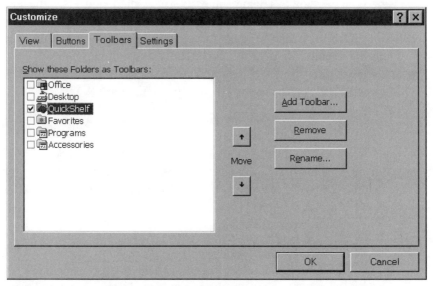

Figure 2-12: Start with a useful OSB toolbar, or create one of your own

While you're still in the Customize dialog, you can play around with the other settings, like the options available on the View tab, as shown in Figure 2-13, until your OSB is configured the way that you'd like.

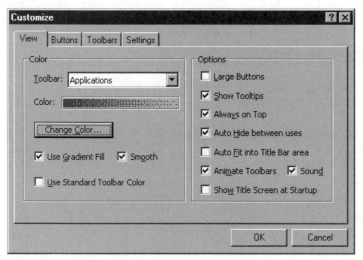

Figure 2-13: Customizing the View settings of the OSB

Table 2-2 shows how we usually set up the OSB on our machines (remember, one man's ceiling is another man's floor). As you can see, we differ somewhat among ourselves on how we adjust our OSB options. This underscores the need to tweak Office wherever possible to make it suit you. A small annoying thing that you have to deal with dozens of times a day can take a real toll on you. Ferret out all the little creature comforts you can by experimenting with these (and other) options. Thoreau said "simplify . . . ;" our mantra is "customize."

Table 2-2: View Options for OSBs

Options	We usually	What it does
Large Buttons	Woody checks it; Jim and Lee don't	This is the equivalent of the Large icon setting we talked about in the last section. If you only have a few buttons on your OSBs, go with large. If you want more buttons, uncheck this box.
Show ToolTips	Check it	Displays text labels when you place the mouse pointer over the button. This feature is called ScreenTips when dealing with toolbars within the actual Office applications. Don't you just love consistency?
Always on Top	Check it	When the OSB is displayed it won't get covered by another window. Most useful when you let the OSB "float" as a free standing toolbar.
Auto Hide between uses	Jim and Lee check it; Woody doesn't	This causes the OSB to disappear when docked to the edge of the display (top, bottom, left, right). Touching your mouse pointer to the docked edge displays the OSB.
Auto Fit into the Title Bar area	Woody checks it; Jim and Lee don't	Melds the OSB into the current application's title bar. More useful if you don't have a great many buttons displayed. With many buttons, you can obscure your title bar information.
Animate Toolbars, Sounds, and Show Title Screen at Startup	None of us check Show Title Screen at Startup, and only Lee checks Animate Toolbars and Sound	These three options deal with special effects and the opening splash screen.

Next, bring up the Windows Explorer. Navigate to *c:\Program Files\Microsoft Office\Office.* (The name of each application's executable

file is shown in Table 2-3.) One by one, click on each Office program
you want to appear on your custom OSB. Drag the program file onto the
OSB and release it. OSB is smart enough to put a shortcut to each
program on the OSB toolbar.

Table 2-3: Executable Filenames for the Main Office Applications

Application	File
Word	Winword.exe
Outlook	Outlook.exe
Excel	Excel.exe
PowerPoint	Powerpnt.exe
Access	Msaccess.exe

You aren't limited to Office programs. Drag any program or document
onto the OSB, and a shortcut icon immediately appears. Adjust the order
of the icons by right-clicking on the tiny Office logo on the bar, choosing
Customize, and working with the Buttons tab. (See Figure 2-14.)

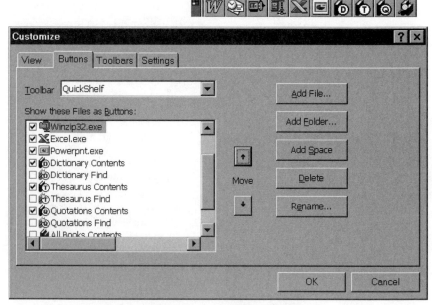

Figure 2-14: Put anything you like on your customized OSB

Get Internet Explorer Installed

When Office installs itself, it places an icon called "Shortcut to Internet
Explorer 3.01 Installer" on your Desktop. It's important that you, as a dedicated Office fan, use IE version 3.01 or later—the widely available IE 3.0

will crash and burn Word and most other Office apps. Versions before 3.0 won't even recognize Office.

If you already have Internet Explorer installed on your machine, start it up, and click Help ➤ About Internet Explorer. Version 3.01 will identify itself as "Version 3.0 (4.70.1215)". If you see any Version number less than 3.0, you need to upgrade IE. If you have Version 3.0 with any build number (the last four digits) less than 1215, it's imperative that you upgrade IE. Otherwise, Word probably will die the next time you try to follow a hyperlink. Install the newest version by double-clicking on that Desktop icon.

Once you're through installing IE, you can safely delete the "Shortcut to Internet Explorer 3.01 Installer" icon from your Desktop.

The Custom Dictionary

Office applications now share a common spell checker, which is a good thing. You get a reasonably comprehensive dictionary and you can store your own list of words in a custom dictionary file (*Custom.dic*).

Whether or not you find it an annoyance (and opinions differ), most of the spelling options are adjustable only on an application-by-application basis (meaning each application maintains its own settings). The number and type of spelling options vary substantially among Office programs. Word has a very rich set of options, as you might expect. Excel has a very limited number of options (bordering on none). For example, if you want to make Word or Outlook ignore words typed in all uppercase, you check the appropriate box in Tools ➤ Options ➤ Spelling and Grammar (just Spelling in Outlook). To do the same thing in Excel, you have to actually start the spell checker (Tools ➤ Spelling), and when the Spelling dialog displays a questionable word, you can check this option. (See Figure 2-15.)

In Word, you can tell the spell checker to ignore words that include numbers, such as Agent99. There is no similar option in Excel at all. Overall, we like the ability to make these settings on an application-by-application basis, but the lack of a uniform set of standard options is annoying in the extreme. Despite Redmond's claims for common interface, common code, common ad infinitum, they have a long way to go to get true uniformity between the applications in the Office suite.

However, all the applications use the *Custom.dic* file. Should you want to edit this file directly (to add a number of words at once or to remove

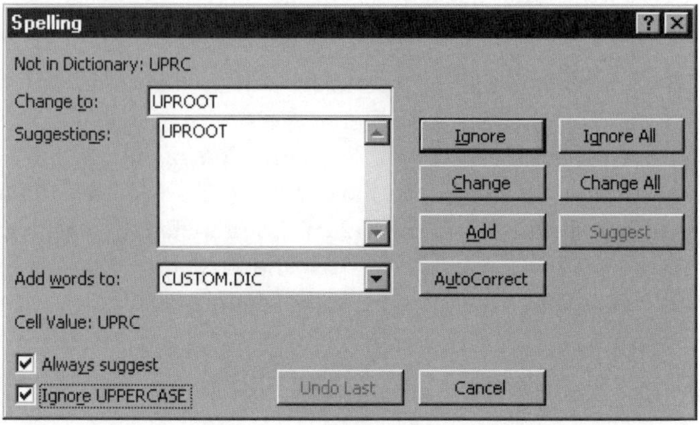

Figure 2-15: Setting the Ignore UPPERCASE option in Excel

something that was added by mistake), go to Word and click on Tools ➤ Options ➤ Spelling and Grammar. Click on the Dictionaries... button. (See Figure 2-16.)

Figure 2-16: Accessing the Custom dictionary

Click on the Edit button and Word opens the *Custom.dic* file (which is a plain text file). When done, just save the file as you would any Word file. When you open the *Custom.dic* file, Word will warn you that the automatic spell check feature will be disabled and you'll have to manually turn it back on when you're done with the file. To turn this feature back on, click on Tools ➤ Options ➤ Spelling and Grammar and check the "Check spelling as you type" box.

File ➤ New and the Templates Folder

Documents, spreadsheets, presentations, databases—whatever type of new document you are creating in Office, it is based on a template of one sort or another. It may be just the plain vanilla *default* template or a fully customized, macro-driven wonder template. Either way, templates are a key concept in creating Office documents.

When you installed Office, it created a hierarchy of folders to hold your templates. What's annoying is that there is very little explanation of how this whole thing works and how you can modify it. Under *C:\Program Files\Microsoft Office\Templates* you'll find a number of folders, which are listed in Table 2-4.

Table 2-4: The File ➤ New Template Folder Hierarchy

Folder	Contents	Appears in the New Dialog as a Tab in These Programs
Access	A collection of HTML pages and JPG graphics. These template files are used when you output a datasheet, form, or report to the Web, or use the Publish to the Web Wizard.	These options do not appear in any New dialog but are used when you output an object to dynamic HTML format.
Binders	A sample Report binder template.	Office Binder
Databases	Sample Access databases.	Access
Legal Pleadings	A Wizard for creating pleading documents.	Word
Letters & Faxes	A collection of Wizards and templates for creating a variety of letters and fax cover sheets.	Word
Memos	A collection of templates and a Wizard for creating a variety of memo documents.	Word
Other Documents	Templates and a Wizard for creating resumes and miscellaneous documents.	Word
Outlook	Sample custom forms for a variety of uses.	Outlook (File ➤ New ➤ Choose Template)
Presentation Designs	A collection of PowerPoint presentation design examples.	PowerPoint

Table 2-4: The File ➤ New Template Folder Hierarchy (continued)

Folder	Contents	Appears in the New Dialog as a Tab in These Programs
Presentations	PowerPoint presentation templates covering a wide variety of business uses.	PowerPoint
Publications	A Wizard for creating newsletters.	Word
Reports	Three sample business report templates.	Word
Spreadsheet Solutions	Three Excel add-ins for Invoices, Purchase Orders, and Expense Statements.	Excel
Web Pages	A Wizard and template for Word and some PowerPoint examples for creating Web documents.	Word and PowerPoint

Each subfolder of the *Templates* folder becomes a tab in the New dialog of the various Office applications. Templates such as *Normal.dot,* stored in the *Templates* folder, appear on a tab called General. Choosing New Office Document from the Start menu on the taskbar displays all the tabs. (See Figure 2-17.)

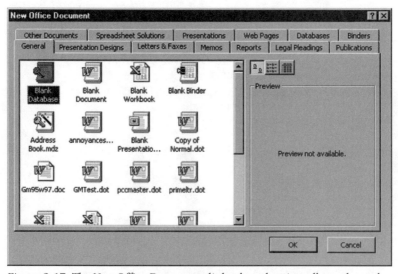

Figure 2-17: The New Office Document dialog box showing all template tabs

If you perform a File ➤ New operation in an application like Excel, the New dialog will look much different, since it only includes tabs for those folders that contain Excel add-ins or templates. (See Figure 2-18.) More generally, each Office application displays only those tabs which contain templates or files for that application.

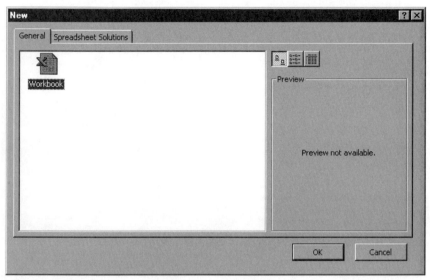

Figure 2-18: Excel's File ➤ New dialog

Most every template option available within the New dialogs (no matter which Office application) is based on a physical file. Clicking on the Word Blank Document icon triggers *Normal.dot*. There are some exceptions. Blank Database, Blank Workbook, and Blank Binder are not actual files, but trigger default documents within Access, Excel, and Binder, respectively. These are "hard coded," as it were. But you can, for example, create your own default template for Excel by creating a workbook and saving it as a template named *Book.xlt* in your *Xlstart* folder (*C:\Program Files\Microsoft Office\Office\Xlstart*).

What is not readily apparent is that you can rework the default structure of the *Templates* folder hierarchy to suit yourself. You can rename, remove, and add new subfolders below the *Templates* folder. To make a folder appear as a tab in the various New dialogs, you just need to put a template for a particular Office application in that folder.

For example, say you only use ten or so Word templates, all of which you've created yourself. Create a subfolder of *Templates* named *Word Stuff* and copy your templates into this folder. As you can see, Figure 2-19 doesn't show any of the usual "New" folders you'd expect. We created the *Word Stuff* template and then relocated all the folders that normally appear in the Word File ➤ New dialog. As long as a folder is not under the *Templates* folder, it will not appear as a tab in any New dialog. We suggest you relocate the folders instead of deleting them, in case you later want to restore the template hierarchy to its original state.

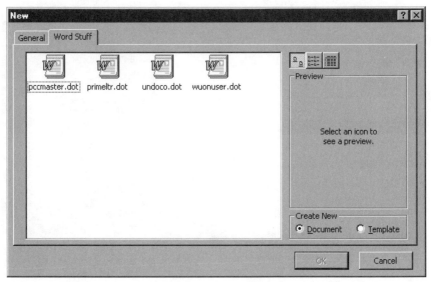

Figure 2-19: A customized tab containing Word user-created templates

A special word about creating sub-subfolders: If you create the *Word Stuff* folder, then create a subfolder of *Word Stuff* named *Godzilla*, the *Godzilla* folder *won't* appear as a tab in the New dialog. But if you put some Word templates or documents in the *Godzilla* folder, those files *will* appear in the *Word Stuff* tab of the New dialog box.

The Office Assistant

Boon or bane, the Office Assistant, disparagingly referred to by its code name "Robert" (son of Redmond's previously failed attempt at a touchy-feely user interface—Bob), is here, and we have to deal with it.

The Office Assistant, which we'll call the OA for short, lets you choose from nine different avatars (from the Cylon-like Hoverbot, to the dippy super mutt called Power Pup) that do cutesy animations as they provide a smart "natural language" question-and-answer system coupled with Office's Help files. To call up the Office Assistant, just click on the ? icon on any Standard toolbar in any Office application, or press F1. If only OA is displayed without its "What would you like to do?" dialog, clicking on it lets you type in a query that the OA tries to answer using the various Help files installed with Office. To get rid of it, you can right-click on the OA window and choose Hide Assistant.

The default character is the paper clip, which is what most people leave the OA set at. The manic Power Pup is good for a laugh, but the Einstein "Genius" character (which is very nicely rendered) is the most animated of the lot. (See Figure 2-20.)

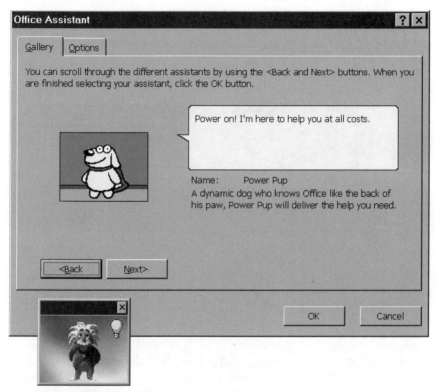

Figure 2-20: Able to leap tall Bobs in a single bound

The OA floats over your applications in a window, watching over your shoulder and occasionally making suggestions or offering tips on how to better do what you've just been doing. But no matter where its little window is, it always seems to be in the way. This is really annoying, and so most advanced users only call up the Office Assistant when needed, then dismiss it immediately after it has answered the question at hand.

The biggest annoyance with the OA? It's an all or nothing kind of thing. If you know Excel backwards and forwards, the last thing you want is an animated paper clip constantly trying to get your attention (and try it does!). But you may be a beginner in Word and would appreciate all the help you can get. If you start the OA in Word, it's displayed in each and every Office application. Shut it down in one application, and it's gone in all of them. Sheesh!

What's more, in Office 95, the Answer Wizard remembered your last six queries, even across multiple Office sessions. (The Answer Wizard was Office 95's predecessor to the OA. It appeared as a tab in the Help dialog of Office 95 applications as well as on the Help menu, and let you type in free-form questions.) With the OA in Office 97, it only remembers your last query, and only during the current Office session.

You can tweak the setting for the Assistant by right-clicking on its window and choosing Options... from the pop-up menu. (See Figure 2-21.)

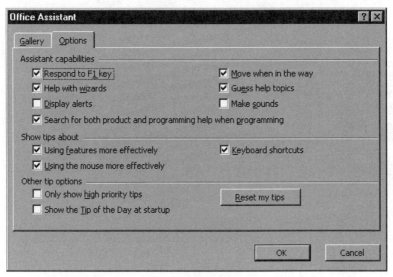

Figure 2-21: Tweaking the Office Assistant settings

There really isn't any way to permanently disable the OA (and if there were, we'd not recommend you do that—while it may be annoying on occasion, it can also be indispensable). But you can lessen its intrusive nature. First uncheck the "Show the Tip of the Day at startup" box at the bottom of the Options dialog tab to prevent the OA from activating itself every time you start up an Office application. Next, uncheck the "Make sounds" box. This goes a long way to restoring your sanity, since it prevents the OA from banging on the screen and performing various other noisy tricks to get your attention (but remember, many folks come to appreciate these sounds, as they provide subtle cues about the state of their Office affairs). Finally, you can uncheck the "Display alerts" check box, and the OA won't usurp your applications' normal message boxes and alerts in an attempt to have a constant dialog with you.

While useful, the Office Assistant query process is by no means perfected yet. If you ask the OA "Microsoft `<application name>` 97 specifications," you'll hit pay dirt for Access. For Excel, you'll get "What's new in Microsoft Excel 97," even though there is a help topic named "Microsoft Excel 97 specifications." You get "Featured highlights in Microsoft Outlook 97" in Outlook, and you'll be plain out of luck in Word and PowerPoint—no relevant topics found. So after trying the "natural language" bit, be sure to try the index of Help topics (Help ➤ Contents and Index) and have a look see for yourself before abandoning online help.

How Office Fits Into Windows

A gadfly once described World War II-era message decryption machines as "devices created by geniuses for use by fools." Unfortunately, Microsoft seems to have taken that slogan to heart. Windows is a magnificently powerful beast that's been intentionally hobbled "for use by fools." At least, that seems to be Microsoft's general attitude.

As far as we know, there aren't many fools using Windows. Inexperienced users, yes. Baffled and frustrated users, definitely. Even people who haven't a clue what's going on. We've all been there before. But real "fools" and "dummies" never make it past the Start button.

So let's take off a couple of Microsoft's condescending Windows training wheels.

You'll find a whole pot full of great Windows tweaks in *Windows Annoyances* (by David A. Karp; ISBN 1-56592-266-2) published by O'Reilly & Associates, the flagship book in this series.

Getting Explorer to Reveal All

To make your life easier, you should undo some of the "I'll protect you from yourself" nonsense that Windows thrusts upon you (if you have not already done so). This is true no matter which Office application you are working with. We're talking about the way the Windows Explorer hides filename extensions. Sure, Microsoft may like everyone to think that DOS is dead and that filename extensions don't matter any more, but whom do they think they're kidding?

Until the basic file format is redesigned to let applications determine a file type in a more sophisticated manner, applications are still partially dependent on the file extension to give them a clue as to what file belongs to which application. Oh, if you rename an extant Excel file, Windows will continue to fire off Excel when you double-click it (assuming the new extension is not associated with another application), but by and large the extension is still important. And as long as the applications are keeping track of the extension, you should too.

Fire up Windows Explorer (Start ➤ Programs ➤ Windows Explorer), click on View ➤ Options, and then click on the View tab (see Figure 2-22). Check the button labeled "Show all files", and uncheck the "Hide MS-DOS file extensions for file types that are registered" (the middle check box at the bottom). These settings affect almost all of your Office (and Windows) applications. The top and bottom check boxes affect only your view within the Windows Explorer application, so you can check them or not, at your discretion.

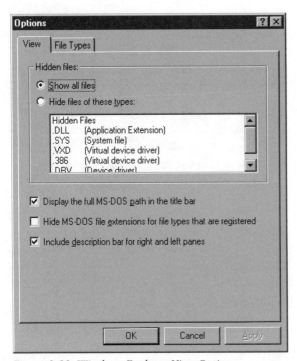

Figure 2-22: Windows Explorer View Options

Max Out Your CD

A lot of Office remains on your CD-ROM even after you've done a complete install, and some of this material you'll want to (or have to) access directly from your CD drive. Things like changing the Office Assistant characters, or, if you have Office Professional, looking up words and phrases in the CD's abbreviated version of Microsoft Bookshelf. So it makes a lot of sense to maximize your CD drive's performance. Surprisingly, Windows doesn't always do this automatically.

Again, maximizing CD-ROM drive performance is easy—once you find the blasted setting in Windows' Byzantine structure. Click Start ➤ Settings ➤ Control Panel. Double-click on the System icon. Click the Performance tab, then the File System button. On the CD-ROM tab, set the "Supplemental cache size" to Large, and "Optimize access pattern for:" to quad-speed or higher. (See Figure 2-23.) Even if you only have a double-speed CD-ROM drive, setting Windows for quad-speed allocates more room in main memory to suck in data from the drive, speeding up CD access.

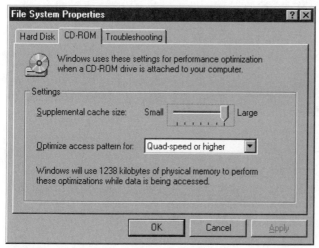

Figure 2-23: Supercharge your CD-ROM drive

Move My Documents

In any Office application, when you click on File ➤ Open, you're propelled to the *My Documents* folder by default. Lots of Office users vilify that *My Documents* folder, and for good reason. It sounds so, uh, touchy-feely. (Note to Redmond: any time you folks feel compelled to put "My" in a name, you're not thinking through the problem!) Fortunately there's a way to work around it.

Go into Windows Explorer (right-click, uh, My Computer, choose Explore). Just for fun, click on *c:\My Documents*, and try to delete it. Windows won't let you take away *My Documents*, instead displaying the error dialog in Figure 2-24. It's a sacrosanct "Windows system folder." But you can rename it: just right-click and pick Rename. You can even move it by clicking and dragging it anyplace you like. As long as you change *My Documents* inside the Windows Explorer (and not, for instance, at a

DOS command prompt), Windows keeps track of its name and location, and notifies all of the Office programs accordingly.

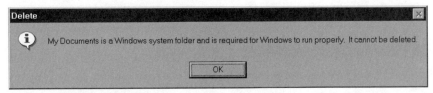

Figure 2-24: No way you can get rid of My Documents

This isn't the only way of attacking the annoyance, of course. You can change the place Word looks for documents—or any other kind of files, for that matter—via the Tools ➤ Options ➤ File Locations dialog. In Excel and Access, use Tools ➤ Options ➤ General to set a default file location. For PowerPoint, it's Tools ➤ Options ➤ Advanced (kind of like hide and seek, no?).

Scan and Defrag

Office has a penchant for scattering temporary files around your hard disk. A file here, a file there, well, more like a dozen files here, two dozen there. They're created, they get deleted (when you're lucky), and all contribute to fragmenting your disk. Between the temporary files being created and deleted at the same time your data files are being created and saved, you wind up with the first part of a file in one location, the middle located someplace completely different, and the end might be a long way from either. A standard scan of a disk drive forces Windows to read and make sure it can reassemble all the files on the disk. It also makes Windows examine its list of unused locations on the disk, and double-check to make sure that list doesn't include a disk location being used by a file. A thorough scan does everything in a standard scan, but also requires Windows to read and write data in every part of the disk, to make sure the surface of the disk is holding up. Both types of scans focus on finding scrambled areas on the disk, and repairing minor problems before they become big problems. Standard scans should be run once a day; thorough scans needn't be run more than once a month, unless you have reason to believe a drive is dying.

A defragmenting run actually rearranges the files on disk, putting far-flung pieces of files close to each other, and consolidating large blocks of unused space. The main reason for running defrag is to speed up access to files, but defrags also entail an often-overlooked benefit: they force Windows to read and write data—something like a thorough scan, but skipping over the unused parts. Thus, a defrag gives many of the benefits

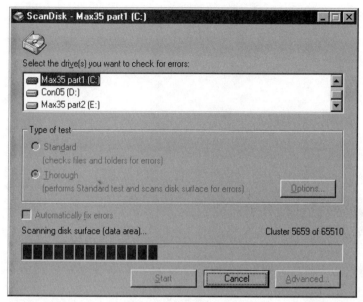

Figure 2-25: Scan and defrag your hard drive(s)

of a thorough scan without taking as much time, or imposing as much wear and tear on the hard drive.

You can run a scan or a defrag by using Windows Explorer (right-click on My Computer, pick Explore). Right-click on the drive you want to check, pick Properties, then look on the Tools tab and select the operation you'd like to perform. (See Figure 2-26.) If you have the Microsoft Windows Plus! Pack, you can use System Agent to schedule nightly scans and less frequent defrags.

NOTE   There's one annoying bug in Scandisk that you may bump into. Changes you make to Scandisk's options don't "take" until you've run Scandisk. For example, if you set up Scandisk to run thorough scans and automatically correct errors (see Figure 2-25), you must actually run Scandisk once before it will remember those settings.

Top Customizing Tips for the Working Office-ianado

Proceeding with our crusade to tweak, poke, and prod Office into working the way you want to instead of the way it wants to, here are several ways you can customize Office.

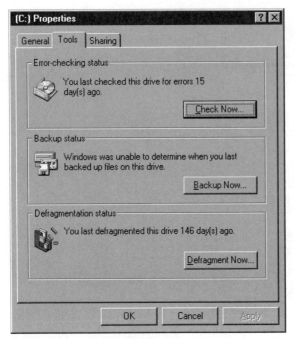

Figure 2-26: Disk maintenance

Do It Yourself Backup

What does the subject of backups have to do with Office? You know how valuable your data is and no doubt have several generations of backup carefully stored away. But have you thought about your hand-crafted custom Word templates? Ditto for your Excel and PowerPoint templates? Your unformatted AutoCorrect entries (you know where they're stored, right?)? Your Windows registry, which, if it gets fried, can ruin your whole month? As Office gets more complex, there are more bits and pieces to keep track of. Sure, you can back up your entire system to tape, but have you ever tried to recover a single file that's gotten toasted when you're under deadline? Read on . . .

Everyone agrees that backups are a good and necessary thing. But they can be long and laborious endeavors, as annoying as sitting and watching paint dry. This tip uses an old and ancient technology (that's right, DOS!) combined with cheap hard disk space, and can be used for everything from quickly backing up whatever your current project is to your entire drive. It's simple, it's fast, and it works.

The key is having a suitable place to copy the files to. One gigabyte hard disks are a fairly cheap backup medium and have the convenience of making your backups accessible without having to go through any restoration process. Read-write CD-ROMs are starting to come down in price. Zip drives, or the larger Jaz drives, phase-change removable media, etc., are all available—there is no shortage of backup media for you to choose from. These all have advantages over tape, and you should really consider one of them.

The only trick is figuring out what you want to backup.

What to backup

Instead of giving you a one-size-fits-all backup routine, we'll show you what you should consider, and allow you to decide what works best for you. Backing up an entire hard disk is pretty straightforward (and we'll give you the command for doing so efficiently), but this is often overkill—your program files are probably on CDs sitting on your shelf. What better backup do you need than that for your programs?

For a subset of your disk, you need to know the folders you want checked and the types of files to be backed up. This covers the groups of files you can go out and scoop up en masse. Then there are a number of specific files that you'll want to backup. Table 2-5 (which lists the extensions of types of files you'll want to back up) and Table 2-6 (which lists folders whose files you'll usually want to back up) are not exhaustive, but cover the most common considerations. If you use your own extensions for certain types of files, you'll want to factor that in as well.

Table 2-5: Office File Extensions and the Programs to Which They Relate

Common File Extensions

File Extension	Relates to
.doc;.dot	Word documents and templates
*.dic	Custom dictionaries
.xls;.xla;*.xlt	Excel workbooks, add-ins, and templates
.ppt;.ppa;*.pot	PowerPoint presentations, add-ins, and templates
.mdb;.mdz;*mde;*mdw	Access databases
.htm;.html;*.shtml	Web pages
*.wiz	Wizards (various applications)
.oft;.pab;*.pst	Outlook templates, Personal Address Book, mailbox contents
*.obd; *.obt; *.obz	Binder documents and templates
*.acl	These files, which are found in the *C:\Windows* folder, contain all your unformatted Office 97 Auto-Correct entries

Table 2-6: Common Office folders and Their Typical Contents

Common Folders

Folder	Usually Contains
C:\My Documents	The default folder where most Office applications want you to store your data files.
C:\Program Files\Microsoft Office\Templates	Templates for all Office applications are stored here and in sub-folders of this folder by default.
C:\Program Files\Microsoft Office\Office\Startup	This folder holds the global templates and *.wll*s that Word loads whenever it starts.
C:\Program Files\Microsoft Office\Office\Addins	Office add-ins.
C:\Program Files\Microsoft Office\Office\Shortcut Bar	The standard shortcut bar folders are found as sub-folders of this folder. They usually contain shortcuts to the applications that are represented on the shortcut toolbars.
C:\Program Files\Microsoft Office\Office\Xlstart	Files that you want Excel to load automatically when it starts.
C:\Exchange	Contains the Outlook *.pab* and *.pst* files. These files can be huge but contain your address book, all your current email and other Outlook data, so you should have a copy.
C:\Windows	Contains the Registry files *system.dat* and *user.dat*. (If the system is configured for multiple users, you'll want to grab *User.dat*, usually stored in *C:\Windows\Profiles\<user name>*.)

The last part of the puzzle that we need are some DOS switches to make our backup solution (the DOS **Xcopy** command) do our exact bidding; these are shown in Table 2-7.

Table 2-7: DOS Xcopy Switches

DOS Xcopy Switches

Switch	What It Does
/d	Copy only files that have been modified on or after a specified date. (For example: /d:07/04/97 copies all files specified that were written on July 4, 1997, or later.) You can omit the date and effectively copy only files that have been updated since the last copy was made. You could also use the /m switch, which copies files whose archive attribute has been set and then resets the file's archive attribute.
/e	Forces **Xcopy** to copy all sub-folders under the source folder, even if those folders are empty.
/r	Forces **Xcopy** to overwrite read-only files in the target folder.

Table 2-7: DOS Xcopy Switches (continued)

DOS Xcopy Switches

Switch	What It Does
/h	Copies hidden and system files.
/k	Copies file attributes along with the files. This would preserve the read-only attribute, for example.

Creating batch files

Whew! Now that you've absorbed all this lore, how do you turn it into a backup solution? Easy, you create a batch file. "A batch file!" you cry incredulously. Yep, a good old-fashioned batch file. Even in this day of URLs, hyperlinks, LNKs, and ACTs, you can still use a plain text batch file to do real, useful work.

For these examples, we'll assume that you've got a nice empty drive E as your destination or target drive for all the stuff to be backed up. To create your batch file, click on Start ➤ Run, type **notepad** into the Run dialog (see Figure 2-27), and click on OK to start Notepad.

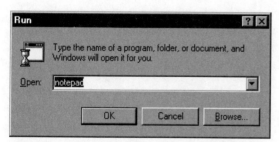

Figure 2-27: Fire up Notepad from the Run dialog

Using the Xcopy command, type one line for each source folder and specify the files to be backed up as well as the destination folder to which the files should be copied. The destination folder's path should always end in a backslash. Using the DOS wildcard characters, * for multiple characters, and ? for single characters, you can copy groups of files with ease. Here are some examples.

To copy all the files in the *C:\My Documents* folder:

```
xcopy "c:\my documents\*.*" "e:\recover\my documents\" /d /e /k /r
```

Notice the /e to grab all sub-folders; and since you may have some read-only documents, the /k preserves the file attributes and the /r allows subsequent backups to overwrite the files as necessary.

For all your templates (or any folder you want to copy including all its contents, sub-folders too) use the same format:

```
xcopy "c:\program files\microsoft office\templates\*.*"
"e:\recover\ microsoft office\templates\" /d /e /k /r
```

Specific file groups or individual files can be set up just as easily:

```
xcopy "c:\windows\*.acl" "e:\recover\windows\" /d
xcopy "c:\windows\user.dat" "e:\recover\windows\" /d
xcopy "c:\windows\system.dat" "e:\recover\windows\" /d
```

Backing up an entire drive is just as simple:

```
xcopy "d:*.*" e: /d /e /h /k /r
```

Enter each Xcopy command on its own line, and save the Notepad file to the C:\Windows\Desktop folder so that the icon is displayed on the desktop for easy access. When you save the file, be sure to give it a *.bat* extension.

A batch file for each occasion

Building these batch files is quick and easy, and you should consider having a collection of them to deal with different situations. For example, when working on a long-term project, you could have a one-line batch file to perform a quick backup that you might run several times a day to copy your working folder contents to a floppy disk in the A: drive.

Customizing Shortcut Menus

We really like the shortcut menus that pop up when you right-click on things in Office applications. We also really despise the annoying shortcut menus that pop up when you right-click on things in Office applications. They never seem to have the options we think should be there. Or worse, as in the case of the Thesaurus command, they seem to have disappeared; this option was on the shortcut menu in Office 95 but was removed in Office 97.

Not to worry. For Word, PowerPoint, and Access, you can manually tweak their shortcut menus so that the commands you want handy are available. It's interesting that you can't customize the shortcut menus manually in Excel (you have to use VBA) or Outlook (you just can't customize them at all). Excel is one of Microsoft's oldest programs and Outlook is one of its newest. If there were ever two applications that you'd think would be consistent, it'd be these two.

Ah well. We'll use Word as the example, but you can also do this in PowerPoint and Access (the commands available for placing items on the menus will be specific to the given application, of course). We'll add the Thesaurus command to the shortcut menu that appears when you right-click on a word in a the body of a document.

1. In Word, right-click on any toolbar and then on the Customize option that appears on the pop-up menu.

2. In the Customize dialog box click the Toolbars tab. Scroll the list of toolbars down to the bottom and check the Shortcut Menus option. This causes the Shortcut Menus toolbar to be displayed, as Figure 2-28 shows.

Figure 2-28: Display the Shortcut Menus toolbar

3. Click the Text menu button on the Shortcut Menus toolbar. You'll see an extensive list of all the shortcut menus that relate to text operations. Different menus appear depending on the context of what you are right-clicking on.

4. Select the Text option. This displays the actual shortcut menu that pops up when you right-click on a single word within a Word document. (See Figure 2-29.)

5. In the still displayed Customize dialog box, click on the Commands tab. From the Categories list, select Tools. In the Commands list, locate the Thesaurus... command. Click-and-drag this command to the shortcut menu. (See Figure 2-30.) Position the command where you want it to appear on the menu and release the mouse button.

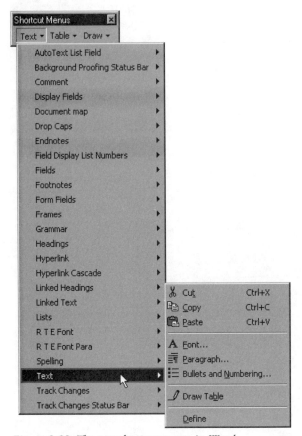

Figure 2-29: The text shortcut menu in Word

Figure 2-30: Placing the Thesaurus command on the shortcut menu

To have the Thesaurus command available in all common right-click contexts, you might want to consider adding it to the Headings, Endnotes, Footnotes, Lists, and Track Changes shortcut menus.

Customizing Your Command Bars

Now that the mystery of tweaking shortcut menus has been dispelled, let's crank up the "I am User, hear me roar!" soundtrack and tackle the various toolbars found in your Office applications.

One of the most annoyance-reducing, productivity-increasing things you can do in your Office applications is to customize the toolbars (okay, okay, it's officially a command bar of the toolbar variety). Command bars are the collections of buttons and menus that each of the Office applications sport. You can easily customize toolbars without having to write any code in Word, Excel, PowerPoint, and Access. Outlook is a separate case, and in its first release (remember, Outlook 97 is an annoying misnomer, it's really Outlook v1.0!), there is no interface for customizing its command bars. Period.

Toolbars are a great, utilitarian feature. One click on a handy icon and something useful happens. But there are many, many commands in each Office application and only limited screen space for displaying the toolbars. You have the Standard and Formatting toolbars in Word, Excel, and PowerPoint. Access, being a horse of a different database color, starts you off with just one toolbar displayed. So who got to decide what buttons receive star billing and which are omitted? Well, to us it looks like the Marketing Department got that plumb assignment.

What else could possibly explain why the Find button is not on Word's Standard toolbar (Edit ➤ Find being a feature you'll use at least hourly if you work with documents) while the Columns buttons is (Tools ➤ Columns being a command you use once in a blue moon)? Our take is that while Find is something that you vitally need and use, the Columns button makes for a better demo. That's where Microsoft gets a bunch of journalists and/or users together and demonstrates all the whoop-de-doo features in Office so you reach for the place that Microsoft wants you to go today, your wallet.

So we like to refer to the default toolbars as the *demoware* versions. They're certainly not the working versions. Changing them to suit the way you work can truly increase your productivity. Saving a few clicks here and there may not seem like enough of a payoff, but it'll make a big difference over the long haul. Trust us, give the changes in this section a chance and see if it doesn't convince you.

Not having the space here to rework all the toolbars in each Office application, we'll settle for getting you started and show you the simple steps needed to add, remove, and rearrange the buttons on the toolbars in

PowerPoint, Excel, and Word (the techniques shown work the same way in Access). The changes we'll suggest are by no means definitive; the point of the exercise is to show you how to customize the toolbars. You need to decide what works best for you given the nature of the work you do in Office.

We cover Excel toolbars in more depth in *Excel 97 Annoyances* (by Woody Leonhard, Lee Hudspeth, and T.J. Lee; ISBN 1-56592-309-X; O'Reilly & Associates). For the complete guide to customizing the Word standard toolbars, see *Word 97 Annoyances* (by Woody Leonhard, Lee Hudspeth, and T.J. Lee; ISBN 1-56592-308-1; O'Reilly & Associates).

Since you may want to experiment a bit before you decide on what works best for you, we'll create new custom toolbars. By creating a new toolbar—rather than modifying the default toolbar—you can swap the new for the old and have a fully customized interface. But should you want to change back to the default, you can just turn the custom toolbar off and the default toolbar on (via View ➤ Toolbars or by right-clicking on any visible toolbar). This also prevents any accidents with the irrevocable Reset button found on the Customize dialog box.

Creating a custom toolbar

Let's start with PowerPoint. Fire PowerPoint up and create a new toolbar; click Tools ➤ Customize, select the Toolbars tab, click New, type in **PowerPointAnnoy Standard**, then press Enter (see Figure 2-31).

Figure 2-31: A new custom toolbar in PowerPoint

Not too impressive at this point, we agree. This is the blank canvas of your new toolbar, where you'll add the buttons that you want, not what some Marketing Suit needs to do a whiz-bang demonstration. This puts the power where it belongs, in your hands. Once this toolbar is populated, you can turn off the default Standard toolbar.

Working with files

The first three buttons on the default Standard toolbar deal with files: creating new presentations with New, opening existing presentations with Open, and saving them to your hard disk with Save.

The first thing to deal with is the way the New button behaves. This button gives you a new presentation, instantly, based on a blank presentation. What's wrong with this, you ask? Well, nothing, unless you are using templates or want to invoke the AutoContent Wizard. Also, we use the button way down at the other end of the Standard toolbar for creating *new slides* much more often than we do the new presentation button. Let's combine the File ➤ New command and the New Slide command on a custom menu control that we'll call, oh, New (how's that for originality?).

The Open button and the Save button are fine as is (we'll just copy them from the default Standard toolbar to our custom toolbar. What's missing from this group is a Close button. If you're like us, you will probably close every file you open at some point. Yes, you can click on the X button, which is on the file's window title bar, to close the child window, unless the child window is maximized, in which case it's in the upper right-hand corner—watch out you don't click a few pixels high or you close the application . . . you get the idea? A close button is a good thing. Trust us.

To summarize, we'll add a custom menu control (called New) that will have a File ➤ New presentation button, plus a New Slide button; the Open button is okay; the Save button is okay; and we're going to add a Close button. If you closed the Customize dialog we used to create your custom toolbar, click Tools ➤ Customize to call it up. Now, follow these steps:

1. To create a menu control named New, select the Commands tab in the Customize dialog box, select New Menu in the Categories list, drag New Menu from the Commands list over to your new custom toolbar (PowerPointAnnoy Standard), then change its name by right-clicking on it and typing **&New** in the Name field and press Enter. To add the New command to the menu control, pull down the File menu, Ctrl+drag (hold down the Control key while dragging with the mouse) the New... command, and drop it on the empty gray square that appears just below the New menu control you just added to the custom toolbar. Right-click on it and rename it `New &Presenta-` `tion. . . .` To add the New Slide command, select Insert in the Categories list, drag New Slide... from the Commands list, and drop it on the menu control just above the New Presentation command you just added.

   This approach—using a menu control as a "front end" to several related controls—is a compelling new feature provided by Office 97 command bars.

2. Since the Open button is not being changed, just Ctrl+drag the Open button from the Standard toolbar to your new toolbar. Remember, holding the Control key lets you copy the button instead of just moving it. Whenever the Customize dialog is displayed, you can use the mouse to move and copy buttons from one toolbar to another.

3. Ctrl+drag the Save button from Standard to your new toolbar.

4. Drop the Close command (it's found in the File category) on your new toolbar.

When you've finished adding these file-related controls, your toolbar should resemble the one shown in Figure 2-32.

Figure 2-32: PowerPointAnnoy Standard under construction—file controls

Printing and spell checking

The next two buttons deal with printing and spelling. The first—which we'll call "print default"—prints one copy of the current presentation—no problem there. Next is Spelling, which none of us here could live without.

What we'll add to this set of buttons is the Find command for searching for text in your presentations and expand a bit on the number of Print commands available to you. For that, we'll add another custom menu control. Here we go:

1. Select Edit in the Categories list. Drag the Find command to your new toolbar (just to the right of the Close button). Right-click on the Find button and click on the Begin a Group menu option. This puts a separator line between the Close button and the Find button. This divider is for cosmetic purposes only, and you can omit it if you don't like separators or are short of display space.

2. Ctrl+drag the Spelling button from the Standard toolbar to your custom toolbar (to the right of the Find command).

3. Create a menu control named Print just as you did earlier for your New menu control. Use &Print for its name. Place it to the right of the Spelling button.

4. Select File in the Categories list and drag the Print command to the new Print menu control you just created on your custom toolbar. Right-click on it and rename it P&rint Presentation. This

button prints one copy of the current presentation. Next, click on the File menu (PowerPoint's regular drop-down File menu from the menu bar), Ctrl+drag the Print... command from the menu to the Print menu control on your custom toolbar. Now you have a command to print the current presentation and one to call up the Print dialog box.

The only other command that would be nice is a button to print just the current slide. There is no built-in command for doing this (although there should be if you ask us). You can use PowerPoint/ VBA to work around this. As PowerPoint only stores macros in presentations you'd have to have a one-slide presentation that you always have open to run your macros. We'll cover VBA in the next two chapters—including a more complex solution involving converting this one-slide presentation to a PowerPoint add-in—but if you're game, close the Customize dialog and start recording a macro via Tools ➤ Macro ➤ Record New Macro. Be sure the "Store macro in" setting is set to your storage presentation, do a File ➤ Print..., check the Current slide option button in the Print dialog, click OK. Stop the recorder (Tools ➤ Macro ➤ Stop Recorder). Next select Macros in the Categories list, and drag your recorded macro to the Print menu control. Right-click on it and rename it `Print &Current Slide`. Neat.

When you've finished with this step, your toolbar should resemble the one shown in Figure 2-33.

Figure 2-33: PowerPointAnnoy Standard under construction—find, spelling, and print controls

That should give you a good start on customizing your PowerPoint toolbars. The techniques for customizing toolbars are the same for Access, Word, and Excel. All are good candidates for the Close button and a Print menu. We also recommend the AutoShapes menu and the Text Box controls for Excel, PowerPoint, and Word (see Figure 2-34). But you need to carefully check out the various commands available to you and craft a toolbar containing the commands you use most often.

Remember, you can just copy buttons from the default toolbars (each Office application has multiple default toolbars, and you can mix and

Figure 2-34: Good candidates for Excel, PowerPoint, and Word toolbars

match buttons all you like) while constructing your custom toolbars. And if you can't find a command in the various Categories, see if it's on a menu somewhere, or on one of the other default toolbars, and copy it. Or you can resort to using a VBA macro.

Consider removing (or not using) any button that just calls up another toolbar. Toolbar space is precious, and you need to fill it with only the buttons that truly help you work faster. Good candidates for the bit bucket are the Web Toolbar button and the Drawing button, both on the Standard toolbar.

Customizing Excel

You can create a very similar set of buttons for an ExcelAnnoy Standard toolbar (at least as far as the first two button groups go). On the New menu control we would add the New button (which gives you a new workbook based on the default template) as well as the New... command (note the ellipsis), which calls up the File ➤ New dialog box and lets you choose from your various templates for creating a new workbook. See Figure 2-35.

Figure 2-35: ExcelAnnoy Standard File New controls

There are a number of Print options that consolidate very nicely on the Print menu control. Putting all these in one very handy menu is a real timesaver. See Figure 2-36.

Figure 2-36: ExcelAnnoy Standard Print commands

Buttons that appear on the Standard toolbar that would just waste space on your custom toolbar are the ones that call up other toolbars (Web Toolbar and Drawing); those you probably seldom use (Paste Function—admirably made obsolete by Excel 97's Formula Palette feature—and Map); and those that represent an actual hazard, like the Sort Ascending and Sort Descending buttons (too easy to accidentally scramble your worksheet).

Good generic candidates for adding are the Paste Names, AutoShapes, Text Box, and Toggle Grid buttons. You might also want to drag a copy of the Contents and Index option from the Help menu and stick it next to the Office Assistant button.

Customizing Word

Word processing is as much art as science, so everyone will probably have their own idea how best to customize the Word 97 Standard and Formatting toolbars. The important thing is that you do customize them. The benefits are manifold, and you'll be amazed how quickly you come to love a work environment tweaked just the way you like it.

You can easily do without the Print Preview, Web Toolbar, Drawing, Tables and Borders, and Columns buttons. They are either obsolete, call up other toolbars, or, as in the case of the Columns button, are used too seldom to rank a spot on your toolbar.

Candidates to add would include Close, Find, Go To, Envelopes and Labels, Shrink One Page, and perhaps a macro to print just the current highlighted selection (easily recorded as we did in the PowerPoint example). See Figure 2-37.

Figure 2-37: WordAnnoy Standard—reengineered for better service

Oh, there is one unique menu item found in Word that is not in any of the other Office applications as of yet, the Work menu. It works like a customizable MRU list. You know how Word tracks the most recently used files at the bottom of the File menu? Only the one you want never seems to be there when you want it? Well, click on the Built-in Menus option in the Categories list, and buried deep down at the bottom of the Commands list is a command called Work. See Figure 2-38.

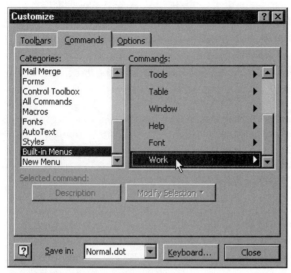

Figure 2-38: The handy Work menu

Drag this menu item up to your menu bar (or custom toolbar, if you'd
like) and drop it. It starts off with only one sub-option on the menu, Add
to Work Menu. Whenever you have a saved document (the file must
have been saved at least once so it can be found and opened) that you'd
like to add to the Work menu for easy recall later, just pull down the
menu and click on Add to Work Menu. Sort of a two-click instant
shortcut to your file. See Figure 2-39.

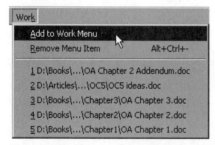

Figure 2-39: The wondrous Work menu

While it's very easy to add documents to this list, it's harder to remove
them. To facilitate being able to prune entries from the Work menu,
we've added a Remove Menu Item command, as you can see in Figure
2-39. This is the built-in command called ToolsCustomizeRemoveMenu-
Shortcuts. You can add this to the Works menu by selecting All
Commands in the Categories list (of the Customize dialog box), and
scrolling down the Commands list to ToolsCustomizeRemoveMenuShort-

cuts. Drag this up to the Work menu and drop it as the second option in the menu. We then renamed it Remove Menu Item (less of a tongue twister).

When you click on this option, the mouse pointer changes into a giant minus sign. *Be careful!* The next menu item/command you click on is deleted from the menu. *Any* menu. Carefully pull down the Work menu (with the minus sign pointer) and then click on the menu option you want to get rid of. Bingo! It's gone to the great bit bucket in the sky. If you accidentally trigger this giant minus sign and don't really want to remove any menu options, you can hit the Escape key to get rid of it.

Quick Change Checklist

What a long strange road it has been! Settings, tweaks, shortcuts, and customizations. The changes recommended in this chapter will easily repay you the cost of this book in time, energy, and a reduced annoyance level.

To keep you on track, Table 2-8 is the Office Annoyances Checklist so you can pick up any changes you may have missed or consult as a quick reference in case you want to change something later.

Table 2-8: Office Annoyances Checklist

Feature	Where to find it	Local or Pan-Office	Recommended setting
Office Assistant always visible	Right-click on OA, click Options, click Options tab, "Show the Tip of the Day at startup"	Local to OA only	Un-checked (off)
Sound feedback - Office Assistant	Right-click on OA, click Options, click Options tab, "Make sounds"	Local to OA only	Un-checked (off)
Sound feedback	Tools ➤ Options ➤ General ➤ Provide feedback with sound	Local to Access, Excel, Outlook, PowerPoint, and Word	Checked (on)
Animation feedback	Tools ➤ Options ➤ General ➤ Provide feedback with animation	Local to Word only	Checked (on)

Table 2-8: Office Annoyances Checklist (continued)

Feature	Where to find it	Local or Pan-Office	Recommended setting
Large toolbar icons	Tools ➤ Customize ➤ Options (In Access use View ➤ Tool-bars ➤ Customize)	Pan-Office; set in any of Access, Excel, Power-Point, and Word[1]	No recommenda-tion
Show ScreenTips on toolbars	Tools ➤ Customize ➤ Options (In Access use View ➤ Tool-bars ➤ Customize)	While this is pan-Office; you should set it only in Excel[1]	Checked (on)
Show shortcut keys in Screen-Tips	Tools ➤ Customize ➤ Options (In Access use View ➤ Tool-bars ➤ Customize)	Pan-Office; set in any of Access, PowerPoint, and Word[1] (this option not supported in Excel)	Checked (on)
Menu animations	Tools ➤ Customize ➤ Options (In Access use View ➤ Tool-bars ➤ Customize)	Pan-Office; set in any of Access, Excel, Power-Point, and Word[1]	Un-checked (off)
MRU List	Tools ➤ Options ➤ General ➤ Recently used file list	Local to Excel, PowerPoint, and Word	9 (or as high as it will go)
Macro virus warnings	Tools ➤ Options ➤ General ➤ Macro virus protection	Local to Excel, PowerPoint, and Word	Checked (on)
Fast Find	To turn off: on all drives, click Start ➤ Settings ➤ Control Panel. Double-click on the Find Fast icon. Click each drive in turn, then click Index, Delete Index, OK	Pan-Office	Turn off

Table 2-8: Office Annoyances Checklist (continued)

Feature	Where to find it	Local or Pan-Office	Recommended setting
User Information	Tools ➤ Options ➤ General In Word: Tools ➤ Options ➤ User Information	Local to Excel, PowerPoint, and Word	Keep current
Office Shortcut Bar	See Table 2-2	Pan-Office	See Table 2-2
Show all files	In Windows Explorer: click View ➤ Options ➤ Show all files	Pan-Office	Checked (on)
Full path visible	In Windows Explorer: click View ➤ Options ➤ Display the full MS-DOS path in the title bar	Pan-Office	Checked (on)
File extensions visible	In Windows Explorer: click View ➤ Options ➤ Hide MS-DOS file extensions for the file types that are registered	Pan-Office	Un-checked (off, meaning, do *not* hide file extensions)
Custom Dictionaries	In Word: click Tools ➤ Options ➤ Spelling and Grammar. Click on the Dictionaries... button	Pan-Office	Keep current
CD-ROM settings	Click Start, Settings, Control Panel. Double-click on the System icon. Click the Performance tab, then the File System button and the CD-ROM tab	Pan-Office	Set the "Supplemental cache size" to Large, and "Optimize access pattern for:" to Quad-speed or higher

[1] There is no way to change this from Outlook although changes made in the other Office applications change the setting in Outlook.

3

Introduction to Office Macros

In this chapter:
- *Jump Start*
- *The VBA Editor*
- *Writing VBA Programs*
- *Controlling Office Applications Using Object Models*
- *Hooking in to the Office Host Application*

Even if you couldn't care less about the difference between a bit and a byte, and break out in hives at the thought of becoming "A Programmer," you owe it to yourself to read through this chapter. Why? Because the Visual Basic for Applications macro language lets you get so much done that you'll quickly wonder how you ever lived without it. Besides, if you have a pretty good handle on how one (or more) of the individual Office applications works, you've already figured out the hard part. Picking up a little Basic and poking around a programming editor pale in comparison.

Think of macros as "leverage," a near-exponential increase in your Office prowess. When you made the transition from green multicolumn dead-tree ledger sheets to Excel or a Selectric typewriter to Word, you should have seen a huge boost in the quality and quantity of documents you were producing. By learning how to create macros, you'll take even greater control over Office and boost the quality and quantity of the documents you produce even farther. Furthermore, VBA—along with the user interface customization techniques we've shown you in previous chapters—is your most powerful weapon in fighting off the annoyance horde. Practically any Office behavior that you find annoying can be reprogrammed your way using VBA. Remember that annoyance is a relative term. An outright bug is annoying, but so is having to click more times than you'd like in order to activate a feature you frequently use. Case in point: it takes five clicks to toggle Excel's R1C1 reference style on or off, and after enough toggles you'll wonder if there's a better way. With VBA, you betcha! In this chapter we provide a seven-line macro that gives you a one-click toggle for R1C1 reference style. One very small VBA macro makes a very big difference in your daily use and enjoyment of Excel and Office.

NOTE   This is a long chapter. We'd like to convince you to tackle it anyway, for three reasons. First, if you understand the logic behind the trickier solutions, you may be able to create your own solutions to the things that bug you. Second, VBA is, without any doubt, the single most powerful feature of Office; you're selling yourself short if you don't learn how to use it. Third, we're going to make it worth your while. We've included several programs in this chapter that are valuable in their own right—programs that are so good you'd probably pay money for them. But you're going to have to wade through this chapter to get them to work. Think of it as intellectual bribery. Heh heh heh.

One more thing . . .

NOTE   You'll be seeing numerous signposts (formatted like this one) throughout the rest of this chapter. Yes, this chapter is a bit bulky. Yes, the material can be tedious. But just remember the pot of gold at the end of the, er, macro. These signposts will appear at junctures and transition points to help you stay oriented and focused. Enjoy!

Jump Start

The macro language that lives inside Access, Excel, PowerPoint, and Word is called Visual Basic for Applications (VBA). (Outlook supports VBScript, a very diluted subset of the Visual Basic language.) VBA was first introduced in Excel version 5.0 (Office 4.x), and at that moment Excel earned the distinction of being Microsoft's first Office application to use VBA.* When referring to the specific dialect of VBA that comes inside an Office application, we usually speak of "VBA/Excel" or "VBA/Power-Point" or "VBA/Word." Microsoft insists that the VBA inside Excel is the same VBA that's inside Word, PowerPoint, and Project, and to a point

---

* Both Excel 5 and Project 4 simultaneously released VBA to the world, but since Project has never been part of the official Office family, we give the vote of pioneering distinction to Excel.

that's true. Still, a program written in VBA/Excel usually won't run, unchanged, in its sibling applications, so we'll continue to draw the distinction. (By *program* here we mean a macro or procedure that calls upon application-specific components or behaviors. It's certainly true that a general-purpose VBA procedure—say, one that hot-swaps a marker in a string variable with incoming replacement text—could be written in Excel/VBA and also be used unmodified in all the other Office applications that host VBA.* It's a subtle but important distinction.)

What's the neatest part about VBA? You don't have to buy anything. It's sitting right there inside its host Office application, waiting for you to bring it to life. All it takes is a little learning and a little gumption, and we hope to give you a good dose of both in this chapter.

Once you're under way, the major conceptual hump involves understanding the behavior and features of the host Office application and its object model. Not to worry. We'll take you by the hand and show you all the important parts.

The Concepts

Practically anything you can do in a host Office application, you can do with a VBA program.† Many things you *can't* do in the host Office application, you can do with a VBA program. Indeed, anything you can accomplish with a program in Windows itself can be done in a VBA program. The full range of Windows programming—from simple offerings for the Windows Gods, to complex delving into Windows' innards—is at your beck and call from a simple (or not so simple!) VBA program. Mind boggling.

Microsoft has licensed VBA to other companies: Visio, for example, was the first company outside Microsoft to come up with a full implementation. Lots of companies are or will be jumping on the VBA bandwagon.

---

* VBScript might, or might not, support all the syntax and constructs used in what we loosely call a "general purpose procedure." Actually, a string-swapping VBA function would probably *not* run unmodified in VBScript, since we all use rigorous data typing but VBScript only supports one generic variable type (Variant), so at the very least you'd have to remark out or remove any Dim statements. But since VBScript is decidedly not VBA, you really have to test your procedures one by one. See *http://www.microsoft.com/VBSCRIPT/US/VBSLANG/VSGRPNON-FEATURES.HTM* for a complete list of VBA features not in VBScript.

† You can call 'em *macros* if you like, but they're really full-fledged programs. We'll use the terms "macro" and "program" interchangeably throughout the book. Technically, in VBA a macro is a subroutine with no parameters. In practice, self-impressed bit twiddlers use macro as a term of derision, e.g., "Oh, it's just a *macro!* I thought you had a program going." Those of us who have been working with macros for many years know better: "Oh, it's just a *program?* I thought you guys knew how to write real *macros.*"

In fact, Microsoft itself has actually swiped the VBA programming editor from the Office group and stitched it into the latest version of Visual Basic. It's that good.

What does that mean for you? You only need to learn VBA once. The skills and tips (and bugs and workarounds) you learn in, say, VBA/Excel transfer over, nearly intact, to Visual Basic, VBA/Word, VBA/PowerPoint, VBA/Visio, and many others. Sure, you have to learn the application—in Excel you're looking at cells and ranges; in Word it's paragraphs and sentences; in PowerPoint it's slides and wipes; in Visio it's shapes and connectors—but the structure that holds all the macros together stays the same. That's leverage on a grand scale.

WARNING   If you plan on working in several of the Office applications that host VBA, keep in mind that although Access 97 includes the VBA language, it definitely *does not include VBA's integrated development environment* (IDE). Oh, it has some of the VBA IDE's nice IntelliSense features—which we cover in this chapter—and an Object Browser, but that's about it. You'll be very frustrated if you enter into the Access coding environment thinking it's the same as the one its Office siblings use. It isn't, and that's too bad. Then there's Outlook. Even though it supports VB-Script and not VBA, keep in mind that Outlook's IDE is even more primitive: Notepad.

Recording Macros

NOTE   The next few sections of this chapter define, describe, and illustrate the features of VBA that are common to all its Office host applications (features like the macro recorder, the VBA Editor, and running some initial simple macros). We use Excel as the host application to demonstrate these core features.

Excel, like many Windows applications, lets you "record" macros.

NOTE   Why would you want to record a macro? In some very lim-
                ited situations, you may be able to record a macro to solve
                a particular problem—after all, macros were originally con-
                ceived as a way to automate repetitive tasks. If you need
                to repeat the same keystrokes over and over again, a re-
                corded macro may save you some time.

                Our intentions are not so pure. We want you to record a
                macro so you can see what a macro looks like, and so you
                have something hanging around later to dissect when we
                start building more capable macros. We'll get you started
                recording a macro, primarily for demo purposes. But in the
                end, all we're really doing is constructing a guinea pig for
                you to play with a bit.

                Macro recording, for us, is a means, not an end.

The mechanism for macro recording is pretty simple, and it's virtually
identical in every computer application that supports it.* There's a macro
Record Start command, not unlike pressing the Record button on a tape
recorder or VCR. Once you start, VBA watches what you do and stores
away your actions in a program, er, macro. When you're done, you press
a Record Stop button, and VBA stops recording your actions. Then you
can "play back" (we would say "run") the recorded program by pushing a
Play button. It's very simple. Let's give it a shot.

Start with a new, blank workbook and the active cell A1 on Sheet1. To
keep this example simple, we ask that you temporarily turn Excel's
"Move selection after Enter" feature off—Tools ➤ Options ➤ Edit, make
sure the "Move selection after Enter" box is not checked (if it is, before
clearing it make a mental note of the Direction setting, as we'll have you
reset this momentarily), click OK.

Click on Tools ➤ Macro ➤ Record New Macro. You should see a dialog
box like that in Figure 3-1.

In the "Store macro in" drop-down list, be sure to select This Workbook.
Then click OK. Doing so informs Excel that you want to record a new
macro (or program) called Macro1, and that you want the recording to
begin immediately. You'll see the Stop Recording toolbar pop up (you
can't read the full title of the toolbar, but it's shown in full in the
Customize dialog's Toolbars list). The recorder is on, so you need to do
something. Next click on the Stop Recording toolbar's right-most button

---

* Excel, PowerPoint, and Word support macro recording. Access and Outlook don't. It's not
surprising that Outlook doesn't (remember, it hosts VBScript), but the continued absence of
macro recording in Access is acutely annoying.

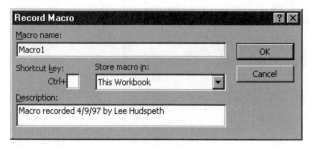

Figure 3-1: Start the macro recorder

(tooltip "Relative Reference"), which we'll explain momentarily, so that it looks as though it is pushed in. We typed

    VBA is oh so cool!

in cell A1, pressed Enter, used Format ➤ Cells ➤ Font to set the font to Comic Sans MS at 26 points blue, then pressed the down arrow key to end up in cell A2. When you're done doing whatever you wanted to do, click the Stop Recording button on the Stop Recording toolbar—the button with the square on it that's supposed to look like a VCR Stop button.

Incidentally, the second button with the tooltip "Relative Reference" tells Excel whether to use absolute or relative references while recording. By default, the macro recorder interprets cell addresses as absolute, so we clicked on the Relative Reference button to have VBA move the active cell cursor down one row from where the active cell was when you started the macro, instead of always going back to the absolute address $A$2.

Congratulations. You've just written your first VBA program.

Want to see how it works? Easy. Activate a different cell, say, C3. Click Tools ➤ Macro ➤ Macros. Click once on Macro1, and click Run (see Figure 3-2). Your program will play back—run, if you will—and insert the text all over again.

You can repeat that as many times as you like. Each time you run the program called Macro1, you'll insert the formatted label into the current cell and select the cell one row down. Nothing to it.

If you want to return Excel's "Move selection after Enter" setting back to its prior state, do so now.

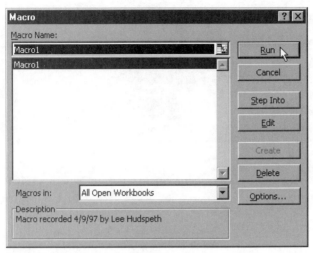

Figure 3-2: Run your first VBA/Excel program, er, macro

The VBA Editor

NOTE   Now we've got you hooked. You have a recorded macro
              sitting in front of you that you can now dissect. This is
              where we start introducing you to the macro surgeon's
              tools: the scalpels, clamps, and sutures you'll use to create
              your own macros. No need to get squeamish. We'll take
              you through the gore, step by step.

Curious to see what your program looks like? Good. Click Tools ➤ Macro
➤ Visual Basic Editor. The window that will appear before your eyes
(Figure 3-3) looks very, very complicated. For good reason. It is.
Remember the first time you saw Excel in all its glory? Well, the VBA
Editor window, in its own way, is every bit as complicated as the Excel
window. Relax a bit, though: once you get into it, the Editor itself—the
part behind this intimidating window—is nowhere near as complicated as
any of the Office Applications. It just looks that way.

Let's start by navigating the various parts of the VBA Editor.

Help in VBA

When you set up Office, you have to specifically tell the installer that you want to include VBA Help. If you go into the VBA Editor and hit F1, the Office Assistant should be ready to answer your VBA questions. If it isn't, insert the Office CD, and reinstall. (This can be done easily using the Add/Remove Programs option from the Control Panel.) This time, make sure you click on Custom, and click the Online Help for Visual Basic box.

For help on VBScript, since Microsoft didn't include VBScript documentation with Outlook, you'll have to look elsewhere.

1. Start by downloading the *VBScript Language Reference* from *http://www.microsoft.com/vbscript.*

2. You'll also want to install the complete version of the Microsoft Outlook Visual Basic Help file (that's the description appearing in its title bar, but to make an ugly mess even uglier, it's called something different in Outlook's Notepad-like Script Editor, namely Microsoft Outlook Object Library Help); the file's name is *Vbaoutl.hlp.* Note that this file really documents the Outlook object model, and *not* VBScript. To install it, go to Outlook and ask the Office Assistant to "get help for visual basic," then select the "Get Help for Visual Basic in Microsoft Outlook" topic. Click the button at the end of the first paragraph, "To do this procedure . . . click," and follow the instructions.

3. Microsoft Outlook Forms Help—an indispensable Outlook add-in—is available at *http://www.microsoft.com/kb/articles/q161/0/82.htm.* It provides much-needed information on Outlook's form design interface and VBScript.

Project Explorer

NOTE   The Project Explorer is to a VBA project as a table of contents is to a book. You'll use it to navigate your way through the different pieces of your VBA projects.

Starting in the upper-left corner, you'll see something called the Project Explorer—a fancy name for something that's very simple once you understand the history of the blasted befuddling terminology. (See Figure 3-4.)

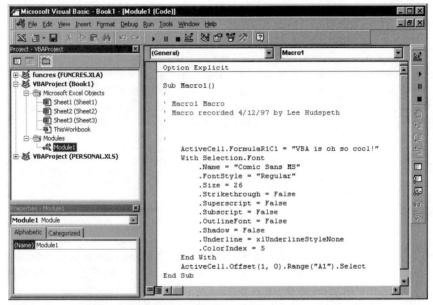

Figure 3-3: Your first program in the VBA/Excel Editor

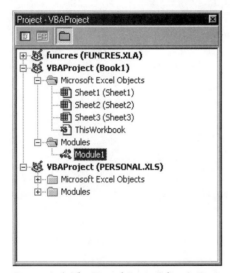

Figure 3-4: The Visual Basic Editor's Project Explorer

This Project Explorer window, probably more than any other single part of VBA, illustrates what happens when Microsoft worlds collide. On the one hand, the people who built Excel started out more than a decade ago with workbooks and sheets. On the other hand, the Visual Basic people—who work in a division of Microsoft that, until recently, was completely separate from the Excel group—speak in terms of projects. A *project* is simply a bunch of programs, custom dialog boxes and the like which, taken together, form what most people would call an *application*. More or less.

Then the Excel world melded with the VB world. The VB folks had to figure out a way to stick their projects inside Excel workbooks. At the same time, the Excel folks had to figure out a way to meld their work-book-oriented way of looking at things into the project-oriented scheme of the VB group. The compromise they reached is embodied in the Project Explorer.

It probably won't surprise you that, given this nice one-to-one correspon-dence, the groups decided that each Excel workbook would contain one, and only one, VBA project. Microsoft essentially equated the concepts of "workbook" and "project." So in the Project Explorer shown in Figure 3-4, VB people will think, "I'm looking at a list of all the *projects* currently available to me," while the Excel people will think, "I'm looking at a list of all the *workbooks* that are currently open." In fact, the two different points of view are both entirely accurate: the Project Explorer lists all open workbooks or, if you prefer, all projects that are open.

In PowerPoint, like Excel, there's a one-to-one correspondence between *presentation* and *project.*

In Word, each document and each template contains one, and only one, project. Microsoft essentially equated the concepts of "document/ template" and "project." So in the VBA/Word Project Explorer, VB people will think, "I'm looking at a list of all the *projects* currently available to me," while the Word people will think, "I'm looking at a list of all the *documents* and *templates* that are currently open."

One Toolbar Button's Worth a Thousand Clicks

The Project Explorer window is different from other Explorer-like win-dows in that you can't open a new project directly in the window, or even in the VBA Editor, for that matter. If you want to have a new project listed in the Project Explorer window, you must go *out to the application you're working in*, and open the workbook/document/ presentation that contains the desired project. That's weird, it's annoy-ing, but that's how it works. (Tip: you can toggle between the VBA Editor and its host with the tried-and-true Alt+Tab technique, but it's even faster to click the "View Microsoft *application*" button on the ed-itor's Standard toolbar; not surprisingly, this button has the icon of whatever application with which you are working on it.)

If you're looking for the VBA program you just recorded, navigate in the Project Explorer window to "VBAProject (Book1)." Then move down to the place where all program code is stored, the Modules folder. Finally, move down to the module called Module1 and double-click it.

Before we do anything else, let's save the workbook we've been practicing in—Book1 if you've been following along—and use it from here on out. By the way, we're choosing not to put these macros into your *Personal.xls* in the event that your working PC is in an office environment where *Personal.xls* is managed—in spite of its name—by your Information Systems protocols or staff.* Let's save this workbook as *Intro to VBA.xls.*

NOTE   Actually, there's a bit more to the list of workbooks (projects) revealed by the Project Explorer at any given time. Obviously, any workbooks you've opened appear in the project list. Any workbooks in the *Xlstart* folder—and your alternate startup folder, if you've defined one—appear in the Project Explorer project list, even if the workbooks are hidden. This means you'll see the special *Personal.xls* workbook that Excel handles for you. (*Personal.xls* is a workbook that Excel creates for you as a general-purpose macro repository; this special file is stored in the *Xlstart* folder, and Excel keeps it hidden by default.) You'll see some but not necessarily all add-ins (workbooks that have been compiled with an *XLA* extension) that are currently loaded. Such add-ins could be add-ins you've loaded manually with the Add-in Manager (Tools ➤ Add-Ins) or that auto-load by virtue of being installed to auto-load themselves.† Typically, although not always, an add-in will be protected, in which case if you try to view its properties in the Project Explorer, you'll be prompted for its password.

Any installed PowerPoint add-ins (with the extension *PPA*) will appear in the Project Explorer list.

Any installed Word add-ins (with the extension *DOT*) will appear in the Project Explorer list. Word add-ins are typically stored in the folder *C:\\Program Files\\Microsoft Office\\Office\\Startup.*

---

* Recall that *Personal.xls* is the door that the macro viruses like XM.Laroux use to gain a toehold and infect a system.

† Being installed to auto-load without user intervention would be common for a third-party or custom Excel solution delivered as an add-in.

Properties Window

Directly below the Project Explorer sits the Properties Window. Whenever
you click on an object, the object's properties appear in the Properties
Window. In the case of Figure 3-5, the object is the project attached to
the workbook called *Intro to VBA.xls*. The only property of this project is
its name, which happens to be, uh, VBAProject.*

*Figure 3-5: The Properties Window, shown here docked to the bottom of Project
Explorer*

Unless you do something to change it, the default name for all VBA/Excel
projects is "VBAProject," and that name appears in the Properties
Window. You can change it by simply selecting the name in the Properties Window and typing in a new name. Although a project does have
other properties—like Description, Help File, etc.—only its Name property is exposed in the Properties Window. That's annoying. If you want to

---

* Remember Major Major Major Major in *Catch-22*? We're absolutely certain he wrote the specs
for default project names in the Office implementation of VBA.

change these other properties, you can't use the Properties Window; instead, you have to right-click on the project in the Project Explorer tree, then choose VBAProject Properties (Tools ➤ VBAProject Properties also works) and change them in the dialog box (see Figure 3-6). Go ahead and do this now: change the name to IntroToVBA and add descriptive text as shown in Figure 3-6. Note that project names must begin with a letter and can include up to 40 characters (letters, numbers, and underscores are all legal). Instead of the VBA Editor's user interface, you could use VBA code to change, say, the description for this project, along with some other properties that are *not* exposed in the Project Properties dialog box. A line of code like this,

```
ThisWorkbook.VBProject.Description = _
"Work in progress VBA project for Office Annoyances readers"
```

does the trick.

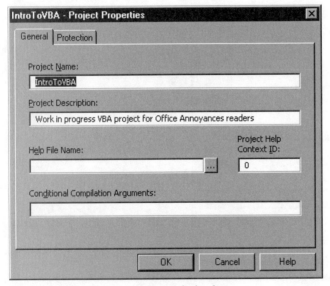

Figure 3-6: The Project Properties dialog box

NOTE   Annoyance alert! In Excel and PowerPoint, the default name for all projects is "VBAProject." In Word, the default name for projects attached to templates is "TemplateProject," and for projects attached to documents, "Project." The name of the VBA property in the Office object model that returns a VBA project for a particular workbook, template, document, etc. is "VBProject" in Excel, PowerPoint, and Word. Go figure.

We'll be seeing a lot more of the Properties Window when we get to things that have more properties.

NOTE   You should get into the habit of changing the name of a project from its default *before* you start working on the workbook. This is a good habit to get into because you'll save yourself grief down the road if the project is referenced by other projects.* Word in particular is a real pain about this. Due to an extraordinarily annoying (read: dumb) design decision, Word "loses" custom settings for a document or template when its project name is changed. Your toolbar changes, keyboard assignments and the like get the deep-six when you change the name of the project attached to a document or template.

Code Window

NOTE   Now we're ready to go beyond the window dressing, into the heart of the matter: the program code itself. Don't be overly concerned if you still haven't figured out exactly what the Project Explorer and Properties Window do; you'll have a chance to see it all work together once we dig into the code.

The Code Window is where you'll be doing most of your work (see Figure 3-7). It takes up the right side of the VBA Editor window, and contains (*mirable dictu!*) your code.

A brief grand tour:

- The Code Window's title bar has all the controls you'd expect of a title bar, but there's a subtle—and annoying—difference between them in Excel, PowerPoint, and Word. In Excel and PowerPoint, the title bar always *includes* the project filename's extension (see Figure 3-7). In Word the title bar always *omits* the project filename's extension (see Figure 3-8). Word's omission of the extension is not just

---

* By changing an Excel VBA project name from the default, you'll avoid the "Name conflicts with existing module, project, or object library" error that occurs when there are several open projects with the name VBAProject and VBA is unable to distinguish between them. You'll also avoid the compiler error "Variable not defined" that occurs when code that worked previously is disrupted by a change in the name of the project that owns a called procedure.

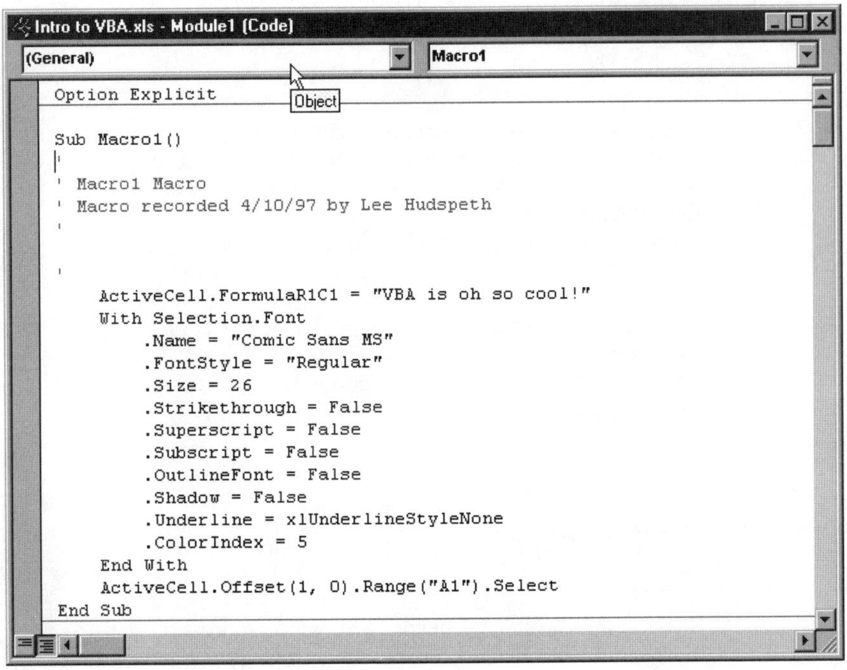

```
Intro to VBA.xls - Module1 (Code)                                      _ □ ×
(General)                                    ▼    Macro1                        ▼
    Option Explicit         Object                                             ▲

    Sub Macro1()
    '
    ' Macro1 Macro
    ' Macro recorded 4/10/97 by Lee Hudspeth
    '

    '
        ActiveCell.FormulaR1C1 = "VBA is oh so cool!"
        With Selection.Font
            .Name = "Comic Sans MS"
            .FontStyle = "Regular"
            .Size = 26
            .Strikethrough = False
            .Superscript = False
            .Subscript = False
            .OutlineFont = False
            .Shadow = False
            .Underline = xlUnderlineStyleNone
            .ColorIndex = 5
        End With
        ActiveCell.Offset(1, 0).Range("A1").Select
    End Sub
                                                                              ▼
```

Figure 3-7: The Code Window—home sweet home

goofy, it makes it harder to quickly see what application is hosting a particular VB Editor window (you have to look at the VB Editor Standard toolbar, then look at its left-most View... button to see what button face is there). Why this difference? Well, there's more. Compare the Project Explorer listing for Excel and Word and you'll discover two differences. First, Word's project listing omits the parenthetical filename listing when the root filename and the project name are exactly the same *and* the file is a global template (whether that global template is open or not), whereas Excel's project listing always shows the parenthetical filename even when the root filename and project name are exactly the same. (Ditto PowerPoint.) Second, Word's project listing never displays a project filename's extension, and Excel's always does (as does PowerPoint's). Again, we ask why? More of Microsoft's little mysteries. If you routinely work in these allegedly consistent applications, these subtly differing visual cues become a jarring distraction.

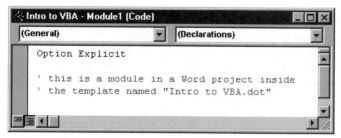

Figure 3-8: Word's Code Window oddly drops the project filename extension

- In the upper-left corner is the Object box, an area where you can pick one of those mysterious objects, in this case objects that can have subroutines or functions* attached to them.

- In the upper-right corner sits the Procedure box, which contains a list of all the subroutines or functions available in the object shown in the Object box.

  If you're looking at the Module1 module of the *Intro to VBA.xls* project (read: the collection of programs called Module1 that's stuck in *Intro to VBA.xls*), the General Object (read: the main collection of programs) should have two procedures. The subroutine you just recorded is a procedure called Macro1. The other procedure is kind of a miscellaneous catch-all thing called (Declarations).

- The stripe down the left side lets you control the way the VBA Editor runs your program, shows you which line of the program is currently running, and lets you set *breakpoints*—lines where VBA is supposed to stop running and wait for you to figure out what's going on. It can come in very handy, as you'll see momentarily.

- The two buttons in the extreme lower-left corner control whether you see just one procedure at a time (this is called *procedure view*) or all the code from all the procedures—arranged alphabetically—that can fit in the window (termed *full module view*).

Believe it or not, you're looking at one of the most sophisticated programming environments available for any programming language. Grown men and women who struggle with wimpy programming editors every day have been known to weep openly at the sight of this marvel. Imagine. All that attention lavished on us lowly macro programmers!

---

* A subroutine is just a program: it's a bunch of VBA/Excel code that does something. A function is just like a subroutine, except that when it's done, it produces a value. For example, a subroutine might print a document, whereas a function might print the same document and return the number of pages that were printed. The distinction is largely academic and tends to become much clearer when you start working with programs.

Docking

NOTE   This section describes the various ways in which you can
              arrange (and hide or make visible) the different windows
              that comprise the VBA Editor.

If you click-and-drag the window title (the blue part) of the Project
Explorer or the Properties Window, you'll see that both windows will
detach themselves from the Editor. You can put them outside the VBA
Editor window, drag them to different corners, even dock the two of
them together outside the Editor. So many choices. Nice of Microsoft to
offer them.

NOTE   You can precisely control which of the VBA Editor's win-
              dows are dockable. Select Tools ➤ Options, click the
              Docking tab, and check or uncheck at your discretion.
              (We recommend you leave all these docking options
              checked except Object Browser, which we find is easier to
              use if not dockable.)

              Furthermore, there is a dragging trick—at least we found it
              to be tricky at first—to getting a window to dock. Let's say
              you want Project Explorer to be left-docked. If it's floating
              aimlessly in the middle of the VBA Editor display space,
              grab it by the title bar and start dragging it left. Often, its
              "in motion" frame will suddenly attach itself—for no appar-
              ent reason—to the bottom of the screen, then suddenly un-
              dock. Very disconcerting. Just hold on and keep dragging.
              When you've left-dragged the window so that about two-
              thirds of its entire real estate is off the left edge of the screen
              (you'll see the thick gray "in motion" frame become a thin
              gray frame), let go and it will be left-docked.

When it comes right down to it, however, most of the time the Project
Explorer and Properties Windows only amount to giant annoyances. Yes,
when you're switching around between projects, the Project Explorer
comes in handy. Yes, when you're setting properties (particularly when
you're designing custom dialog boxes), the Properties Window is indispensable. But when you're really hunkered down writing VBA programs,
you rarely need either.

We recommend that you hide them both, by clicking on the X in the
upper-right corner of each window. When you need them, calling them
back takes just a click on the VBA Standard toolbar.

The Access Programming Environment

After enticing you with the alluring details of VBA's multi-window IDE and docking capabilities, we're sorry to report that you must set all those advances aside when working in the Access programming environment. You get one window—the Code Window, as shown in Figure 3-9, except it's called the Module Window by the Access Help file—plus the Object Browser and some IntelliSense features. That's it. Furthermore, Access doesn't support Forms 2.0, the forms engine for UserForms (dialog boxes) provided with Excel, PowerPoint, and Word; instead Access uses its own proprietary forms engine.

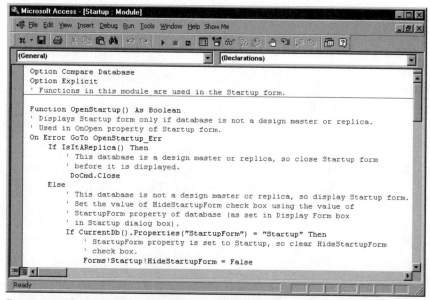

Figure 3-9: The Access programming environment (no Project Explorer, no Properties Window, no User Forms)

Toolbars

The VBA Editor, like most Office applications, has a handful of toolbars. When you first start the Editor, you'll see the two most important ones: Standard and Debug (see Figures 3-10 and 3-11). Surprisingly, there's a substantial amount of overlap between the two. Not so surprisingly, some parts of both toolbars are very poorly designed.

Figure 3-10: The Editor's Standard toolbar

Figure 3-11: The Editor's Debug toolbar

We won't go into a lot of detail about customizing the VBA toolbars, except to note that it can be done—if you know the trick. Word, Excel, and PowerPoint let you change toolbars by clicking on Tools, then Customize. Not so the Editor. You'll have to right-click on a toolbar, pick Customize, then click and drag from that point.

NOTE   Don't bother trying to get that huge "Ln X, Col Y" button
                 off your Standard toolbar, or to shorten it. The button
                 won't come off, and you can't make it any smaller. You
                 can drag the Standard toolbar anywhere you like—make it
                 float, dock it on the left, do whatever you can—and that
                 gargantuan, ugly button stays put. Man, talk about annoy-
                 ing. You'd think that Microsoft would put it down in the
                 lower-left corner, to the left of the horizontal scroll bar.

The most important three buttons on both toolbars (so important they put 'em there twice!) are the right-wedgie Play button, the two-vertical-line Pause button, and the square block Stop button. Clicking on those buttons respectively play, pause, and stop execution of the current subroutine. For all you tooltip-philes out there, these buttons' tooltips read like this, though for semantic sanity we'll stick with the VCR-type terminology:

- Play—Run Sub/User Form (F5)
- Pause—Break (Ctrl+Break)
- Stop—Reset

The next important button is the one in the middle of the Debug toolbar that looks like a stack of pancakes with a loopy arrow. When you click on that button, VBA runs just the next line of your program. It's called a "Step Into" button because when you run programs with it, VBA "steps into" each subroutine and function that gets called.

Finally, you can bring back up the Project Explorer window by clicking the button near the end of the Standard toolbar that looks like a sheet of paper with squares and pills on top of it. (We call the picture "Portrait of Project with Descending Quaaludes," but your impression may vary.) The button immediately to its right—the one with a finger on a sheet of paper—brings up the Properties Window.

Some of the other buttons do nifty things—the three Debug toolbar buttons that look like sheets of paper invoke tremendously powerful debugging aids (the Locals Window, Immediate Window, and Watch Window, respectively)—but we'll limit our exploration in this book to the buttons mentioned. They'll get you started. You can strap on the warp drive later.

NOTE   So much for the orientation. You've seen the macro surgeon's tools. Now let's put them to use.

Annoying Settings

Before you start using the VBA Editor, there are two groups of settings you need to fix.

First, everybody who uses VBA should click on Tools ➤ Options, and under the Editor tab, check the box marked Require Variable Declaration. (See Figure 3-12.) In Access, it's Tools ➤ Options ➤ Module.

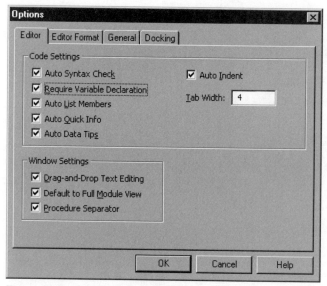

Figure 3-12: Always require variable declaration

The mechanics behind this setting are unimportant, but this requirement outstrips all others. With this box checked, VBA will require you to declare any variable names before using them in any code that you write. By forcing you to declare variables (you'll see how shortly), VBA effectively minimizes the number one source of programming bugs: misspellings.

NOTE   To find out more about the data types supported by VBA,
                see the Help file topic "Data Type Summary."

Second, if you have installed any Office components or any other applications that VBA will use, it's important that you tell VBA about them. Do
so by clicking on Tools ➤ References, and checking the box next to any
programs you expect to be using with VBA, as shown in Figure 3-13.

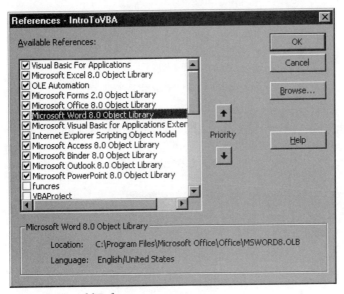

Figure 3-13: Add References

If you plan to use VBA aggressively (and, hey, you paid for it—why
not?), consider adding references to any programs you might want to
control from Excel. We check all of the following:

- Microsoft Office 8.0 Object Library

- Microsoft Word 8.0 Object Library

- Internet Explorer Scripting Object Model

- Microsoft Access 8.0 Object Library

- Microsoft Binder 8.0 Object Library

- Microsoft Outlook 8.0 Object Model

- Microsoft PowerPoint 8.0 Object Library

- DAO 3.5 (especially if you're going to use Access)

Adding each of these references involves a small amount of overhead. They can also lead to a bit of confusion when VBA asks questions like, "Do you want to look at Help on the Windows collection for Excel or for Word?" But by and large, it's much better to have these around should you need them.

Basic Functions

NOTE   So far VBA is just a disembodied ghost, floating around in some promised land of milk and programmatic honey. Let's take a look at how the VBA Editor works with Excel, and vice versa. We'll haul out that little recorded macro, just to give you a look-see.

Microsoft hooked the Code Window into Excel itself: you can run your program in the Code Window and watch the effects of your program in Excel. We find it most useful to run Excel and VBA in windows that don't overlap, or overlap just a little bit, so we can see everything that's going on.

TIP   To precisely split your desktop between two application windows, minimize all applications (right-click the taskbar tray and choose Minimize All Windows), right-click the taskbar icon of the first application and choose Restore, right-click the taskbar icon of the second application and choose Restore, then right-click the taskbar tray and choose Tile Horizontally (or Tile Vertically).

To get a feel for what's happening, arrange VBA and Excel itself so you can see both of them at the same time (see Figure 3-14). Make sure Macro1 is showing in VBA. If you have recorded more than one macro, put the cursor somewhere in Macro1.

Now click the right-wedgie Play button a few times. See how VBA puts text in successive cells (moving down one row at a time) in the blank worksheet?

To put it all under a microscope, here's what's happening:

1. You push the Play button. VBA runs the program called Macro1.

2. VBA sets the contents of the active cell to the formula—in this case a text label—comprised of the text "VBA is oh so cool!"

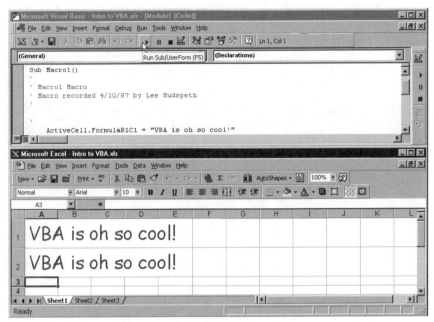

Figure 3-14: Testing VBA's interaction with Excel

3. VBA applies all the properties you set while in the Font tab of the Format Cells dialog (font name, font style, size, and so on).

4. VBA selects the cell that is in the same column but one row down from where the active cell had been when you started the macro.

If you then push the Play button again, everything starts all over at Step 1.

Try playing with this a bit. Change the text in Macro1 to, oh, "Excel is the King of Spreadsheet Hill!" Click the Play button a few times. Do something different. Change the font to be even more outlandish or plain vanilla or whatever, activate some random cell, and click the Play button again. See how that works? Pretty straightforward.

Are you curious about that last expression, the one that reads:

```
ActiveCell.Offset(1, 0).Range("A1").Select
```

Here's an explanation:

1. The `ActiveCell.Offset(1, 0)` part of this expression returns a Range object that is offset from the specified range (in this case, the range defined by `ActiveCell`). The offset is 1 row positive (read: 1 row down) and 0 columns (read: same column), meaning, one cell directly down from where you started.

   So, if the active cell was cell A1, `ActiveCell.Offset(1, 0)` refers to cell A2.

2. `.Range("A1")` is a relative expression—and, it turns out, super-fluous, but the recorder put it in for reasons known only to the folks who wrote the recorder. It means "same column, same row": in other words, no change to the range defined in Step 1. How do we know this? Well, carefully read the last paragraph of the Help topic "Range Property (Application, Range, or Worksheet Object)" and you'll get the drift in the sentence, "For example, if the selection is cell C3, then `Selection.Range("B1")` returns cell D3 because it's relative to the Range object returned by the Selection property." Here, think of `Range("B1")` more like a relative reference of RC[+1] because B1 has a relative offset of one column relative to A1 (A1 is the upper-left corner or origin of any Excel worksheet), and B1 has a relative offset of zero rows relative to A1, and that's RC[+1].

   So, if the range resulting from Step 1 is cell A2, at the end of Step 2 you're still at cell A2. Really!

3. The expression `.Select`, not surprisingly, selects the range defined by everything that went on so far in the VBA expression.

   So, at the end of Step 3 you've selected cell A2. Whew! Moral: when writing VBA/Excel code manually to accomplish this, drop the `.Range("A1")` part of this expression and simply say `Active-Cell.Offset(1, 0).Select`.

Writing VBA Programs

NOTE   See how it all fits together? No, we didn't think so. Hang in there. The more you work with it, the more it'll make sense. Honestly. This is one humdinger of a programming environment.

Just so you understand where we've been and where we're heading: At this point, that recorded macro has served its purpose—it has given you something to play with on your way to VBA understanding. You can forget about it now. You're old enough to make your own toys, from scratch. With a little bit of help, of course.

Before we dive into the big, bad world of events and object models, let's take a few minutes to write and run a couple of simple VBA programs.*

---

* We use the term "VBA" here because these programs rely on Visual Basic for Applications alone. In other words, they'll run precisely the same way in VBA/Access, VBA/Excel, VBA/ Word, VBA/PowerPoint, VBA/Visio, and probably any other VBA flavor you can find. They'll also run the same way in Visual Basic itself.

These won't cure any of Excel's annoyances, but they'll give you a fighting chance to ease into the VBA way of thinking.

If You've Never Written a Program, Don't Panic

Computer languages, like human languages, don't unveil themselves immediately. You have to memorize little snippets—"Hello, how are you?" or "Where is the bathroom?" or "I can count to ten"—and then work on tying the snippets together.

Computer languages, like human languages, have all sorts of rules and conventions. There are phrases that "sound right"; there are phrases that don't quite go together, even if they do work.

You wouldn't expect to learn French in one sitting. It's amazing how many folks get frustrated because they can't learn Basic in one sitting. In many ways, Basic is more difficult than French. Of course, in other ways, it's considerably simpler.

If you concentrate on getting the feel of a language—again, human or machine—you'll often find that the nit-picky rules fall into place, sooner or later. You'll get better at it with practice. That's precisely the method we think you'll find easiest for learning VBA.

Creating a New Program

Our first program puts a series of message boxes up on the screen that count from one to ten. The last of these is shown in Figure 3-15.

To create this program, start by ensuring that you're still working in IntroToVBA's Module1 module.

NOTE   For simplicity's sake, from this point forward we're going to refer to a project by its project name as opposed to its filename. So when we say "put a new procedure in IntroToVBA's Module1 module" you'll know we're referring to the IntroToVBA project stored inside the file called *Intro to VBA.xls*, even though the VBA Editor's title bar in Excel uses the filename, not the project name (unlike VBA/PowerPoint and VBA/Word, which use the project name, as we discussed earlier in this chapter).

Use Your Choice of Excel, PowerPoint, Word, or Access for the First Two Exercises

The first program you work on in this section is called `LoopPractice`. The second is called `PowerOfTwo`. These two programs, and the instructional steps we present to describe them, work *precisely* as shown in these three Office 97 applications: Excel, PowerPoint, and Word. That's really no surprise since these three applications all support the very same implementation of VBA and the VBA IDE. Feel free to work through the exercises associated with `LoopPractice` and `PowerOfTwo` in any of these three applications.

In Access, these two programs run the same way as they do in Excel, PowerPoint, and Word. The minute details of our step-by-step instructions won't match precisely with Access' proprietary programming environment, but the overall steps are reasonably close—close enough that you should be able to get the code entered and running without too much fuss. (As an example of the subtle differences imposed by Access, for Excel, PowerPoint, and Word, we say "If you can see Macro1 in the Code Window, you're in good shape. If not, bring up the Project Explorer (possibly by clicking the "Portrait of Project with Descending Quaaludes" button on the Editor's Standard toolbar), navigate to the project called IntroToVBA, then Modules, then double-click on Module1." In Access you have a Module Window, not a Code Window; there's no Project Explorer; and the main toolbar is named Visual Basic, not Standard. But the code still runs the same.

What about Outlook? We're going to take this opportunity to point out that Outlook's programming environment is so *poorly implemented, feeble,* and *irksome* that to even scratch the surface of how to get oriented there is beyond the scope of this book. However, for those among you who are willing to test these cold, deep waters, check out the section entitled "Testing LoopPractice and PowerOfTwo in Outlook VBScript." There we present the skeletal steps needed to create a test Outlook form to host a button by which you can then call the programs `LoopPractice` and `PowerOfTwo`. Yes, sadly, that's how you have to do it, because although the Outlook Script Editor (Notepad in flimsy disguise) has a Run command, it doesn't work.

If you can see Macro1 in the Code Window, you're in good shape. If not, bring up the Project Explorer (possibly by clicking the "Portrait of Project with Descending Quaaludes" button on the Editor's Standard toolbar), navigate to the project called IntroToVBA, then Modules, then double-click on Module1.

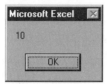

Figure 3-15: The final message box

We're going to create a new program called `LoopPractice`. Start by clicking on Insert ➤ then Procedure as shown in Figure 3-16.

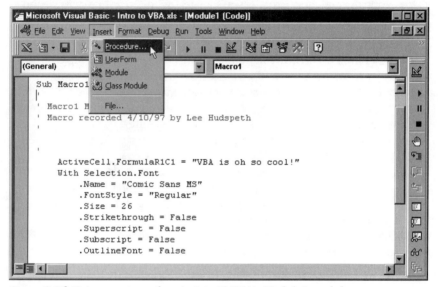

Figure 3-16: Put a new procedure in IntroToVBA's Module1 module

When the Add Procedure dialog comes up, type in the name **LoopPractice**. Leave the option buttons alone, and click OK, as shown in Figure 3-17.

VBA will create a new subroutine called `LoopPractice`, complete with `Sub` and `End Sub` statements, which mark the beginning and end of the subroutine. Your cursor is already in position for you to start typing your program. (If you're following along, it will be sitting at the beginning of the empty line following the `Sub` statement, as shown in Figure 3-18.) Type the code shown in Example 3-1 (remember, VBA has already provided the first and last lines).

Example 3-1: The LoopPractice Subroutine

```
Public Sub LoopPractice()
Dim i As Integer
For i = 1 To 10
   MsgBox i
Next i
End Sub
```

Figure 3-17: Create a subroutine called LoopPractice

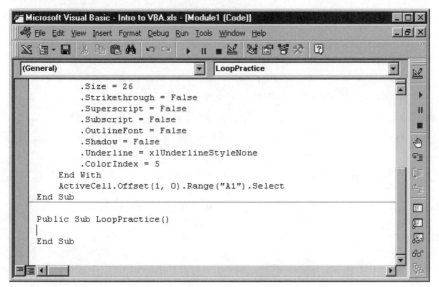

Figure 3-18: LoopPractice() appears in the Code Window

| *NOTE* | Notice that we've indented code inside the `For...Next` loop construct by one tab stop. If you're new to programming, the practice of indenting code is a long-standing tradition and definitely makes your code more readable. |

That's a fully functional VBA program. Translated into English, it goes something like this:

1. This is a subroutine called `LoopPractice` that's Public, i.e., other programs can use it.

2. Set aside room for a variable called *i*. It will hold integer values.

3. Do the following, with *i* first set to 1, then to 2, then to 3, etc., and finally with *i* set to 10.

4. Put a message box up on the screen that contains the current value of *i*.

5. Repeat with the next value of *i*.

6. This is the end of the subroutine called `LoopPractice`.

It probably won't surprise you too much to know that `LoopPractice` will put a series of ten message boxes on the screen, each with a number from one to ten. Verify the results by running `LoopPractice`; simply push the Play button and watch what happens.

If you were watching closely as you typed in the program, you probably noticed little cheat boxes that popped up, offering to help you with your program. The first one (Figure 3-19) listed all the different variable types that could go in a `Dim` statement. You wanted `Integer`.

This capability, where VBA offers you a list of valid commands at a particular point in building a line of code, is called Auto List Members. You can scroll down the proffered list with the up and down arrow keys, or you can simply type more letters in the command to scroll down the list. Either way, when VBA has found the item you want, hitting the Tab key will automatically fill out the remainder of the command and leave the cursor on the current line. It's a wonderful feature.

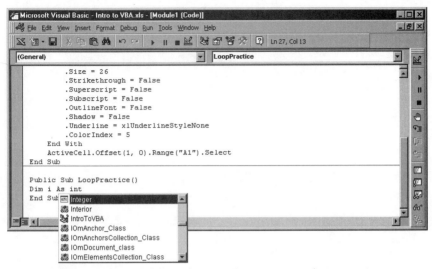

Figure 3-19: VBA offers valid variable types as Auto List Members

---

NOTE	Pressing the Tab key to accept the desired item in the list may feel awkward at first, but you'll get used to it. You can press Enter to accept the desired item in the list and start a new line.
	The Auto List Members list will differ depending on the References you've defined for the current project. You'll recall from earlier in the chapter that we've thrown our References net fairly wide to include several other applications' object models.

The second cheat box that popped up (Figure 3-20) listed the parameters that could go along with a message box function. You only used the first parameter—in this case the variable i—in place of the Prompt parameter.

This capability, where VBA prompts you with the various parameters for a particular command, is called Auto Quick Info. It can also come in very handy, especially if you're forever forgetting which parameters are available, and what sequence they come in. The shorthand VBA uses can sometimes grow cryptic, and VBA doesn't offer to complete commands for you as it does with Auto List Members. Still, you'll come to rely on this feature over and over again.

If you find type-ahead looking-over-your-shoulder features like these annoying—and some people do—you can turn them off by choosing Tools ➤ Options ➤ Editor, and unchecking them individually or en

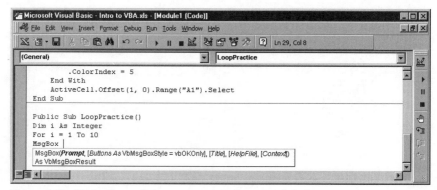

Figure 3-20: VBA offers valid parameters as Auto Quick Info

masse, as desired. For additional information about the VBA Editor's settings, click this dialog's Help button.

NOTE   Note that when you type the command form of a com-
           mand—MsgBox i—instead of the function form—rc =
           MsgBox(i)—VBA's Quick Info pops up at different times.
           In the command form, you won't see Quick Info until you
           type a space character following the command. In the func-
           tion form case, you'll see Quick Info as soon as you type
           the opening parenthesis of the parameter list.

Embellishment

The best way to learn about VBA is to play with it a bit. You have a great little sandbox here, so take advantage of it! Try these variations.

The For statement can do lots of things. Replace For i = 1 to 10 with one of the following:

```
For i = 5 to 10
For i = 1 to 10 Step 2
For i = 5 to 1 Step -1
```

The MsgBox command has three commonly used parameters. The first parameter is just the message that appears in the box. The second param-eter specifies the types of buttons (OK, Cancel, etc.) and the icon (none, exclamation mark, question mark, etc.) that appear in the box. The third parameter appears as the box's window title. Try these in place of MsgBox i. In each case try to guess what will happen before you run the program:

```
MsgBox i*10
MsgBox i, vbOKOnly
```

```
MsgBox i, vbYesNoCancel
MsgBox "The value of i is: " & i, vbExclamation, "My Loop
Practice Routine"
```

A message box produced by the last `MsgBox` statement is shown in Figure 3-21.

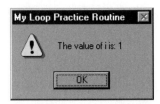

Figure 3-21: A fancier MsgBox

`vbOKOnly`, `vbYesNoCancel`, and `vbExclamation` are examples of VBA constants. They're numbers predefined by VBA and given relatively easy to remember names. For example, `vbYesNoCancel` is preassigned the value 3 by VBA. You could try to remember that the number 3 will produce Yes, No, and Cancel buttons on a VBA `MsgBox`. But you'll undoubtedly find it much easier to remember the constant `vbYesNo-Cancel`. Since these general-purpose constants are the same across all the Office applications that support VBA, your learning curve is lessened dramatically.

NOTE   If you need help with a particular object, method, property, or function in your source code, inside the Code Window simply click next to (or anywhere inside) the keyword you want help on and press F1.

A More Interesting Program

Let's try a slightly more complex program, and see if we can take advantage of several additional VBA features. Get VBA going, click Insert ➤ Procedure, type **PowerOfTwo**, and click OK. Then type in the program shown in Example 3-2.

Example 3-2: The PowerOfTwo Subroutine

```
Public Sub PowerOfTwo()
Dim iMax As Integer, i As Integer
Dim sMsg As String
iMax = InputBox("Enter a number between 1 and 32766", "Find Power")
If iMax > 0 And iMax < 32767 Then
    If iMax = 1 Then
        i = iMax
```

Example 3-2: The PowerOfTwo Subroutine (continued)

```
    Else
        i = 1
        Do
            i = i * 2
        Loop Until i > iMax
    End If
    sMsg = "The greatest power of two less than or equal to " _
            & iMax
    sMsg = sMsg & " is " & i & "."
    MsgBox sMsg, vbOKOnly, "Find Power"
Else
    MsgBox "You typed an invalid number.", vbOKOnly, "Find Power"
End If
End Sub
```

In English, the program goes more or less like this:

1. This is a subroutine called `PowerOfTwo` that other programs can use.

2. Set aside room for integer variables called *i* and *iMax*, and a string called *sMsg*.

3. Ask the user to type in a number between 1 and 32766.* Set *iMax* to that value.

4. If the user typed a valid number, keep calculating progressively larger powers of two. Stop when you've reached a number bigger than *iMax*, and display in a message box the power of two that's closest to but less than *iMax*.

5. If the user didn't type a valid number, tell him so.

6. This is the end of the `PowerOfTwo` subroutine.

Look like a reasonable program? Good. Click the Play button and run it.

The dialog in Figure 3-22 appears, asking you to enter a number between 1 and 32766. Let's start by seeing how fast this program will go when it works on a significant problem. Feed it a big number like, oh, 20000.

Oops. Something went wrong. You've hit an overflow—programmer's jargon for "the result you got when you did a calculation that is too blasted big to fit into the variable it's supposed to go into." (Click the Help button in Figure 3-23 and you'll see a somewhat less understandable description.) What went wrong? And why?

---

* Note that integer variables can only hold values up to and including 32,767. To learn that, hit F1 and ask VBA Bob, "What is the maximum value of an integer?" After you've seen that he hasn't a clue what you're talking about, ask Bob "integer data type," then select the Integer Data Type topic.

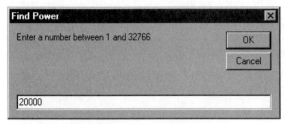

Figure 3-22: The PowerOfTwo input box

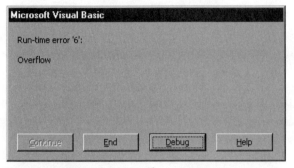

Figure 3-23: Run time error 6

To help find out, click the Debug button in Figure 3-23. VBA will immediately highlight the line it was running when the error occurred, as Figure 3-24 shows. A yellow arrow appears in the vertical bar to the left of the line that was being executed.

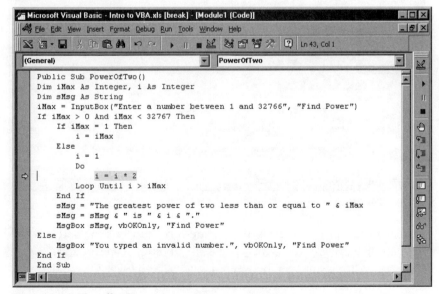

Figure 3-24: The offending statement

Somehow, the variable *i* is getting too big. (You'll also notice that if you enter a smaller value, say 4, the program reports a result that's larger than what you entered. This is obviously wrong. You'll see why, and fix this bug, in the ensuing paragraphs.) That's the only possible reason why you'd hit an overflow on that particular line. Let's use a couple of VBA's cooler features to track down the error.

While it's true that we could step through the program line by line by clicking on the Debug toolbar button that looks like a stack of pancakes, doing so could take a while—particularly if the program is calculating lots of powers of two. Let's take a different tack and insert a breakpoint in the program.

One of the most useful debugging tools, breakpoints tell VBA, "Pause when you reach this line." Breakpoints don't affect the flow of the program, don't change any variable values, don't do anything but get VBA to wait while you look at how things are going. You can insert a breakpoint at the line that says `Do...` by left-clicking at that point in the vertical bar on the left of the Code window, as shown in Figure 3-25. Do so now.

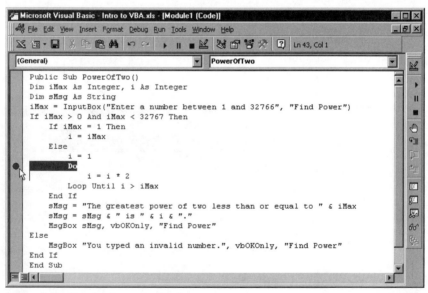

Figure 3-25: Breakpoint set at "Do"

Now, stop the program (click the square-box Stop button) and run the program again, using the right-wedgie Play button. Type in 20000 again when asked for a number between 1 and 32766. Click OK, and boom! VBA stops dead in its tracks when it hits the breakpoint. Note how nothing has changed: the program simply paused so you could take a look-see.

Now simply hover the cursor next to any variable. See how its value appears, in a yellow box, as a so-called tooltip? (See Figure 3-26.) Amazing.

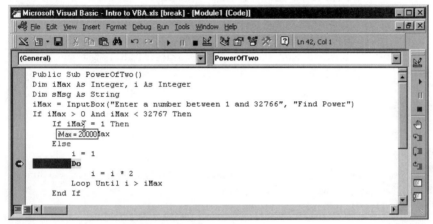

Figure 3-26: Variable value tooltips—a to-die-for feature

Once you've ascertained the value of *i*, hit the Step Into (**F8**) button again and again, until VBA triggers another overflow. Do you see where the problem lies?

There's a bug in the program. If you don't see it yet, click the Stop button, then start the program all over again using the value 20000. Once you reach your breakpoint, keep hitting the Step Into (**F8**) button until the value of *i* gets up to 16384, then pause reflectively. Aha! Your program is about to multiply 16384 by 2 again, and the resulting number, 32768, will trigger the overflow. It'll also send the value of *i* higher than the number that the user typed in. If you think about it, you'll come to the conclusion that the Until part of the loop should stop at iMax / 2.

Okay. No need to let that little bug stop you. If the value of *i* is at 16384 and the yellow arrow is pointing to the i = i * 2 line, you can skip farther down in the program by simply picking up the yellow arrow and sticking it on the next statement that you want VBA to execute!

If you put the arrow on the first sMsg = line and click the Play button, as we've done in Figure 3-27, VBA will continue to run from that point on, and you can get on with your testing. Just don't forget to change the Loop line to say:

```
Loop Until i > iMax / 2
```

```
     Else
          i = 1
          Do
               i = i * 2
          Loop Until i > iMax
     End If
     sMsg = "The greatest power of two less than or equal to " & iMax
     sMsg = sMsg & " is " & i & "."
```

Figure 3-27: Bypassing the bug

As we said, it's quite an editor. It's a treat to use, once you get the hang of it. And we haven't even scratched the surface of all its features. As you grow more proficient at VBA—and your programs get longer and longer, and buggier and buggier—you'll learn about the other editor debugging features, including:

- The Locals window, which lists all defined variables and their current values

- The Immediate window, which lets you run any VBA statement manually, while a program is executing

- The Watch window, which lets you pause the program when a variable's value changes

Unfortunately all of these topics are beyond the scope of this book, but a few hours spent kicking around the VBA Editor's Help file will reap big rewards. Most of all, you should come away with the belief that the VBA Editor is a world-class program editor—quite possibly the best ever created.

And, it's at your beck and call.

NOTE   As your VBA programs grow larger and more complex, you may find yourself longing for some guidelines on how to systematically name your variables, constants, controls, procedures, etc. There is a lot of material on this subject out there. In terms of what's readily accessible from Microsoft's Web site, you might want to start with the TechNet CD's article *Using Consistent Naming Conventions for Solution Development with MS Office.* Also check out the Microsoft Knowledge Base article Q110264 *LONG: Microsoft Consulting Services Naming Conventions for VB.* Wherever you turn for naming conventions, the payback for adopting a convention and using it consistently will be tremendous.

PrintCbarControlList: A Genuinely Useful Program

NOTE   Congratulations on surviving your first VBA programming experience. Now may be a good time to take a break. From this point on, we're going to tackle a variety of problems, just so you can get some experience working with VBA and the VBA Editor. There's no way we could squeeze a full introduction to VBA into this chapter, so we'll sacrifice completeness for broad exposure.

Even if you're thinking of picking up a VBA book or reference later (the *Mastering Office Development* CD* produced by Microsoft is a good starting point), try wading through the remainder of this chapter. You'll have a chance to see VBA in action, solving real problems. If you follow along closely, you may pick up a number of tips and insights that the other sources don't touch.

Besides, the `PrintCbarControlList` program's pretty cool, and you won't find it anywhere else!

The best way to get to know VBA is to trace through working programs, trying to figure out exactly which commands accomplish what tasks. Just as there's no substitute for practice in a foreign language—and complete immersion works even better—diving head first into real, working VBA programs will give you a great opportunity to absorb the language and its nuances.

Back in Chapter 2, *Vital Changes and Settings*, we showed you how you can fight back against the demoware factory-default Standard toolbars that ship with Excel, PowerPoint, and Word. We use a VBA macro called `PrintCbarControlList` to uncover a variety of interesting command bar control properties, and now we'll walk you through building this macro.

To create your own copy of the macro, bring up the VBA Editor (Tools ➤ Macro ➤ Visual Basic Editor). Like the `LoopPractice` and `Power-OfTwo` macros you worked with earlier, `PrintCbarControlList` can

---

* You can order the *Mastering Office Development* CD from Microsoft Internet Platform and Tools Division at 800-621-7930, part no. 087-00047_99 for $99.95 plus tax, shipping, and handling.

be developed and used inside Access,* Excel, PowerPoint, or Word. Make sure you're in the IntroToVBA project, navigate down to the Module called Module1, and add a new procedure to the module by clicking Insert ➤ Procedure, typing the name **PrintCbarControlList**, and clicking OK. Next, since the program uses Excel to produce a report— even if the current application isn't Excel—you need to establish a reference to Excel's object library; to do so in the Code Window, select Tools ➤ References, check the "Microsoft Excel 8.0 Object Library" box, then click OK. (While the References dialog is displayed, also make sure that "Microsoft Office 8.0 Object Library" is checked.) Then type in the program in Example 3-3. You should be able to step through the macro and see more or less what's going on.

Example 3-3: The PrintCbarControlList Routine

```
' -----------------------------------------------------------------
' Purpose:   List all interesting property values for each control
'            in the specified command bar. Works from within any
'            Office application.
'
' Inputs:    None
'
' Updated:   03/28/97 (PCG)
'            04/14/97 (PCG) - version 1 of ? for Excel Annoyances
'                             Chapter 5 "Intro to VBA"
'            07/22/97 (PCG) - modified to work from any Office
'                             application
' -----------------------------------------------------------------
Public Sub PrintCbarControlList()
    ' ----- Initializations/declarations
    Dim blnExcelHost As Boolean
    Dim cbarControl As CommandBarControl
    Dim lngRowIndex As Long
    Dim rngHeadings As Excel.Range
    Dim strCBarName As String
    Dim strDefault As String
    Dim strPrompt As String
    Dim strTemp As String
```

---

* If you try to run the **PrintCbarControlList** macro as-is in Access, Access will throw you one curve ball. Access' implementation of the Application object is non-standard by its omission of the Name property. OLE Automation object model guidelines stipulate that the Name property is one of a group of core properties for the high-level Application object, as it is in Excel, PowerPoint, and Word. Since Access doesn't support this particular standard, you'll see a compiler error, "Method or data member not found," on the **Application.Name** expression. Here's the fix: in the seven-line block of code beginning with **If Application.Name = "Microsoft Excel" Then**, remark out lines 1-4 and 7. (Remarks or comments are indicated either by the keyword **Rem** or by the apostrophe character preceding the text that's turned into a remark.) Next change the statement **.Cells(1, 1) = Application.Name & " Command Bar name: " & _** to **.Cells(1, 1) = "Application.Name" & " Command Bar name: " & _** (you're simply converting the unsupported expression to a literal string). Now the macro will run in Access.

Example 3-3: The PrintCbarControlList Routine (continued)

```
Dim strTitle As String
Dim strType As String
Dim oxlApp As Excel.Application
Dim oxlTargetSheet As Excel.Worksheet
Dim oxlWorkbook As Excel.Workbook
strTitle = "OfficeAnnoy Command Bar Control Lister"
strDefault = "Web"
strPrompt = "Please enter the name of the command bar " & _
    "you're interested in:"
strCBarName = InputBox(strPrompt, strTitle, strDefault)
' ----- Main body
' don't bother with an empty string or Cancel from user
If strCBarName = "" Then
    Exit Sub
End If
' make sure we don't process a bogus command bar name
On Error Resume Next
strTemp = CommandBars(strCBarName).Name
If Err <> 0 Then
    Exit Sub
End If
' reset normal error handling
On Error GoTo 0
' handle Application and other OLEAuto object references
If Application.Name = "Microsoft Excel" Then
    Set oxlApp = Application
    blnExcelHost = True
Else
    Set oxlApp = CreateObject("Excel.Application")
    blnExcelHost = False
End If
Set oxlWorkbook = oxlApp.Workbooks.Add
Set oxlTargetSheet = oxlWorkbook.ActiveSheet
With oxlTargetSheet
    ' put the command bar name in A1
    .Cells(1, 1) = Application.Name & " Command Bar name: " & _
        CommandBars(strCBarName).Name
    ' starting in A2, add the column headings
    lngRowIndex = 2
    Set rngHeadings = .Range(.Cells(lngRowIndex, 1), _
        .Cells(lngRowIndex, 10))
End With
rngHeadings.Value = Array("Index", "BuiltIn", "Caption", _
    "DescriptionText", "Id", "OnAction", "TooltipText", _
    "Type (Value)", "Type (Name)", "Visible")
rngHeadings.Font.Bold = True
' starting in A3, add the data
' On Error to avoid run-time error 438 on some .OnAction calls
On Error Resume Next
lngRowIndex = lngRowIndex + 1
For Each cbarControl In CommandBars(strCBarName).Controls
    With cbarControl
        oxlTargetSheet.Cells(lngRowIndex, 1) = .Index
        oxlTargetSheet.Cells(lngRowIndex, 2) = .BuiltIn
```

Example 3-3: The PrintCbarControlList Routine (continued)

```
oxlTargetSheet.Cells(lngRowIndex, 3) = .Caption
oxlTargetSheet.Cells(lngRowIndex, 4) = .DescriptionText
oxlTargetSheet.Cells(lngRowIndex, 5) = .Id
oxlTargetSheet.Cells(lngRowIndex, 6) = .OnAction
oxlTargetSheet.Cells(lngRowIndex, 7) = .TooltipText
oxlTargetSheet.Cells(lngRowIndex, 8) = .Type
Select Case .Type
    Case 0
        strType = "msoControlCustom"
    Case 1
        strType = "msoControlButton"
    Case 2
        strType = "msoControlEdit"
    Case 3
        strType = "msoControlDropdown"
    Case 4
        strType = "msoControlComboBox"
    Case 5
        strType = "msoControlButtonDropdown"
    Case 6
        strType = "msoControlSplitDropdown"
    Case 7
        strType = "msoControlOCXDropdown"
    Case 8
        strType = "msoControlGenericDropdown"
    Case 9
        strType = "msoControlGraphicDropdown"
    Case 10
        strType = "msoControlPopup"
    Case 11
        strType = "msoControlGraphicPopup"
    Case 12
        strType = "msoControlButtonPopup"
    Case 13
        strType = "msoControlSplitButtonPopup"
    Case 14
        strType = "msoControlSplitButtonMRUPopup"
    Case 15
        strType = "msoControlLabel"
    Case 16
        strType = "msoControlExpandingGrid"
    Case 17
        strType = "msoControlSplitExpandingGrid"
    Case 18
        strType = "msoControlGrid"
    Case 19
        strType = "msoControlGauge"
    Case 20
        strType = "msoControlGraphicCombo"
    Case Else
        strType = "unknown"
End Select
oxlTargetSheet.Cells(lngRowIndex, 9) = strType
oxlTargetSheet.Cells(lngRowIndex, 10) = .Visible
```

Example 3-3: The PrintCbarControlList Routine (continued)

```
        End With
        lngRowIndex = lngRowIndex + 1
    Next
    ' reset normal error handling
    On Error GoTo 0
    ' center cbar name as title across A1...
    oxlTargetSheet.Range("A1:J1").Select
    With oxlApp.Selection
        .HorizontalAlignment = xlCenter
        .VerticalAlignment = xlBottom
        .WrapText = False
        .Orientation = 0
        .ShrinkToFit = False
        .MergeCells = False
    End With
    oxlApp.Selection.Merge
    ' AutoFit the entire range we just entered
    oxlTargetSheet.Range("A1").CurrentRegion.Columns.AutoFit
    If Not blnExcelHost Then
        ' make sure closing Excel via OLE Automation doesn't lose
        '    the new file
        MsgBox "You must save the new Excel workbook.", _
            vbOKOnly + vbInformation, strTitle
        oxlApp.Visible = True
        Do While oxlApp.Dialogs(xlDialogSaveAs).Show <> True
        Loop
        oxlApp.Quit
        Set oxlTargetSheet = Nothing
        Set oxlWorkbook = Nothing
        Set oxlApp = Nothing
    Else
        ' nothing required
    End If
End Sub
```

Translating that into English goes something like this:

1. This is a subroutine called `PrintCbarControlList`.

2. Save space for a variety of different variable types: one Boolean variable, one CommandBarControl object variable, one Long variable, six String variables, and four different Excel.*something* object variables (Range, Application, Worksheet, and Workbook). These Excel object variables allow the program to quickly refer to and interact with objects inside Excel's object model from outside Excel (more on object models later in the chapter).

3. Ask the user which command bar she wants a report on (the default is the Standard toolbar). If the user enters no command bar name or a bogus command bar name, exit quietly.

4. Create a new Excel workbook.

5. Put the command bar name in the active worksheet's cell A1.
6. Starting in A2, add the column headings.
7. Starting in A3, add the data.
8. Use the `For Each...Next` construct to walk through the `CommandBarControls` collection for this particular command bar, and put property values into cells in the current row.

NOTE In object model lexicon, a collection is an ordered set of objects that you can refer to as a single item. You can also refer to its individual component objects.

---

9. Perform some nice AutoFit formatting on the Excel columns.
10. If the host application isn't Excel, make sure that the Excel workbook is saved before Excel is shut down. This program demonstrates the techniques for gracefully opening and closing another application.

To run the macro, put the cursor anywhere inside the subroutine, then click the Play button. See Figure 3-28 for a sample report.

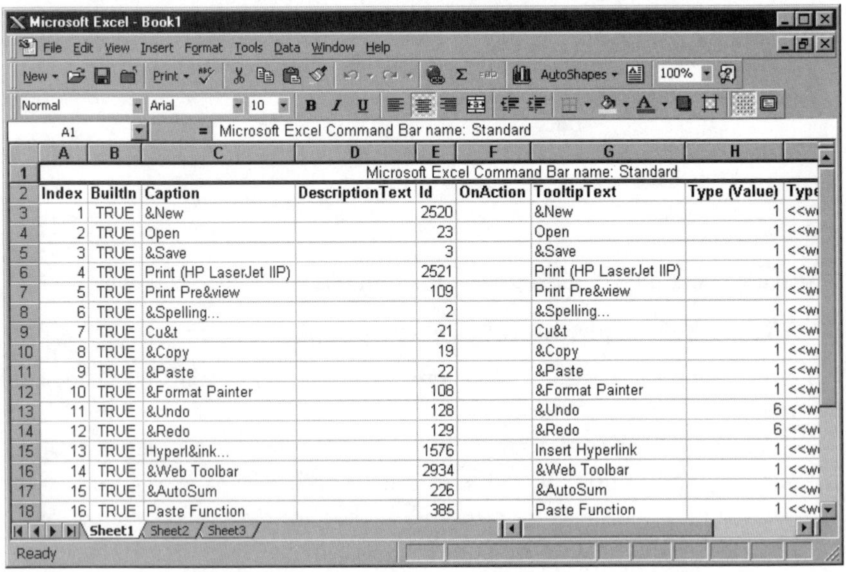

Index	BuiltIn	Caption	DescriptionText	Id	OnAction	TooltipText	Type (Value)	Type
1	TRUE	&New		2520		&New	1	<<w
2	TRUE	Open		23		Open	1	<<w
3	TRUE	&Save		3		&Save	1	<<w
4	TRUE	Print (HP LaserJet IIP)		2521		Print (HP LaserJet IIP)	1	<<w
5	TRUE	Print Pre&view		109		Print Pre&view	1	<<w
6	TRUE	&Spelling...		2		&Spelling...	1	<<w
7	TRUE	Cu&t		21		Cu&t	1	<<w
8	TRUE	&Copy		19		&Copy	1	<<w
9	TRUE	&Paste		22		&Paste	1	<<w
10	TRUE	&Format Painter		108		&Format Painter	1	<<w
11	TRUE	&Undo		128		&Undo	6	<<w
12	TRUE	&Redo		129		&Redo	6	<<w
13	TRUE	Hyperl&ink...		1576		Insert Hyperlink	1	<<w
14	TRUE	&Web Toolbar		2934		&Web Toolbar	1	<<w
15	TRUE	&AutoSum		226		&AutoSum	1	<<w
16	TRUE	Paste Function		385		Paste Function	1	<<w

Figure 3-28: PrintCbarControlList output for Excel's Standard command bar

TIP	There are two quick ways to call up a list of all 42 Excel collections in Visual Basic Help. First, the Item topic: ask the Office Assistant "item" and choose the Item topic. Second, the "Add Method" topic: ask Robert "add method" and choose the "Add Method (Workbooks Collection)" topic, then click the See Also link and choose the second "Add Method" item in the list. The former lists all collections as jump topics (topics you can click on and go to immediately). The latter lists what happens when the Add method is applied to each collection, also with jump topics.

Fleshing Out VBA

So far we've covered the "Basic" part of VBA: a very powerful programming language, tied into a world-class programming editor and debugger. As you've seen in `PrintCbarControlList`, the Basic part of VBA, all by itself, can do all sorts of things to Excel—and alleviate all sorts of annoyances. But the programming language itself is only part of the story and only one of the tools at your disposal to customize Office to work for you and, if you develop custom Office applications for others, your users.

The "visual" part of VBA consists of an enormously powerful kit for drag-and-drop construction of custom dialog boxes, plus built-in hooks to associate controls* on the dialog boxes—push buttons, text boxes, check boxes, spin buttons, and much more—with your program code.

NOTE	In this section and the two that follow ("Custom Dialog Boxes" and "Control Events and Control Event Handlers") we take a quick look at the other parts of VBA—valuable parts that you may want to exploit in your programs, somewhere down the line. As before, we won't even try for completeness. Instead, our goal is to give you an idea of the major chunks of the language that are available, and how they all fit together.
	Although we're still using Excel as the Office host application to demonstrate VBA, remember that PowerPoint/VBA and Word/VBA provide these same capabilities.

---

* As far as we're concerned in this discussion of VBA, *controls* are simply the things that sit on a dialog box. In the larger Windows world, controls can sit in dialogs, Excel sheets, Word documents, on Web pages, and many other places. You can create your own controls with Visual Basic 5.0, Control Creation Edition.

Four kinds of hooks between the visual and the Basic—the dialog boxes and program code—come into play:

1. Your program can set many of the controls' characteristics. For example, you can write a program that changes the name that appears on a push button, or one that changes the color of the entire dialog box. These characteristics are called control *properties*.

2. Your program can retrieve controls' characteristics. For example, if you set things up so your custom dialog box can be resized, you can write a program that retrieves the dialog's current size or location on the screen. If you have check boxes on the dialog, your program can look to see if a particular box has been checked.

3. You can set up certain programs to be run when specific things happen to the custom dialog. For example, you can tell VBA "run the program called Foobar whenever the user double-clicks on this picture." The things that can happen are called *events*. We call the programs that handle control events *event handlers*.

4. Finally, you can make your program "trigger" or "fire" events. For example, you can write a program to tell VBA, "behave precisely the same way you would've behaved if the user had clicked the OK button." Think of this as an invisible hand that you can manipulate from inside your programs. Sure, the user can click a Cancel button. But your program can click the Cancel button just as well.

Let's take a look at custom dialog boxes, how they're constructed, and what options are available to you. Then we'll tie together the "visual" and the "Basic" with a demonstration of control event handlers.

NOTE   The terms "event" and "event handler" need a context in order to be correctly understood. In the context of custom dialog boxes, these terms refer to *control* events. In the context of an application's event model (referred to in some Microsoft documentation as the "code behind documents" feature), these terms refer to application and/or object events that you can control with VBA code, for example, events occurring at the application (Excel and Word), document (Word), sheet (Excel), and Workbook (Excel) level. PowerPoint doesn't support application events, not even the old Auto macros (except for a loaded add-in, which runs an `Auto_Open` macro when loaded and when PowerPoint starts, and an `Auto_Close` macro when the add-in is unloaded or PowerPoint closes).

Custom Dialog Boxes

VBA calls the dialog boxes you construct *User Forms* (originally code named Forms^3 and pronounced "forms cubed," but now the forms engine is referred to as Forms 2.0). The term *form* has come to be synonymous with *dialog box*. We'll try to stay consistent here and only refer to custom-built dialogs, dialog boxes, or simply *dboxes*. The Forms 2.0 forms engine is shared by Excel, PowerPoint, and Word. Access uses its own proprietary forms engine, and to add insult to injury, Outlook uses yet another proprietary forms engine. Since Microsoft is shifting to Forms 2.0 as the common forms engine, and it's only a matter of time before *all* Office applications use it, we'll focus on that technology for this next example.

NOTE   If you develop any applications in Word, be aware that Word includes yet another type of Form, which is a particular kind of document (template) that has certain parts locked out so they can't be modified. A VBA User Form is decidedly not a Word Form.

To see what's going on, let's construct a simple custom dialog box. If you're not in the Visual Basic Editor, click on Tools ➤ Macro ➤ Visual Basic Editor. Bring up the Project Explorer and the Properties Window by clicking on the two buttons on VBA's Standard toolbar. Navigate to the IntroToVBA project, which should have a Module called Module1 that contains the macros you worked on earlier.

To create a new custom dialog box, click on Insert ➤ UserForm. VBA will place a new dbox in the window that used to hold program code. It will call the new dbox UserForm1, and put UserForm1 in the dbox's title area (see Figure 3-29). At the same time, a window marked Toolbox will appear. It contains controls that you will probably want to paint on your dbox.

For starters, let's change the caption at the top of the dbox. To do so, locate the Properties Window, which probably sits just below the Project Explorer. The top of the Properties Window should say Properties— UserForm1, which is meant to inform you that you are looking at the properties of the thing called UserForm1. Underneath sits a drop-down list box that says UserForm1 UserForm, which repeats the name of the dbox, and informs you that the dbox called UserForm1 is a UserForm. Rocket science.

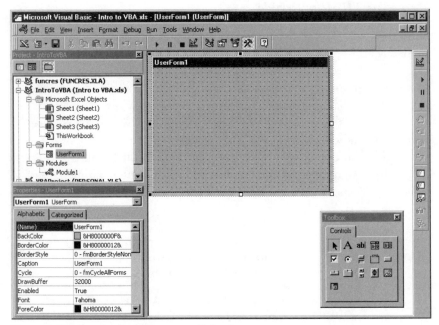

Figure 3-29: Creating a new custom dialog box

Look down in the body of the Properties Window and locate a line that says Caption. The Caption property of UserForm1 is nothing more or less than the text that appears in the title bar of the UserForm1 dbox. Change the Caption to "My Custom Dialog" and watch as VBA changes the title bar of UserForm1 while you type. (See Figure 3-30.)

For this simple exercise, we're going to place a single Command Button control on the dbox. To do so, first make sure the Toolbox is visible by single-clicking anywhere inside your custom dbox. Then locate the Command Button control in the Toolbox. It's the last control on the second row and has a tooltip of "CommandButton." Click it once. Now click on the custom dbox and click-and-drag to paint a Command Button on it. (See Figure 3-31.)

We want the Command Button to say something slightly more intelligent than "CommandButton1." The text that appears on a Command Button face is simply the Caption property of the Command Button. Go over to the Properties Window, scroll down to Caption, and change it from CommandButton1 to "PUSH ME!". (See Figure 3-32.)

Congratulations. That's all it takes to build a custom dialog box in VBA. Granted, it doesn't do much just yet, but adding intelligence to a dbox remains the provenance of event handlers. For now, think of this nascent dbox as an exceedingly pretty face that can perform a few airhead tricks.

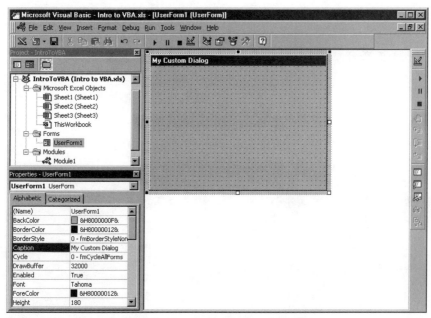

Figure 3-30: Changing the title (Caption) of the custom dialog box

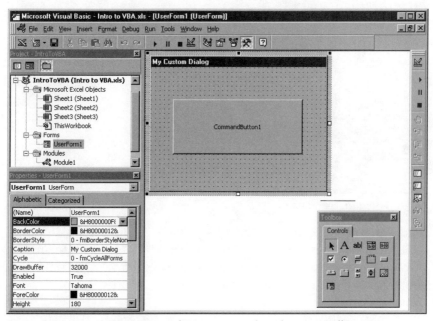

Figure 3-31: Painting a Command Button control on the custom dbox

To see the entire UserForm1 repertoire, click the VBA Play button. Your custom dbox will spring to life, as shown in Figure 3-33.

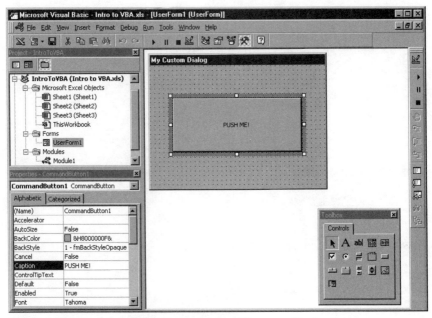

Figure 3-32: Changing the Caption property of CommandButton1

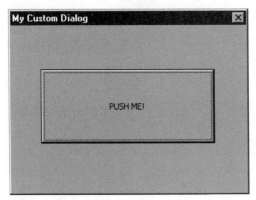

Figure 3-33: Run UserForm1

Note how you can push the Command Button, but it doesn't do much, aside from looking marvelous. You can also move the dbox around, placing it anywhere on the desktop. But that's about it. When you're bored (should take about two seconds), click the X in UserForm1's upper-right corner, and you'll return to VBA.

Control Events and Control Event Handlers

Let's write an event handler that will accomplish something when you push UserForm1's Command Button. While we won't try to create anything as fancy as `PrintCbarControlList`, we think you'll be pleasantly surprised by how easy it is to make programs work with VBA custom dialog boxes, and how little effort it takes to change the dboxes from inside a program.

We're going to write a program that runs whenever the user clicks the Command Button. In VBA-speak, the program should run when the CommandButton1.Click event occurs (or "fires"). VBA's method of associating events with their event handlers is simplicity itself, and relies on the names of the event handler subroutines. For example, when the CommandButton1.Click event fires, VBA looks for a subroutine called `CommandButton1_Click`. If that subroutine exists, Excel runs it. Easy.

So if we want to write a program that will run when the user clicks on CommandButton1—or, if you want to impress your boss, a "handler for the CommandButton1.Click event"—we apparently need to construct a subroutine called `CommandButton1_Click`. VBA makes that incredibly simple, too.

Design Time vs. Run Time

The official documentation makes a big distinction between *design time* and *run time*. No need for you to get hung up about it. The difference is really quite simple.

Sometimes you're writing a program. Other times you're running the program. That's the whole difference. When you're writing a program, *design time*, you don't expect things in the outside world to suddenly affect your program. When you're running a program, though, you expect it to respond to everything.

Since VBA gives you so many ways to run and stop programs—breakpoints, single-line stepping, and much more—sometimes it's hard to remember when you're running, and when you're programming. The basic rule is this: if you click something or push something, and you don't get the response you were expecting, check to make sure you're in the mode you thought you were in. To move from design mode to run mode, just click once inside the VBA editor and hit F5, or click the Play button. To move from run mode to design mode, click the Stop button.

Whenever you want to write an event handler for any control's most common event, you just double-click on the control and VBA will get the subroutine going for you. In this case, the Click event is far and away the most common event for a Command Button. So if you double-click on CommandButton1, VBA will get rid of the custom dialog box, move you into the code writing window, and start a subroutine for you that's called CommandButton1_Click.

We prefer to get rid of the Project Explorer and Properties Window as soon as we start writing code. You might want to do the same by clicking the X in the upper-right corners of each. You can see the result in Figure 3-34.

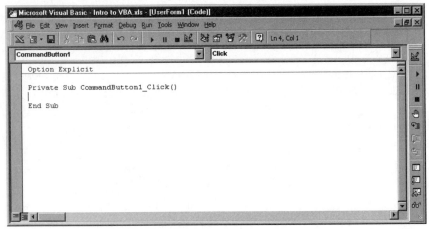

Figure 3-34: Double-click on the Command Button, and VBA/Excel sets this up for you

Type in the simple program shown in Example 3-4. (VBA has already supplied the first and last lines.)

Example 3-4: The CommandButton1.Click Event Handler

```
Private Sub CommandButton1_Click()
If CommandButton1.Caption = "PUSH ME!" Then
    CommandButton1.Caption = "Push Me AGAIN!"
Else
    CommandButton1.Caption = "PUSH ME!"
End If
End Sub
```

No doubt you can figure out what the program does without our help. It works by looking at and changing the text on the face of the Command Button. Or, in VBA-speak, it examines and sets the Caption property of the CommandButton1 control.

Once you're done typing in the code, you can run the whole thing by clicking on the Play button. Click on the Command Button a few times to make sure all is well (see Figure 3-35). Then click the X in the upper-right corner to flip back into VBA.

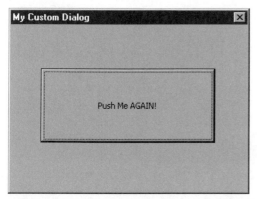

Figure 3-35: The CommandButton1_Click() event handler in action

One last note before we start tying VBA/Excel into Excel itself. Back in the coding window, take a look at the Object and Procedure drop-down lists. On the left side you'll see a list of all the controls available in the current custom dialog box. On the right—as shown in Figure 3-36—there's a list of all the events associated with whatever control you've chosen. The enormous number of available events (e.g., MouseMove, which fires whenever the user passes the cursor over a Command Button) gives you unprecedented leeway in making custom dialog boxes work the way you want them to work.

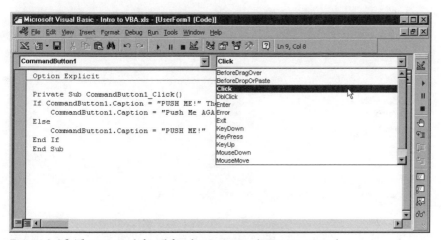

Figure 3-36: The events defined for the CommandButton1 control

Testing LoopPractice and PowerOfTwo in Outlook VBScript

> *"Things are always darkest before they go pitch black."*
>
> —From "I Spy"

This section is provided for those of you who are interested in seeing what is involved in writing and testing even a simple program in Outlook VBScript. If you follow along carefully step by step, the end result will be successful execution of these two programs. As we suggested earlier in this chapter, if you're going to be doing any Outlook development work, you need to get all the Help updates we mentioned. Scouring the third-party market for books is also a good idea. O'Reilly & Associates publishes an excellent tome on VBScript by Paul Lomax, *Learning VBScript*, ISBN 1-56592-247-6; note that it is written in the context of VBScript for Internet Explorer and Web page development. Here are the steps required to create and run either `LoopPractice` or `PowerOfTwo` using Microsoft Outlook:

1. Create a new scratch record (say, a Contact).
2. Select Tools ➤ Design Outlook Form.
3. Click on the (P.2) tab.
4. Click on the Control Toolbox button.
5. Add a command button to the form (it will be named CommandButton1).
6. Click the View Code button on the toolbar (to start the Script Editor).
7. Enter a one-line statement for the `CommandButton1_Click` subroutine procedure to call `LoopPractice`, as shown in Example 3-5.

Example 3-5: The CommandButton1_Click Subroutine in Outlook VBScript

```
Sub CommandButton1_Click
LoopPractice
End Sub
```

8. Paste (or type) in your code for `LoopPractice` and `PowerOfTwo`.
9. Remark out all `Dim` statements in both macros, because VBScript doesn't support data types other than Variant.
10. Change `Next  i` to `Next` because VBScript doesn't accept the counter being listed in the `Next` closing statement. (Alternately, leave it as `Next  i` if you want to see how painfully crippled VBScript's debugging capabilities are.)
11. Switch back to the form in Design view (the title bar says "(Design)").

12. Select Tools ➤ Design Outlook Form (to exit Design view and enter Run mode).

13. Click the command button to fire `CommandButton1_Click`, which calls your procedure. When done, select Tools ➤ Design Outlook Form to toggle out of Run mode.

14. To test `PowerOfTwo`, edit the call to `LoopPractice` to `PowerOfTwo` and repeat Steps 11-13.

Controlling Office Applications Using Object Models

So much for the whirlwind introduction to VBA, its programming environment, and the way VBA influences—and is influenced by—custom dialog boxes. Much of what you've seen so far in this chapter is applicable to VBA/Excel, VBA/PowerPoint, VBA/Word, VBA/Visio, and even Visual Basic itself. Once you've spent a few hours learning VBA, a substantial portion of what you've discovered will be immediately useful in any of those other programming languages.

NOTE   In this section we'll delve into the concept of an application object model—the set of hooks that let you write programs to control the way the application behaves. What does an application object model have to do with annoyances? Just about everything. The application object model defines (and limits!) precisely how your programs can manipulate that application, be it Excel, PowerPoint, Word, and so on. If you've never hit an object model before, the concept can be a bit confusing. Not to worry. We'll take you through step by step, give you a handful of examples, and then turn you loose to try it for yourself.

Now let's turn to the ways in which VBA can control Office applications. It's not an exaggeration to say that you can write a VBA program to do just about *anything* in an Office application that hosts VBA.

Objects, Properties, and Methods

Buzzwords, buzzwords.

Wherever you look in VBA land, you'll find references to objects, properties, and methods. They constitute the ruling triumvirate of the VBA party. You'll see the terms mentioned so often that you might be tempted to believe they represent some sort of cosmic truth. That they're a literary shorthand for The Fundamental Concept Behind VBA, Life, the Universe, and Everything. That somehow understanding the difference between an object, property and method will bestow instant transcendental illumination on your road to VBA enlightenment.

Ha.

Chances are good that you're reasonably well versed in the tenets of grammar. If so, here's what you need to know: an object is a noun; a property is an adjective; and a method is a verb. That's it.

Fortunately, object modeling hasn't yet descended to the level of adverbial clauses and the subjunctive mood. But those days are coming.*

Objects are things. In Excel, that includes workbooks, sheets, cells, ranges, shapes, built-in dialog boxes, and much more. One of the most fundamental objects in Excel is the range—a conglomeration of cells that could be a single cell, an entire column or row, a selection of cells that includes one or more contiguous blocks of cells, or a 3-D range. In Word, this includes documents, paragraphs, words, bookmarks, footnotes, built-in dialog boxes, and much more. One of the most fundamental objects in Word is also the range—a block of text with a beginning point and an ending point, that includes everything in between the two. In Power-Point, you'll work most with the presentation object (analogous to a Word document or Excel workbook), which in turn contains slide objects.

There are object models for the following shared Office components: Office Assistant, Office Binder, Office CommandBars, Office FileSearch, Data Access for ODBCDirect Workspaces, Data Access for Microsoft Jet Workspaces, Microsoft Forms, Microsoft Map 97, and Visual Basic Editor. To view these object libraries in Object Browser, simply go into any VBA code module and select Tools ➤ References then check the appropriate library in the list and click OK (some are already included in another object library). Now you can browse through that component's object library; try it with Microsoft Map 97 (called "MSMap" in the Object Browser). MSMap's first-level objects are Templates (map templates), Features (features in the specified map), Datasets (a range of cells used to create a map), Themes (themes that are displayed in the specified map), and PinMaps (pinmaps that you can plot on the specified map).

---

* Quick question to you object modelers out there—and we know you're reading this. What do you call a property of a property? (Grammatically that's an adverb.) How long before you draw a distinction between methods that operate directly on associated objects, changing the object itself, and methods that merely change the contents or appearance of an object? (Akin to the distinction between transitive and intransitive verbs.) Better brush up on your Latin, guys.

In VBA itself, programs are considered to be objects, as are custom dialog boxes and controls on the boxes. Whenever you're tempted to point at something on the screen and call it a "thing," chances are very good VBA considers it to be an object.

Properties refer to the characteristics of objects. You've worked with the Caption property in custom dialog boxes and Command Buttons. It probably won't surprise you to learn that Font is a property of Range or that Name is a property of Workbook.

Methods do things to objects. For example, the Add method applied to Excel's Workbooks object (a collection object, actually) adds (creates) a new Excel workbook. The Delete method applied to a Sheet object deletes the specified Excel sheet. In Word, the expression `Application.GoBack` applies the GoBack method to the Application object and moves the insertion point back through its last three locations (same as pressing Shift+F5), one for each execution of the `Application.GoBack` statement.

In modern parlance, the difference between nouns, adjectives, and verbs has blurred somewhat: nouns take on the appearance of adjectives, verbs become nounified, and so on. The same is true of objects, properties, and methods—in some cases it isn't completely clear if a property should in fact be a method, or vice versa. Only the most anally retentive grammarian would deny this blurring in modern language. Only the most anally retentive object modeler would deny the blurring in VBA.

This can lead to a great deal of confusion. For example, in Excel, Find is a method (or verb) and this is the way most people would think of it. But in Word, Find is an object (or noun). In Excel, Zoom is a property (or adjective); but in Word, Zoom is an object.

Don't get too hung up in the terminology, and don't be overwhelmed by the huge number of objects, properties, and methods available in VBA. The terminology ultimately comes to make some sense. And your work will commonly concentrate on a small subset of all the available objects, properties, and methods.

Application, the Tip of the Object Iceberg

According to the *Mastering Office Development* CD, to see a graphic display of the entire object models for Excel and Word, ask Robert about "Microsoft Excel Objects" and "Microsoft Word Objects." This worked for us only in Word, and you have to query Robert from Word's VB Editor in order to get a hit. We weren't able to find a graphic for the Access, Excel, or PowerPoint object models using this technique. How annoying.

However, there's a quick and easy way to start at the top of any Office application's object model and drill down from there just by using Help. Each Office host application's object model begins with the Application object. The Application object represents the entire application. Let's use Excel as an example:

1. From inside the VBA/Excel Editor, ask Robert "application," then select the "Application Object" topic.

2. Inside the Visual Basic Help file click on the Multiple Objects rectangle immediately below the Application rectangle (see Figure 3-37).

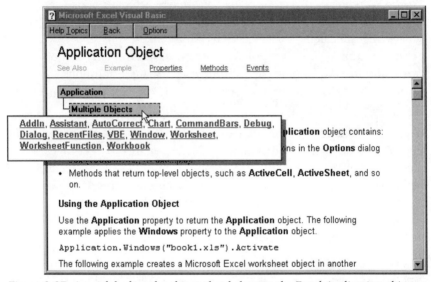

Figure 3-37: A quick look at the objects that belong to the Excel Application object

3. From inside the resulting pop-up, you can select any of the green underlined topics, each of which represents an object (or object collection) that belongs to the parent Application object. You can also use VBA's Object Browser to navigate through, and get help on, an Office component's object library (more on the Object Browser shortly).

NOTE   Microsoft has posted detailed graphic displays of all the Office 97 component object models on its Web site, along with indispensable information such as the name of the component's object library, Help file, and additional notes (see Figure 3-38). We highly recommend you bookmark *http://www.microsoft.com/OfficeDev/Docs/OMG/default.htm.* Now!

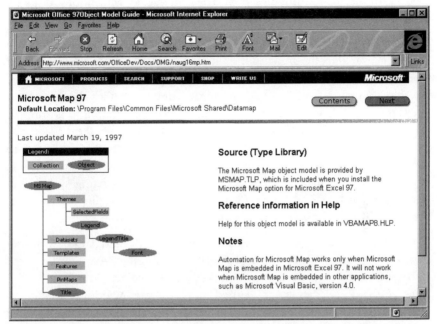

Figure 3-38: Microsoft Map 97's object model—on the Web and in sizzling color

---

Is This Object Oriented Programming?

Most Office users, upon learning that VBA works with things called "objects," want to know if VBA actually incorporates Object Oriented Programming (or OOP).

In a word, the answer is no.

While the precise definition of OOP has seen more changes than Michael Jackson's nose, most OOPers (OOPophiles?) agree that a true Object Oriented language must provide solid support for techniques with odd sounding names—encapsulation, inheritance, polymorphic operators, and such. While VBA 5 has built-in support for some aspects of those features, typically via Class Modules, in fact VBA is still a long, long way from the OOP ideal.

A Brief History of Office Application Object Models

Sooner or later almost every computer program has to interact with the outside world. Very simple, old-fashioned DOS programs interacted with the user by waiting for the user to type something and then acting on whatever key was typed. They interacted with a printer by writing lines, one at a time, to the printer's port. They interacted with floppy disks by reading or writing a record of data at a time.

As they became more sophisticated, those old programs rarely interacted with the user directly. Instead, they took advantage of the programs built into DOS so they didn't have to muck around with nitpicking details (e.g., the location of a particular file on a hard drive, whether the user hit a backspace to delete the preceding character, spooling output to a print file so the program didn't have to check constantly whether the printer was busy). Gradually, programs shifted from working with the user over to working with the operating system. By and large, that was A Good Thing. Sure, the programmer had to learn how to call the operating system, but the additional hassle of figuring out operating system calling conventions far outweighed, say, building your own print spooler from scratch.

Then came Windows, and all hell broke loose. By and large, Windows insulated programs from the user effectively—so effectively that very few programs attempted to bypass Windows and interact directly with the user. Instead, programmers learned how to use Windows routines— learned to "call the Windows Application Programming Interface," or Win API—to get things done. The Windows API just describes all the routines that can be called by Windows programs, along with a definition of variables to be passed to the routines, and the meaning of the values that should be returned. While it was, and is, difficult to write a solid Windows program, much of the complexity was tamed by setting the Windows API in concrete and making programmers work through the Win API.

Object models in general, and an application object model in particular, take this abstraction one step farther. Where an API defines the routines a program can use, along with their parameters and values, an object model defines the things—the objects—a program can manipulate, along with valid operations on the objects. It's a subtle distinction, but one we've found useful for thinking about any Office application object model.

Hidden here is a fundamental secret behind an Office application object model: it makes virtually every nook and cranny of that application available to you for manipulation in your VBA programs, and it does so in a very nonprocedural (no, we won't say "object oriented") way.* Microsoft has gone to great pains to ensure that the Office application object

---

* Note our use of "virtually" in that sentence. It's fair to say that 99% of the things you can do interactively—manually—with an Office application can be done programmatically with VBA. An example of the 1% coming 'round to bite you on the hindquarters is Word's insidious insistence on putting pictures and objects and what-all in its drawing layer by checking the "Float over text" box for you. Stuff in the drawing layer flip-flops all over the place, unless you remember to un-float pictures each and every time you insert one. Out of five "Float over text" holes we identified, we could only plug three—and one of the plugs involved the ultimate VBA/Word kludge, *SendKeys*. For the nitty gritty, see Chapter 5 of *Word 97 Annoyances*.

models describe all the things inside the host application (objects), along with characteristics of those things that you can change (properties), and activities you can perform on the things (methods). It's a significant step forward in the evolution of macro programming languages.

An Office application object model doesn't look like an API, like a set of procedures and their parameters. In VBA, the emphasis focuses strictly on objects, properties, and methods. Lots and lots and lots of objects, properties, and methods.

The Excel object model

In Excel, the high-level objects you'll be dealing with most often are as follows: The Application object provides access to Excel itself and its application-wide settings and behaviors. The Workbooks collection and individual Workbook objects point to open workbooks whether saved or unsaved. Window and Pane objects allow you to control the appearance of Excel's windows and splits (panes). The Sheets and Worksheets collections grant access to all sheet types (Sheets) or just worksheet sheets (Worksheets), and the individual Worksheet and Chart objects provide access to those sheet types respectively. The Range object is probably the most useful navigational and referencing tool in Excel. It represents a conglomeration of cells that could be a single cell, an entire column or row, a selection of cells that includes one or more contiguous blocks of cells, or a 3-D range. You'll do well to carefully study the "Range Object" Help topic and all associated properties and methods, plus the online Help's example code.

The Excel object model has changed in Excel 97. (This may only be of interest to you if you've worked with VBA in earlier versions of Excel, or plan to do multi-version coding.) Changes have been made to support the application's new features. For backward source code compatibility, older components have been hidden. For example, you wouldn't refer to a Line object any longer, but rather the Shapes collection, the Shape object, or the ShapeRange collection and their relevant methods and properties. You can unhide these hidden components in the Object Browser by right-clicking on the Excel Application class and then choosing the Show Hidden Members menu item; hidden components are shown in light gray type. (A complete list of these hidden components appears in the Help topics "Hidden Objects" and "Hidden Properties and Methods.") Pre-Excel 97 VBA code still runs fine in Excel 97 in most cases. You should use (and benefit from) the new components unless your code needs to run unmodified across multiple versions of Excel/VBA. Figure 3-39 shows the Help topic "Changes to the Microsoft Excel 97 object model." If you've worked with VBA in earlier versions of Excel then you should read and print copies of this and its eight Help sub-topics.

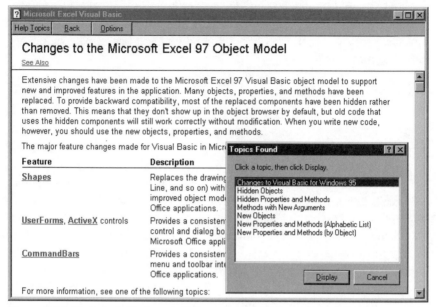

Figure 3-39: The crucial help topic "Changes to the Microsoft Excel 97 object model"

The Word object model

Keep in mind that Word's object model really begins with Word 97. Yes, there was (and still is) a Word.Basic object for Word 6 and Word 95; it was simply the non-VBA WordBasic language's 900+ commands and functions wrapped up in the guise of an object model. This made Word 6 and 95 dance as slaves (but not masters) to applications like Visual Basic and VBA/Excel 95.

Word 97 Annoyances contains a section titled "The Most Common (and Confusing) Word Objects" in which we devote 10-plus pages to, well, the most common and confusing Word objects. Specifically, we cover the Document object, stories (precisely, Range objects that belong to the intriguing StoryRanges collection), the Selection object, the Range object, and the Excel Conspiracy Theory. Space constraints prohibit including that material here, but the salient point is not to accept the Word documentation's counsel to use the Range object instead of the Selection object. Au contraire, the Selection object and its manifestations almost always proves superior to its sibling, the Range object.

Don't Throw Away Your Word 6 Reference Books!

So much of VBA/Word behaves precisely the same way as Word 6 and Word 95 that those old Word 6 and Word 95 reference books can come in very handy. We used the *Hacker's Guide to Word for Windows*, 2nd Edition, by Woody Leonhard, Vincent Chen, and Scott Krueger (Addison-Wesley, ISBN 0-201-40763-9) extensively while writing the *Word 97 Annoyances* chapter on VBA.

You might think that the *Hacker's Guide* would be hopelessly obsolete—after all, it hasn't been updated since Word 6—but many of the "gotchas" in the *Hacker's Guide* continue to appear in VBA/Word 97. The language changes a bit, but the underlying weird behavior of Word, in so many instances, remains the same. Two prime examples: the Table selection oddities and the admonitions for clearing formatting in Finds and Replaces (all discussed in detail in *Word 97 Annoyances*). Both are key problems—and obscure sources of devastating bugs—in VBA/Word, just as they were in Word 6 and Word 95.

Don't throw away the old books! Until somebody comes up with a definitive list of VBA/Word commands and their oddities (a chore that would take years, in our opinion), a quick scan at the old *Hacker's Guide* can save you hours, even days, of frustration.

The Access object model

In the Access object model, the Application object is at the top of the hierarchy; all other Access objects are referenced through it. The Application object contains the Forms, Reports, and Modules collections; the Screen object; and the DoCmd object, a peculiar and very useful Access object that allows you to run almost all Access commands, including functions and macros. The Screen object references the Access object that has the focus—it can be a form, report, or control. It is useful when you want to perform an action on the object the user is working on, without knowing its name. Moving down the (rather sparse) Access object model hierarchy, the Forms object contains a collection of Controls, as does the Reports object. The Modules object has no sub-objects. One important note: to reference a Form, Report, or Module object from VBA or VBScript code, you must first open the object in code (though you can keep it from displaying by not making the Access object visible). Note that the Access object model lets you work with the components of the Access interface— primarily tables, forms, reports, and commands. In order to manipulate Access *data*, you need to use the DAO object model instead.

The DAO object model

The Data Access Objects (DAO) object model is used to manipulate data stored in standard database formats, including Access. Its highest level is the DBEngine object, referencing the entire data structure. The DBEngine object has two subobjects: Errors and Workspaces. Errors contains error messages, as you might expect, while Workspaces contains named user sessions. Under Workspaces there are Groups, Users, and Databases collections, of which the Databases collection is the most commonly used. Users and Groups and their sub-objects are used to set up or modify security options, while Databases and its sub-objects are used to manipulate data. Under Databases there are further collections of Containers, QueryDefs (queries), Recordsets, Relations, and TableDefs (tables), each with its own subobject collections: Containers have Documents; QueryDefs have Fields and Parameters; Recordsets have Fields; Relations have Fields; and TableDefs have Fields and Indexes. By using DAO objects, you can manipulate Access data programmatically, without having to open an Access object.

The Outlook object model

Outlook's object model is very rich and rather strange. At the top there is the Application object, and underneath the Application object there are several objects that contain all the lower objects in the hierarchy. The Explorer and Inspector objects are Outlook's interface objects. The Explorer object is a window that displays a folder's contents (for example, the Inbox), and you need to set a reference to this object to manipulate an open Outlook folder. Use the Explorer object and its sub-objects to get at the Outlook object with which the user is working. Beneath the Explorer object is the MAPIFolder object, which references individual folders. The Inspector object displays an item, such as a contact or task, and has Item and Pages (tabs) objects beneath it. The Assistant object is the familiar Office Assistant, for some reason considered as an Outlook object. Not much use here. The other main Outlook object under the Application object is the NameSpace object, referencing Outlook data stored in MAPI format, and containing a Folders collection with subsidiary Items. The NameSpace object and its sub-objects are used to reference specific items in folders by name, without the need to first open them—these objects are used to manipulate Outlook data. Note that although there are CommandBar objects beneath the Explorer and Inspector objects, in the current implementation of Outlook you can't manipulate command bars programmatically, so they aren't much use.

The PowerPoint object model

The Application object provides access to PowerPoint itself and its application-wide characteristics. The Presentations collection and its constituent Presentation objects correspond to open presentations. The Slide object (there's also a Slides collection) refers to a specific slide within a presentation. You'll also want to become familiar with the SlideRange collection that is an on-the-fly grouping of just the slides you specify. The Master object denotes a slide master, title master, handout master, or notes master. Drawing objects on PowerPoint slides are represented by the Shapes collection, the ShapeRange collection, and the Shape object. The Shapes collection gathers together all the Shape objects on a specific slide; this collection doesn't extend beyond one specific slide. The ShapeRange collection is analogous to the SlideRange collection described earlier, but restricted to a single slide. To access the text inside a shape, you'll want to study the TextFrame object, the TextRange object, and the HasTextFrame and HasText properties.

Other Office object models

Office 97 is absolutely rife with object models. To see them all (specifically, the ones currently available on your system), take a quick stroll among the dozens of available references from inside any VBA project. As we demonstrated earlier in this chapter, select Tools ➤ References, then revel in the plethora of object and control libraries that are available to you. Table 3-1 provides a list of all the object models available to you in Office 97 Professional, along with the corresponding descriptive text that appears in the VBA Editor's References dialog box.

Table 3-1: Office Object Model Names Plus Descriptions (As They Appear in the VBA Editor's References Dialog Box)

Object Model's Application/ Component Name	Description text in the References dialog box
Access 97	Microsoft Access 8.0 Object Library
Excel 97	Microsoft Excel 8.0 Object Library
Outlook 97	Microsoft Outlook 8.0 Object Library
PowerPoint 97	Microsoft PowerPoint 8.0 Object Library
Shared components available to all Office 97 applications	
Office Assistant	Microsoft Office 8.0 Object Library

Table 3-1: Office Object Model Names Plus Descriptions (As They Appear in the VBA Editor's References Dialog Box) (continued)

Object Model's Application/ Component Name	Description text in the References dialog box
Office Binder	Microsoft Binder 8.0 Object Library
Office CommandBars	Microsoft Office 8.0 Object Library
Office FileSearch	Microsoft Office 8.0 Object Library
Other Office 97 components	
Data Access for ODBCDirect Work-spaces	Microsoft DAO 3.5 Object Library
Data Access for Microsoft Jet Work-spaces	Microsoft DAO 3.5 Object Library
Microsoft Forms (as in "User Forms," meaning dialog boxes)	Visual Basic for Applications
Microsoft Map 97	Microsoft Map
Visual Basic Editor	Microsoft Visual Basic for Applications Extensibility

It's really annoying that, while in the References dialog box, the frame along the bottom of the dialog box truncates the full path shown in the Location: line. For a particularly long path and filename—for example, in the case of the Microsoft DAO 3.5 Object Library—you can't see all of it. *Attention Microsoft: fix this!* (Turns out the default location is *C:\Program Files\Common Files\Microsoft Shared\Dao\Dao350.dll,* but you'd never know that by looking at this dialog.)

The Object Browser

We've spent several pages introducing you to the notion of an object model and how one relates to VBA. Since the Excel object model, for example, contains more than 150 objects and collections of objects, along with innumerable properties and methods, you might get the impression that we've only scratched the surface. You'd be right.

Your closest source of information (it's free, too) on any of the numerous Office object models is something called the Object Browser. It's a frequently overlooked component of the VBA Editor. We find it indispensable. (See Figure 3-40.)

The Object Browser displays all the valid objects, properties, and methods accessible to your programs. It also has very good hot links from the objects, properties, and methods to the on-line Help screens for each of them (right-click an item in any of the browser's many panes and choose Help). If you learn to use the Object Browser as your reference of first resort, you'll stand a fighting chance of writing programs that actually work.

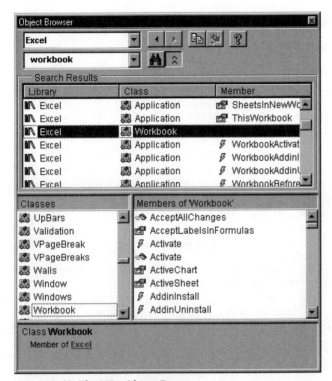

Figure 3-40: The VBA Object Browser

To get into the Object Browser, go into the VBA Editor and click View ➤ Object Editor (or simply hit F2). The interface is decidedly nonstandard and a bit obtuse, but stick with it and entire object models are at your fingertips. If you want to copy the named arguments list for a particular method (*including custom procedures in any of your own projects*), once that method is displayed in the Display pane (the pane at the bottom of the browser), highlight it with your mouse, as shown in Figure 3-41, and copy it to the clipboard by clicking the right mouse button and selecting the Copy option from the pop-up menu or by pressing Ctrl+C.

NOTE   Be ever vigilant. No program documentation is ever complete—or completely accurate—and the VBA online Help is no exception. Some of the descriptions are just plain wrong. Some of the code samples don't work. And many, many "gotchas" are left unexplored. Still, if you take the documentation with a grain of salt, you'll find an enormous amount of important information there. And the easiest way to get to the information is via the Object Browser.

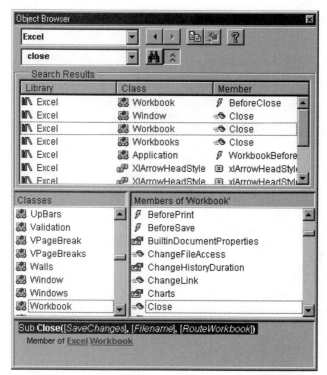

Figure 3-41: Use Object Browser to grab the named arguments for the Close method (when applied to an Excel Workbook object)

In summary, if you need to learn about a particular Office application (or control, or shared component) and its associated object model, follow these steps:

1. If the thing of interest is a full-blown application that supports VBA, fire up the VBA Editor, ask Robert "application," then drill down on the Application Object Help topic. As described earlier in this chapter, click on the Multiple Objects rectangle immediately below the Application rectangle (see Figure 3-37) and explore from there. You can also use the Object Browser to jump to a specific Office application's Application object. How fast it is to use the Office Assistant versus the Object Browser in such a case is merely a matter of which one is already running!

2. Otherwise, in any application's VBA Editor, look for the appropriate library in the References dialog's list and select it, then click OK (see Table 3-1). Now use the Object Browser to focus on that particular item's library in the Project/Library Box. For example, change it from "<All Libraries>" to "DAO" and then browse the Classes and Members

of... lists, right-clicking and choosing Help from the pop-up menu whenever you want more information on a specific component.

3. Fire up your Web browser and check out *http://www.microsoft.com/ OfficeDev/Docs/OMG/default.htm.*

Hooking in to the Office Host Application

We hope you've seen enough to get a feel for the nouns, verbs, and adjectives that your programs can use to harness an Office application's power, and turn it to your own devices. Let's focus our attention now on the way you shoe-horn your own programs into a host application, so they look and feel like they're part of the application itself. After all, you may come up with a great way to solve an annoying problem, but it won't mean much if you can't make it easy to use.

Even if you never write a custom macro or program a single lick, this information is important because it will let you tie other peoples' solutions into your own copy of the Office host application of choice.

Let's take a look at all the different ways you have to weave your programs into the fabric of an Office host application.

Where to Put Macros

In Excel, you can store macros in several different project locations if you want them available every time you start Excel:

* The special *Personal.xls* workbook. (*Personal.xls* is a workbook that Excel creates for you as a general-purpose macro repository; this special file is stored in the *Xlstart* folder, and Excel keeps it hidden by default.)

* A workbook that is always loaded by virtue of being in the *Xlstart* folder or your alternate startup folder, if you've defined one. (Excel's installation routine creates a folder called *Xlstart*, usually just below the location of the folder that houses *Excel.exe*. When Excel starts, it attempts to load any files it finds in *Xlstart*. The alternate startup setting lets you specify a folder of your choice to be the equivalent to *Xlstart*. Any files in this alternate folder get loaded automatically *in addition to* those in *Xlstart*. This is handy if you're on a network and

want to auto load some files from the net and some from your local disk. To change this setting, select Tools ➤ Options ➤ General, and manually type the full path into the "Alternate startup file location" edit box.)

- An add-in that is always loaded by virtue of its presence in the Add-In Manager's internal tables.

Using *Personal.xls* is convenient, but this special workbook is an easy target for macro viruses; this makes it a less useful candidate for storing macros. Auto-loading workbooks is the solution we suggest in *Excel 97 Annoyances*, primarily because you won't be saddled with the complex and Byzantine behavior of Excel add-ins. The trick is to finish the workbook's feature set and then hide it; this way it auto-loads but isn't visible when you start Excel. Furthermore, although hidden, you can still edit its macros from the VBA Editor just as you would those in any other open workbook.

Excel add-ins offer greater protection capabilities and an entire set of behaviors that you may find helpful, especially if you're developing custom Excel solutions for more users than just yourself. But for day-to-day use for storing your custom programs, we suggest using *My Macros.xls* as an auto-loading workbook. Here are the steps:

1. Create a new workbook and save it as *My Macros.xls* in the *Xlstart* folder (typically *C:\Program Files\Microsoft Office\Office\Xlstart*).

2. Select Window ➤ Hide.

3. Exit Excel and respond Yes when prompted "Do you want to save the changes you made to 'My Macros.xls'?".

In Word, most people put their macros in *Normal.dot*, Word's special, global, "always running" template. It's easy, and you're always assured that a *Normal.dot* macro will be available (and editable) with minimum hassle.

Unfortunately, there are two problems with that approach:

- Some programs (including a few viruses!) overwrite key programs in *Normal.dot*. For example, if you have a macro in *Normal.dot* called `AutoOpen`, and you happen to open a W97M/Wazzu infected file (see *Word 97 Annoyances*, Chapter 8, on *The Viral Threat*), whatever you put in `AutoOpen` will be wiped out—overwritten by the infection routine in Wazzu. Some installation programs, particularly for older Word macros, can be very impolite and blithely overwrite macros without checking to see if macros with certain names already exist.

- If you use Microsoft's anti-virus program, WordProt (again see *Word 97 Annoyances*, Chapter 8), it will password protect *Normal.dot*. If you forget that password, you're simply up the ol' creek without a paddle—there's no way to unprotect the file, no way to retrieve your old macros in *Normal.dot*. This threat is actually more sinister than it first appears. If somebody uses your PC and runs the WordProt installer, they can effectively lock you out of your own *Normal.dot*. Permanently. There's nothing you can do about it, unless you happen to have a very recent, unprotected backup copy of *Normal.dot*. You do, don't you?

Because of those two problems, we like to put our Word macros in a separate global template, which we call *My Macros.dot*. By locating *My Macros.dot* in the Word *Startup* folder, we're assured that they're always available—although locating the macros in a separate template does mean that you'll have to open the template in Word before you can edit the macros.

In Access development circles, the term "macro" refers to a now effectively vestigial architecture that has been around since the dawn of the Access era. *An Access macro is not a VBA procedure*, it is a collection of actions (much like a script), and Access macros are rarely if ever used today for professional Access development work (the primary exceptions being `AutoKeys` and `AutoExec`). Your general-purpose VBA procedures can be stored in either Access *.MDA* files (which you can create yourself, but the process is not nearly as straightforward as when creating Office add-ins; for a complete discussion on how to manage this chore, see the Help topic "Create your own wizards, builders, and add-ins") or within separate utility modules within each database.

Outlook doesn't support manual or programmatic changes to its own user interface. (Outlook add-ins are developed in C/C++.) Any VBScript code you write is stored with its host form, and is only available when that form is open and/or running.

PowerPoint has no equivalent to Excel's *Xlstart* folder technology or Word's global template architecture. So if you want to keep general-purpose PowerPoint macros on hand and open for any PowerPoint session, you can set up a shortcut that opens a specific PowerPoint presentation—say, *My Macros.ppt*—and start PowerPoint that way. Alternately, as described in Chapter 4, *VBA Fights Office Annoyances*, you could create and load a PowerPoint add-in to hold your general-purpose VBA procedures.

Assign to Toolbar Button

You can put your Excel/VBA programs, er, macros on Excel toolbars with a few simple clicks. Whenever the user clicks on that particular toolbar button, your macro gets run. Here's how to assign a toolbar button to the `PrintCBarControlList` macro that we presented earlier in Example 3-3: click on Tools ➤ Customize, then click the Commands tab. On the left, scroll down to Macros. On the right, choose either the Custom Menu Item or Custom Button control, then drag and drop it onto the toolbar of your choice. Now right-click the new control and choose Assign Macro from the popup menu. When the Assign Macro dialog opens, choose This Workbook in the "Macros in" list (you can also choose All Open Workbooks, as shown in Figure 3-42, or just *Personal.xls*), scroll down to the `PrintCBarControlList` macro, and click OK.

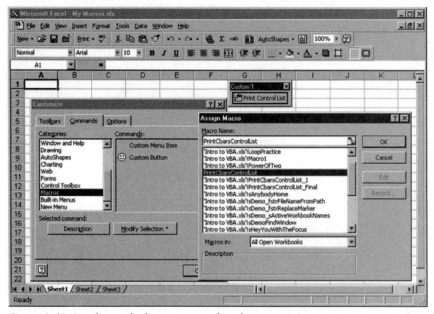

Figure 3-42: Excel's got the best user interface for assigning macros to command bar controls

In Figure 3-43, we used the name "Print Control List" and the button image from the Format ➤ AutoFormat control.

From this point on, the button you just put on the toolbar will run the macro you chose. In this case, clicking on the button will run the `Print-CbarsControlList` macro in the Module1 module in the IntroToVBA project. As Figure 3-43 shows, Excel even picks up a tooltip that's the same as the name you give the control (not necessarily the same as the underlying macro name, by the way).

Figure 3-43: The button is ready

In PowerPoint, the process is vaguely similar to that described for Excel, except that there's no Assign Macro menu option that opens an Assign Macro dialog. Instead, once you choose Macros in the Categories list, the Commands list displays the names of available subroutines (without their parameters, if they have any) in all open presentations. Annoyingly, if multiple presentations have subroutines with the same name; you won't be able to tell them apart because the dialog box lists them by subroutine name only with no hint of who owns which one. Absurd. Someone in Redmond was in way too big a hurry when designing this dialog. (The only workaround is to use VBA code to set the OnAction property for the toolbar button control to the desired presentation's module and subroutine.)

In Word the process is similar to that described for Excel, sort of. Once again, there's no Assign Macro pop-up menu item that produces an Assign Macro dialog. Instead, once you choose Macros in the Categories list, the Commands list displays *all* the available subroutines (without listing any parameters) from all available templates: the current document's parent template (or, if the current document is in fact a template, then the template itself), *Normal.dot*, and any loaded global templates. At least in Word (unlike the wayward PowerPoint), you see a rational listing of subroutines in the form of `projectname.modulename.subroutinename`, e.g., `MyWordVBAProject.MyModule1.MySubroutine1`.

In Access the process is somewhat similar, but there are some differences to be aware of. If you want to hook up an Access macro (not an Access VBA procedure) to a command bar control, in the Categories list box look for "All Macros" not "Macros." Alternately—again, here we're talking about Access macros, not Access VBA procedures—from the Database window, click the Macros tab, then click the name of the macro you want to create a toolbar for, then select Tools ➤ Macro, Create Toolbar from Macro.

The process of assigning a VBA procedure to an Access command bar control is annoyingly different from Excel, PowerPoint, and Word, so get ready to jump through some hoops. From the Module Window, add a built-in command (say, File ➤ New Database…) to the toolbar, right-click the control, choose Properties, which displays the <toolbar name>

Control Properties dialog box, manually type the procedure name in the On Action combo box (unlike Excel, PowerPoint, and Word, there's no predefined list here, ouch), edit the other control properties as you see fit, click Close, click Close again. Or you can do it the way the Access Help file describes it (see Help topic "About running Visual Basic code"), which is a double-kludge—assign an Access macro to the toolbar button and have the macro call the VBA procedure.

Sadly, in PowerPoint and Word, you can't manually reassign a macro to an extant control. Instead you have to delete the control and add it back with the new macro reference. Excel is light-years ahead of its Office siblings in this arena. All the other Office applications should take their cue from Excel's handling of manual macro assignments.

Assign to Menu Bars

The method for assigning macros to locations on menu bars in Access, Excel, PowerPoint, and Word resembles the toolbar procedure covered in the previous section. Outlook, of course, can't play this tune because its user interface can't be modified.

Assign to Keyboard

When it comes to assigning keyboard shortcuts to Excel macros, there's good news, annoying news, and more annoying news.

First the good news: you can actually assign a keyboard shortcut. But even the good news is a bit annoying; you can assign any keyboard combination you want, as long as it is Ctrl plus some other key. Meaning, you can't do Alt+ or Shift+ or combinations thereof; the key combination must always begin with Ctrl.

Annoyingly, to assign a shortcut key, you must be in Excel (not the Visual Basic Editor) and click Tools ➤ Macro ➤ Macros. You should also be able to do this from the Visual Basic Editor but you can't, and that's a real disappointment. Select the macro you want from the displayed list and click the Options button. (See Figure 3-44.)

In the Macro Options dialog shown in Figure 3-44, you can select a key to use in combination with the Ctrl key, as well as type in a description of the macro. This is where you hit another major annoyance—if you use a key combination that you've already assigned, the new assignment over-writes the old without any warning whatsoever.

When it comes to assigning keyboard shortcuts to PowerPoint macros, there's only bad news. It can't be done.

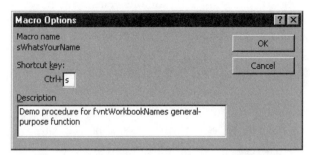

Figure 3-44: Excel's Macro Options dialog box assigns shortcut keys and a macro description

Word is a bit more flexible than Excel in this regard. To assign a Word/ VBA macro called `ShowMsgBox` to, oh, `Ctrl+Alt+Shift+T`, here's all you have to do:

1. Click on Tools ➤ Customize, bring up the Commands tab, and click the Keyboard button. Make sure "Save changes in:" shows the template you want to contain the keyboard assignment. On the left of the dialog shown in Figure 3-45, under Categories, pick Macros. On the right, pick ShowMsgBox.

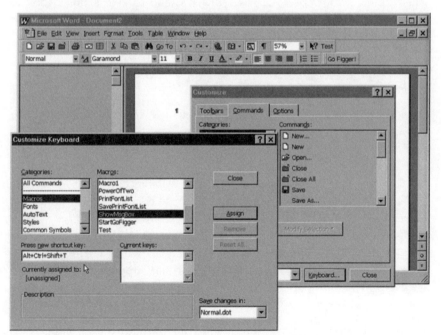

Figure 3-45: Assign a Word/VBA macro to a key combination

2. This Customize Keyboard dialog is a bit strange. First, you have to click inside the box that says "Press new shortcut key." Then you should press whatever key combination you want to assign to invoke the macro—in this case, we held down the Ctrl, Alt, Shift, and T keys simultaneously. When you have the combination you want in the box, click Assign. (You might be tempted to click Close, but make sure you click Assign first.)

3. Click Close all the way back out. From this point on, pressing `Ctrl+Alt+Shift+T` will run the `ShowMsgBox` macro.

Unfortunately, Word doesn't have an easy way to reset one single key assignment. Your only option is to reset all the keyboard assignments, all at once. Blecch.

Events for the Application Object and Other Objects

Earlier in this chapter we discussed controls on dialog boxes, and the events and event handlers for these controls, like the Click event for the CommandButton1 control, which is handled by a procedure automatically called `CommandButton1_Click`. Now it's time to take a quick look at events and event handlers for objects like the application itself (say, Excel) along with that application's primary objects. By "primary" objects we mean the high-level objects users interact with most often, for example, Workbook and Worksheet objects in Excel and Document objects in Word.

Excel possesses rich event-handling capabilities. You can associate code with application object events, but to do so requires that you write a class module. Class modules are beyond the scope of this book, but you can read about them in Excel's on-line Help, the *Mastering Microsoft Office 97 Development* CD, and various books on Visual Basic 4 and 5. The relevant Excel Visual Basic Help topic is "Using Events with the Application Object." Associating code with Workbook, Worksheet, and Chart object events doesn't involve class modules. You can write macros that are associated with any of 17 Workbook object events shown in Figure 3-46. (For more information about other Excel objects that support events, see on-line Help.) Here's what happens when the two most common Workbook object events fire:

• The `Workbook_Open` subroutine runs when the workbook is opened.

- The `Workbook_Close` subroutine runs before the workbook closes. (If the workbook has changed, this event occurs before the user is asked to save changes.)

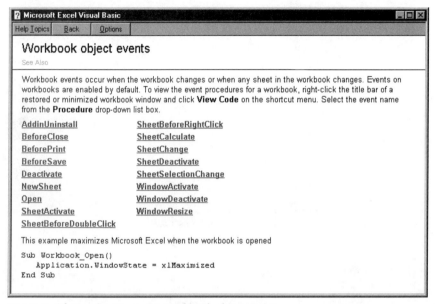

Figure 3-46: Excel supports 17 Workbook object events

To see how to construct these event handlers, open up a convenient test workbook. (We used one called *test.xls*.) In the VBA Editor's Project Explorer, navigate to the Microsoft Excel Objects folder and double-click on This Workbook. On the left, in the Code Window's Object box, pick Workbook. By default, the editor creates an empty, private `Workbook_Open` subroutine as shown in Figure 3-47. (If you want a different event you would choose it from the list on the right.)

Now type in the simple program in Example 3-6. Close your test workbook. Yes, you want to save changes.

Example 3-6: Code for a Workbook_Open() Event Procedure in Excel

```
Private Sub Workbook_Open()
MsgBox "Opening test.xls"
End Sub
```

Now open the test workbook. Excel will greet you with its Virus warning message. Click "Enable macros." As soon as you clear the Virus warning message, Excel "fires" the Workbook.Open event. VBA goes looking for an event handler and finds one in *test.xls* called `Workbook_Open`. The result is a message box on the screen, as shown in Figure 3-48.

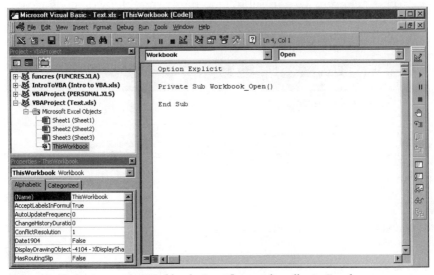

Figure 3-47: Setting up the Workbook_Open() event handler in Excel

Figure 3-48: The Workbook.Open event handler kicks in

Access has a rich architecture for data, error and timing, filter, focus, keyboard, mouse, print, and window events. Like its Office siblings, it uses VBA as a repository for event procedures; however, the techniques by which you create these event procedures are different from those described for Excel and Word. For more information, ask Robert "events" and study the various relevant topics; see in particular the Help topic "Create an event procedure."

A discussion of Outlook's event-handling capabilities can be found in the Microsoft Outlook Visual Basic Help file described earlier in this chapter. Outlook supports the following events: Close, CustomAction, CustomPropertyChange, Forward, Open, PropertyChange, Read, Reply, ReplyAll, Send, and Write.

PowerPoint has no application or object event-handling capabilities.[*]

---

[*] Strangely (but you can use the quirk to your advantage), PowerPoint add-ins do support the old `Auto_Open` and `Auto_Close` macros. This is not true for regular PowerPoint presentations.

Here's an annoying bug that afflicts Word but *not* Excel. As soon as you set up a document event handler in a Word document, *every* time you open that document, you'll trigger the Virus warning message. Even if you delete the document event handler macros entirely, Word continues to believe that there are macros attached to the document, and continues to bedevil you with that warning message. Since there's no way to delete the Microsoft Word Objects component, there's no way to completely clean the document once it's been soiled. Your only option is to copy the entire contents of the document to a clean new document, and refrain from writing event handlers! *We repeat—this bug does not occur in Excel.*

For additional information about Word's event model, an extensive discussion of how the new Word/VBA events relate to the old Auto macros used in WordBasic, and numerous warnings about Word firing sequence bugs, see *Word 97 Annoyances.*

Onward

You made it! It was a long but informative journey from the outset of this chapter to this, the end of the trail, and we sincerely hope you enjoyed it. You should now find yourself well-prepared for using VBA in an Office application to conquer annoyances, be they egregious or just plain, well, annoying.

4

In this chapter:
- *Fighting Excel
  Annoyances*
- *VBA Does Battle with
  Wonder Word*
- *A VBA/PowerPoint
  Shape Grabber*

VBA Fights Office Annoyances

If you're joining us from Chapter 3, *Introduction to Office Macros*, let's review where we've been so far with our introductory grand tour of VBA and Office macros. We began with an overview of what macros (a.k.a. programs, procedures, and subroutines) are and how they will change your life forever. This was followed by a tutorial on recording macros and using the VBA Editor—with its myriad bells, whistles, and ministrations—to edit your recorded macros or to enable you to build them from scratch. Then we moved doggedly on to examine three (two small and one large) VBA programs to see what makes them tick. Next came a tutorial on custom dialog boxes and event-driven programming. In the most recent section, you learned about object models, and about Office application object models in particular, and then got a practical lesson in how to explore object models using online Help and the Object Browser.

So much for concepts and the fundamentals. It's time to get down to brass tacks. In this chapter, we'll devote ourselves exclusively to VBA programs that will go a long way toward reducing your Office annoyance level. We present a group of Excel macros that extend Excel's existing feature set by offering single-click access to often-used auditing features, along with another single-click macro for displaying the handy Go To Special dialog that's normally three clicks and a second dialog box away. Following this are two Word macros that vastly reduce the amount of effort required to produce commonly desired effects: typing em dashes and toggling the current document in its "how it will print" display mode and its "underpinnings" display mode. Last is a turnkey, step-by-step exercise in which you create—from scratch—a PowerPoint utility called ShapeGrabber. This program includes a custom dialog box that allows

the user to pick and choose among PowerPoint's numerous shape types—
from AutoShape to TextEffect—in order to select or delete them in
batches, including a presentation-wide deletion capability. So not only do
you get more VBA code to work with, it's put together in the context of a
utility with a user interface (dialog box).

Fighting Excel Annoyances

Excel annoyances come in three distinct flavors:

- Excel doesn't work the way it's supposed to.

- Excel doesn't work the way you want it to.

- Procedures should be a darn sight easier than they are. This includes
  the hidden jewels that seem to have been buried in this incredibly
  powerful spreadsheet program, or that could certainly be more intuitive or obvious. This is the most common type of Excel annoyance.

In *Excel 97 Annoyances* we doggedly pursue Excel's elusive mindset, all
the while exposing annoyances from all of the above sources. Most often
you'll find yourself using VBA in Excel to either smooth a rough edge
here and there, calibrate Excel precisely to your liking, or provide a
custom user interface for data gathering and analysis. Here are three
programs that will greatly reduce your "Excel doesn't work the way you
want it to" annoyance level.

For these macros, create a workbook called *My Macros.xls.* We'll create
these macros in Module1. Save this file to your *Xlstart* folder. To make it
hidden, make your last edits to the macros, click Windows ➤ Hide and
then close Excel. When asked if you want to save changes to *My
Macros.xls* click on Yes.

Formula/Results Flipper

A cell can contain a number, text, or a formula. But what you *see* in a cell
may not be what was entered into a cell. Formatting can control what
you see in a cell. For example, 34547 formatted as a date might display as
Aug-94. The formula =3+5 displays as 8.

There are two faces to a sheet: what a cell really contains, and what the
cell displays. Normally, Excel shows the results of formatting and calcula-
tions in the cell grid. We'll call this the "results" side. What was really
entered into the cells we'll call the "formula" side, since the actual
formula and not the formula's result is what we're interested in here.
Changing a sheet's display from results to formulas is called "flipping the

sheet" and is a powerful tool for auditing spreadsheet models because it quickly exposes hidden formula errors.

You can flip a sheet by going to Tools ➤ Options ➤ View and checking the Formulas box. Or you can press `Ctrl+`` `. As handy as this keyboard shortcut is, we recommend you add a button to your Auditing toolbar to toggle this state with a single click. Oddly, you won't see the Auditing toolbar listed in the popup menu when you right-click on a toolbar. Instead, you have to get there the long way: either Tools ➤ Auditing ➤ Show Auditing Toolbar or Tools ➤ Customize ➤ Toolbars, check Auditing, Close.

Open Module1 in your hidden *My Macros.xls* and enter the code from Example 4-1, then assign this macro to a new button on your Auditing toolbar.

Example 4-1: The Formula_Flipper Program

```
Public Sub Formula_Flipper()
'
' Formula_Flipper Macro to flip the worksheet display
'    between formulas and results
' Written xx/xx/xx by YourNameHere
'
    On Error GoTo EndMacro
    ActiveWindow.DisplayFormulas = Not ActiveWindow.DisplayFormulas
EndMacro:
End Sub
```

From A1 to R1C1 Reference Style and Back

Cell references can be absolute, relative, or mixed (a combination of absolute and relative), and you'll never get out of the minor league of spreadsheet building until you are completely comfortable with the difference.

A1 is a relative address. $A$1 is an absolute address.

What's the difference? An absolute address refers to a specific cell. $A$1 refers to the cell that is at the intersection of column A and row 1. Type the reference =$A$1 into any cell you want, then copy it to any other cell, and you'll always get column A, row 1.

But A1 is a horse of a different color. Type =A1 into a cell. Now copy it one cell to the right. Is the formula still =A1? No, it now reads =B1. The cell reference changed *relative* to the new location of the formula. You moved the formula one cell to the right, so it now references the cell one cell to the right of the original reference.

Annoying? No, definitely not. This is by design, and it enables many of the wonderful things for which you use spreadsheets. Imagine you have several columns of numbers, a formula that totals the first column, and you use the fill handle to copy that formula across the bottom of the other columns. The formula changes (well, it *appears* to change) so that each column is totaled, courtesy of relative referencing.

To understand what's going on here, you have to realize that this business of column letters is an elaborate fiction. Excel actually thinks in terms of row and column *numbers*. Let's see how this works by changing the reference style to R1C1:

1. In cell B2 enter =A1.

2. In cell B3 enter =$A$1.

3. Now, from the Tools menu, click on Options.

4. In the General tab, check the "R1C1 reference style" box.

5. Click on OK.

Your formulas should now look like Figure 4-1.

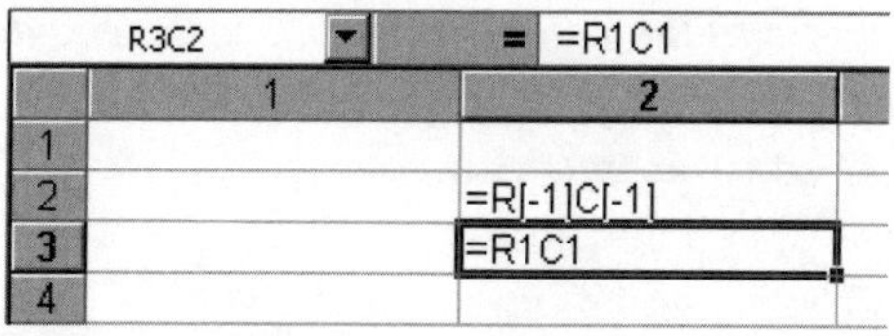

R3C2	▼	■	=R1C1
	1		2
1			
2		=R[-1]C[-1]	
3		=R1C1	
4			

Figure 4-1: The difference between relative and absolute

Notice that the columns are now numbered, not lettered. This is how Excel really thinks, in terms of row numbers *and* column numbers. The formula in cell R2C2 (that's B2 in the old notation) looks pretty odd until you get comfortable with this notation. Reading the formula from left to right, it says, *"From this cell up one row, from that cell one column to the left."*

R stands for row, C for column, and numbers in brackets tell you what direction and how far to travel to find the referenced cell. A minus sign means up or left. Positive numbers (no sign) mean down or right. Easy.

In Figure 4-1, the formula =R1C1 in cell R3C2 is an absolute reference. It refers to the intersection of row 1, column 1. That intersection never changes no matter where you copy this formula.

Here's an R1C1 style relative example. Switch the notation back to A1. Enter the formula =B6+B7 in a new worksheet's cell B8. Use the fill

handle to copy this formula to C8 and D8. Your formulas look like those
in Figure 4-2.

B	C	D
=B6+B7	=C6+C7	=D6+D7

Figure 4-2: Adding the two cells above, in A1 notation

The individual formulas *appear* to have changed as you copied them into
the adjacent cells. This is because the original formula was entered using
relative references—references that are meaningful only in the context of
the relative positions of the cells. In this case all three formulas are identical. They look different, but they are all identical to Excel. To see this,
switch to R1C1 notation, as shown in Figure 4-3.

2	3	4
=R[-2]C+R[-1]C	=R[-2]C+R[-1]C	=R[-2]C+R[-1]C

Figure 4-3: Same formula adding the two cells above, in R1C1 notation

Each formula says, in effect, "*Start from this cell and go up two rows but
stay in this column, and add that value to the value in the cell up one row
from this cell, in this same column.*" Drag any of these formulas to any
spot on the sheet and it will try to add the two cells directly above the
current cell. If you try to reference a cell location that is off the sheet
(say, by copying this formula up to row 1) you'll get a #REF! error.

You can create a formula that contains a mix of absolute and relative
references. The formula =R1C[3] refers to row 1 (absolute) and three
columns to the right relative to the cell containing the reference. Type
=R1C[3] into cell R1C1. Flip back into A1 notation and you get =D$1.
The column reference D is relative. The row number $1 is absolute.

If you really want to get a feel for what formulas are all about, turn on
the R1C1 reference style for a month or so. You may never turn it off.

The R1C1 reference style is good for more than just getting comfortable
with absolute/relative referencing. It is an invaluable troubleshooting and
auditing strategy.

A formula that gets overwritten can be readily discovered using the
Formula_Flipper program discussed in the previous section. But formulas
that are off just a bit are harder to ferret out, and this is where R1C1 can
help.

In Figure 4-4, we show the same column of relative formulas in R1C1 style on the left and A1 style on the right. Which style makes it easier for you to spot the error?

6	6
=RC[-4]-RC[-3]*RC[-2]	=C4-D4*E4
=RC[-4]-RC[-3]*RC[-2]	=C5-D5*E5
=RC[-4]-RC[-3]*RC[-2]	=C6-D6*E6
=R[1]C[-4]-RC[-3]*RC[-2]	=C8-D7*E7
=RC[-4]-RC[-3]*RC[-2]	=C8-D8*E8
=RC[-4]-RC[-3]*RC[-2]	=C9-D9*E9
=RC[-4]-RC[-3]*RC[-2]	=C10-D10*E10
=RC[-4]-RC[-3]*RC[-2]	=C11-D11*E11
=RC[-4]-RC[-3]*RC[-2]	=C12-D12*E12
=RC[-4]-RC[-3]*RC[-2]	=C13-D13*E13
=RC[-4]-RC[-3]*RC[-2]	=C14-D14*E14
=RC[-4]-RC[-3]*RC[-2]	=C15-D15*E15

Figure 4-4: R1C1 versus A1 reference style

Yes, we agree. R1C1 style makes it easier to spot the error (fourth from the top). So let's create a macro to toggle between A1 and R1C1 notation with one click, and assign it to your Auditing toolbar.

Open Module1 in your hidden *My Macros.xls* and enter the code from Example 4-2, then assign this macro to a new button on your Auditing toolbar.

Example 4-2: The Style_Flipper Program

```
Public Sub Style_Flipper()
'
' Style_Flipper Macro to switch between R1C1 and A1 reference style
' Written xx/xx/xx by YourNameHere
'
    With Application
        If .ReferenceStyle = xlA1 Then
            .ReferenceStyle = xlR1C1
        Else
            .ReferenceStyle = xlA1
        End If
    End With
End Sub
```

A One-Click Edit Go To Special

Excel's Go To Special dialog box (Edit ➤ Go To, Special) is chock full of useful tools for troubleshooting errant spreadsheets. The major annoyance is that you have to drill down to the Go To dialog box, then choose a button on that dialog to get to the Go To Special dialog. The one-click solution is to add another custom button to your Auditing toolbar.

Enter the code shown in Example 4-3 into Module1 in your *My Macros.xls* and add a new button for it on your Auditing toolbar.

Example 4-3: The EditGotoSpecial Macro to Open the Go To Special Dialog

```
Public Sub EditGotoSpecial()
'
' EditGotoSpecial Macro to pop up the Go To Special dialog
' Written xx/xx/xx by YourNameHere
'
    If TypeName(ActiveSheet) = "Worksheet" Then
        On Error GoTo EndMacro
        Application.Dialogs(xlDialogSelectSpecial).Show
    Else
        Beep
    End If
    Exit Sub
EndMacro:
    If Err = 1004 Then
        MsgBox "No cells (or objects) found.", vbExclamation
    End If
End Sub
```

For additional material on VBA/Excel, as well as numerous other VBA/Excel program code listings, see Chapter 5 in *Excel 97 Annoyances*. You can also go to *http://www.oreilly.com* and download *Intro to VBA.xls* and *My Macros.xls*.

Another source of VBA/Excel utilities, including step-by-step instructions on how to build them, can be found in *Office Computing* and on its Web site, *http://www.zdnet.com/pccomp/oc/*. In particular, see the October 1997 issue's articles on the Excel utilities TimeIt and ShapeNotes.

TimeIt helps you enter your project time and analyze it. You build a data entry form using a custom VBA dialog box and store the data in Excel lists (databases). You then add time calculation formulas and learn how to use pivot tables to analyze the data once you've captured it.

ShapeNotes addresses a feature that's sorely lacking in Office 97's Office Art—a way to assign comments to a shape, for example, performance review notes about an employee in an org chart. In this project you build a small program with a dialog box that displays all the diagram's shapes and allows you to add, view, and edit the comments you attach to these shapes.

VBA Does Battle with Wonder Word

Word's galling annoyances can be divided into three parts:

- Annoyances that arise from the complexity of the problem itself. These are annoyances that Microsoft really couldn't avoid. They have more to do with the conceptual leap from the typewriter era (or the pen-and-pencil era) to the typesetting era than anything else.

- Annoyances attributable to the way Word was designed or implemented. Microsoft could have worked around these problems, but they didn't. Often these annoyances are perpetuated with the excuse that they're needed "for backward compatibility." You're the one left holding the compatibility bag, until you see how Word is put together, and can think your way around the problems.

- Annoyances that are just plain stupid. Word's full of them.

In *Word 97 Annoyances*, we expose Word's innermost thoughts and use that perspective to understand and solve numerous annoyances. This section contains several programs to do just that.

Em Dash

Why does Word insist on making the em dash so difficult?

As you may know, an em dash is a loooooooong dash, used to set off subordinate clauses in sentences. We use 'em all the time. It's stunted younger sister, the en dash, isn't nearly as impressive.* And the piddling-poor hyphen (also known as a minus sign, or sometimes simply a "dash") doesn't cut any mustard.

If Word actually *did* what it says it does (see Figure 4-5) and set things up with AutoFormat As You Type so two hyphens turn into an en dash and three turn into an em dash, at least you'd have a little bit of control over things. As it stands though, Word doesn't even come close. Word's symbol replacement behavior is governed by the AutoCorrect dialog (Tools ➤ AutoCorrect), in particular, by check boxes on that dialog's Auto-Format As You Type tab. As best we can tell, here's what really happens when you check that "Replace symbol characters with symbols" box in the Tools ➤ AutoCorrect, AutoFormat As You Type dialog:

- If you type a space, followed by a single hyphen, followed by any alphanumeric characters (or at most one space, followed by any

---

* In most fonts, the en dash is character number 150; the em dash is character number 151.

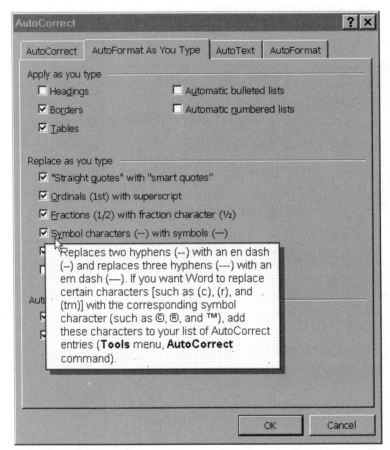

Figure 4-5: Word lies once again

alphanumeric characters), Word turns the single hyphen into an en dash.

*   If you type a space, followed by two hyphens, followed by any alpha-numeric characters (or at most one space, followed by any alphanu-meric characters), Word turns the double hyphen into an en dash.

That's it. Both single and double hyphens turn into en dashes; there's no way to create an em dash out of hyphens. Worst of all, though, you have to type a series of characters before Word changes the hyphens into en dashes. Why is that so annoying? Start Word and type this sentence:

> I really think, this is a subordinate clause, that I should use em dashes.

Now go back and pretend you're editing the sentence. You want to replace the commas with em dashes, but you'll settle for en dashes. How long does it take for you to get the sentence to look like this:

> I really think – this is a subordinate clause – that I should use em dashes.

The problem stems from the fact that you have to be typing, continuously, for Word to kick in and replace hyphens with en dashes. It's all a major pain. Unless you have the right macro, of course. Heh heh heh.

You'd think Microsoft would make it easy to set up some other key as an em dash key: after all, most keyboards have a virtually unused "minus" key in the upper-right corner of the number pad; it would make a dandy em dash key. The traditional technique for modifying a key's behavior is as follows. (Let's practice this on a new document—we'll assume its temporary name is Document2.) Select Tools ➤ Customize; click the Keyboard button; choose the appropriate document or template to "Save changes in" (which here is Document2); then pick a category (typically you'd scroll to the bottom of the list and select either Macros, Fonts, Auto-Text, Styles, or Common Symbols), say, Common Symbols. Next select Em Dash in the "Common Symbols" list; type a key sequence in the "Press new shortcut key" field (let's use Ctrl+Alt+A); click Assign; click Close; click Close again. To test, type Ctrl+Alt+A in the current document and you should see an em dash.

But if you try this Tools ➤ Customize, Keyboard route, you'll find that Word won't let you reassign the behavior of the NumPad minus key. If you try to use AutoCorrect to replace a NumPad minus with an em dash, Word will suddenly start changing all your hyphens, regardless of source, into em dashes. Blecch.

Here's how to change that vestigial NumPad minus key into a full-fledged em dash:

1. Start Word. If you have a template called *My Macros.dot* in your *Startup* folder, open it. Otherwise, create one now and save it in *Startup*.

2. Click Tools ➤ Macros, Visual Basic Editor.

3. In *My Macros.dot*, navigate to its Production module (add a Production module if you don't already have one).

4. Click Insert, Procedure, type **TypeEm** and hit Enter.

5. Type in one line between the two provided (the em dash is character number 151) as shown in Example 4-4.

Example 4-4: The TypeEm Subroutine

```
Public Sub TypeEm()
Selection.TypeText Chr$(151)
End Sub
```

We need to assign `TypeEm` to the NumPad minus key. And we need a macro to do it. Here's a case where what *cannot* be accomplished manually *can* be done with VBA. By some design quirk in Word, you can't manually assign the NumPad minus key to the em dash symbol, but you can assign the NumPad minus key to a custom macro (named `TypeEm`), and that macro can insert the em dash for you. However, in order to get the rabbit to pop out of this hat, you need a throw-away macro (we've named it `Temp`) to assign the key to the `TypeEm` macro. Click on Insert ➤ Procedure. Type **Temp**, click Private, and hit Enter. Then type the program shown in Example 4-5.

Example 4-5: The Temp Subroutine for a One-Time Custom Key Assignment

```
Private Sub Temp()
CustomizationContext = NormalTemplate
KeyBindings.Add KeyCategory:=wdKeyCategoryMacro, _
    Command:="TypeEm", KeyCode:=BuildKeyCode(wdKeyNumericSubtract)
End Sub
```

Run this macro by clicking the right-wedgie Play button.

WARNING   Bug Alert! If you have any customized toolbars in the current document when you run the macro, they'll get replaced by the standard *Normal.dot* Toolbars. DON'T PANIC! Close down Word, saving changes, start Word again, open the document again, and the customized toolbars will be reinstated.

Once the assignment macro is done, every time you hit the NumPad's minus key, you'll get a big, beautiful em dash in your document. Use it with wild abandon.

ShowAll

Every time you click on the toolbar button that looks like a paragraph mark (its official tooltip reads "Show/Hide ¶ (Ctrl+*)," Word runs a built-in command that looks to see if the Nonprinting characters' All box is checked in the Tools ➤ Options ➤ View dialog. If it is checked, the built-in command clears it out; if it isn't checked, it gets turned on. Easy.

Unfortunately, the All box doesn't do what we want to do when we're looking closely at a document. It shows some things we aren't interested in—those pesky dots in place of spaces, for example, and optional hyphens that rarely concern us—while ignoring other invisible things that can make a big difference (including Word's {field} codes).

Hijacking Word's Built-In Commands

One of the most important decisions the early Word designers made was to allow Word macro programs to run like any other Word programs, even supplanting the built-in operations of Word itself. Think about that for a second. It's quite important. Fundamental, in fact. This means your VBA/Word programs can run in place of Word's built-in commands. If you don't like the way Word performs a Show All operation, for example (and we don't), you need only create a global macro called ShowAll. Then, every time Word would normally run the ShowAll command, instead it passes control over to your macro. That may be Word's most powerful feature. It's certainly VBA/Word's most powerful feature.

Want to take over that button and make it work the way you want? Good. Here's how you'd do it:

1. The hardest part of commandeering a built-in command lies in figuring out which command to commandeer. Unless you know the trick. Hold down Alt and Ctrl, and push the plus key on the numeric keypad. Then click the cloverleaf icon on the Show/Hide ¶ button (see Figure 4-6).

2. In this particular case, the button's command is ShowAll, as Figure 4-6 shows. If you scan down the list of 965 possible built-in command names, you'll find that one of the listed commands is called ShowAll. Let's make sure that's the one we want.

3. Open *My Macros.dot.* Click on Tools ➤ Macro ➤ Visual Basic Editor. Navigate to the Production module in *My Macros.dot.*

4. Click Insert ➤ Procedure, type **ShowAll** and hit Enter. You should have a new Sub...End Sub pair.

5. Start by verifying that this is the correct built-in procedure name by typing in a simple program like the one shown in Example 4-6.

Example 4-6: An Early Version of the ShowAll Macro

```
Public Sub ShowAll()
MsgBox "In ShowAll"
End Sub
```

6. Go back out to Word, click the Show/Hide ¶ button on the Standard toolbar, and ensure that you get a message box with the appropriate message.

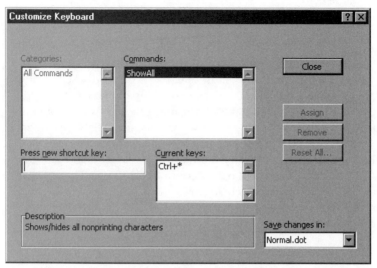

Figure 4-6: Searching for the Show/Hide ¶ button's built-in command name

The best way we've found to flip back and forth between observing a document and looking at the underpinnings behind a document does *not* involve the All box in Tools ➤ Options, View. Instead, we prefer to see if field codes are visible, or if field code results appear on screen (the "usual" setting), and flip-flop based on that value.

After going around with this for quite some time, we decided to let ShowAll flip-flop between these two groups of settings:

* The way that shows how a document will appear when it's printed: Page View, with paragraphs and tabs appearing on the screen, but bookmarks, field codes, optional hyphens, and hidden text not appearing. A document in Page View is shown in Figure 4-7.

* The way that shows the structure behind what appears: Normal View (may as well not go through all the hassle of paginating raw field codes), with paragraphs and tabs appearing on-screen, as well as bookmarks, field codes, optional hyphens, and hidden text. Figure 4-8 shows a document in Normal View.

If you would like to do something similar, using the Visual Basic Editor, click on Insert, then Procedure, type **ShowAll**, and type the code shown in Example 4-7.

Example 4-7: The Final ShowAll Program

```
Public Sub ShowAll()
If ActiveWindow.View.ShowFieldCodes Then
    ' Field codes are showing, return to default settings
```

Figure 4-7: The usual settings, which show how the document will print

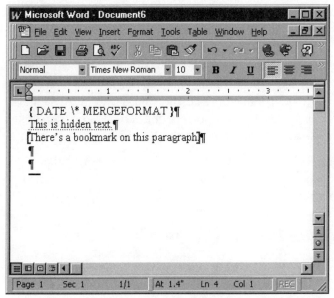

Figure 4-8: The behind-the-scenes settings, which show the structure of the document

Example 4-7: The Final ShowAll Program (continued)

```
    With ActiveWindow.View
        .ShowBookmarks = False
        .ShowFieldCodes = False
        .ShowHyphens = False
        .ShowHiddenText = False
        .ShowParagraphs = True
        .ShowTabs = True
    ' And flip into Page View
        .Type = wdPageView
    End With
Else
    ' Field results are showing, so show everything behind the
    ' scenes
    With ActiveWindow.View
        .ShowBookmarks = True
        .ShowFieldCodes = True
        .ShowHyphens = True
        .ShowHiddenText = True
        .ShowParagraphs = True
        .ShowTabs = True
    ' Then go into Normal View
        .Type = wdNormalView
    End With
End If
End Sub
```

You may not agree with our division of views, of course. That's the beauty of macros: you can change them around any way you like. You might want to show picture "anchors" (the points at which floating pictures attach themselves to the underlying document). For a complete list of all valid .View parameters—all the things you can change by simply adding them to this macro—go into the VBA Editor, ask Robert "view object," and look through the Properties listed.

For additional material on VBA/Word, as well as numerous other VBA/ Word program code listings, see *Word 97 Annoyances*. You can also go to *http://www.oreilly.com* and download *My Macros.dot*.

A VBA/PowerPoint Shape Grabber

PowerPoint provides no way, with its current user interface, to manually do the following:

- Select all shapes of a specific type—just AutoShapes, just Comments, just Freeforms, etc.—on the current slide.

- Delete any such group of shapes, either on the current slide or all slides.

It is possible to manually select all the shapes on a slide (Ctrl+A), but you can only manually select and then delete shapes on the current slide. You can manually Shift+left-click your way through various shapes on the current slide to produce a multi-shape selection, but it's impossible to tell what type of shapes they are as you're manually selecting them, or to extend the selection beyond the current slide. But with VBA these challenges are answered by an amazingly straightforward yet powerful little VBA/PowerPoint utility, one we call ShapeGrabber. In this section you'll build ShapeGrabber—from scratch. The utility consists of a dialog box with nine controls (see Figure 4-9), plus two code modules comprising about 250 lines of source code.

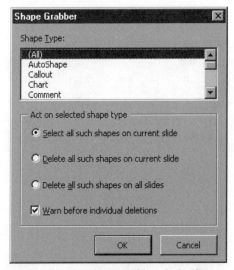

Figure 4-9: The ShapeGrabber dialog box

NOTE   A completed *ShapeGrabber.ppt* and *TestShapeGrabber.ppt* are available for downloading at *http://www.oreilly.com.*

To see how difficult it is to manually differentiate between shape types on a PowerPoint slide, conduct this experiment:

1. Create a new PowerPoint presentation using the "Title Only" Auto-Layout (third row, third column).

2. Select Insert ➤ Picture ➤ Clip Art, pick any image that tickles your fancy, then click Insert.

3. Select Insert ➤ Comment, type in some notes, press Esc twice.

4. Repeat the process in Step 3 again to add a second comment. Now you've got four shapes on this slide, representing three shape types: the title is a Placeholder type, the clip art image is an Embedded OLE Object type, and the comments are Comment type shapes.

5. Insert a new slide (Slide2) and add a comment to it, then return to Slide1.

6. If you wanted to manually select—either for review, highlighting, property modification, or subsequent deletion—all three Comment shapes on Slide1 and Slide2, well, you can't! You could manually select each of the two Comments on Slide1, press Del, switch to Slide2, select the Comment shape, and press Del again (go ahead and walk through these steps now). But imagine repeating this process across even a smallish 20-slide presentation. Tedious, to say the least. That's because PowerPoint doesn't allow selections to extend across slides. But ShapeGrabber gives you the ability to delete shapes across slides, as well as to narrow down the type of shapes you want to select or delete.

ShapeGrabber's dialog box displays a list of the names of the 18 different shape types supported by PowerPoint (19 if you count our "(All)" custom category):

- AutoShape
- Callout
- Chart
- Comment
- EmbeddedOLEObject
- FormControl
- Freeform
- Group
- Line
- LinkedOLEObject
- LinkedPicture
- Media
- OLEControlObject
- Picture
- Placeholder
- ShapeTypeMixed

- TextBox

- TextEffect

You can see the constants behind these shape types by using the Object Browser and searching for "msoshapetype," as shown in Figure 4-10.

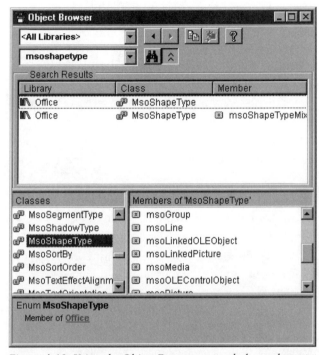

Figure 4-10: Using the Object Browser to track down shape type constants

Below the list in Figure 4-9 are three radio buttons that determine what action ShapeGrabber should take: one check box that instructs Shape-Grabber to warn you (or not) before each individual shape's deletion, and the ubiquitous OK and Cancel command buttons.

Step 1: Create Two New Presentations

Here are the steps to create two working presentations:

1. Create a presentation to host the VBA project, save it as *Shape-Grabber.ppt* in your *My Documents* folder.

2. Create a presentation to host test shapes, save it as *TestShape-Grabber.ppt* in your *My Documents* folder.

Step 2: Design the Dialog Box

Now you can follow along with us step by step as we construct the dialog box:

1. Activate *ShapeGrabber.ppt.*

2. Start the Visual Basic Editor (Tools ➤ Macro ➤ Visual Basic Editor).

3. Select `VBAProject` (`ShapeGrabber.ppt`) and rename it to `ShapeGrabber` (Tools ➤ VBAProject Properties, type **Shape-Grabber** in the Project Name edit box, click OK). It should then read `ShapeGrabber` (`ShapeGrabber.ppt`) in the Project window. As we have discussed, you should always give your projects unique names and not use the defaults.

4. Create a new dialog box (Insert ➤ UserForm). Refer back to Figure 4-9 for the general layout of the controls in this and the following steps.

5. Change the dialog box's Caption property; in the Properties Window, select the value UserForm1 for the Caption setting, type **Shape-Grabber**, then press Enter.

6. You may want to enlarge the dialog box at this point by dragging its lower-right corner down and to the right, as shown in Figure 4-11

NOTE   Adding any type of control to a VBA dialog box follows the same sequence of events: select the control from the Toolbox, drag and drop it on the dialog box, reposition and resize it if necessary, then set its other properties as needed. The Toolbox is only visible when the focus is on a UserForm (i.e., dialog box) object, as shown in Figure 4-11. If it's still not visible, select View ➤ Toolbox..

---

7. Add a Label with the caption "Shape Type:".

8. Below the Label, add a ListBox. This pair of controls displays the names of all the shape categories.

NOTE   When you look at a ListBox control in design mode, you won't see its vertical scroll bars. They do appear at run time, but only if there are more items in the list than can be displayed in the control's vertical space. This is by design.

---

9. Now you need to change some of ListBox1's properties in order to prepare it to be populated with a two-dimensional array. The reason

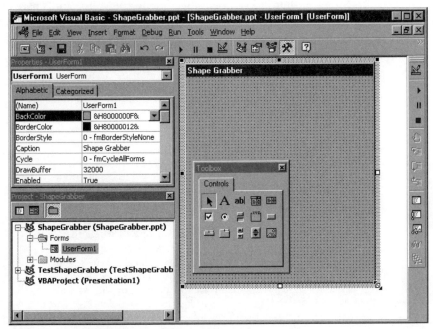

Figure 4-11: ShapeGrabber's dialog box in its birthday suit

for all this fiddling is to display some human-readable shape type information in the list box while making some numeric values (that are meaningless to the user but very important to your utility) available to the program code. It's like telling VBA, "Show stuff like 'AutoShape' and 'Callout' in the list box while hiding the values `msoAutoShape` and `msoCallout` behind them."

So, the array's first column contains human-readable values like "(All)," "AutoShape," "Callout," etc. The array's second column contains matching constant values for these values: `ALL_SHAPES` (a global constant you've created), `msoAutoShape`, `msoCallout`, etc. (These constants are all listed in the subroutine `sLoadShapeTypes` shown later in Example 4-15.) Set ListBox1's BoundColumn property to 2; this causes the list box's *.Value* property to return the contents of the second column. Set the TextColumn property to 1; this causes the list box's *.Text* property to return the contents of the first column. Change the ColumnWidths property to `-1;0` (that's a dash, a one, a semicolon, and a zero with no spaces, trust us), which the Properties Window echoes back as `;0 pt`. This setting causes the first column to be displayed normally while hiding the second column.

10. Add a Frame and change its caption to "Act on selected shape type."

11. Add three OptionButton controls, align them vertically, and change their Caption properties as follows: change OptionButton1's caption to "Select all such shapes on current slide"; change OptionButton2's caption to "Delete all such shapes on current slide"; and change OptionButton3's caption to "Delete all such shapes on all slides."

12. Add a CheckBox below the third OptionButton and change its Caption to "Warn before individual deletions."

NOTE   Good user interface design is not rocket science, but it does have rules and regulations. Studies show that these guidelines help people (your users) quickly understand and work with dialogs. Case in point: when you're providing a deletion feature, provide the user with a safety net. Here it's in the form of a preference setting that defaults to a conservative value to prevent a non-warning deletion (conservative is "on," which displays a message box with options to delete, not delete, or cancel altogether before a deletion). A user familiar with the utility can opt to turn this off and not get any warning prior to deletions. For more information about user interface design, see *The Windows Interface Guidelines for Software Design* (Microsoft Press, ISBN 1-55615-679-0).

---

13. Outside the frame, add two CommandButtons along the bottom of the dialog box. Change their Captions to "OK" and "Cancel" respectively.

14. Set CommandButton1's Default property to True. This indicates that the user pressing the Enter key is the equivalent of clicking the OK button.

15. Save your work (File ➤ Save, ShapeGrabber.ppt). As when creating any document or macro, you should always save your work whenever you type more than you'd care to retype. We'll not include specific steps for saving your work from here on out.

Step 3: Write the Code

Now it's time to write the code for control event procedures, as well as the code for starting the utility and handling various general-purpose operations. But first you need a separate module to store variables and constants that are available to the entire project—referred to as public or global variables and constants:

1. Create a new module: Insert ➤ Module, change the module's (Name) property to modGlobals, and press Enter.

2. Type the declarations as shown in Example 4-8.

Example 4-8: Public Variables and Constants Go in the modGlobals Module

```
Public objStartingSheet As Object
Public vntShapeTypes() As Variant
Public Const ALL_SHAPES = -999
Public Const MACRO_TITLE = "ShapeGrabber"
```

3. Switch back to the dialog box by double-clicking on the UserForm1 icon in the Project Window.

The next trick is picking your own preferred shortcut for moving between the Code Window for the code behind the dialog box (meaning, control event procedures) and the UserForm Window itself. If you're where you left off at the last step, you're in the UserForm Window looking at UserForm1. To activate the Code Window for this dialog box, you can do any of the following:

- Select View ➤ Code

- Press F7

- Click the View Code button in the Project Window as shown in Figure 4-12

- Double-click anywhere on the dialog box itself (although this has the possibly undesirable effect of creating a default event procedure for whatever control you double-clicked, e.g., CommandButton1_ Click in the case of CommandButton1)

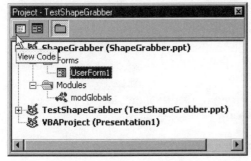

Figure 4-12: Use the Project Window's mini-toolbar buttons to quickly move between code and object

Switching back is easy: View ➤ Object; Shift+F7; or click the View Object button in the Project Window.

There are three control event procedures in ShapeGrabber:

- UserForm_Initialize

- CommandButton1_Click

- CommandButton2_Click

Let's add the code for these control event procedures now:

1. To create `UserForm_Initialize`, the procedure that runs after a form is loaded but before it's shown (you'll trigger it with a `UserForm1.Show` expression in a moment), double-click on UserForm1 in the Forms folder, View ➤ Code, then choose UserForm from the Object list on the left and Initialize from the Procedure list on the right. Type the code shown in Example 4-9. This procedure calls the subroutine **sLoadShapeTypes**, which in turn creates the array used to load the shape categories and then assigns that array to the list box. Next it makes sure the Warn… box is checked.

Example 4-9: ShapeGrabber's UserForm_Initialize() Procedure

```
Private Sub UserForm_Initialize()
' set up the list box
sLoadShapeTypes
' set first option button as default
OptionButton1.Value = True
' set to conservative Warning state
CheckBox1.Value = True
End Sub
```

2. Next add the `CommandButton1_Click` procedure that's triggered whenever the user clicks on the OK button. The quickest way to add this procedure is to double-click on the CommandButton1 control in the UserForm Window. Type the code shown in Example 4-10. This procedure follows different logic paths depending on which of the three mutually exclusive option buttons is selected when the user clicks OK: if OptionButton1, then call the **sSelectShapes** subroutine; if OptionButton2, then call **fintDeleteShapes**; if OptionButton3, then loop through all the slides in the presentation, calling **fintDeleteShapes** for each slide therein.

Example 4-10: ShapeGrabber's CommandButton1_Click() Procedure

```
Private Sub CommandButton1_Click()
Dim intRC As Integer
Dim sld As Slide
If OptionButton1 Then
    sSelectShapes ListBox1.Value
ElseIf OptionButton2 Then
    intRC = fintDeleteShapes(objStartingSheet, ListBox1.Value)
ElseIf OptionButton3 Then
    For Each sld In ActivePresentation.Slides
```

Example 4-10: ShapeGrabber's CommandButton1_Click() Procedure (continued)

```
        intRC = fintDeleteShapes(sld, ListBox1.Value)
        If intRC = vbCancel Then
            Exit Sub
        End If
    Next sld
End If
End Sub
```

3. Add the `CommandButton2_Click` procedure for responding to a click on the Cancel button. This one-liner simply unloads the dialog box. Type the code shown in Example 4-11.

Example 4-11: ShapeGrabber's CommandButton2_Click() Procedure

```
Private Sub CommandButton2_Click()
Unload UserForm1
End Sub
```

There are nine other functions and subroutines in ShapeGrabber:

- Auto_Close (this procedure is covered in the following section)
- Auto_Open (this procedure is covered in the following section)
- fintDeleteOneShape
- fintDeleteShapes
- flngShapeCount
- sLoadShapeTypes
- sMsgNoShapes
- sSelectShapes
- StartShapeGrabber

Let's build these procedures, except for the two Auto procedures that we cover in the following section:

1. To create a new procedure, you need a new module, so select Insert ➤ Module. This creates Module1 and puts you in its Code Window.

2. Now select Insert ➤ Procedure, type **fintDeleteOneShape**, select the Function option button, leave the Public scope option button selected, click OK. Type the code shown in Example 4-12. This function deletes the shape that's passed to it as the argument *shpTarget*. If the argument *blnWarning* is True, it warns the user first with a message that can cancel the operation. Another of the function's chores is to include the shape's text (if any) in the message box to help identify the shape for the user.

NOTE   The naming convention we use here is to identify function
               procedures with a lowercase "f" and prefix and subroutine
               procedures with a lowercase "s." The next three letters—
               for functions only—indicate its return type (e.g., "int" for
               Integer or "str" for String). That's followed by the rest of its
               name. So "f" + "int" + "DeleteOneShape" = "fintDeleteOne-
               Shape."

Example 4-12: ShapeGrabber's fintDeleteOneShape Function

```
' -----------------------------------------------------------------
' Purpose:   Delete a single Shape object; query user first if a
'            flag is true.
'
' Inputs:    blnWarning - Boolean to indicate if user wants to be
'                         warned before each deletion
'            shpTarget  - an object variable (the target shape)
'
' Returns:   Integer; vbYes, vbNo, or vbCancel (in this case the
'            caller is expected to do an Exit Sub or whatever is
'            needed)
'
' Updated:   06/25/97 (PCG)
'            07/17/97 (PCG)
' -----------------------------------------------------------------
Public Function fintDeleteOneShape(blnWarning As Boolean, _
                shpTarget As Shape) As Integer
' ----- Declarations/initializations
Dim intAnswer As Integer
Dim strPrompt As String
Dim strShapeText As String
' ----- Main body
If blnWarning Then
    ' ask before deleting
    strShapeText = "<<empty>>"
    ' note use of .HasTextFrame etc. which is unique to PowerPoint!
    If shpTarget.HasTextFrame Then
        If shpTarget.TextFrame.HasText Then
            strShapeText = shpTarget.TextFrame.TextRange.Text
        End If
    End If
    strPrompt = "Are you sure you want to delete shape " & _
        shpTarget.Name & _
        " (text '" & strShapeText & "')" & _
        " on slide " & shpTarget.Parent.Name & "?"
    intAnswer = MsgBox(Prompt:=strPrompt, _
        Buttons:=vbYesNoCancel + vbQuestion + vbDefaultButton2, _
        Title:=MACRO_TITLE)
    If intAnswer = vbYes Then
        shpTarget.Delete
    ElseIf intAnswer = vbNo Then
        ' do nothing
```

Example 4-12: ShapeGrabber's fintDeleteOneShape Function (continued)

```
    ElseIf intAnswer = vbCancel Then
        ' the caller will do an Exit Sub
    End If
    fintDeleteOneShape = intAnswer
Else
    ' don't ask, just delete
    shpTarget.Delete
    fintDeleteOneShape = vbYes
End If
End Function
```

3. Insert a new function procedure named `fintDeleteShapes` and type the code shown in Example 4-13. This function handles the process of deleting more than one shape, based on a particular shape type. The argument *objSourceDoc* allows the function to act on any slide, whether it's the current slide or not. The argument *lngShape-Type* indicates what shape types to look for and delete. For example, all Comment shapes have the constant value `msoComment`. (These constants are all listed in the subroutine `sLoadShapeTypes` shown in Example 4-15.)

Example 4-13: ShapeGrabber's fintDeleteShapes Function

```
' ----------------------------------------------------------------
' Purpose:   Wrapper to delete shapes of a specific shape type,
'            which might be our own designation of "all" (-999).
'
' Inputs:    objSourceDoc - an object variable (the target slide)
'            lngShapeType - the shape type
'
' Returns:   Integer; vbNo or vbCancel (in this case the caller is
'            expected to do an Exit Sub or whatever is needed)
'
' Updated:   06/25/97 (PCG)
'            07/17/97 (PCG)
' ----------------------------------------------------------------
Public Function fintDeleteShapes(objSourceDoc As Object, _
                lngShapeType As Long) As Integer
' ----- Declarations/initializations
Dim intRC As Integer
Dim lngCount As Long
Dim lngRC As Long
Dim lngMax As Long
Dim shp As Shape
' ----- Main body
fintDeleteShapes = vbNo
lngMax = objSourceDoc.Shapes.Count
If lngShapeType = ALL_SHAPES Then
    ' ------------------------------------------------------------
    ' Note: the following code works but only en masse so you can't
    '   warn user prior to each individual object's deletion:
```

Example 4-13: ShapeGrabber's fintDeleteShapes Function (continued)

```
' With ActiveWindow.View.Slide
'      .Shapes.SelectAll
' End With
' ActiveWindow.Selection.ShapeRange.Delete
' --------------------------------------------------------------
If lngMax = 0 Then
    sMsgNoShapes objSourceDoc, UserForm1.ListBox1.Text
    Exit Function
End If
' --------------------------------------------------------------
' Note: don't delete from within a collection via For Each,
'    instead use an explicit stepping technique otherwise
'    internal collection indexing goes awry and you won't delete
'    all the desired objects.
' --------------------------------------------------------------
For lngCount = lngMax To 1 Step -1
    Set shp = objSourceDoc.Shapes(lngCount)
    intRC = fintDeleteOneShape(UserForm1.CheckBox1, shp)
    If intRC = vbCancel Then
        fintDeleteShapes = intRC
        Exit Function
    End If
Next lngCount
Else
    lngRC = flngShapeCount(objSourceDoc, lngShapeType)
    If lngRC = 0 Then
        sMsgNoShapes objSourceDoc, UserForm1.ListBox1.Text
        Exit Function
    End If
    For lngCount = lngMax To 1 Step -1
        If objSourceDoc.Shapes(lngCount).Type = lngShapeType Then
            Set shp = objSourceDoc.Shapes(lngCount)
            intRC = fintDeleteOneShape(UserForm1.CheckBox1, shp)
            If intRC = vbCancel Then
                fintDeleteShapes = intRC
                Exit Function
            End If
        End If
    Next lngCount
End If
End Function
```

4. Insert a new function procedure named `flngShapeCount` and type the code shown in Example 4-14. This function uses the `For Each...Next` construct to walk through the Shapes collection of the specified slide, and count how many match the specified shape type.

Example 4-14: ShapeGrabber's flngShapeCount Function

```
' -----------------------------------------------------------------
' Purpose:   Given a host (slide), return a count of the number of
'            shape objects of a particular type.
'
' Inputs:    objSourceDoc - an object variable (the target slide)
'            lngShapeType - the shape type
'
' Returns:   Long
'
' Updated:   06/25/97 (PCG)
' -----------------------------------------------------------------
Public Function flngShapeCount(objSourceDoc As Object, _
                  lngShapeType As Long) As Long
Dim lngCount As Long
Dim shp As Shape
lngCount = 0
For Each shp In objSourceDoc.Shapes
    If shp.Type = lngShapeType Then
        lngCount = lngCount + 1
    End If
Next shp
flngShapeCount = lngCount
End Function
```

5. Insert a new subroutine procedure named **sLoadShapeTypes**, and type the code shown in Example 4-15. This subroutine loads the two-dimensional array that stores human-readable shape type descriptions in its first column and the associated built-in constants in its second column, then assigns the array to the dialog's list box.

Example 4-15: ShapeGrabber's sLoadShapeTypes Subroutine

```
' -----------------------------------------------------------------
' Purpose:   Load a two-dimensional array of values into the listbox
'            control. First column contains human-readable shape
'            categories, second column contains corresponding Office
'            object model constants.
'
' Inputs:    None
'
' Updated:   06/25/97 (PCG)
' -----------------------------------------------------------------
Public Sub sLoadShapeTypes()
ReDim vntShapeTypes(18, 1)
' ----- init first column (0-based col 0)
vntShapeTypes(0, 0) = "(All)"
vntShapeTypes(1, 0) = "AutoShape"
vntShapeTypes(2, 0) = "Callout"
vntShapeTypes(3, 0) = "Chart"
vntShapeTypes(4, 0) = "Comment"
vntShapeTypes(5, 0) = "EmbeddedOLEObject"
vntShapeTypes(6, 0) = "FormControl"
```

Example 4-15: ShapeGrabber's sLoadShapeTypes Subroutine (continued)

```
vntShapeTypes(7, 0) = "Freeform"
vntShapeTypes(8, 0) = "Group"
vntShapeTypes(9, 0) = "Line"
vntShapeTypes(10, 0) = "LinkedOLEObject"
vntShapeTypes(11, 0) = "LinkedPicture"
vntShapeTypes(12, 0) = "Media"
vntShapeTypes(13, 0) = "OLEControlObject"
vntShapeTypes(14, 0) = "Picture"
vntShapeTypes(15, 0) = "Placeholder"
vntShapeTypes(16, 0) = "ShapeTypeMixed"
vntShapeTypes(17, 0) = "TextBox"
vntShapeTypes(18, 0) = "TextEffect"
' ----- init second column (0-based col 1)
' ------------------------------------------------------------------
' Note: this control's BoundColumn property = 2 (2nd col) so that
'    these values are returned when user clicks the control
'    (.Value); TextColumn property = 1 (1st col) so the
'    human-readable values are returned by the Text
'    property; and to render normal display of 1st col and
'    to hide 2nd col, type "-1;0" into ColumnWidths property
'    in Property Window (echoes back ";0 pt")
' ------------------------------------------------------------------
vntShapeTypes(0, 1) = ALL_SHAPES
vntShapeTypes(1, 1) = msoAutoShape
vntShapeTypes(2, 1) = msoCallout
vntShapeTypes(3, 1) = msoChart
vntShapeTypes(4, 1) = msoComment
vntShapeTypes(5, 1) = msoEmbeddedOLEObject
vntShapeTypes(6, 1) = msoFormControl
vntShapeTypes(7, 1) = msoFreeform
vntShapeTypes(8, 1) = msoGroup
vntShapeTypes(9, 1) = msoLine
vntShapeTypes(10, 1) = msoLinkedOLEObject
vntShapeTypes(11, 1) = msoLinkedPicture
vntShapeTypes(12, 1) = msoMedia
vntShapeTypes(13, 1) = msoOLEControlObject
vntShapeTypes(14, 1) = msoPicture
vntShapeTypes(15, 1) = msoPlaceholder
vntShapeTypes(16, 1) = msoShapeTypeMixed
vntShapeTypes(17, 1) = msoTextBox
vntShapeTypes(18, 1) = msoTextEffect
' load 'em into the control
With UserForm1
    .ListBox1.List = vntShapeTypes
    .ListBox1.ListIndex = 0
End With
End Sub
```

6. Insert a new subroutine procedure named **sMsgNoShapes** and type the code shown in Example 4-16. This subroutine displays some common message text that is called in several places in the program.

Example 4-16: ShapeGrabber's sMsgNoShapes Subroutine

```
' ------------------------------------------------------------------
' Purpose:   Displays a common-text message box that there are no
'            shapes of a particular category on slide x.
'
' Inputs:    objSourceDoc      - an object variable (the target
'            slide)
'            strShapeCategory - human-readable shape category
'                               description text
'
' Updated:   06/25/97 (PCG)
'            07/17/97 (PCG)
' ------------------------------------------------------------------
Public Sub sMsgNoShapes(objSourceDoc As Object, _
        strShapeCategory As String)
Dim strPrompt As String
If strShapeCategory = vntShapeTypes(0, 0) Then
    strPrompt = "There are no shapes at all on slide " & _
        objSourceDoc.Name & "."
Else
    strPrompt = "There are no " & strShapeCategory & _
        " shapes on slide " & objSourceDoc.Name & "."
End If
MsgBox Prompt:=strPrompt, Buttons:=vbOKOnly + vbInformation, _
    Title:=MACRO_TITLE
End Sub
```

7. Insert a new subroutine procedure named **sSelectShapes**, and
   type the code shown in Example 4-17. This subroutine first makes
   sure that it doesn't try to act on a slide with no shapes of any kind
   (or no shapes of the designated type). Next it proceeds to use the
   handy *SelectAll* method if the user wants to select all shapes; otherwise, it walks through all shapes and compares them one by one
   against the desired type, selecting the shape if there's a match

Example 4-17: ShapeGrabber's sSelectShapes Subroutine

```
' ------------------------------------------------------------------
' Purpose:   Select shapes of a specific shape type, which might be
'            our own designation of "all" (-999).
'
' Inputs:    lngShapeType - the shape type
'
' Updated:   06/25/97 (PCG)
'            07/21/97 (PCG)
' ------------------------------------------------------------------
Public Sub sSelectShapes(lngShapeType As Long)
' Note: PowerPoint doesn't allow shape object selection to extend
'   beyond a single slide.
' ----- Declarations/initializations
Dim lngCount As Long
Dim lngRC As Long
Dim shp As Shape
```

Example 4-17: ShapeGrabber's sSelectShapes Subroutine (continued)

```
' ----- Main body
' force use of objStartingSheet because our UI points to
'   the current slide only (not other slides in Slides collection)
If objStartingSheet.Shapes.Count = 0 Then
    ' always exit if total count is zero
    sMsgNoShapes objStartingSheet, UserForm1.ListBox1.Text
    Exit Sub
ElseIf lngShapeType <> ALL_SHAPES Then
    lngRC = flngShapeCount(objStartingSheet, lngShapeType)
    If lngRC = 0 Then
        sMsgNoShapes objStartingSheet, UserForm1.ListBox1.Text
        Exit Sub
    End If
End If
If lngShapeType = ALL_SHAPES Then
    objStartingSheet.Shapes.SelectAll
Else
    lngCount = 0
    For Each shp In objStartingSheet.Shapes
        If shp.Type = lngShapeType Then
            If lngCount = 0 Then
                ' start a totally fresh selection
                shp.Select Replace:=msoTrue
            Else
                ' extend the extant selection
                shp.Select Replace:=msoFalse
            End If
            lngCount = lngCount + 1
        End If
    Next shp
End If
End Sub
```

8. Insert a new subroutine procedure named `StartShapeGrabber`, and type the code shown in Example 4-18. This subroutine fires when the user clicks the custom toolbar button. It makes sure the user is in Slide View, then displays the dialog with the `UserForm1.Show` expression.

Example 4-18: ShapeGrabber's StartShapeGrabber Subroutine

```
' ----------------------------------------------------------------
' Purpose:  Parameterless subroutine for connection to UI to start
'           this utility.
'
' Inputs:   None
'
' Updated:  06/25/97 (PCG)
' ----------------------------------------------------------------
' Copyright © 1997 PRIME Consulting Group, Inc.
' ----------------------------------------------------------------
```

Example 4-18: ShapeGrabber's StartShapeGrabber Subroutine (continued)

```
Public Sub StartShapeGrabber()
Dim intAnswer As Integer
If ActiveWindow.ViewType <> ppViewSlide Then
    intAnswer = _
        MsgBox(Prompt:=MACRO_TITLE &_
        " runs in Slide View. Switch?", _
        Buttons:=vbYesNo + vbQuestion, _
        Title:=MACRO_TITLE)
    If intAnswer <> vbYes Then
        Exit Sub
    Else
        ActiveWindow.ViewType = ppViewSlide
    End If
End If
Set objStartingSheet = ActiveWindow.View.Slide
UserForm1.Show
End Sub
```

Step 4: Add a Custom Toolbar and Button

To make ShapeGrabber available to act on other presentations, and to prevent it from displaying its own "host" presentation (one blank slide), you're going to turn it into a PowerPoint add-in. Through a quirk of PowerPoint's application event model, PowerPoint presentations themselves (*.PPT* files) don't support the special `Auto_Open` and `Auto_Close` macros, but add-ins (*.PPA* files) do.

`Auto_Open` fires whenever (1) the user manually loads the add-in, or (2) PowerPoint starts and the add-in is in the loaded add-ins list (more on how the add-in load/unload interface works in a moment). `Auto_Close` fires whenever (1) the user manually unloads or removes the add-in, or (2) PowerPoint shuts down and the add-in is in the loaded add-ins list. So all you need is code in `Auto_Open` to create a custom toolbar and one button to trigger ShapeGrabber's `StartShapeGrabber` macro, plus cleanup code in `Auto_Close` to quietly delete this custom toolbar.

First, let's create these two Auto macros.

1. Insert a new Public subroutine procedure named `Auto_Open`, and type the code shown in Example 4-19.

Example 4-19: ShapeGrabber's Auto_Open Procedure

```
' --------------------------------------------------------------
' Purpose:   Auto_Open runs only when the add-in is loaded (this
'            includes when PowerPoint starts, or the user manually
'            loads it); it does _not_ run when the PPT opens.
'
' Inputs:    None
```

Example 4-19: ShapeGrabber's Auto_Open Procedure (continued)

```
'
' Updated:  07/17/97 (PCG)
' ----------------------------------------------------------------
Public Sub Auto_Open()
Dim cbb As CommandBarButton
On Error Resume Next
' just in case our toolbar already exists at load time, delete it
'    (ignoring errors) and then re-add it
CommandBars("ShapeGrabber").Delete
On Error GoTo 0
CommandBars.Add(Name:=MACRO_TITLE).Visible = True
Set cbb = _
    CommandBars(MACRO_TITLE).Controls.Add(Type:=msoControlButton, _
    Before:=1)
With cbb
    .Caption = "Start ShapeGrabber"
    .FaceId = 675
    .OnAction = "StartShapeGrabber"
    .Style = msoButtonIconAndCaption
End With
End Sub
```

NOTE   It's imperative that these Auto macros be declared as Pub-
                lic or they won't fire.

---

2. Insert a new Public subroutine procedure named `Auto_Close`, and
   type the code shown in Example 4-20.

Example 4-20: ShapeGrabber's Auto_Close Procedure

```
' ----------------------------------------------------------------
' Purpose:  Auto_Close runs only when the add-in is unloaded or
'           removed (this includes when PowerPoint shuts down, or
'           the user manually unloads/removes it); it
'           does _not_ run when the PPT closes.
'
' Inputs:   None
'
' Updated:  07/17/97 (PCG)
' ----------------------------------------------------------------
Public Sub Auto_Close()
On Error Resume Next
' delete our toolbar (ignoring errors)
CommandBars(MACRO_TITLE).Delete
End Sub
```

NOTE   If you're using the *.PPT* from *http://www.oreilly.com* you
can skip this note.

If you've been typing in the code manually, you might
want to check for errors before saving the presentation
and the add-in. In the VB Editor from any Code Window,
select Debug ➤ Compile ShapeGrabber. Fix any errors, or,
if there are none, proceed with the next step. You might
also want to test the *.PPT* version before compiling as an
add-in, then return to this step.

3. Save the presentation (*ShapeGrabber.ppt*).

4. To create the add-in, activate PowerPoint, select File ➤ Save As,
change to the folder *C:\Program Files\Microsoft Office\Office*, select
PowerPoint Add-In (**.ppa*) in the "Save as type" drop-down list, then
click Save. This creates a file called *ShapeGrabber.ppa*. You can save
the add-in to any folder you like, but Office is the traditional repository for PowerPoint add-ins (several ship-with *.PPA* files are in this
Office folder). (See Figure 4-13.)

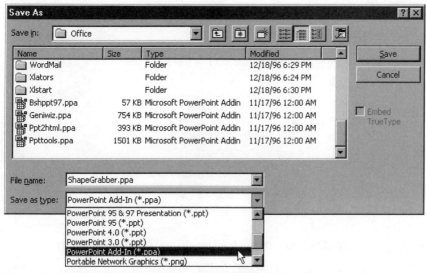

Figure 4-13: Saving a presentation as a PowerPoint Add-In file

5. To load the add-in, select Tools ➤ Add-Ins, then—after what may
seem like an interminable wait with lots of hard disk whirring and
grinding—when the Add-Ins dialog box appears (as shown in Figure
4-14), click Add New and browse until you find *ShapeGrabber.ppa*.
When you find it, click OK; when warned about macros, click Enable
Macros, click Close (if the ShapeGrabber toolbar appears somewhere

on top of the Add-Ins dialog box, that's okay, just drag it out of the way). Figure 4-15 shows PowerPoint's Add-Ins dialog box after loading ShapeGrabber.

6. Close *ShapeGrabber.ppt.*

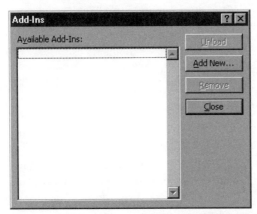

Figure 4-14: PowerPoint's Add-Ins dialog box before loading ShapeGrabber

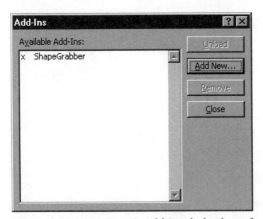

Figure 4-15: PowerPoint's Add-Ins dialog box after loading ShapeGrabber

Step 5: Add Test Shapes to the Test Presentation and Take ShapeGrabber for a Spin

Now that you've finished developing ShapeGrabber, and have set it up as an add-in, you need a presentation on which to test it. That's what the file *TestShapeGrabber.ppt* you created earlier is for. Here's how to test it:

1. Open *TestShapeGrabber.ppt.*

2. Add a variety of shapes to Slide1, add a new slide, and add some shapes there too. You may instead want to download our prepared version of *TestShapeGrabber.ppt* (see Figure 4-16).

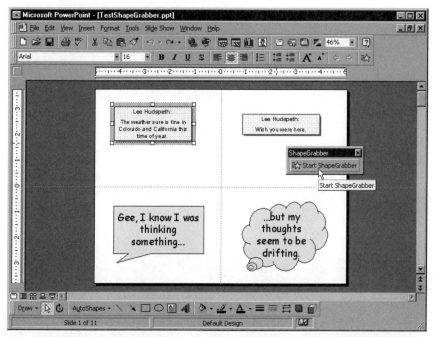

Figure 4-16: This version of TestShapeGrabber.ppt is chock full of different shape types, grab it from our Web site

3. Save *TestShapeGrabber.ppt* so you can always close-no-save it after experimenting on it, thereby keeping it full of shapes for future testing.

4. Now run ShapeGrabber through its paces.

As we mentioned earlier, if you want to work with ShapeGrabber in the Visual Basic Editor's debug mode either to learn how the code works or to correct any typographical errors, keep the non-add-in version (*Shape-Grabber.ppt*) open and do your tests on it. It's also advisable, although not absolutely necessary, to do this testing with the add-in not loaded. If you make any changes to the *.PPT*, then remember to save the *.PPT*, save it again *as an add-in*, and repeat the add-in loading process described earlier. Enjoy!

NOTE   There's a free bonus macro in the downloadable *ShapeGrab-ber.ppt* project called ShowShapeType. Select one shape on a slide, then run this macro to see a message box reveal the shape's type in human-readable form. This is handy in case you thought something you inserted via Insert ➤ Picture ➤ Clip Art was actually a Picture shape type instead of its true identity—an EmbeddedOLEObject shape type.

5

In this chapter:
- *Access*
- *Excel*
- *Outlook, New Kid on the PIM Block*
- *PowerPoint*
- *Word*

Hard-Core Office

Microsoft Office 97 is comprised of five main pieces: Access, Excel, Outlook, PowerPoint, and Word. In this chapter we'll take a look at the best and the most annoying features of each application. The goal is to point you towards any hidden gems you might not be aware of and to help you avoid some of the bogs and pitfalls that are lurking here and there. With workarounds and fixes wherever possible, natch!

Access

Office 95 was the big upgrade for Access, Microsoft's flagship database product. Access got the real VBA language, became a full OLE server (previously it was only an OLE client), and picked up a number of miscellaneous improvements and fixes. However, along with all the new goodies came an annoying decrease in stability, and absolutely no improvement in performance for most real-life database operations. A number of corporations have stuck with Access 2 (the last 16-bit version) solely because of its superior performance. Sure, the Marketing Suits can always find an esoteric scenario or two for their presentations, in which performance shows tremendous improvement, but in the real world, developers (and their clients) found Access 95 to be no faster than Access 2.0—and it was considerably less reliable. Many database developers chose not to do significant development in Access 95 for these reasons, and hoped that Microsoft would soon rectify the situation.

Well, the wait is over! Access 97 is significantly faster than Access 2.0/ Access 95, and much more reliable to boot. Microsoft has added new

Internet capabilities, and there are a number of enhancements to the interface. Yep, there is a lot to like in Access 97.

There are a few annoyances lurking about as well. Consider that you still cannot record a macro in Access 97. You can create a macro from scratch. But record one like you can in Word, Excel, or PowerPoint? Nope, you just can't do it. And while the MRU lists in Word, Excel, and PowerPoint can be set to show from zero up to the last nine files you worked on (Tools ➤ Options ➤ General), in Access you get four. It's static, with no way to change it.

No multiple undo in Access 97 either. Excel finally got multiple undo with Office 97, Word has had it for a while now, PowerPoint has it, but Access (as well as Outlook) missed out. You have only a single undo level, which on the surface may not seem like much of an annoyance, but often problems with database records become noticeable only at some point after you change them. With multiple levels of undo, assuming that there are enough levels, you can just roll back your data as soon as you notice the error(s). With a single level of undo, you can't. Then you have the problem that you'll very quickly get used to having and relying on the multiple undo ability in the other Office applications. "Relying on" being the key phrase here. Be careful that when you switch to Access you're consciously aware that you can't get carried away, counting on being able to unwind a series of actions with undo. Beware.

In the next few sections we'll look at some of the bane as well as the boon in Access 97.

Accessing Word

It's annoying when Office applications don't work the way you think they should. Consider how easy it is to insert some Excel data into a Word document. Copy a range in Excel, switch to Word, and you can Paste Special the Excel table as either a linked or embedded object. Piece of cake.

Not so easy with Access. Try this with an Access table (using Paste Special or by dragging the table* onto a Word document) and you wind up with a plain Word table filled with text. To get a true link between

---

* By dragging the table's icon from the Tables tab of the Database window and dropping it onto a Word document.

data in Access displayed in Word, you have to start jumping through hoops:

1. In Word, display the Database toolbar. View ➤ Toolbars ➤ Database.

2. Click on the Insert Database button (fourth from the right).

3. Click on the Get Data command button. (See Figure 5-1.)

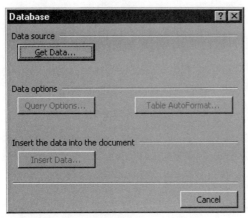

Figure 5-1: The Database box

4. A standard File Open dialog box appears. Select the MS Access Data-bases in the "Files of type" list box. Select the Access database that contains the information you want and click on Open.

5. In a few seconds you'll be able to choose the specific table or query you want. (See Figure 5-2.)

Figure 5-2: Choose the table or query you want to link to from your Word document

6. Next, click on the Insert Data command button (see Figure 5-1). On the Insert Data screen, check the "Insert data as field" box to create an updateable link to the Access table. (See Figure 5-3.)

Figure 5-3: Check the "Insert data as field" box to create a link to the Access data

While Word is churning away getting the data, take a look at the status bar. You will see that Word is using DDE (Dynamic Data Exchange) to get the data from Access. Wait a minute, wasn't DDE supposed to have died several years ago, being replaced successively by OLE, OLE Automation, Automation, and now ActiveX, its latest incarnation as the hot buzzword? Apparently there is a group at Microsoft that is still using DDE. While DDE is slow and cranky, if you must have a link to an Access table in a Word document, this is the only option available at present.

The database field in the document is quite complex in field code view:

```
{ DATABASE \d "D:\\My Documents\\Address Book\\Address Book.mdb"
\c "TABLE zstlkpObjectType" \s SELECT * FROM [zstlkpObjectType]"
\h }
```

Toggling the field code display in Word (Alt+F9) reveals the table itself (see Table 5-1); it's not as nicely formatted as the dragged table you'd get if you did a non-linked drag-and-drop, but you can modify the column widths and styles in Word. Note that the fonts have been lost, as well as column alignment and table borders.

Table 5-1: How the Linked Access Data Appears in Word

ObjectType	ObjectDesc
1	Table
5	Query
6	Attached Table
-32768	Form
-32761	Module
-32764	Report
-32766	Macro
-327860	Table Format
4	ODBC table

Pretty gruesome, no? You can reformat the table of course. Make it a thing of wonder and beauty to behold. Trouble is, when you update the link you'll lose all the formatting unless you do a little surgery on the default link field that was created. You'll have to manually add the * MERGEFORMAT switch yourself to preserve local formatting. The revised field would look like this:

```
{ DATABASE \d "D:\\My Documents\\Address Book\\Address Book.mdb"
\c "TABLE zstlkpObjectType" \s SELECT * FROM [zstlkpObjectType]"
\h \* MERGEFORMAT }
```

Annoying, but at least you can manually work around it.

Another method that uses DDE to achieve pretty much the same result involves copying a table in Access, switching to Word, and selecting Paste Special from the Edit menu. You'll see the dialog box shown in Figure 5-4.

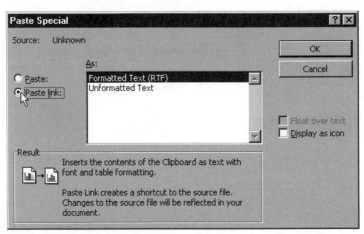

Figure 5-4: Pasting linked data

Check the "Paste link" option button and choose between formatted and unformatted text. If you change the data in Access, it is automatically updated in Word. The "link" is actually a field code in Word that looks like this (the \r denotes that the Formatted Text (RTF) option was selected):

```
{ DDEAUTO MSAccess "D:\\My Documents\\Address Book\\Address
Book.mdb;Table Addresses" All \r }
```

Unfortunately, Paste Link is fraught with annoyances. Large tables consisting of several hundred records may come across garbled and unreadable. Even smaller tables may appear fine but suddenly start "increasing in size" while Access constantly sends data to Word. In Access, the status bar will show that it's copying data, seem to complete this task, and then cycle through the data again. The mouse will alternate between an hourglass and a normal pointer while this seemingly endless loop runs over and over.

This tendency of Access to behave in a non-standard manner is not limited to its interaction with Word within the Office family. You can't drag Access forms as OLE objects to other Office applications either—say to embed an Access form on an Outlook form as a sub-form. In fact, the interface between Access and Outlook is almost nonexistent. Ideally, we should be able to use Access tables as the data source for Outlook contact items—via a live link, of course. But all that is currently available is a set of limited built-in Outlook Import and Export utilities—which don't handle custom fields—and the very problematic Exchange/Outlook Wizard, which we'll discuss in a bit.

The Access Database Wizard

When you first fire up Access, you can choose to create a blank database (one where you are going to build everything yourself), open an existing database (equivalent to File ➤ Open Databases), or you can run the Database Wizard. The Database Wizard in Access makes creating a ready-to-run database a snap. It is really an impressive piece of software engineering. Novices, experts, and everyone in between will like this feature.

You can also kick off the Database Wizard when you click on File ➤ New Database. Choose the Databases tab in the New dialog and choose one of the many database templates that ship with Access. (See Figure 5-5.) The Database Wizard kicks in after you select a template and assign a name to the file using the File New Database dialog.

NOTE   For some reason known only to Microsoft, some of the template names are in all caps, while most are in mixed case.

The list of templates is pretty complete. Which is good, because you can't open, modify, or easily create your own Database Wizard templates. In this respect Access operates in a different universe from Word, Power-Point, and Excel. Part of this is due to the nature of databases, but most is due to how the Wizard works and the amount of code behind it. In any event, using the Database Wizard lets you quickly generate a database containing tables, entry forms, and a ready to use interface. The Wizard displays the tables that it will create (based on the template you started

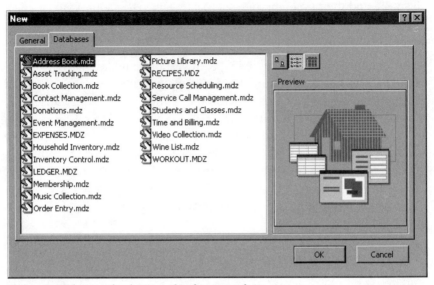

Figure 5-5: The standard Access database templates

with) and lets you choose from a number of fields that can be used for a particular table. You check and uncheck the appropriate boxes to control what fields are used. You can also have the Wizard populate the table with sample data (by checking the "Yes, include sample data" check box). This lets you work with the database immediately; you can experiment to see if it meets your needs before populating it with your own data. (See Figure 5-6.)

The next few panels of the Wizard let you pick display styles for the various screens, much like the AutoFormat features in the other Office applications. This is another nifty way to create a very presentable database in a hurry. The style elements are used throughout the various on-screen forms. You can also choose a style for any printed reports that are a part of the database. Next, you can choose a database report format (styles and colors) that controls things like headings and layout.

Lastly, you can specify a title for your database that is automatically inserted on the database's main Switchboard screen. If you want a particular picture, like a logo, to appear on all your reports, you can specify that as well. (See Figure 5-7.)

When you're done, Access creates all the components of the database. When you open the database, the main Switchboard form greets you. As you can see, the Switchboard serves as a user interface for working with your newly generated database. (See Figure 5-8.)

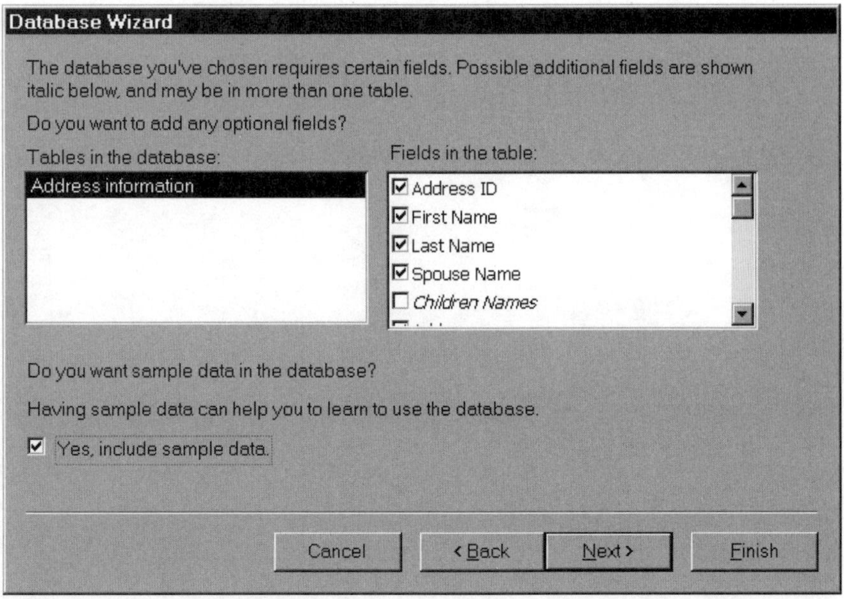

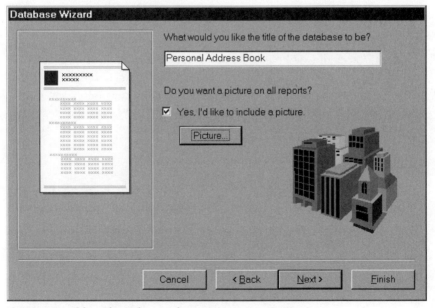

Figure 5-6: Selecting database fields

Figure 5-7: Add a title and a graphic to jazz up your reports

As you can see, the Switchboard is already set up with command buttons for the main functions of the application. If your needs are basic, you can

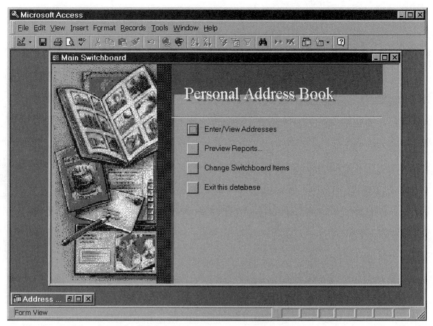

Figure 5-8: The Switchboard form—instant user interface

probably use your database as is; or you can start customizing it and go on from there.

Although you could quibble at some of the design features of a database created via the Wizard (spaces are used in field names, database objects are not named according to any accepted naming convention, etc.), most would find these considerations quite immaterial. Instant database in just a few clicks! Very nice.

Query Wizards

Access has always had an easy-to-use query interface, letting users make joins* by dragging a field from one table to another, and creating SQL statements in the graphical query grid. And this method is still the most flexible and the fastest once you're familiar with the way queries work.†

---

* A *join* associates a field in one table with a field of the same (or compatible) data type in another table. This determines how your data is related. A record with CustomerID 996 could be related to all purchase order records where the CustomerID is 996.

† For more on queries and those that are not supported by Access' drag-and-drop query interface see *Access Database Design & Programming* by Steven Roman (O'Reilly & Associates, ISBN 1-56592-297-2).

But those of us who don't think of SQL as their first language can use any of several Query Wizards that make it a snap to find things like unmatched or duplicate records in a table. There's a Wizard that will walk you through cross-tabulations and one that will help you create simple queries to extract subsets of data from tables. Click the Query tab and click on New. The New Query dialog box appears, and you select the Wizard you want. (See Figure 5-9.)

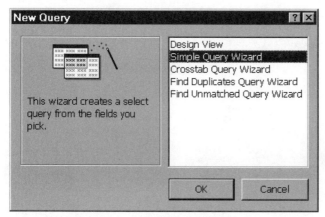

Figure 5-9: Selecting your query methodology

From there you just make selections, and the query is created for you. In Figure 5-10, you see the Simple Query Wizard that allows you to select the table to query and the fields you want to use. The Wizards in Access are very well-bred and polished.

For the experienced database user, the process of working through the screens in a Wizard can take longer than doing things manually. But that is one of the most outstanding aspects of Access: there is plenty of power available to the database guru, and this power is carefully made accessible to the casual user.

Hyperlinks in Access

Since we're talking about Office 97, you know it's only a matter of time before you run into the wowie-pow-zowie Internet connectivity features again. All the Office applications sport new Internet features. Some of them are actually useful, some are just annoying. Hyperlinks are a great example of both.

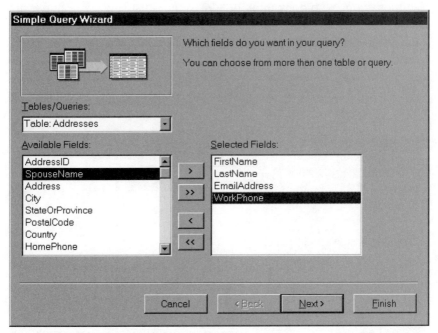

Figure 5-10: Choosing table fields to include in a query

Hyperlinks in Access 97 manifest themselves as a new data type called, simply enough, Hyperlink. You can store URLs, UNC paths, or paths to local files, as shown in Table 5-2.

Table 5-2: A Hyperlink by Any Other Name

Valid Hyperlinks	Example
URL (Universal Resource Locator)	*http://www.primeconsulting.com*
UNC (Universal Naming Convention) path	*\\ripley\ripley_c_drive*
Local path	*c:\data\books\oa\oa4\chapter4.doc*

Click on a hyperlink and wonderful things can happen. If you click on a URL, your favorite browser is triggered and off Web surfing you go. Click a path to a local document and that document is fired up. Great.

The problem (and you knew one was coming, didn't you?) is this: Access is effectively brain-dead about what makes a good link. Okay, Excel is nearly as bad, but in Excel you pretty much have to enter a hyperlink using the Insert Hyperlink dialog box, which gives you a fair chance of browsing for the link or at least being awake enough to type carefully (see Figure 5-11).

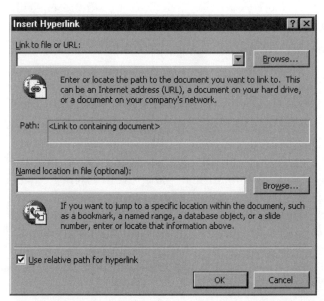

Figure 5-11: Creating a hyperlink in Excel via Insert Hyperlink

In Access, though, even before you can use the Insert Hyperlink command, you have to set the field type to Hyperlink (see Figure 5-12). Once you do that, any text entered into that field (or text that is already there) is considered a valid link. URL, path, or street address—it makes no difference.

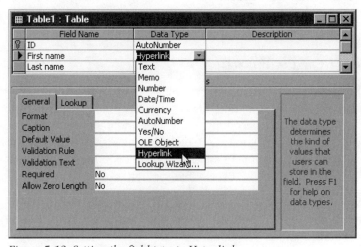

Figure 5-12: Setting the field type to Hyperlink

Click on that field and Access tries to initiate a link. Needless to say, without a valid link your computer will waste cycles as it fires up your browser and tries to connect to a bogus reference. Be sure to enter the right information when you set up a Hyperlink field in Access.

Another major annoyance is that with Hyperlink fields containing URLs, Access opens a new instance of your browser every time you click a link. You can quickly wind up with multiple instances of Internet Explorer or Netscape running, which takes a toll on system resources.

Developers find the Hyperlink Column option on the Insert menu to be annoying (along with the Insert Column command, though to a somewhat lesser extent). You'd think that modifications to the structure of a database would not be allowed in anything other than Design View, but you can insert a Hyperlink Column into a table in Datasheet View. What's more, if you are in Design View and you add a column (field), your changes are automatically saved to the database. But make an addition to the field structure in Design View and then try to switch to Datasheet View and you are told you must first save the table (see Figure 5-13). Inconsistent, peculiar, and very annoying.

Figure 5-13: In Design View you have to save, in Datasheet View it's automatic . . . go figure

Publish to the Web Wizard

A very useful Internet feature of Access is the Web Wizard. The Web Wizard makes it a snap to generate HTML pages that contain Access table data. With Web publishing becoming more and more critical to Office users, this feature is sorely needed. The Access Web Wizard is superior to the one found in Excel (which generates the HTML code but requires that you create the page to house the Excel table separately).

Open a database and select Save As HTML from the File menu. In the second panel of the Wizard you can select any combination of Tables, Queries, Forms, and Reports. (See Figure 5-14.)

Be sure to check the box next to each component for which you want to generate a page. Selecting a table, for example, will highlight it but does not select it for page generation. Check the box!

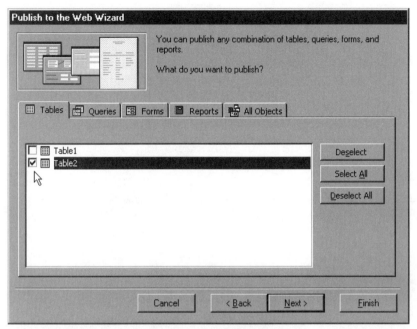

Figure 5-14: Selecting components for Web publishing

You can specify a default template to be used in the next Wizard panel. You can browse for HTML pages to use, and Access ships with a number of HTML documents for this purpose. You'll most likely find them in *C:\Program Files\Microsoft Office\Templates\Access* (which we'll just refer to as the "HTML template folder"). Doing a little snooping through these HTML files reveals how you can easily create your own templates. For instance, Example 5-1 shows the code listing from the *Stones.htm* template that comes with Access. The key is the tag `<!-- ACCESSTEMPLATE_BODY-->`. Wherever this tag appears in an HTML document that you then specify as the template to be used in the Publish to the Web Wizard, that is where the Access data is inserted (thereby replacing the tag). By putting this tag in your own HTML pages, you can effectively create your own HTML templates for use with Access.

Example 5-1: The Stones.htm HTML Source Listing

```
<HTML>
<TITLE><!--ACCESSTEMPLATE_TITLE--></TITLE>
<BODY leftmargin = 110 background = stones.jpg>
<!--ACCESSTEMPLATE_BODY-->
</BODY>
<BR><BR>
<IMG SRC = "msaccess.jpg">
</HTML>
```

NOTE   If you use one of the HTML templates that ship with Ac-
                cess, but you save your newly created Web pages in a loca-
                tion other than the HTML template folder, you'll need to
                copy the *.jpg* files appropriate for the template you're us-
                ing from the HTML template folder to where you are stor-
                ing your Web pages. Otherwise, you won't get the logos
                and background graphics to appear in your page. It's an-
                noying that the Wizard does not do this for you since you
                can specify where you want your new page created.

Next, you can specify that you are creating either a static Web page or
one that will update dynamically when the underlying Access data
changes (provided you have the necessary Web server infrastructure, i.e.,
Microsoft Internet Information Server or Active Server Pages). (See Figure
5-15.)

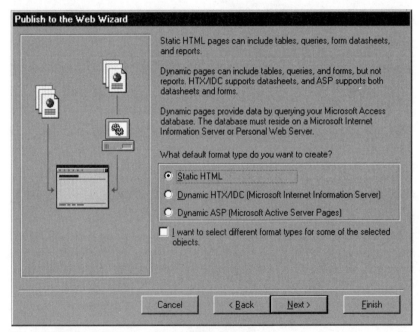

Figure 5-15: Several choices for the type of page to create

The Wizard also lets you choose a folder to store the created pages,
either locally or via the Web Publishing Wizard that ships with Office (see
Figure 5-16). The Web Publishing Wizard can be found on your Office
CD-ROM in the *\Valupack\Webpost* folder. Run *Webpost.exe* to install it.
This utility lets you upload your web pages via the FTP protocol, direct to

your Web site. When the Publish to the Web Wizard is finished, it fires off the Web Publishing Wizard automatically.

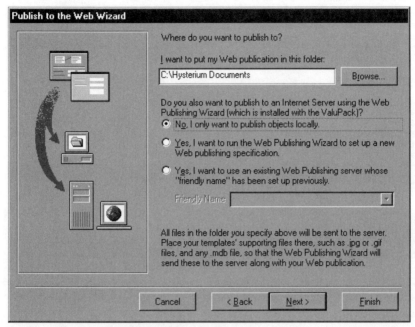

Figure 5-16: Choosing a location for your pages

One annoyance is that each component you selected back in Figure 5-14 is spun out as a separate page. You can select a different HTML template for each of these components (which gives you some degree of formatting control), but if you want two tables to appear in the same Web page, you'll have to do some manual surgery on the files once the Wizard has generated them. The good news is that the code is reasonably simple, particularly if you have any HTML experience.

You can have the Wizard create a Home page for you, which generates a page like that shown in Figure 5-17. The table is labeled Switchboard and lists each of the components that you selected when generating the pages. A link to each page created by the Wizard appears in the Object column. This is functional but not too aesthetically pleasing.

Oddly enough, once you've completed generating the pages, the Wizard doesn't offer to open any of them. You'll have to navigate to the file and open it yourself. Perhaps this is because the Wizard could be generating a number of pages and doesn't want to presume which one should be opened. But if you only generated one page how hard could it be to have the Wizard open it for you? You'd think that it would at least automatically

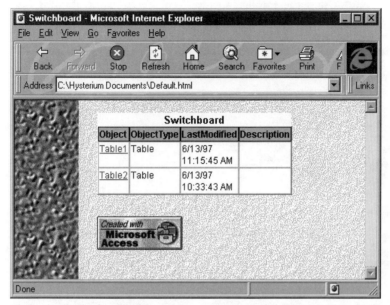

Figure 5-17: The final Web page shown in Microsoft Internet Explorer

open the Home page (if one were specified) or the last HTML file generated by the Wizard at the very least. Or even better, the Wizard could
provide a step for you to choose among these behaviors. At least that's
how we would have designed it.

Performance Analyzer

Access 95 garnered a number of catcalls for poor performance. To deal
with some of the fallout from that debacle, Microsoft made major improvements to Access 97 and also built in the Performance Analyzer. This
special tool tries to pinpoint possible performance problems and even
makes suggestions about how to correct them.

NOTE   The Performance Analyzer is installed as a Wizard. If you
            did not install the Wizards that come with Access 97, the
            menu options for Analyzer will not appear. Rerun setup
            and install the Access Wizards in order to use the Perfor-
            mance Analyzer.

To run the Performance Analyzer on the current database, pull down the
Tools menu, select Analyze, and then click on Performance from the
cascading menu. In the Performance Analyzer dialog box you can select

some or all of the particular database objects to be analyzed. (See Figure 5-18.)

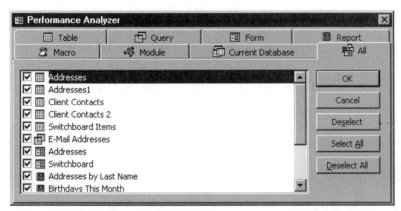

Figure 5-18: Analyzing all the objects in the current database

After churning through the objects you specified for analysis, you'll be presented with a number of recommendations, suggestions, and ideas for your consideration. (See Figure 5-19.)

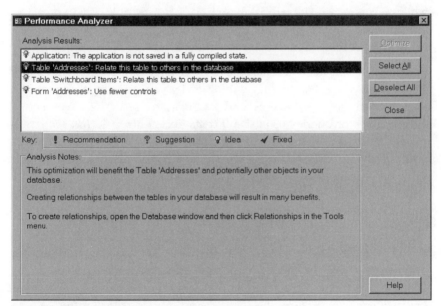

Figure 5-19: The Performance Analyzer pay off

When you select an item in the list, you can see information and suggestions about improving performance in the Analysis Notes box at the bottom of the dialog. The information is not always as specific as one could hope for, but it can be quite helpful all the same. Great feature overall.

Access and Outlook

Access is a powerful relational database application; Outlook isn't. And therein lies the tale.

Outlook is billed by Microsoft as your "Desktop Information Manager" and acts as your universal address book. You keep your email addresses there—Outlook replaces the Exchange client and is the new and improved email program in Office, well, new in any event—as well as street addresses for everyone you do business with. There is no set of information more crucial than the names and addresses you use to conduct your business dealings.

Wouldn't it be wonderful if Outlook could serve as a front-end for a single Access database containing all your name and address information? If you could make changes in Access and have those changes instantly reflected in Outlook? And vice versa? Alas, according to the word from Mount Microsoft, since Outlook uses a MAPI flat-file database structure while Access is a relational database, this is not feasible. There is still no end in sight for the hodge-podge of address book databases, Personal Address Book files, Contact lists, ad infinitum.

So what can you do when it comes to moving data between Access and Outlook? If you're handy with writing code, you can use Automation to transfer data between Access and Outlook, or set up a reference to Access tables or queries using DAO (data access objects). *But there is no way to set up a live link between an Access table (or set of linked tables) and a folder of Outlook Contact items.* The VB Data Control, which works so well in Visual Basic to display Access data, does not work on Outlook forms. Microsoft has been promising an ActiveX database connector control to Outlook developers for quite a while now, but as of this writing, it has not yet seen the light of day.

If you're willing to resort to VBScript or VBA code to transfer data between Outlook and Access you can find a few code samples on the Outlook Developers Home Page at *http://www.outlook.useast.com/outlook/ OutlookCodeExample.htm*. If all you want is basic data transfer—a one-way import or export between Outlook and Access with no linking—you can use File ➤ Import and Export from the Outlook menu.

There is a tool for creating a table in Access that is linked to the Contact list in Outlook: the Microsoft Exchange and Outlook Wizard. This Wizard was recently (February 1997) made available for download at *http:// www.microsoft.com/accessdev/accwhite/exchwiz.htm.* Download the file *WZMAPI80.EXE.* Run this file on your system and it installs itself as a set of Access Add-Ins. You get both a Link Exchange/Outlook Wizard for creating a linked table in Access, and an Import Exchange/Outlook Wizard for doing straight imports. Both options are found on Access's Tools ➤ Add-ins cascading menu.

With either utility, you get to choose a folder of contacts to bring into Access, as shown in Figure 5-20.

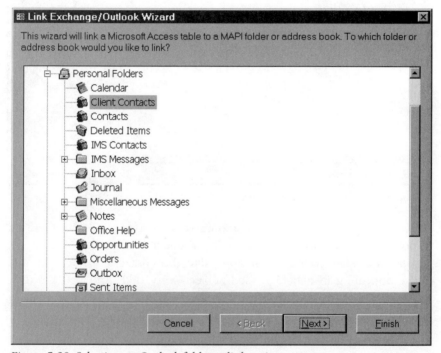

Figure 5-20: Selecting an Outlook folder to link to Access

NOTE   You will see all your Outlook folders on this screen, al-
            though some of them are clearly inappropriate for linking
            to Access, such as the Notes folder.

You can then give the table that will be created in Access a name (the default name is the name of the folder in Outlook). After you have made all your selections, Access grinds away and creates the table. (The length of time this takes depends on the number of records you are linking to or importing.)

If you're creating a linked table, it shows up in Access with an Exchange icon in the Access Tables list and an arrow indicating that the data is in a linked table. (See Figure 5-21.)

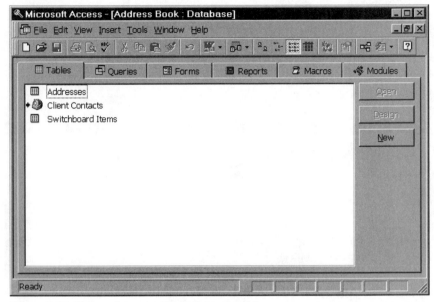

Figure 5-21: The newly created linked Access table

The latest linking and importing add-in works as described. But there's a problem with the tables of information generated in Access. You do get Contact items in your Access table—like the contact's name, their full name appearing in a field named Subject. Very odd. And you get their business phone number, but not the address. Plus you get a number of strange and useless MAPI fields like Has Attachments.

As a useful means of linking and/or importing usable data from Outlook to Access, these Wizards are just plain annoying. They won't capture all the useful Outlook built-in fields, and they omit any custom fields you may have created in Outlook. The Import Exchange/Outlook Wizard seemingly lets you exclude fields you don't want imported, but in our tests, every field, whether excluded or not, was imported. Clearly, these Wizards both need work to be of any value to Access users.

Annoying Printing Problems

In general the Access Report Wizards do a fair job when it comes to printing reports and such from a database. Not great perhaps, but adequate. And if you're willing to familiarize yourself with all the advanced features of the Report module, you can make sophisticated and elegant reports by designing them yourself in the report design window. But some procedures that by all means should be slam-dunks are instead—you guessed it—annoying.

Unhappy relationships

Consider joining fields between tables in the graphical Relationship window. From the Database window select Tools ➤ Relationships. You pick the tables and queries you want and then simply drag the fields you want to relate from one table to another. It is a very slick and powerful utility. (See Figure 5-22.)

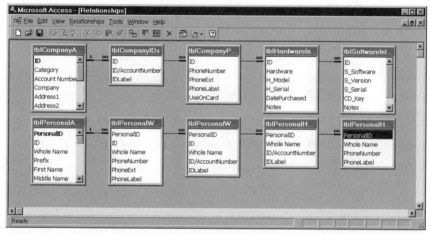

Figure 5-22: The Access Relationship diagram showing one-to-many links between several tables

But once you have everything defined, you'll probably find you want a printed copy for reference. Nope. Once you're in this window, there are no available print commands. This is a major annoyance. There are two workarounds. First, assuming you can get the entire gestalt on screen, you could use a screen capture utility to snap a picture and then print out the graphic file. Or you can use the Documenter feature to generate a report that shows you the relationships. Click on Tools ➤ Analyze ➤ Documenter. Click the Tables tab and select all the tables. Then click the Options button and check the Relationships check box. Click on OK and Access will produce an object definition that you can print out. (See Figure 5-23.)

This is a poor substitute for the intuitive Relationship diagram, which shows all the joins at once, but it does provide you with a report of the links between the tables.

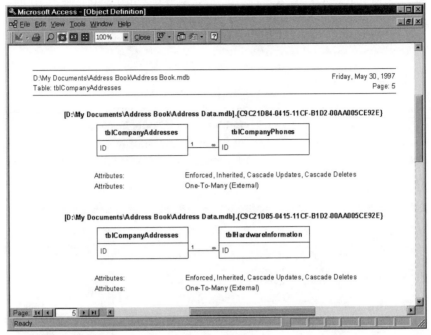

Figure 5-23: Table relationships in the Database Documenter report

Design views

Trying to print out a table, or especially a query, in design view so you can have a hard copy of the various relationships can also be quite irritating. See Figure 5-24 as an example.

You can't print out these views either. Like the relationships, you can get the information from the Documenter, although in a less intuitive format.

Reports in other formats

To save an Access report in another format, you select the report and choose Save As ➤ Export from the File menu. Check the "To an External File or Database" option button and you'll see the familiar Save As dialog. Your choices for anything resembling word processing are a bit limited; you can go to a text file or RTF format. Once you choose the appropriate format, you can check the AutoStart box, which fires up the proper application and loads the exported file.

There's also an OfficeLinks button on the toolbar when a report is selected in the Database window's Report tab that offers to publish the report with Word or analyze it with Excel. The former spins out an *.RTF* file and opens it in Word, and the latter creates an *.XLS* file and opens it in Excel.

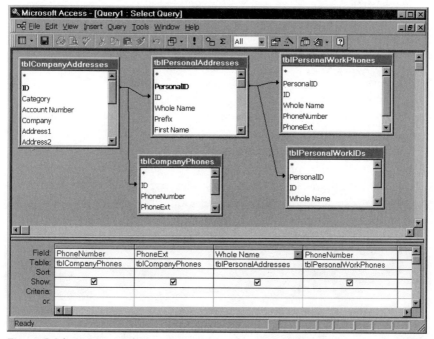

Figure 5-24: A query in design view

RTF will get your report close to where you want to go today but not all the way. Lines are stripped out, some spurious characters get introduced, some characters are removed—for example, the full report title—and what's more annoying, the report footer is not converted to a true Word footer. It's just text down where you hope the bottom of the page is. It might be the top of page two, as happened to us in our testing lab.

Going to a text format is not the road to report nirvana either. You get a lot of the same problems as with RTF, plus you get a sprinkling of low-number ASCII characters (10 and 13, for example) throughout your document. So either way you're going to have to do some manual cleanup.

Excel

Excel 97 is Microsoft's flagship spreadsheet product—king of the spreadsheet hill for both the professional number cruncher as well as the occasional user. Excel is a cornerstone of the Office suite and the oldest product in the group. As befitting its position as Office elder, Excel has fewer of the "this doesn't work like it's supposed to" annoyances simply because it has gone through more revisions than some of its Office siblings.

New in Excel 97 are revised specifications that address some of the most annoying aspects of previous versions, plus a bevy of very useful new features.

Cell Capacity

The upper limit on the amount of text you can type into a cell has undoubtedly frustrated and annoyed more Excel users than any other limitation we can think of. Up until Excel 97, the upper limit was a paltry 255 characters. We can't think of a single Excel user we've encountered in either a personal or a professional setting who didn't rail against this headbanger. The Excel designers made sure they exceeded this constraint—by two orders of magnitude! Now you can loquaciously type up to 16 pages of material in a cell—well, 32,000 characters to be exact. (See Figure 5-25.)

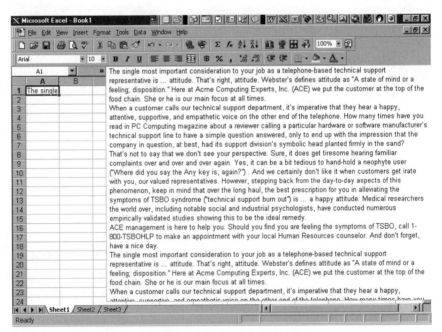

Figure 5-25: A single Excel cell loaded with 32,000 characters

More Rows, Same Columns

Excel 95 supported a maximum of 16,384 rows. Excel 97 ups the ante four-fold to 65,536 rows per worksheet. The maximum column count remains unchanged at 256. That's roughly 15 feet wide by about 850 feet from top to bottom. Ah ha. That's 16,777,216 cells, thank you, so everyone run out and upgrade your RAM to 64 MB so you can begin to use all that real estate.

Take a look at the view from the dark recesses in Figure 5-26.

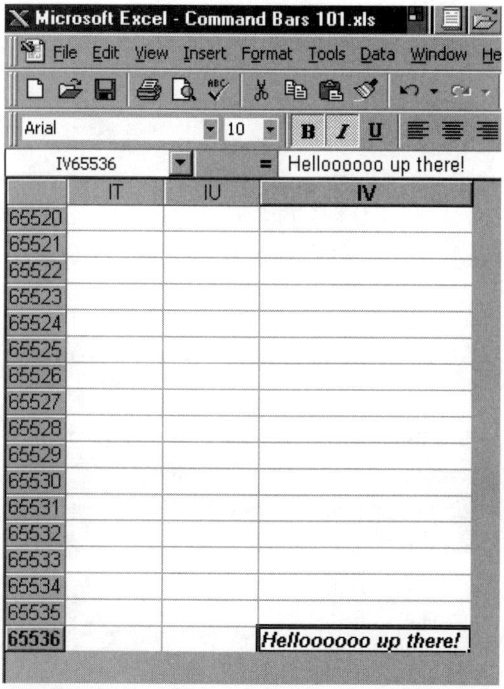

Figure 5-26: Cell IV65536 sure knows what lonely's like

This increase solved a serious size limitation for users who developed flat file databases using Excel (or imported large chunks of data from external databases). Since each record consumes one row, this increase quadruples the size of a database table that can be worked with in a single sheet.

Reefing in the Sheets

Speaking of sheets, Excel 95 annoyingly produced new workbooks with 16 sheets by default—based on the logic that most users want every workbook to have twelve sheets (one for each month) plus four more (one for each quarter for a recap). We'd like to have seen the usability lab-rat research that came up with that result.

Anyway, unless you went in and sniffed around the Tools ➤ Options tabbed dialog long enough to find the setting to make it a more reasonable number, say, three (Tools ➤ Options ➤ General ➤ Sheets in New Workbook), you were stuck with deleting empty sheets or just leaving them in your workbooks.

We all complained loudly about this one and the Redmond Rangers listened up. Excel now creates a sensible three worksheets in a new workbook unless you ratchet it up yourself (the maximum in a default workbook is 255).

Multi-Level Undo

Until Excel 97 came along, Excel was hamstrung by a single-item undo stack. Harking waaaaaay back to the good old Office 4 days, this is one area in which Word definitely had—and still has—its big brother beat. While Word 6 introduced a 100-action undo capability, Excel 5 shamefully stopped short at one. No changes from Office 4 to Office 95 for either application—Excel 95 held its ground stubbornly (still just one item), with Word 95 at 100 items.

Excel 97 still lags mightily on this dimension, providing a mere 16-item undo stack whereas Word 97 weighs in with a whopping 2,417 item undo capability. We'll take 16 undos over a scanty one undo any day, but there's plenty of room for improvement here.

You'll like the user interface of the undo button (located on Excel's Standard toolbar), as shown in Figure 5-27. It provides an amazing amount of detail in a relatively small, compact space. Cool.

Figure 5-27: Excel's undo stack after creating a small sales table

Hyperlinks in Excel

Everything these days has to somehow be tied into the Internet, the über-buzzword extraordinaire. Not to be left behind by the hyperbole media machine, Excel 97 (along with all the other Office applications) has its share of Web and Internet features. These features range from the useful to the "that's very interesting but why would anyone want to do that?" variety. Hyperlinks fall into the former category.

NOTE   Hyperlinks work the same whether you're creating them in Word, Excel, PowerPoint, or Access. Access, as discussed in the previous section, actually has a Hyperlink data type. PowerPoint has some interesting actions—mouse-over and mouse-click—that are associated with a hyperlink.

Hyperlinks are a new name for an old idea, that of creating a link between documents. Only instead of a link that just returns a value from one sheet and displays it on a sheet in another book (or somewhere within the same book), you can have a *hyperlink*, a "hot spot" that, when clicked on, takes you right to the other sheet/book. (See Figure 5-28.)

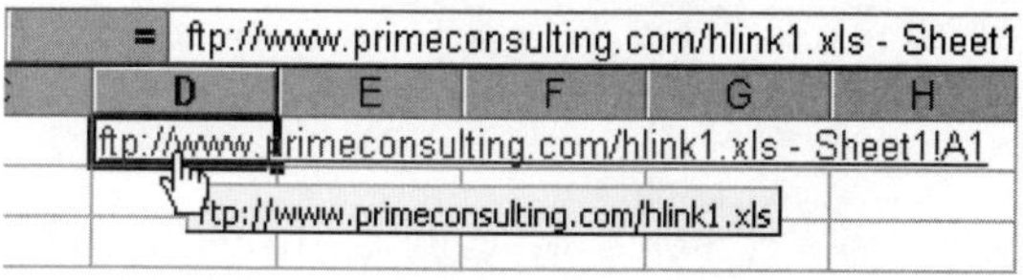

Figure 5-28: A hyperlink to a workbook stored on a Web site

The buzz about this feature (according to the Microsoft Marketing Machine) is the ability to link across (you guessed it!) the Internet. But whether you use hyperlinks in conjunction with the Internet, an intranet, or just your local disk, it's a very cool and useful feature.

A hyperlink that jumps you from the link to another location can easily be created via the Insert ➤ Hyperlink command or by clicking on the Insert Hyperlink button on the standard toolbar. Doing so pops up the Insert Hyperlink dialog box. (See Figure 5-29.)

You can browse for the file you want to link to as well as the optional location within that file. In Excel, a location can be an address (A1, A1:B2) or a named range. In Word you would reference a bookmark to locate a specific place within a document.

To provide a link to a value *and* provide a jump point from one Excel sheet to another (this would apply more to going across the Internet or an intranet) you use a hyperlink within a formula. The hyperlink feature can link to external data using both the HTTP and FTP protocols. For example:

```
='http://www.somewhere.com/[hlink1.xls]Sheet1'!A1
```

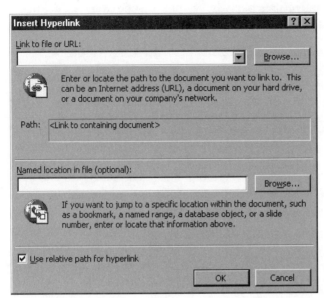

Figure 5-29: Creating hyperlinks

The preceding formula *returns* the contents of cell A1 from a sheet named Sheet1, in a workbook named *hlink1.xls*, in the root folder of the *http://www.somewhere.com* domain. The next formula returns the contents of the range name MyNamedCell from the sheet named Anamed-Sheet, in the *myfile.xls* workbook, in the *stuff* folder on the *ftp.myserver.com* ftp site:

```
='http://ftp.myserver.com/stuff/
[myfile.xls]AnamedSheet'!MyNamedCell
```

The simplest way to create a hyperlink like this is to open both the source and destination workbooks and copy the data in the source file, click on the destination sheet, and then choose Edit ➤ Paste Special ➤ Paste Link. If you're linking in a range, select the upper-left cell of the area in the destination sheet where you want the linked data to appear.

Interestingly enough, if you create the link by the copy-paste link method, the returned value is also a hyperlink to the source spreadsheet. If you just type in the formula, you get the linked value but it is not a hyperlink, since you cannot click on it to activate that sheet/location.

The Formula Palette

A spreadsheet cell can contain text, a number, or a formula. Formulas are the primary means of programming your spreadsheet models, and Excel goes the extra mile with the new Formula Palette feature to simplify building formulas. Just click on the equal sign button on the formula bar to start entering your formula, and the Formula Palette automatically appears. (See Figure 5-30.)

This feature is primarily designed to help you enter functions into your formulas, but it offers numerous features for formula construction.

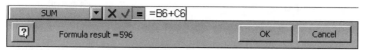

Figure 5-30: Clicking on the equal symbol activates the Formula Palette

In Figure 5-30, the equal symbol at the left of the formula bar was clicked and a simple formula was entered, one that adds the values in two cells. The formula bar is modeless, meaning you can have it active and still click on cells, pull down menus, switch workbooks or applications, etc. Cell B6 in the active sheet was selected, the plus symbol was typed, and cell C6 was clicked on.

The Palette displays the result of the formula at this point (Formula result = 596) and displays a Help button on the left, and an OK and Cancel button on the right. Click on the OK button (or the little checkmark symbol to the left of the equal symbol) and the formula is entered into the active cell. Click on the Cancel button (or on the X next to the check-mark symbol) and the formula is discarded and no changes are made.

Excel has over 300 built-in functions. You can peruse them by pulling down the Insert menu and clicking the Function option, which calls up the Paste Function dialog. You can also access this dialog from the Palette by pulling down the drop-down list of functions (the down-pointing triangle to the left of the X button). This list tracks the last 10 functions you used in formulas, and at the bottom is an option for More Functions, which calls up the Paste Function dialog. (See Figure 5-31.)

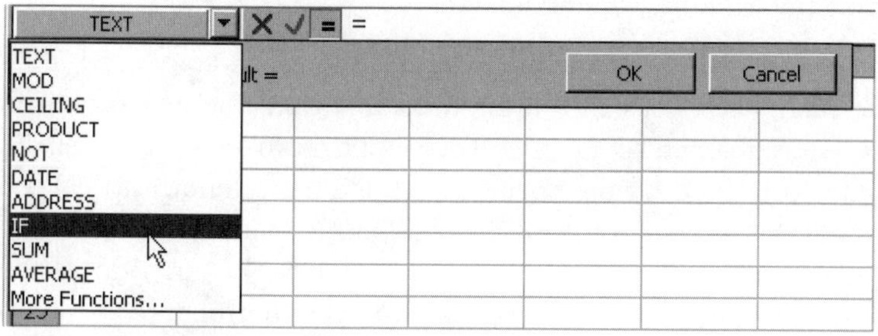

Figure 5-31: The Paste Function dialog box

The Formula Palette replaces the clunky Function Wizard of Excel versions past. In Figure 5-32, the IF function was selected from the drop-down list in the Palette, which provided us with information about the function and the arguments that it accepts. The IF function lets you perform a logical test—in this case we're checking to see if the total of several columns is equal to the total of the rows, called a crossfoot. It then returns one result if the logical test is TRUE, and a different result if the test is FALSE.

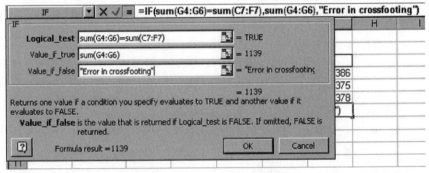

Figure 5-32: Entering functions with the Formula Palette

The Palette is truly a mind-bogglingly useful implementation of the Wizard concept. Note the buttons at the end of the input boxes. They cause the Palette to roll up, out of your way while you look at the sheet or make selections with the mouse. By simply filling in the blanks you can construct a powerful conditional formula.

Range Finder

Excel provides some excellent tools to make both building and maintaining formulas a snap. New in Excel 97 is the Range Finder. The Range Finder is a feature that visually displays the cells being referenced by a formula when the formula is being edited.

Range Finder assigns each reference in a formula a color and then outlines the referenced cells in the same color. In the formula shown in Figure 5-33, the reference to B6 in cell E5 appears in blue, and cell B6 itself is bordered in blue on the sheet. In cell E5, the reference to cell C6 is in green and the reference to cell E3 is in purple, with those cells like-wise colored. A black and white picture like Figure 5-33 cannot do justice to this feature. It is exquisitely implemented and very useful.

	A	B	C	D	E
1	North Division Sales				
2		Qtr.1	Qtr.2		
3	Widgets	98	101	COGS per unit	$3.98
4	Doohickeys	110	92		
5	Gizmos	109	86	Total COGS	=B6+C6*E3
6	Totals	317	279		
7					

Figure 5-33: Range finder in action

Data Validation

We'll bet this has happened to you: You carefully craft your spreadsheet, checking the formulas and clearly labeling the input areas. Then you distribute it to your department, and someone immediately renders your work useless by entering invalid data hither and yon with wild abandon. Text where values should go, numbers where you expect to be grabbing text to concatenate, zeros where you need to have divisors, thereby making your sheet break out with #DIV/0 errors like it had the measles. Talk about annoying! Fear not though, with Excel 97's Data Validation feature, this is one annoyance you can do something about.

You can now establish validation rules for entries made into specific cells in your worksheet. Select the target cells—from a single cell to an entire range—and then choose Validation from the Data menu. Excel 97 displays the Data Validation dialog shown in Figure 5-34.

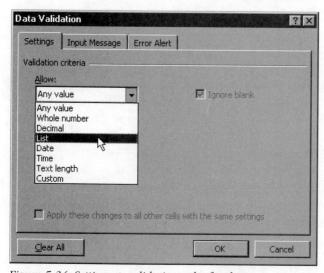

Figure 5-34: Setting up validation rules for data entry

You get wide-ranging control over the type of data that a cell will accept. You can indicate that whole numbers, decimals, and dates, for instance, should lie within a specified start and end range, or you can restrict the length of a text entry to a minimum or maximum length, to name just a couple of the dialog's options and features. If you started off with a range selected, any rules you establish are applied to each cell within the range when you click OK.

This technique of adding validation rules is so important to ensuring a spreadsheet's integrity that you really should fully explore this feature. Once you have established validation on a cell, you can copy that cell and then do a Paste Special on a destination cell to paste just the validation rules. This makes applying existing rules to new cells and ranges of cells very easy.

You can also set up an Input Message—sort of like a custom cell tip—that pops up when the target cell is selected. This is massively useful, since you can create an Input Message for a cell whether you validate any information or not. This lets you have instructional messages appear whenever certain cells are activated. (See Figure 5-35.)

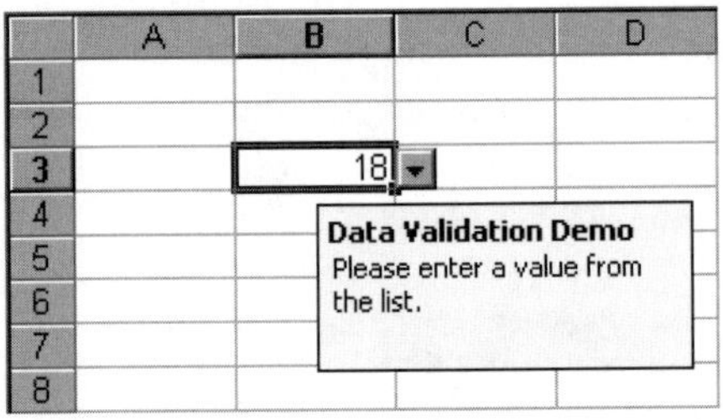

Figure 5-35: Pop-up instructions when a validated cell is selected

One of the best methods of validating data is to allow the user to choose from a predefined set of values; this is precisely what an interface object like a drop-down list box does. Excel 97 allows you to create such a list box without using a form or an external control. The List validation shown in Figure 5-35 warrants a bit of discussion. You create a list of valid entries on a sheet. Select the List choice in the Allow drop-down list box in the Data Validation dialog. Then click in the Source box and highlight the valid entries in your worksheet. Click OK. There is now a drop-down list associated with the target cell that only appears when that cell is selected. Very nifty indeed. Well, perhaps one minor annoyance—you can't pick a default value. If the user does not make a selection, the cell remains blank.

Last but not least, you can create your own error alert message that is displayed when an attempt is made to enter a value outside of the specified parameters, as Figure 5-36 shows. You can control the dialog's icon, caption, and message text by providing the appropriate information in the Error Alert tab of the Data Validation dialog.

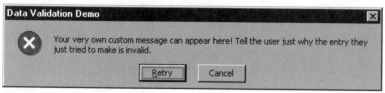

Figure 5-36: Your message here

One minor annoyance is that once you have associated validation rules with a cell, you don't have any visual clue that you've done so unless you select the cell and it has an Input Message. What you can do is pull up the Go To dialog box (press the F5 function key) and click the Special button. In the dialog box, click the "Data validation" option button and then the OK button. All cells with rules will then appear as a noncontiguous selection on the sheet. Use the Tab key to cycle through all the selected cells.

Conditional Formats

The slickest feature available in Excel 97, next to Data Validation, is the ability to change cell formatting if the value of a cell meets some predefined condition. Say you're calculating percentages and you know you have a problem if any values in the range hit 1.0 or higher. Just set a conditional format. If any value in the range equals or exceeds 1.0 then that cell is automatically formatted to have borders and a bright yellow shading. (See Figure 5-37.) Sorta hard to miss, no?

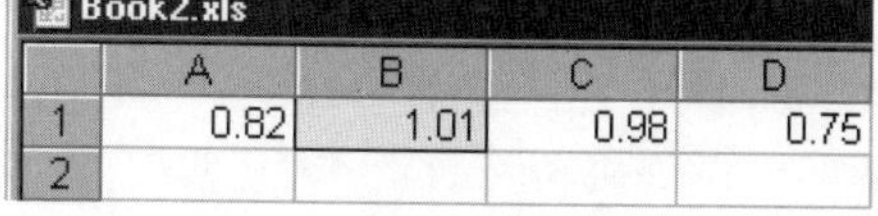

	A	B	C	D
Book2.xls				
1	0.82	1.01	0.98	0.75
2				

Figure 5-37: Formatting changes automatically based on value

To create a conditional format, select Conditional Format from the Format menu. When you first display the dialog box shown in Figure 5-38, it lets you set a single condition. If you click the Add button, you can add a second. Click Add again and you can set a third (as shown here). You can test the value of a cell (Cell Value Is), or you can enter a formula that evaluates to TRUE or FALSE. This latter ability is very powerful, letting you change the formatting of cells based on what's happening in other cells on the active sheet, or on other sheets in the workbook.

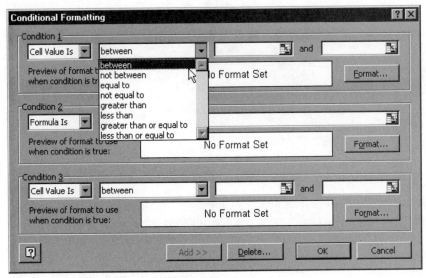

Figure 5-38: Set up to three conditional formats

Formats you can specify are font, borders, and patterns (shading). A minor annoyance is that you can't adjust the weight of borders. Also, like the regular Format ➤ Cells ➤ Borders, you aren't able to specify a color for the border settings. You can choose one, but it won't appear— Microsoft's version of "any color you want, as long as it's black."

Conditional formats are a dynamite way to build in visual cues to show what is happening in your model.

Outlook, New Kid on the PIM Block

PIM stands for Personal Information Manager. And Outlook is the new kid on the PIM block. Rumors of a Microsoft PIM code-named Ren and Stimpy have been around for years. Regardless, don't be fooled by a version number of 8.0 (soon to be patched up to 8.02, we hear); this is a "1.0 release," and in many ways, it shows. In many other ways, particularly its nice integration into the Office suite, it is head and shoulders above its PIM rivals. So prepare to swallow a bittersweet pill with "Outlook" etched all over the capsule (we could make a bad pun here— advising you to "look out" so, well, there it is). As the prescription works its magic, and you feel the effects of various contraindications, we'll be at your side offering our best advice. Remember, we've been there too.

Since Outlook is the brand new kid on the block, we'll touch on each of its main features and most annoying habits in this section.

Outlook comes chock-full of features, bells, and whistles, some of which are gewgaws, others priceless jewels. In fact, as a newcomer to Outlook, it's very easy to become distracted by the baubles. Let's get started by talking about Outlook's core features, and the annoyances that come with them.

Outlook's designers might disagree with our algebra here, but from where we sit, Outlook has six primary, core features:

- Calendar (Appointments, Meetings, and Events)
- Contacts
- Email
- Journal
- Notes
- Tasks

NOTE   Throughout this book, when we refer to Outlook data types or modules, we use a convention of normal capitalization, e.g., "Outlook Appointment" instead of "Outlook appointment."

Notice how we have lumped three different types of Outlook data—Appointments, Meetings, and Events—into a single category—Calendar. We do this purposefully, to help simplify the enigma. Officially, an Outlook Appointment involves only you (no other people or resources); an Outlook Meeting is an appointment involving other people and/or resources; and an Outlook Event is an activity spread over more than a 24-hour period or an annual event like a birthday. But they all have one simple thing in common: they live on your Calendar.

The Outlook Bar (see Figure 5-39), the non-dockable bar along the left side of the Outlook window, provides quick one-click access to Outlook's core features. The Bar comes with three built-in buttons labeled Outlook, Mail, and Other that represent Outlook's three built-in Shortcut groups. To manipulate groups, right-click anywhere in or on the Bar while that group is displayed. Each group comes with its own set of built-in Shortcuts (like Inbox, Calendar, Contacts, etc. in the Outlook group). You can add new Shortcuts (right-click the Bar, click Add to Outlook Bar, select File System in the "Look in" drop-down list box, scroll down the Folder name list, select My Computer, and the display becomes an Explorer-like tree from which you can select folders) and otherwise freely manipulate the Shortcuts in each group (including drag-and-drop within and among groups).

Figure 5-39: This is Outlook's "Outlook Bar"

An annoyance worth noting before we journey into the heart of the beast: those of you who prefer the mouse to the keyboard should be using the New button (leftmost on Outlook's toolbar) quite often. The button's face changes as you move from one module to another, so in the Calendar module the button's face is for an Appointment (its ToolTip reads "New Appointment"), and in the Notes module the face is for a Note (its ToolTip reads "New Note"), and so on down the line. If you want to use this button to create a new entry from among Outlook's many entry types, that's fine. Just get into the habit of first touching the button with the mouse *before* clicking; this way you'll see its ToolTip and know for sure what entry type it will create for you. Alternately, you could get into the habit of always clicking on the button's down-arrow (along its right edge), thereby producing a nice cascading menu of all the entry types from which to choose, as shown in Figure 5-40.

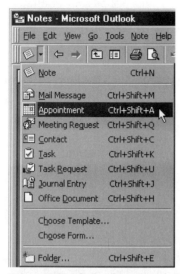

Figure 5-40: The toolbar's handy New menu button—use it!

That extra click is worth it while you're learning the Outlook labyrinth. For those keyboard types among you, get busy memorizing your cherished entry shortcuts: `Ctrl+Shift+M` for Mail, `Ctrl+Shift+A` for Appointment, etc. See Table 5-3 for more shortcuts.

Table 5-3: Handy Outlook Shortcuts

Outlook Item:	Keyboard Shortcut:
Create email message	Ctrl+Shift+M
Create Appointment, Meeting, or Event	Ctrl+Shift+A
Create a new Contact	Ctrl+Shift+C
Create a new Task	Ctrl+Shift+K
Create a new Note	Ctrl+Shift+N
Create a new Journal entry	Ctrl+Shift+J

Outlook's Most Egregious Annoyances

Here are Outlook's three most egregious annoyances:

- Outlook has no customizable toolbars.

  In fact, Outlook doesn't use the nice, new, Office-wide Command Bars object model. So if you want to customize Outlook's user interface to march to the beat of your drummer, forget it. By a loooooong stretch of the imagination, one could argue that the Outlook Bar feature with its editable groups and Shortcuts represents a pseudo-toolbar (we wouldn't, but some might). It just ain't so. Sure, you can rename, add, delete, and otherwise rearrange groups and Shortcuts, but these are simply storage locations for Outlook data. You can't customize the way Outlook presents its feature set to you via its toolbars or menu bar. And that's a shame.

- Outlook doesn't support VBA and doesn't include its integrated development environment.

Instead, Outlook supports VBScript, a very diluted subset of the Visual Basic language. If you've bought into the tremendous benefits of an Office-wide programming language and its associated development environment—and you should—then you'll be very disappointed and frustrated when working with VBScript to control Outlook. For a detailed—and very depressing—look at what VBA and Visual Basic have that VBScript doesn't, check out *http://www.microsoft.com/vbscript/*, find the question "How does VBScript compare to Visual Basic and the Visual Basic language in the Microsoft Office applications (Word, Excel, and so on)?", then click on the link marked "differences between VBScript and Visual Basic for Applications."

Keep in mind that VBScript isn't crippled capriciously. Microsoft purposefully designed it to be small, lightweight, and "Internet-safe" (here meaning with no direct access to file input/output operations or the underlying operating system); thus, the missing features. That's fine for Internet Explorer, which also hosts VBScript, but it's completely unacceptable for Microsoft's inaugural PIM.

- Outlook is modal when it is uploading and downloading messages.

You can forget about using Outlook for anything else while it's gathering or sending email messages. We'll discuss this more a bit later on.

Add an Appointment

Have you ever been a passenger in a Volkswagen Beetle skittering down an unfamiliar highway at about 65 m.p.h. with all the windows down, at night, a flashlight in one hand and a road map in the other, late to some milestone event in your life, trying to give directions to the driver? That's a very close approximation of how it feels to be an Outlook neophyte trying to add a new piece of information. Solution: memorize keyboard shortcuts for your most frequently created entry types, or, if you're a mouse-ophile, click the New toolbar button and choose from there (see Figure 5-40). Furthermore, don't waste any time thinking about Outlook's self-imposed three different types of calendar activities. An Appointment can easily be rendered into a Meeting, which can easily be rendered into an Event, ad infinitum. We'll show you how. Of course, if you personally prefer to think about what data type you're about to create, then you may do so up front. Just rest assured that if you slip up, you can easily shuffle a particular calendar activity among Outlook's three calendar event types.

TIP   Create *every* new calendar activity as an Appointment using `Ctrl+Shift+A`. Then, put this common dialog box and its options to use as needed to add attendees or establish the activity as an annually recurring birthday or whatever (more on Meetings and Events in a moment).

So to schedule a one-time appointment, press `Ctrl+Shift+A` (or click the New button and choose Appointment). Type in the subject and location (if appropriate), choose your start and end date/times, set a reminder if you want one, then click the Save and Close button. (See Figure 5-41.)

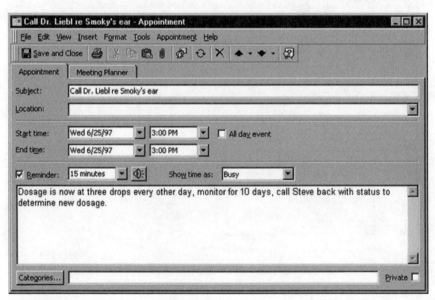

Figure 5-41: Outlook's Appointment form

When it comes to entering dates, Outlook recognizes "tomorrow," "next week," "two weeks," etc., as correct dates, using the current date as the starting reference. Very handy.

Add a Meeting

If you're an Outlook neophyte, we suggest you add every calendar
activity—including Meetings—by using the `Ctrl+Shift+A` shortcut (or
click the New button and choose Appointment). Now fill in the Appointment tab's fields as needed, then simply flip this entry to a Meeting by
clicking on the Meeting Planner tab, invite your attendees by clicking the
Invite Others button, then click Send. (See Figure 5-42.) Note that as soon
as you click on the Invite Others button, the dialog box's title bar
changes from "Your Subject Goes Here - Appointment" to "Your Subject
Goes Here - Meeting"—it's that simple. It's annoying that Outlook only
provides one Send mode: clicking Send puts this email invitation into
your Outbox for later sending. We'd like very much to see Microsoft
change this button's label to "Send Later" and add an additional button
labeled "Send Now" that would connect to the appropriate mail service
and send the message immediately.

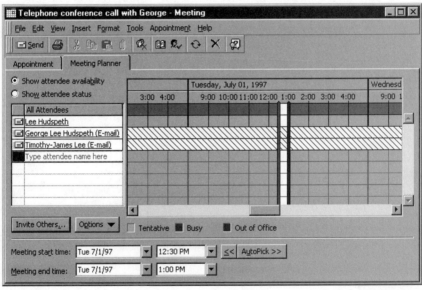

*Figure 5-42: Use the Meeting Planner tab of the Appointment dialog box to flip an
Appointment to a Meeting*

NOTE	Remember that all Outlook calendar activities—Appointments, Meetings, and Events—share this same two-tabbed dialog box: the first (left-most) tab is always labeled "Appointment" and the second tab is always labeled "Meeting Planner." Don't worry about it, just take our `Ctrl+Shift+A` prescription and you'll be fine.

Add an Event

Keeping pace with our `Ctrl+Shift+A` shortcut advice, to plan a non-recurring event (where by non-recurring we mean a vacation or a seminar, as opposed to a fixed-frequency repeating event like a birthday), press `Ctrl+Shift+A` (or click the New button and choose Appointment). Fill out the Appointment card as usual (in Figure 5-43 we manually checked the "All day event" box, and selected Out of Office in the "Show time as" drop-down box, all in keeping with the nature of the 7-day vacation), then click the Save and Close button. It's the "All day event" box being checked that identifies this entry as an Event instead of an Appointment.

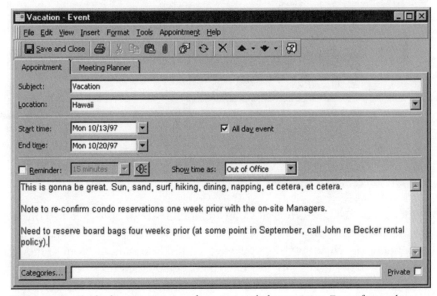

Figure 5-43: Outlook's Appointment form instantly becomes an Event form when you click the "All day event" check box

Add a Contact

Creating a Contact is simple: from the Contacts module, select Contacts, New Contact. See Figure 5-44. Fill in the fields in the General tab, and Outlook automatically parses the entered data, breaking down a name as you type it into Title, First, Middle, Last, and Suffix, and automatically stores each item in a separate field (click the Full Name button to view or edit these detail fields). Ditto for the address. The Details tab lets you enter contact details like an assistant's name, a birthday, an anniversary date, and so on. Outlook's database structure supports a plethora of fields. On the All Fields tab, you can enter almost any conceivable type of information. Filter the display from a handy pull-down list (the "Select from" control).

Figure 5-44: Outlook's Contact form

Outlook confusingly offers a variety of different ways to get to contact information that is stored somewhere other than the Contact list, depending on what services you have currently installed. From Outlook, you could have access to the Exchange Personal Address Book (PAB), Outlook's Contacts list, a CompuServe address book, the MSN address database, among others, all depending on your configuration. You should stick to the Contacts feature set and avoid the PAB, the latter being a relic from the by-gone days of Schedule+ and Exchange. (In Chapter 7, *Strategies*, we'll show you how to migrate your PAB entries—if you're a former Exchange user—to Outlook's Contacts module.)

Here's what irritates us most about Outlook's management of contact data: there's no connection to Access, which is vastly superior to Outlook as a storage database for contact information. If you don't have a flavor of Office that comes with Access (i.e., Access is not installed), Outlook should use the relational .mdb file format and store contact information in its own .mdb file. If Access is detected during Outlook setup, the installation program should ask whether you want to store contact data directly in Access and offer to fire up a Contacts Wizard to create the appropriate links from an existing Access address information database to the Outlook Contacts module, which would then be a dynamic interface to the data in the user's existing Access tables. That's what should happen, but alas, it does not.

And a major data-entry annoyance: there's no way to set defaults for frequently entered—and often static—fields, like a default area code for all new Contact phone numbers, or a default Title for all new Contacts. To tell Outlook to search for contact information in your Contacts module instead of some other repository, choose Tools ➤ Services ➤ Addressing, then choose the desired default in the "Show this address list first" drop-down. Annoyingly, this setting affects only Outlook, meaning it is not a pan-Office sticky setting. So in Word, if you add an Insert Address button and click it, you most likely will see a different repository defaulting in the selectable list.

Send Email

If you're familiar with the Exchange email client, then you'll be right at home with Outlook's email interface. Even if you aren't a former Exchange user, Outlook's email user interface, which is shown in Figure 5-45, is easy to use and master (for help, ask Robert "email" or "e-mail"). There are, however, numerous annoyances.

In the Outlook Mail Bar, the Inbox icon shows—in parentheses—how many unread messages the inbox contains. The Deleted Items icon shows how many deleted items it contains, but only if they are unread. The Outbox icon is strangely silent on this score. We appreciate the logic behind no count in the icon description for Sent Items at any time, but the Outbox icon should always reveal its count of waiting items.

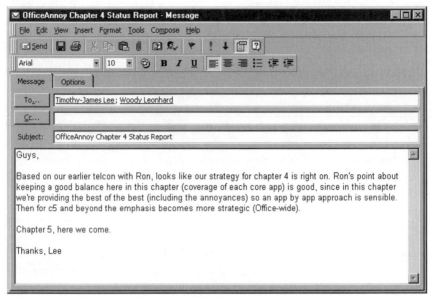

Figure 5-45: Outlook's Message form for outbound messages

NOTE   When Outlook is connected to a mail service, it becomes
                application-modal. This is a fancy way of saying that you
                can't interact with Outlook's interface at all until the cur-
                rent mail session is completed—so you can't read the first
                few messages while more are coming in, you can't create
                an outgoing message, or you can't interact with Outlook in
                any way whatsoever until the mail session is done. The Ex-
                change email client was not like this (application-modal)
                when connected, so why is Outlook? Two steps forward,
                three steps back.

We've been scratching our heads over this one for a while now. Why
aren't there keyboard shortcuts for each Go data category (as in the Go
command on the menu bar)? Only Inbox and Outbox have shortcut keys:
Ctrl+Shift+I and Ctrl+Shift+O, respectively. Why not Calendar,
Contacts, Tasks, Journal, Notes, Sent Items, Deleted Items, and My
Computer? These are brain-dead omissions.

No matter what folder you're in, the default Outlook toolbar should
always display Inbox, Outbox, and Check for New Mail buttons for one-
click access to these folders/features. And it's utterly amazing that there's
no button at all for the Check for New Mail feature; instead you have to
use the mouse or F5. The latter only invokes the all-service Check for
New Mail behavior, which typically processes the services in a different

order than those currently checked in the Check for New Mail On dialog and sporadically misses some of them altogether.

Checking Mail

How Outlook checks your mail when you have multiple services installed is controlled (in theory) by the two commands on the Tools menu: Check for New Mail, and Check for New Mail On. (See Figure 5-46.)

The Check for New Mail command checks for mail on any installed services listed in the Tools ➤ Options ➤ Email tab. (See Figure 5-47.)

In this example, we have checked both The Microsoft Network and the CompuServe Mail services. When you click on Check for New Mail or press the F5 key in Outlook, it runs an "all services" check and connects to all the email services you have checked here.

To control which services are checked on a session by session basis, you click on the Check for New Mail On command on the Tools menu. This presents you with a dialog box listing all the installed email services. You check only those services you want polled and click on OK. (See Figure 5-48.)

Figure 5-46: Checking the mail

If you've ever used the "CompuServe Mail for Microsoft Exchange" service drivers[*] with Outlook (or Exchange), then you're no doubt very impressed with its message-by-message progress dialog. Or Microsoft's own Internet Mail and News reader, which reports the total number of messages to send and to receive. Outlook should meet or exceed these features. (See Figure 5-49.) Instead, Outlook just grinds away, and you have no idea if you are waiting for it to pull in 5 messages or 150. Should you just go grab a quick cup of coffee or go to lunch? *Sheesh.*

---

[*] You can download the CompuServe Mail for Microsoft Exchange service drivers (the filename is *CSMAIL.EXE*) from CompuServe's CSMAIL section (GO CSMAIL). Be sure to print out and follow the downloading/installation instructions.

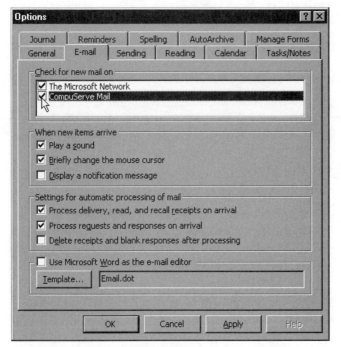

Figure 5-47: Selecting services to check

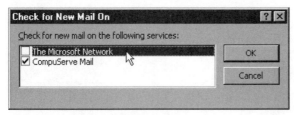

Figure 5-48: Choosing specific services

On the upside of Outlook email (you may already know this trick, but if you don't, it's priceless) type the first few characters of an email recipient's name in the To field, then press Ctrl+K. If Outlook can uniquely identify the characters you entered, it automatically finishes the recipient's name/address for you; otherwise, you get a list of close matches to choose from.

Receiving Email

As with Exchange's email client, receiving mail is a matter of selecting which currently installed services in the current profile you want Outlook to check, then choosing Tools ➤ Check for New Mail or Check for New

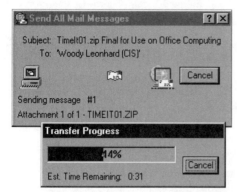

Figure 5-49: The CompuServe Mail for Microsoft Exchange service (works with Exchange and Outlook) displays an informative transfer progress dialog

Mail On.... We long ago became habituated to the Check for New Mail On... form of this procedure so we can choose which services to check, depending on which of our numerous mail providers is operational (or not, which is usually a 50/50 proposition these days <sigh>). Once you have received incoming mail, you'll peruse individual messages in Outlook's Message form, as shown in Figure 5-50.

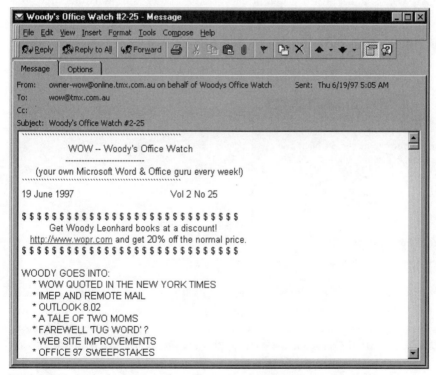

Figure 5-50: Outlook's Message form for received messages

Perhaps you've seen the warning, "A message could not be delivered. Make sure there is sufficient memory and disk space and that the message store is accessible, then try again." Although the warning suggests trouble on your system, what's actually happening is that for some reason, Outlook can't handle an incoming message from your service's mail server. The program reacts by refusing to download anything. This is an Outlook bug as yet unacknowledged by Microsoft. To resolve the problem, you need to remove a honked-up message from that provider's mail server. How? Simple: download your mail with another email application. We have yet to encounter an incoming message that confounded Outlook but couldn't be downloaded by something else. Internet Mail and News (IMN)—bundled with Microsoft Internet Explorer 3.01 and higher—is a good choice. (If it isn't already on your system, download it from *http://www.microsoft.com/ie/imn/*.) IMN includes a facility on its file menu for exporting messages to your Outlook/Exchange Inbox so you can still store them there. And you can't knock the price: it's free.

Add a Note

A Note is a free-form container for notes, ideas, and whatnot, that gets automatically date/time stamped when created and updated. You can stuff it full to about 32,000 characters of text only (no graphics). Creating a Note is easy: press `Ctrl+Shift+N` (or click the New button and choose Note). (See Figure 5-51.)

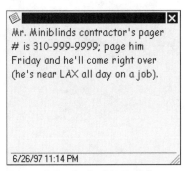

Figure 5-51: Outlook's Note form

For a quick peek—without having to invoke an Object Browser or punch up a help file—at all the data Outlook is managing behind a Note, click View ➤ Show Fields, select "All Note fields" from the "Select available fields from" drop-down list box, and scan the fields listed in the "Available fields" and "Show these fields in this order" list boxes, as shown in Figure 5-55 (click Cancel to dismiss the dialog).

Outlook provides a feature for organizing your data: categories. Outlook comes with a Master Categories list, and you can easily add your categories to it. See Table 5-4.

Table 5-4: Outlook Master Categories

Outlook Master Categories

Business	Key Customer
Competition	Miscellaneous
Favorites	Personal
Gifts	Phone Calls
Goals/Objectives	Status
Holiday	Strategies
Holiday Cards	Suppliers
Hot Contacts	Time & Expenses
Ideas	VIP
International	Waiting

To add your own categories to the Master List (thereby making them available to all of Outlook's various types of items), pull down the Edit menu and click Categories. Click the Master Categories List button. Type in your category name in the "New category" text box, and click Add. (See Figure 5-52.)

Figure 5-52: Adding new categories to the Master list

To avoid having your Notes (or any other class of items in Outlook) become a tangled mass of undifferentiated stuff, we suggest you assign

Notes to categories. When you create the Note, click on the note icon in the upper-left corner of the Note. From the pop-up menu, click on Categories, as you see in Figure 5-53.

Figure 5-53: Assigning a Note to a category

When you click on the Categories option you'll see the dialog box shown in Figure 5-54. You can assign as many categories as you'd like. When done, click OK.

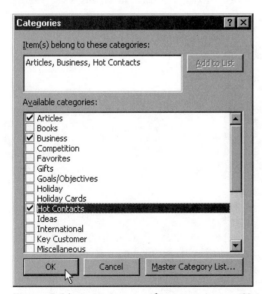

Figure 5-54: Assigning specific categories to a Note item

There's a handy default View to take advantage of this: select View ➤ Current View, By Category.

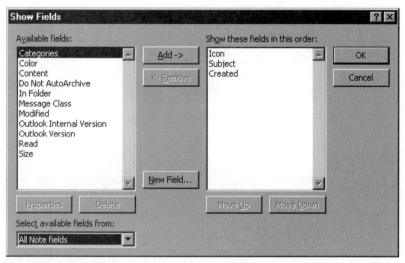

Figure 5-55: The Show Fields dialog box looking at all Note fields

Add a Task

Tasks are your handy-dandy to-do items. There's a shortcut to adding a bare-bones Task once you're in the Task module: click inside the edit box that reads "Click here to add a new Task" (in light gray type), enter a description, then press Enter. You can open the Task later to tweak its numerous settings (see Figure 5-56) or use the keyboard shortcut Ctrl+Shift+K from anywhere. (Hmmm, K? Who knows, guess all the good letters were taken.) Although a Task can be non-time dependent, you'll find that you often assign time parameters—including recurrence patterns—to Tasks.

PowerPoint

Presentation software has evolved from a "read the bulleted items to your audience" level to full-blown, multimedia, whiz-bang, special effects-filled sensory extravaganzas. PowerPoint is at the forefront of this evolution. Whether you create presentations every day or only once or twice a year, PowerPoint is the state-of-the-art software that blah, blah, etc., etc.

Okay, so you only have PowerPoint 97 because it came "free" with Office. But it's really an extraordinary package, and if your copy has become shelfware—still sitting quietly, pining away on your Office CD-ROM—you might want to actually install it and see what it can do. It might surprise you.

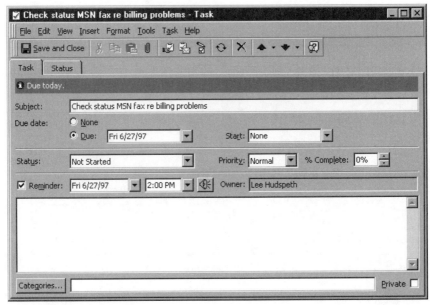

Figure 5-56: Outlook's Task form

Check the Settings

First, make some adjustments. Most of the Tools ➤ Options settings will be familiar—like setting the number of entries on the MRU (see Figure 5-57). But there are other settings that you've not seen in the other Office applications. On the General tab, you can set a threshold at which sound files are linked instead of embedded to a presentation file. This helps you keep the size of your presentations more manageable. The default is shown here at 100Kb. Be careful though! It is really annoying to install your presentation on the boss's computer and get to the third slide when you realize that your killer sounds are all links to files that aren't on that particular computer.

Another departure from the standard Office settings (those found in most other Office applications) is the Maximum number of undo operations found on the Edit tab (see Figure 5-58). In Excel you get a flat maximum of 16 undos. In Word you get over 2,400 undo levels. But in PowerPoint you get to set it yourself—any number you want, up to a maximum of 20 (which also happens to be the default setting).

Why this is user-selectable in PowerPoint and not the other Office applications is anyone's guess. It sounds like a halfhearted attempt to let the user save resources in a pinch. Since presentations are often graphic intensive, tracking undo levels can eat up precious system resources if you're

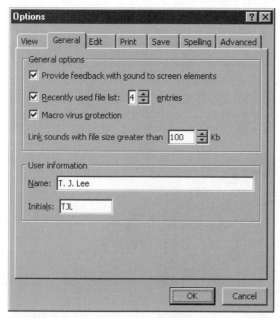

Figure 5-57: Setting the MRU and link sounds settings

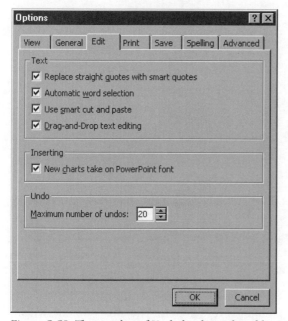

Figure 5-58: The number of Undo levels is selectable up to twenty

working in a constrained environment. But the default is cranked up to
the maximum setting, and most users probably never even realize that

they can change it. It's annoying that there is not more consistency across the Office applications where Undo is concerned.

Here's another interesting setting unique to PowerPoint: you can set a default file type in which you want all your presentations saved. This is handy if you're doing a lot of presentations and you always want them saved in the dual Microsoft PowerPoint 95 & 97 Presentation format. On the Save tab (see Figure 5-59), there is a drop-down list from which you can choose the default save file type.

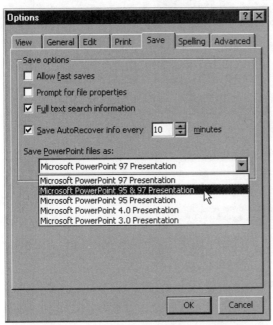

Figure 5-59: Changing the default save as file type

AutoContent Wizard

For some people, a blank canvas really gets their creative juices flowing. Others live in terror of the dreaded blank page. For the latter sort, Power-Point 97 provides a terrific AutoContent Wizard that can kick off the presentation you're developing with a batch of preformatted slides complete with sample content.

You just take this basic set of slides and tweak them until you have created your own award-winning presentation. The AutoContent Wizard can be run by selecting the appropriate option button when PowerPoint first starts up. (See Figure 5-60.)

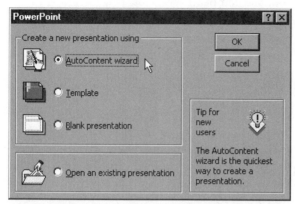

Figure 5-60: Running the AutoContent Wizard at start up

If you're already past startup, you can run the AutoContent Wizard by selecting New from the File menu, then clicking the Presentations tab. Choose the *AutoContent Wizard.pwz* file and click OK. The first panel gives you a brief overview of the process. The next panel is where things get interesting. (See Figure 5-61.)

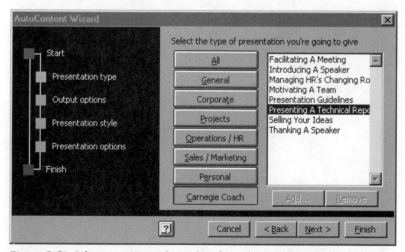

Figure 5-61: Selecting a Wizard template from the categorized selections

PowerPoint 97 comes with 23 templates, broken down into categories that cover the majority of business and personal presentation needs. These templates are stored in the *C:\Program Files\Microsoft Office\Templates\Presentations* folder. In Figure 5-61 we've selected one of the templates that was prepared for Microsoft by the folks at Dale Carnegie. These templates are actually mini-tutorials on how to give an effective presentation broken down by various types.

It gets even better. Most of the templates come in two flavors. One for traditional presentations where you stand in front of a computer or projection screen, lecturing a room full of the VIPs in your company. But you also (in the next Wizard panel) can choose to create a presentation that you'll make available online, on your company intranet or on the Internet. Very cool.

If you selected the traditional presentation option earlier (Presentations, informal meetings, handouts), you can further refine your choices in the next panel, e.g., on-screen, color or black and white overheads, even 35mm slides. PowerPoint will even help you generate handouts to go along with your presentation. These options are called the *Presentation style*. (See Figure 5-62.)

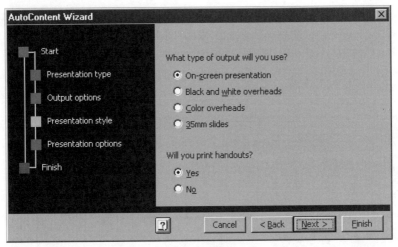

Figure 5-62: Choosing your presentation style

Once you've made your choices in the Wizard, you get a presentation in Outline view. Outline view is definitely the best view for working with slides in PowerPoint. (See Figure 5-63.)

Titles, bullets, and body text all appear in a traditional outline view. Click on the title or text for any slide (each slide is numbered) and that slide appears in the Slide Miniature window (shown in the upper-right corner of Figure 5-63). This gives you a thumbnail view of the slide you're working on.

If you've ever worked with outlines in Word, then you can easily manipulate an outline in PowerPoint. This is one area where Microsoft has gotten its pan-Office act together. Each first-level heading is a separate slide. You can promote and demote levels using the mouse. Just position the

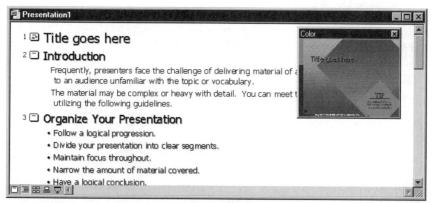

Figure 5-63: Your presentation with sample data in Outline view

mouse pointer at the beginning of a title, bullet, or paragraph and it will change into a four-headed icon. You can drag the item left (promote), right (demote), or you can relocate the item up or down. You can also move text and bullets between slides and/or reorder the slides, all with the mouse. It's fast and easy.

One annoyance: you cannot expand and collapse your outline with the same amount of control as you can in Word. You can either collapse the outline to just the slide titles, or expand it to all levels. Nothing in between. Nuts.

Design Templates

PowerPoint 97 also ships with a number of templates that have very distinctive backgrounds, fonts, color schemes, slide and title masters, and the like. You can choose one of these designs when you first create your presentation (File ➤ New ➤ Presentation Designs) or you can create your presentation first—using a blank template or the AutoContent Wizard— and apply a design later.

Open an existing presentation and click Format ➤ Apply Design. Choose from any of the 17 templates provided by Microsoft. You can also create your own custom templates (File ➤ Save As, and choose Presentation Template (*.pot) from the "Files of type" drop-down list), which will appear in this list. (See Figure 5-64.)

Applying a design lets you quickly reformat your presentation. Of course, if you don't want your presentations looking like those created by everyone else who happens to own a copy of PowerPoint, you'll want to create your own templates.

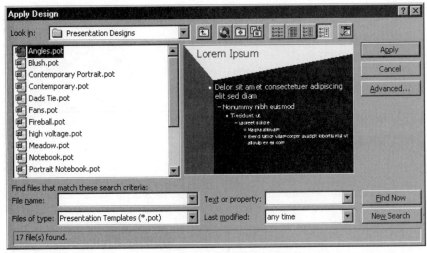

Figure 5-64: Choosing a Design template to apply to your presentation

Slide Finder

Slide Finder is a new utility in PowerPoint 97 that lets you go into existing presentations and find a slide that you want inserted into the presentation you're currently working on. Pull down the Insert menu and select the Slides from Files option. From the Slide Finder dialog box you can browse for presentation files in the Find Presentation tab. Files that you will want to search regularly can be added to the List of Favorites, as shown in Figure 5-65. Either tab will let you display thumbnails of all the slides in that presentation, and you can click on the one you want inserted.

This feature is a two-edged sword. On the one hand, you can go out and snag that exquisite epitome of slide-dom for your current presentation. On the other hand, it lets you recycle slides with wild abandon, creating rehashed and potentially mediocre slide shows.

Multimedia Features

Laser sounds, flashing text, sound tracks, special effects . . . Lights! Camera! Action! PowerPoint 97 has really gone Hollywood as far the multitude of whiz-bang animations and sounds you can add to your slide presentations. This is not necessarily a bad thing, considering how a bit of flash can certainly spice up a presentation. But overdoing it will have your audience heading for the door, so use some common sense and restraint.

Figure 5-65: Using Slide Finder to snag slides for your current presentation

Adding animation is as easy as selecting a title, bulleted item, or text on a slide and choosing a preset animation option. Select your text and click on Preset Animation on the Slide Show menu. The cascading menu offers you a number of animations to choose from. (See Figure 5-66.)

Animations are just the tip of the "jazz up a presentation" iceberg. In the *ValuPack* folder on the Office 97 CD-ROM, there's a sub-folder named *Musictrk* where you can install the Music Tracks add-in. With this program, you can add a sound track to your slides. No kidding. (See Figure 5-67.) Once you've installed the add-in, you can choose Custom Soundtrack from the Slide Show menu. You get a number of types of music that play while your slides are on screen.

One really annoying aspect of all this is that some multimedia options are on the Slide Show menu, while some options falling in the multimedia category are hung on the Insert ➤ Movies and Sound menu option.

You can even create a "voice-over" narration, which lets you create a self-running slide show. Create your slides and then choose Record Narration from the Slide Show menu. Sound recording consumes disk space at an alarming rate, so you'll be informed how much recording time you have based on the available free disk space. (See Figure 5-68.)

The sound files can be embedded (one to each slide) or they can be linked (just check the "Link narrations in" box and choose a suitable directory). Click on OK and record your narration as you move through the

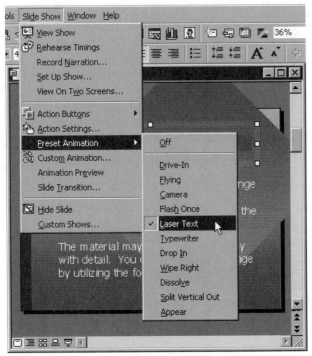

Figure 5-66: Selecting a preset animation

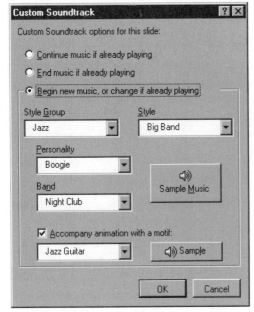

Figure 5-67: Mixing your own sound track

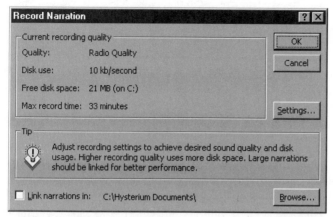

Figure 5-68: Recording a narration

slides. The narration for each slide is stored in a separate linked or embedded file. You remove narrations by deleting the speaker icon from the lower right-hand corner of each slide. Narrations are great! Just start up your slide presentation, and you can sneak to the back of the room to scarf down the danish and coffee while the audience sits in (hopefully) rapt attention, staring at the screen.

PowerPoint and the Web

Not only does the AutoContent feature offer to walk you through the creation of a personal home page for posting on the World Wide Web, one of the flat-out most useful enhancements in PowerPoint 97 is its ability to take a slide presentation and transform it into a ready-to-publish Web page. The Save As HTML Wizard builds all the components discussed in this section.

NOTE   If the Save As HTML option in PowerPoint is grayed out, or is missing altogether from your other Office applications, chances are you haven't installed the Web Page Authoring HTML add-in. To install ths add-in, run Office Setup again.

This Wizard is capable of generating two types of Web presentations out of a series of slides. The first is what could be considered a "traditional" series of Web HTML coded pages linked by <HREF> tags. Each slide becomes a graphic on a page, and each page is set up with navigation buttons that move you forward and backward through the series of Web pages. The second is an ActiveX presentation that lets you view a slide show across the Web as though PowerPoint were running on your local machine. In this section we'll look at an overview of these two types of presentations. In Chapter 7 we'll walk you step by step through creating each type.

A series of pages

In this example, the HTML Wizard was used to generate a traditional series of Web pages. The advantage here is that any graphics-capable browser can view the presentation without having any special add-ins installed. Each slide is turned into a single graphic that is referenced by a standalone HTML page. Pages are linked using standard HTML tags, and you navigate by clicking on the buttons provided (the small graphics images) to jump from page to page. (See Figure 5-69.) PowerPoint generates all the images you need for your pages, including the navigation buttons. In Figure 5-69, you see a group of four buttons (from top to bottom): First, Previous, Next, and Last. (The precise button location is user selectable when you create the pages.) These quickly let you walk forward and backward through the presentation. The second group of three buttons are the Index, Home, and Text buttons.

The Index button takes the user to a PowerPoint-generated Index page. (See Figure 5-70.) The index page has hyperlink jumps to each of the individual slides. It also provides links for your email address and to a home page you define. You can include additional information and even a link so that the presentation source (the *filename.ppt* file) is downloadable. Check a box, and PowerPoint even includes an ad for Microsoft Internet Explorer complete with animated logo (which acts as a jump to the Microsoft Web site).

The Home button provides a hyperlink jump to your defined home page (which is the same as the page shown in Figure 5-70).

The Text button takes you to a different series of pages that the Save As HTML Wizard generates at the same time as the pages we've been discussing. Only this set is devoid of any graphics. Someone without the bandwidth to readily view your graphical wonder, or someone on Unix running Lynx as their browser, can simply click on the Text button to view a complete set of "text only" slides. Figure 5-71 shows you the text only equivalent of the slide shown in Figure 5-69.

It would be nice if the HTML Wizard gave you a choice of whether you want to have a "text only" version or not. If you don't want the option of text-only slides, you have to delete the created HTML files (look for *.htm*

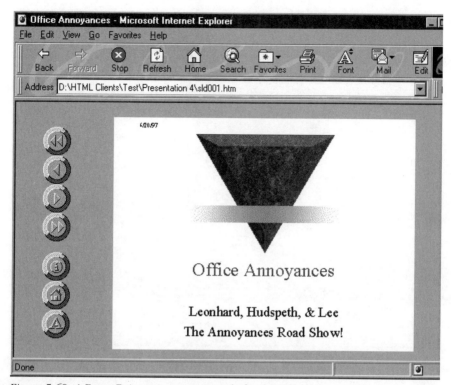

Figure 5-69: A PowerPoint presentation ready for the Web

files that have a letter "t" prefix, like *tsld001.htm*), and then remove the link to the equivalent text slide from each of the presentation slides. That's an annoying amount of HTML hacking if you want to bypass a text-only version of your presentation.

ActiveX Animation player

Instead of the usual series of linked pages, you can opt to have Power-Point 97 generate an ActiveX Animation that you can embed on a Web page. At first glance it may seem no different than the first example. Consider Figure 5-72.

You can use the N and P keys on your keyboard to show the Next and Previous slides just as you can in PowerPoint. With the mouse you can left-click on the slide image and your browser advances to the next slide. Right-click on the image (as shown in Figure 5-72) and you get a Previous option to go back one slide. Click the Expand option and enlarge the slide to the full window space available to your browser, or—and this is really the icing on the ActiveX cake—you can expand the slide to your full monitor screen. This is the exact equivalent of running a slide

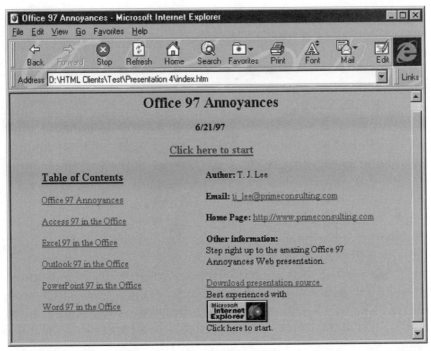

Figure 5-70: Automatically generated index page

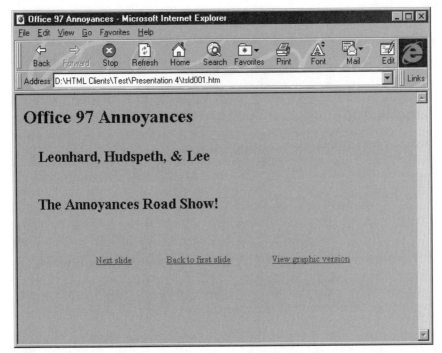

Figure 5-71: Plain vanilla presentation

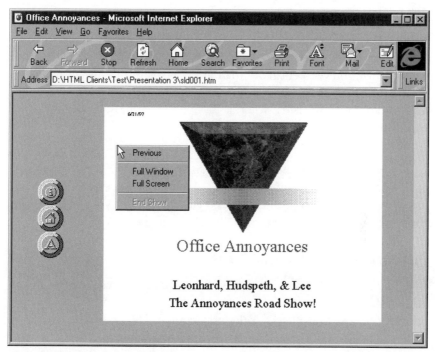

Figure 5-72: ActiveX Animation

show on your local computer (except for the possible delays, since the source data is coming across your intranet or the Internet). This is very hot stuff.

One annoyance you may run into: once you go to Full Window view, there is no shortcut menu option to restore the view to what you see in Figure 5-72. Just hit your browser's Back button to return to that view. When you go to Full Screen view, you can get out of it by right-clicking on the slide and selecting End Show (or hit Escape).

NOTE Using this method (PowerPoint Animation) requires that the browser used to view the Web page be Microsoft Internet Explorer 2.0 or later, or Netscape Navigator 1.22 or later, and have the Animation Player add-in installed. You'll find the Animation Player on the Office CD-ROM: *\Valu-pack\Pptanim\Axplayer.exe*, or you can download the latest version from *http://www.microsoft.com/powerpoint/internet/player/default.htm*.

Word

Word is the part of Office that everyone loves to hate, including us. We love Word. We hate Word. We love to hate Word. And we'd hate to live without it. If you've spent more than a few weeks using the program, it's dollars to donuts that you've probably come to the same conclusion. We love Word because it is without a doubt the most powerful word processor available on the PC for all-around general use. We hate it because, well, because it's just so annoying at times.

Word is probably the richest source of annoyances in Office. It is also the most often used application and one of the least understood. Word 97 has added several new features and enhanced some of your old favorites. In this section we'll point out both the good and the bad.

Paragraph Marks and Tabs

When you install Word, it keeps you from seeing two vital "hidden characters," the paragraph mark and the tab, that sit inside Word documents. Neither of those "characters" prints on your printer. Both are crucial to understanding what's happening with your documents.

Word's designers chose to hide the paragraph mark and the tab from Word users so they wouldn't be confused when a character on the screen didn't print on the printer. In our experience, even utterly clueless Word users get used to the discrepancy within minutes. (Remember, we were once completely clueless too!) What newbies *can't* get used to is Word's odd behavior, the behavior that can only be explained by the presence of "invisible" tabs and paragraph marks!

We've been railing against the invisible paragraph mark for years.

NOTE   You have to be able to see paragraph marks in order to use Word. If you can't see paragraph marks, you're fooling yourself. It's really that simple. Paragraph marks contain most of the information used by Word to control fonts, formatting, tab stops, lines, boxes, shading, language proofing, styles, picture locations, widow/orphan gathering, line spacing, bullets, numbering, and much more.

The single greatest conceptual jump you'll have to make in order to master Word is the mental conquest of paragraph marks. And you can't work with them unless you can see them.

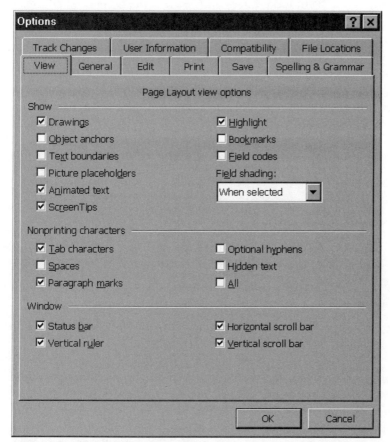

Figure 5-73: Always, always make tab characters and paragraph marks visible

To make tab characters and paragraphs marks both visible, click on Tools ► Options, and bring up the View tab. Under "Nonprinting characters," check the boxes next to Tab Characters and Paragraph Marks. Click OK. (See Figure 5-73.) This is the very first change many Word gurus make to any Word installation. We won't even look at a document unless Word's paragraph marks are showing.

Word's Hyperconundrum

Word is always looking over your shoulder as you type. Microsoft calls it IntelliSense™,* but we like to poke fun at the Redmondians and call much of it IntelliNONSense. IntelliSense is not new in Word 97, but it has been punched up a bit in this version. Its most notable addition by far is the new *hyperlinks* feature.

When you type a Web address (say, *http://www.oreilly.com*) or an email address (e.g., *woody@wopr.com*) in a document, Word automatically identifies what you've typed as a reference to the Net. Word then takes it upon itself to automatically convert the address into a hyperlink. (See Figure 5-74.) Once converted, anyone who clicks on the hyperlink will be transported (at least theoretically) to the Web address, or be invited to create a mail message to the indicated person. It's a great theory, but there are several problems.

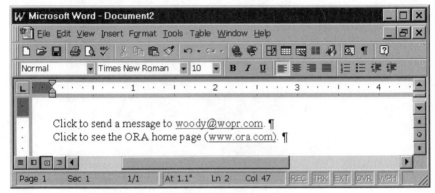

Figure 5-74: Automatically generated hyperlinks—what you see

Word shows hyperlinks on the screen with a garish blue-underlined emphasis. Looking at a document with many hyperlinks can be a painful experience. (If you use WordMail to read email in Outlook, some of the hyperlinks appear bold, blue, and underlined. Nothing like tasteful understatement, eh?) When you print documents with hyperlinks, even on a black and white printer, the underscores and bold come through and make the document virtually unreadable.

In spite of appearances, a hyperlink isn't the same thing as real text. Word creates a hyperlink by using something called a "hyperlink field," which you can see in Figure 5-74. Fields don't behave the same way as text. You can't backspace and correct typos inside a field—if you misspelled *woooody@wopr.com*, backspaced and deleted the extra "o"s, you'd end up with a hyperlink that still sent mail to *woooody@wopr.com*, in spite of how the hyperlink appears on-screen. (Don't believe it? Give it a shot!) Try to delete the first character in a hyperlink, and you'll end up

---

* Here's a little known fact: Microsoft claims a trademark on IntelliSense, and uses it rather liberally (even indiscriminately) for any Microsoft product feature that the marketing folks think is cool enough to sell more software. Whirlpool also claims a trademark for the term Intellisense™. In Whirlpool's case, the word refers to their washing machines' ability to determine how much water is in the tub. There's a metaphysical hyperlink lurking in there somewhere.

deleting the whole link. Also, it's incredibly hard to select a hyperlink with a mouse without triggering the link itself—try to copy a hyperlink, and you're likely to end up on the Web. Sooner or later.

Finally, the hyperlink IntelliSense program isn't very intelligent. It has a nasty habit of picking up extraneous flotsam along with the link. If you look closely at Figure 5-75, you'll see how the hyperlink identification program picked up a trailing right parenthesis along with the Web address. If you clicked on that hyperlink, your Web browser would go out looking for the address *www.ora.com)* and end up in a blind alley.

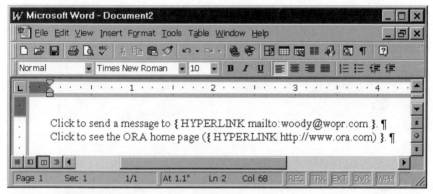

Figure 5-75: Automatically generated hyperlinks—what you really got

Get rid of the IntelliSense auto hyperlink annoyance by clicking Tools ➤ AutoCorrect, bringing up the AutoFormat As You Type tab, and clearing the box marked "Internet and network paths with hyperlinks." (See Figure 5-76.) Once it's turned off, if you really want to create a hyperlink, just click on the main toolbar's Insert Hyperlink icon, the one with a picture of the world and two chain links—we're debating whether it's really a stylized infinity symbol—at the bottom.

Even if you like the auto hyperlink IntelliSense and can put up with the bugs in Word's hyperlink identification program, you're probably very tired of those blue underscored links by now. Here's how to turn hyperlinks into something more legible. Note that this change will apply to any hyperlink you create in Word, either with the auto hyperlink identifier, or ones that you insert manually via the Insert Hyperlink icon on the main Toolbar. Follow these steps:

1. Click Format, Style.

2. In the List box on the lower-left, choose "All styles."

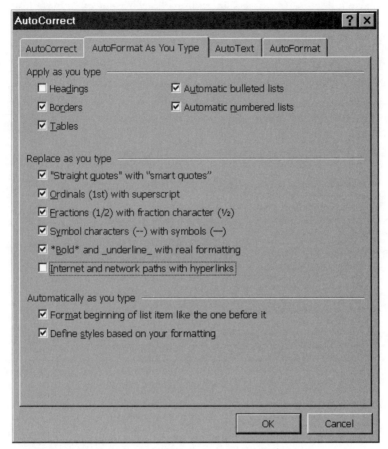

Figure 5-76: Turn the hyperlink annoyance off here

3. In the Styles box in the upper-left, click on Hyperlink. ("Hyperlink" is the name of the character style Word applies to all identified hyperlinks.)

4. Click Modify.

5. At the bottom of the Modify Style dialog, check the "Add to template" box. Then click Format, Font.

6. In the Font dialog, choose whatever font formatting you want to apply to identified hyperlinks. In this case, we chose no underline, in preppy Teal. (See Figure 5-77.)

7. Click OK all the way back out.

While you're at it, you might want to change the "Followed hyperlink" style as well. This controls the physical appearance of hyperlinks that have been clicked on—thus, "followed."

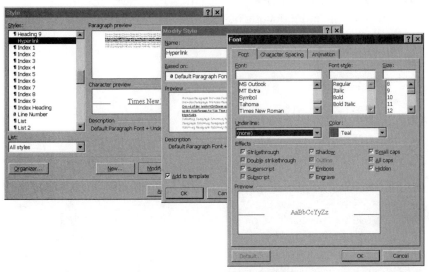

Figure 5-77: Cut the glare and change the Hyperlink style

People won't have a hard time identifying hyperlinks, even after they lose the blue, underlined formatting. They'll notice the slightly different color. Most of all, when the cursor approaches a hyperlink, it turns into a pointing finger, with the hyperlink destination appearing as a yellow ToolTip. And when you print the document, the hyperlinks won't stand out at all.

AutoText

Long the poor stepchild of AutoCorrect, AutoText has found new respectability in the latest version of Word. No doubt you've seen AutoText in action: you'll be typing along when a yellow ToolTip appears above the text you're typing, offering to complete a word, or in some cases an entire phrase. As soon as the ToolTip appears, if you hit the Enter key (or the Tab key, or the F3 function key), Word automatically fills in the phrase.

This is quite different from AutoCorrect: with AutoCorrect, the changes take place automatically, and there's nothing (short of yanking the Auto-Correct entry) you can do to stop it. AutoText, on the other hand, requires you to actively pick the word and hit Enter, Tab, or F3.

Some of the AutoText entries are pretty lame. Others, including the days of the week, can be helpful. And some of the entries are very nice. For example, if you start typing today's date, when you get past the month Word will offer to fill in the rest: type July on Independence Day, and the

ToolTip will read July 4, 1998, as Figure 5-78 shows. Hit Enter, and the full date appears in the document.

Figure 5-78: AutoText appears as a ToolTip

When Word installs itself, it picks up two AutoText settings that you may not want: the name and company name on the registration screen. You might find one or the other most annoying. For example, if you registered your software with the company name "Widgets Inc.," but company policy requires that you spell out "Widgets Incorporated" in your documents, you should probably get rid of the "Widgets Inc." entry, and add one for "Widgets Incorporated." Anyway, if any of the AutoText entries bug you, click on Insert ➤ AutoText, AutoText, click once on the entry you no longer want, and click Delete.

You can make an AutoText entry out of anything you can select (highlight) in a Word document. Just select the text, table, image, or whatever in your document, and then click Insert ➤ AutoText, AutoText. You'll see the AutoCorrect dialog box with the AutoText tab selected as shown in Figure 5-79.

Your selection appears in the Preview box. Type a name for your entry in the "Enter AutoText entries here" text box and click on the Add button. Simple.

Auto Bulleting and Numbering of Lists

One of Word's less successful implementations of IntelliSense occurs when the program, in its infinite wisdom, determines that you're typing in a numbered or bulleted list and attempts to help you construct it. Some people love the feature. Most advanced Word users detest it. After all, buttons for applying bullets and numbering sit on the Formatting Toolbar, and when you manually apply your own bullets and numbers, you don't have to suffer through Word second-guessing what you really meant.

There's a very long list of rules Word is supposed to use when autoformatting documents. You can see the official list by clicking Help ➤

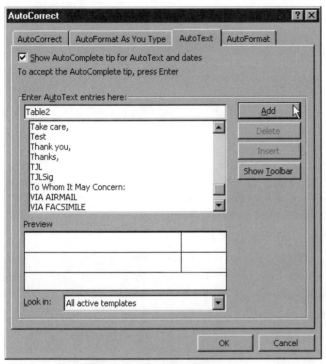

Figure 5-79: Setting up an AutoText entry

Contents and Index, bringing up the Find tab, typing AutoFormat, and clicking on the topic called "Learn about AutoFormat changes Word makes." Unfortunately, Word doesn't obey those rules very closely; worse, the rules Word actually uses are horribly convoluted. Try this little example:

1. Start with a new, clean document.

2. Type 1. (note the period), followed by some text. Hit Enter.

3. Word should kick in its autoformatting, indent the earlier paragraph and start the next paragraph with a 2. Good. Type some more text. Hit Enter twice.

4. You should now have a list with entries numbered 1 and 2, followed by two empty paragraphs. Type in some more text, lots of text if you like—you could even type a whole book at this point—and hit Enter.

5. Now type 4. and a word or two, then hit Enter.

See how Word behaves? It starts autoformatting again, *changing the 4 into a 3* in spite of what you typed, and kicks you back into autonumbered paragraphs one more time. (The same thing happens if you type a

2 instead of a 4, but the behavior is very different if you type a 1 or 5.) Apparently Word thinks you wanted to type a 3 even if there are dozens of intervening pages: it's correcting your obvious mistake. You might think of that as IntelliSense. Many people find it plain annoying whenever a computer thinks it's smarter than its operator, even when that's demonstrably not the case.

Worse, if you start a paragraph with a 1., then type some text, hit Enter and type some more, you can never go back and change the "1." If you subsequently decide that the old number 1 really should've been a 2, and that you need a number 1 at the beginning of the list, you're SOL* as far as the "automatic" part of autonumbering goes. You have to manually select the starting paragraph, Format ➤ Bullets and Numbering, click the Customize button, choose the desired starting value in the Start at spinner control, then click OK. Whew.

In spite of what you might read in the Word online Help, Autonumbering kicks in when you type a 0 or 1 followed by a period, hyphen, closing parenthesis, or greater-than sign, then either a space or a tab, and then some sort of text. It will also kick in if you type a number that is equal to, or one or two greater than, the number on the last autonumbered paragraph, followed by one of the punctuation marks, a space, or tab, and some text. (E.g., if the last autonumbered sequence stops at 6, and you type a 6., 7., or 8., followed by a space and some text, autonumbering will start in at 7.) If you don't follow one of these precise sequences, autonumbering doesn't take effect.

Similarly, autonumbering will start if you begin a paragraph with a I, A, a, or i, followed by the punctuation, a space, or tab, and text. Paragraphs will be numbered with Roman numerals or letters, as appropriate. Sequences that leave off and start again obey the same rules as with Arabic numerals.

Autonumbering not only places a number at the beginning of each paragraph, it inserts a tab and then formats the whole paragraph with a hanging indent, so the number appears to the left of all text. The size of the indent varies depending on what kind of list you're using and, oddly, on whether you type a space or a tab after the punctuation mark. In the U.S. English version of Word, lists with Arabic numerals or letters typed with a space lead to an indentation of 0.25 inches, but those typed with a tab lead to an indentation of 0.50 inches. Lists with Roman numerals always go out to 0.50 inches.

---

* Strictly Outta Luck. A technical term.

If you've ever wondered why your Arabic numeral-numbered lists don't line up with your Roman numeral-numbered lists, now you know.

Autobulleting behaves in a totally different way. Word kicks in autobullets when you type in one of the punctuation marks listed in Table 5-5, followed by a space or a tab, and then text.

Table 5-5: Autobulleting Bullets

"Auto" Punctuation	Resulting Bullet
*	●
-	▬
--	■
>	➤
->	➜
=>	⇨

Word also starts autobullets when you insert a symbol (from the Insert ➤ Symbol menu), follow the symbol by two or more spaces or a tab character, then type in some text. In this case, the Symbol becomes the bullet character.

What's wrong with autonumbering and autobulleting? Several things:

*   They're subject to some strange behavior—although admittedly the way Word works today is far, far superior to similar "features" in earlier versions of Word and competing products.

*   They're hard to undo if you don't catch the autoformatting immediately.

*   If you come to rely on them, they don't give a whole lot of flexibility. For example, how do you automatically start a list at the number 3

(without manually rooting your way around in the Bullets and Numbering dialog)?

- Many people object to computer programs making judgment decisions based on flimsy evidence—a point that describes autonumbering quite specifically.

- Mostly, though, all of the flexibility (and none of the hassles) already appear on the formatting Toolbar: the numbering, bulleting, indent, and "undent" buttons couldn't be simpler.

Why surrender your options to Word when you can do it just as easily, and much more accurately, by yourself? To keep Word from taking over this small part of your freedom, click on Tools ➤ AutoCorrect, then click on the Autoformat as You Type tab, and clear the "Automatic bulleted lists" and "Automatic numbered lists" boxes. You're free!

Prior Version Compatibility

If you have to exchange Word 97 files with users still running Word 95, you've discovered that the files are incompatible when going upstream (from Word 97 to Word 95).

No problem, you say? You just call up the Word 97 file, click on File ➤ Save As, select Word 6.0/95 (*.doc) in the Save as type drop-down list box, and you get a native Word 6.0/95 file (Word 6 and Word 95 shared a common file format), right?

Wrong. What you get under this scenario is an RTF file. Wait a minute, what about the Rich Text Format (*.rtf) Save as type? It gives you *exactly* the same result as the Word 6.0/95 (*.doc) setting: an RTF file, which you should be aware are humongous files. An RTF file is much larger than a binary Word file. Add a few embedded graphics and we're talking huge, bloated files.

If you don't want to exchange RTF files with your Word 95 users, you have two choices. First, you can pop over to the Microsoft Web site and download *wrd6ex32.exe* (*http://www.microsoft.com/Officefreestuff/word/dlpages/wrd6ex32.htm*). This installs a real Word 6.0/95 binary file converter in Word 97. And it's worth going through the trouble to get it installed. Consider the size of a single file, saved under each of the three file formats shown in Table 5-6.

Table 5-6: File Types and Sizes

File Name	File Type	File Size
OA Chapter 5.doc	Word 97	644KB
OA Chapter 5.doc	Word 6.0/95	11,190KB
OA Chapter 5.rtf	Rich Text Format	23,355KB

To accentuate the differences in file sizes, we chose a file that contains a number of embedded graphics (a data type that RTF admittedly does not handle very compactly). As you can see, the replacement converter helps by reducing the file size by just over 50%.

An alternative is to tackle the problem from the other end. You can install a converter (*Wrd97cnv.exe*) for the Word 6 or Word 95 program that needs to read native Word 97 files. This file is available on the Office 97 CD-ROM in the *\ValuPack\Wrd97cnv* folder. You can also download it from *http://www.microsoft.com/word/freestuff/converters/wrd97cnv.htm*, where you can also get a list of features in Word 97 that are not supported in the Word 6/95 version. This file installs *Msword8.cnv* or *Mswrd832.cnv* on your computer, depending on whether you're running a 16 or 32-bit version of Windows.

Our sample native Word 97 file, opened in Word 95 and resaved as a native Word 95 file, has a file size of 11,193KB. Therefore, there is almost no difference—a mere 3KB—in converted file size between (a) saving the file from Word 97 in the Word 6/95 format as opposed to (b) opening the native Word 97 file in Word 95 and saving it (assuming you have the latest converters installed on each end).

The most efficient way to exchange files is to deal with the "highest level" file format available to both correspondents. Obviously, this may not always be the Word 97 binary file format, but the converters are available to ease this pain somewhat. Don't forget when emailing files to do everyone on the distribution list a big favor and zip first.

The moral of this particular story is to get the latest converters for all versions of Word that you work with, and you'll have the most flexibility in exchanging files between the versions.

6

More Hard-Core Office

When application suites re-emerged as a real marketing force on the software landscape, they were little more than conglomerates of individual applications haphazardly tossed together, sharing only a single price tag and some shrink-wrap. Granted, as a whole the suite encompassed most application needs, but no one would have accused suite components of actually working together as a team. But more and more, a real effort is being made to integrate the individual pieces, and to provide common interfaces and utilities. Microsoft Office is the hands-down winner in this regard.

In this chapter we'll sojourn through the features that make Office greater than the sum of its individual parts.

Office Assistant Overt or Covert?

In Chapter 2, *Vital Changes and Settings*, we briefly discussed the "natural language" help system that ships with Office, and how you can modify some of its settings. The Office Assistant (code-named Robert, son of Bob) is the culmination of years of dabbling with artificial intelligence by software developers. (Anyone remember Hal, once the must-have add-on for Lotus 1-2-3?) The much ballyhooed but misfired "Bob" interface to Windows went nowhere, but Microsoft doesn't like to give up, so the Office Assistant was born.

The OA is pan-Office. Once fired up, it sits on your screen (consuming precious pixels) watching and waiting as you try to get your work done. You get nine different avatars or personalities with Office 97. Clippit, the paper clip; The Dot, a bouncy ball; The Genius, a claymation Einstein; the ubiquitous Office Logo; Mother Nature; Power Pup; Scribble, an origami cat; and Will, as in a cartoon Bard. If you can't find one of these that doesn't make you gag, then you can download new avatars from Microsoft's Web site. A nice quiet blank one—maybe just a tad smaller than a dime—would be nice, minus animation please. The animations are cute at first, but the blinking, winking, swooshing, boinnnng-ping gets old and annoying remarkably fast.

The OA window can be positioned anywhere you like and it jumps out of your way if it senses you are trying to work on the screen where it's situated. It "watches" what you are doing and if it thinks it has a worthwhile suggestion on how you can do something better or more efficiently, it displays a light bulb. Click on the light bulb and you'll get the tip. (See Figure 6-1.)

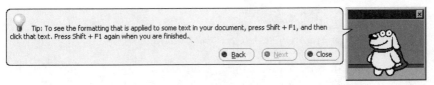

Figure 6-1: Standard size Office Assistant window with a better idea

If you ignore the OA long enough, it'll even reduce its size. Unfortunately, its only two sizes are too big and still too big. Compare the relative sizes of Figure 6-1 and Figure 6-2.

Figure 6-2: Ignore it and the Office Assistant gets about 56% smaller

But the big whoop-dee-doo over the OA is that you can ask it questions, and, to the best of its ability, it will try to find relevant help for you in the current application's help file. You start this process by clicking anywhere on the OA window. (See Figure 6-3.)

Still trying to anticipate your needs, you notice that the Power Pup has already displayed some help topics (again, based on the last operation you performed). You can type in a question and hit Enter or the Search

Figure 6-3: Ask and your Office Assistant will try to find

button. You can type a few words, a phrase, or an actual question. The OA parses your text and tries to match what you typed with the help index keywords using natural language algorithms.

The OA gets into the act in other ways as well. If you perform an operation that normally results in a message box displaying some information or prompting you to make a choice, the OA takes over that job. In Figure 6-4, for example, OA has preempted the message box that would ordinarily have been displayed by an unsuccessful search using Edit ➤ Find. Annoyingly, when it replaces a message box with only an OK button, in direct violation of all that is holy in contemporary user interface design, the OA omits the button. The first time it happens, you'll be surprised, if not flabbergasted. Yes, pressing Esc or clicking the balloon both dismiss the message box, but the missing button is totally inconsistent with traditional message box behavior.

Putting the cute factor aside for a moment, the underlying natural language engine, while getting better with each revision, still needs a considerable amount of work. If you don't enter the proper key words, it won't matter how lucid your query is, the OA will either come up empty-handed or provide topics that are completely off target. Furthermore, Office help behaves differently between various Office applications. As

Figure 6-4: Office Assistant performing the function of a message box

we touched on in "The Office Assistant" in Chapter 2, you can pose the same query in several of the Office applications; in one you may find exactly what you want, in another you get topics that have nothing to do with your question, and you may stump another one completely. It may tell you it does not know what you mean and to please rephrase your question, the OA equivalent of "Reply hazy . . . ask again later."

If you find all this annoying, you can avoid the OA and simply work with the traditional Contents and Index help option located on the Help menu of each Office application's menu bar. This gets you the familiar Help Topics dialog box with its Contents, Index, and Find tabs. Figure 6-5 shows the Index tab selected.

Using the index can often get you better results than asking the OA. You can add a button for this dialog to each application's Standard toolbar, right next to the OA button. Then if you can't get some help with one, you can try the other. (See Figure 6-6.)

The single most annoying, maddening, infuriating aspect of Office Assistant is its forgetfulness. This manifests itself in two ways. First, when you come back to it after selecting one of its suggested topics, it no longer displays the list of suggested topics. Try this:

1. In Word, click OA, ask it "hyperlink," and click Search.

2. You get a five-topic list plus the "see more" triangle. Now click the "Move around in a document" topic.

3. Either minimize the help window or Alt+Tab back to Word. *The five-topic list is gone*, even though the OA remembers your query ("hyperlink" is still displayed in the text box). The OA dialog box should provide a check box entitled "Preserve prior topic list," or even better, the OA should always remember and redisplay the prior topic list when you return to it.

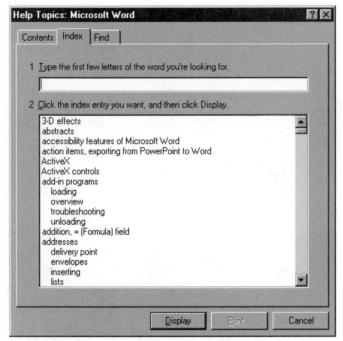

Figure 6-5: The traditional Help dialog

Figure 6-6: A choice of Help options

Second, the OA forgets all but your most recent query text when you shut down the application or Windows. But its predecessor, the Office 95 Answer Wizard, remembered your six most recent queries and stored them in a convenient combo box, even after you closed Office or Windows. Why the blasted Office 97 Office Assistant lacks this indispensable feature is beyond us.

Keep in mind that the OA is pan-Office. It provides help topics by looking at what application is current at the moment. So if you change the avatar in Word to Clippit, that's what you'll see in Excel. If you dismiss the OA window in PowerPoint, it's closed in all your Office applications. Start it in one Office application and there it is in all the others. This is really an annoyance, since you may want the OA always on in PowerPoint if you are just learning that program, but not want it on in another program with which you are competent. It would really be nice if some of the OA options were configurable on an application by application basis.

Binder Gets Better But . . .

Office Binder was introduced in Office 95, and it's really an interesting concept. Binder allows you to take a number of documents and roll them all into a single binary file. This makes transporting a group of related files much easier than tracking each file separately. The magic that makes this work is the ability of Binder to manipulate each file as an OLE object or, more specifically, an OLE document stream.

When you work with Binder in Office, you simply work on each document contained within a particular binder as though you were working with the individual document. In the example in Figure 6-7, a Word document, a PowerPoint presentation, and an Excel workbook have been bound into a single binder file, *Spiff Project.odb*. In Figure 6-7, the Word document is active, and in the right pane of Binder, you see the document and the familiar Word command bars. Basically, you have Word running within Binder, complete with any custom menus, toolbars, macros, etc., and you can work on the document just as if you were in Word. Ditto for Excel and PowerPoint.

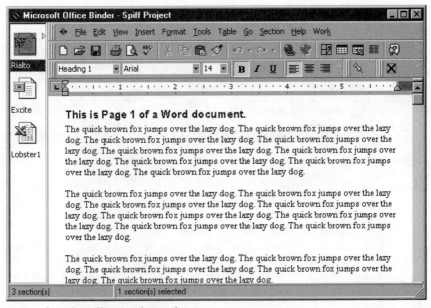

Figure 6-7: The Office Binder application

However, this ability comes at a price. In our example, we have bound files from Word, PowerPoint, and Excel; activate each one in turn and you'll have hidden copies of Word, PowerPoint, and Excel running on your system, eating up system resources just as if the applications were running and visible. Once activated, they stay loaded in memory until you close any running instances of Binder that originally invoked these Office applications. (Unlike Excel, PowerPoint, and Word, Binder can only manage one file at a time, meaning that if you want to have two binders open simultaneously, each one runs its own copy of *Binder.exe*.) The good news is that if you run multiple copies of Binder, they share the hidden copies of the underlying applications.

Melded with the encapsulated copy of the primary application for the active section, two additional menus appear: Go and Section. These and several of the options on the other menus are now specific to Binder. Clicking on the Save button on the toolbar, for example, saves the entire binder, not just the section you are working on.

Each file in a binder is called a *section*. You can add a new section via Section ➤ Add, which then creates a new document—i.e., a Word, Power-Point, or Excel document—as a section within the binder file. And Word, PowerPoint, and Excel cover all the section types you can have in a binder. No Access, no Outlook data.

More often, we find ourselves adding existing files to a binder. To do this select "Add from File" from the Section menu. (See Figure 6-8.)

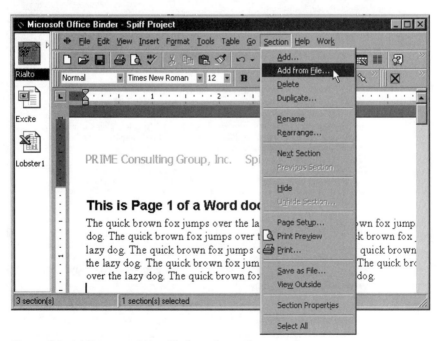

Figure 6-8: Adding an existing file from the section menu

Clicking on "Add from File" gets you the standard, common Open dialog box—here in a binder it's entitled Add from File—and you can pick the extant file to be added to the binder. Now this can be tricky. When you Add from File, you are actually adding a *copy* of the file you select to the binder binary file. The original file is still sitting right where you left it, and will not reflect any changes you make to its copy in the binder. This can cause confusion and annoyance if you or someone else makes changes to the unbound version when they intended to be working with the version in the binder, or if you expect that the two versions should remain in synch.

NOTE   Here's a good rule to follow when adding a file to a bind-
            er: once you've added a file to a binder, you should delete
            the standalone version, move it to a floppy, or otherwise
            archive and remove it from general circulation.

Because the Office file you add to a binder remains as a separate file, some users have erroneously assumed that the data in the standalone file is dynamically linked to the binder section. This is not the case. There is no connection between the unbound file and the section within the binder—we repeat, *changes in one are not reflected in the other.*

Binder has improved a lot from Office 95, where it was a 1.0 release. You can now split panes with the mouse within the Right Pane (that's the clever name Microsoft has given to the area of Binder that displays your individual documents) in the same way that you'd split a pane within Word or Excel. But since the Window menu is removed from each of the individual applications within Binder, you can't freeze panes in Excel, or unfreeze them if you add a section that already has frozen panes. Also, you lose the handy Split and Remove Split menu commands. While you can use the mouse for this, it's still annoying to lose the menu options.

The File Open buttons on the Word and Excel toolbars now are functional (they had some problems in the previous version). You can create templates with sections of the file types you want. And you can now display the entire filename in the Left Pane when you mouse over a section icon (see Figure 6-9). The names don't wrap in the pane but are fully displayed.

Binder-wide headers and footers still need work. You can really bollix up page numbering if you print or print preview any sheet other than Sheet1 (the first sheet in the workbook) in an Excel section. If this happens to you, look up the MS Knowledge Base article Q163679. Sporadically, we

Figure 6-9: Displaying long filenames in the Left Pane

have experienced problems with page numbering on files added to a binder where the headers and footers were already set up within the individual document.

Here's a real slap in the face: Unbelievable as it may seem, there's still no MRU in Binder, a feature that is quite annoying in its absence. Plan on keeping all your binders in a central location if you don't want to spend a lot of time searching for the binder files you just were working with.

Office 97 binders are not backward compatible with Office 95. To share files in a binder with someone running a previous version of Office, you have to unbind the binder and give them the individual files. Just select the binder in Explorer, right-click on it, and choose the Unbind option from the pop-up menu.

But by far the most annoying aspect of Binder is that it's just not stable enough for constant use. It's prone to GPFs, and you can't do a shutdown in Windows 95 with a binder open (Windows displays a message box telling you to close any binders first). We hope Microsoft keeps working on the concept and rounds off some of the rough corners that plague Binder.

IntelliSense at Every Click and Press

The basic idea behind what has become a buzzword at Microsoft, *IntelliSense*, had a very humble beginning. Back in Word 2 there was a feature called the Glossary. You could type in some keystrokes, save them as a "glossary" entry with a specific name, and later type the name and press F3 and those keystrokes were dropped in the current document. The Glossary feature evolved into the current AutoText feature in Word 97. Then somewhere along the way some bright Microserf had an epiphany. Why wait for the user to overtly do something before changing something in the document? The user presses the spacebar after every word typed in a document. Why not check what the user just typed every time the spacebar key is pressed and determine if something should be done? So AutoCorrect in Word was born and that begot the concept of IntelliSense.

An awful lot of IntelliSense is annoying IntelliNonSense. As good as the various applications are at guessing what you want, it really gets annoying when they start changing information you enter when you'd rather just have your entries be accepted at face value. Fortunately most IntelliSense features can be turned off, ignored, or tweaked to suit your needs.

IntelliSense in Word

Every time you press trigger keys on your keyboard, like the spacebar, Word checks what you just typed against a list of pieces of text that it maintains. Pull down the Tools menu and click on AutoCorrect to see this list. In the AutoCorrect tab you'll see a two-column list box. (See Figure 6-10.) Word checks the first column to see if this is what you just typed. If it finds an exact match, it replaces the text you typed with what is in the second column. It's automatic and nearly instantaneous. This is how Word corrects common typos and spelling mistakes on the fly and replaces (c) with © as if by magic.

Note that Word AutoCorrect lets you control the TWo INitial CApitals, first letter of sentences, and names of the days of the week. It'll even watch to see if you are banging away with the cAPS LOCK key on and, if you are typing lower case where usually things should be uppercase and vice versa, Word will reverse things for you.

The key setting is the last check box, "Replace text as you type." Unchecking this box lets you turn off the "if you see this when the user presses the spacebar, replace it with this" feature of AutoCorrect.

NOTE   The hot tip for AutoCorrect is if it kicks in where it shouldn't—say you want an open parenthesis, letter c, close parenthesis and you don't want AutoCorrect to switch that to a copyright symbol—just type, hit the space-bar (AutoCorrect will change what you typed into the copy-right symbol), then hit Ctrl+Z (undo) to nullify the effect of AutoCorrect.

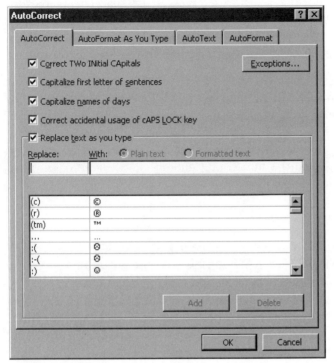

Figure 6-10: AutoCorrect - IntelliSense

Word has a number of other IntelliSense features such as AutoFormat As You Type (see Figure 6-11). Type an asterisk, a space or tab, and some text and then hit Enter. Bingo! A bulleted list is started. Type a plus sign, one hyphen, a plus sign, one hyphen, and a plus sign; hit Enter and you have an instant two-column table. The more hyphens you type, the wider the columns. (We're not sure how useful that particular feature is though.)

Word guesses and creates headings and borders, will replace straight quotes " " with smart quotes " " (what everyone else calls publisher's quotes), and handles ordinals and fractions. Type a word with a leading and following *asterisk* and it becomes **bold**, use _underline_ to get *italic*; create automatic hyperlinks; and control list items and styles. A whole lotta autoformatting goin' on!

The AutoFormat tab is almost identical to the AutoFormat As You Type tab, the difference being the "As You Type" qualifier. The AutoFormat As You Type does just that, changes things as you type. The AutoFormat tab controls what happens when you manually run the AutoFormat option from the Format menu.

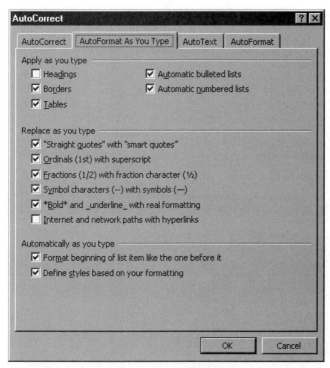

Figure 6-11: AutoFormat the IntelliSense way

Word has extended the IntelliSense concept to spell checking and even grammar checking. On the Tools ➤ Options ➤ Spelling and Grammar tab you can tweak the IntelliSense features for spelling and grammar. (See Figure 6-12.)

With the "Check spelling as you type" box checked, potential spelling errors appear in your document with a squiggly red line under the suspect word. A quick right-click with the mouse and some suggested alternatives appear. Select the "Check grammar as you type" check box and grammatically suspect sentences and phrases get a green squiggly. A right-click on the squiggles will get you some suggestions on correcting your grammar. While the grammar checker is not as slick as the spell checker, it's another long step in the right direction.

IntelliSense in Excel

Excel has some interesting new IntelliSense features. The same basic Auto-Correct feature set you enjoy in Word is now available in Excel; in fact, in all the Office applications save Outlook. Tools ➤ AutoCorrect in Excel displays the AutoCorrect dialog box. (See Figure 6-13.)

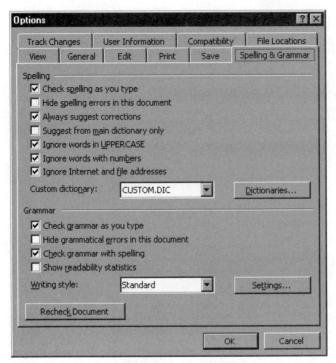

Figure 6-12: Spelling and Grammar IntelliSense

NOTE   The default AutoCorrect entries that come with Office are
           stored in *MSO97.ACL,* while any custom entries you create
           are kept in **username.ACL.** Both files can be found in the
           C:\Windows folder.

Excel also boasts some unique IntelliSense features. Formula AutoCorrect will fix 15 of the most common mistakes made when entering formulas into a cell. Transposed cell references, two equal signs starting a formula, or a semicolon where a colon is required, a missing closing parenthesis, and other common typos all are corrected automatically.

Another IntelliSense feature in Excel is AutoComplete. This is a big time-saver and has the added benefit of letting you use it or ignore it with very little effort. Excel watches what you type in a column of data and if it detects that you're entering a label that you've previously entered in the same column, it offers to complete the entry for you. (See Figure 6-14.) As soon as Excel has enough unique characters to guess what you might want, it completes the cell entry. In Figure 6-14, as soon as the N in National was typed, Excel guessed we were typing City National Bank

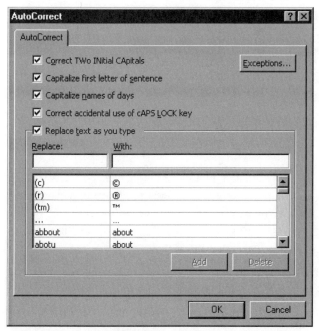

Figure 6-13: AutoCorrect in Excel

and filled in all the characters shown in black. You have the option of hitting Enter and using the offered entry to complete your label, or you can just keep typing whatever you want.

9	Num	Date	Payee
143	5778	6/30/97	City National Bank
144	5779	6/30/97	City Advertising
145	5780	6/30/97	City Bank
146	5780	6/30/97	City National Bank
147			

Figure 6-14: Excel's AutoComplete

IntelliSense in PowerPoint

PowerPoint, in addition to the AutoCorrect feature you've seen in Word and Excel, has the unique AutoClipArt feature. While it doesn't presume to start changing things automatically, AutoClipArt goes a long way towards helping the casual presentation creator. Create a presentation and click on Tools ➤ AutoClipArt. If any of the text in your presentation matches keywords that AutoClipArt recognizes, you'll see the AutoClipArt dialog. (See Figure 6-15.)

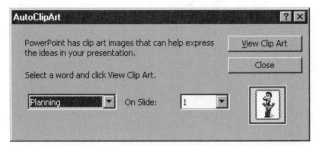

Figure 6-15: IntelliSense in PowerPoint—multimedia help with slides

The drop-down list box on the left in Figure 6-15 gives you a list of all the words in your presentation for which PowerPoint wants to suggest a matching piece of clipart, picture, video clip, or sound file, all in the interest of punching up your presentation. The list box to the right shows you on which slide or slides that keyword appears.

On the Tools ➤ Options ➤ Edit tab you can tweak some of the "edit while you type" features like smart quotes (which we talked about in the previous section), whether entire words are automatically selected when editing, and smart cut-and-paste that controls how spaces are added or removed when cutting and pasting text into your slide. (See Figure 6-16.)

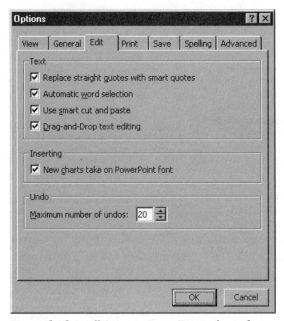

Figure 6-16: IntelliSense in PowerPoint—basic features

IntelliSense in Access

Access enjoys the basic AutoCorrect feature that is common to all Office applications, but due to the nature of a database development environment, you don't find the same types of IntelliSense in the Access user interface that you find in its Office siblings.

There are some spiffy control Wizards in Access that pop up when you create new controls of various types (and assuming the Control Wizard button on the toolbox is depressed). There are also a number of VBA IntelliSense features in Access/VBA. Access offers to complete typing a language element for you (or makes a suggestion of possibilities for completing it). These are great features but are more geared to the developer. For example, type "DoCmd" in a code module, and Access pops up a list of the available methods of the DoCmd object. (See Figure 6-17.)

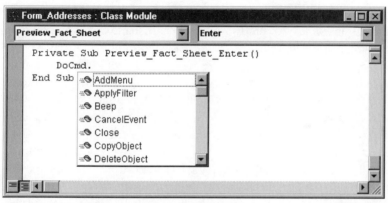

Figure 6-17: IntelliSense in Access code module

IntelliSense in Outlook

While it lacks many of the IntelliSense features found in its Office siblings, Outlook does have one very cool IntelliSense feature that helps make your life easier. When you enter Contact item information, you can type in someone's entire name. For example, type in James T. Kirk, and Outlook will automatically parse the name into FirstName, LastName, and MiddleInitial and store them in the appropriate fields. Ditto for the Contact's address: you type the entire address in a single textbox control, and the Street, City, State, and zip are all broken out and placed in the appropriate individual fields.

Outlook also recognizes English terms when it comes to dates. Type "next Tuesday" and you'll get the correct calendar date. "A week from tomorrow," "yesterday," "next month," etc., all are recognized and translated instantly to their equivalent calendar dates using the current date as "today."

When entering an address in an outgoing email message, you can type in a few characters and press `Ctrl+K`, and Outlook will match and complete the address for you from the Contact list or address books in the current profile.

Wheelin' It with IntelliMouse

The IntelliMouse is bundled with several flavors of Microsoft Office as well as being available as a separate product. So while not an actual part of the Office Suite, the Office applications do provide specific support for it, and chances are fair to good that if you don't already have one, there's probably one in your future.

Okay, when it comes to hardware—especially hardware we come in close personal contact with for 12, 16, or more hours a day—we're awfully opinionated. As far as we're concerned, with one exception, Microsoft's forays into hardware have been uniformly disastrous, stretching back almost a decade. We hate the "natural" keyboard. But we've always loved Microsoft's old dove bar mouse. It just feels "right"— and none of the hundred-plus competitors we've tried has weaned us away from the plain little beast. Until Magellan, er, IntelliMouse, uh, IntelliPoint. (All right, the official terminology is IntelliMouse for the device itself and IntelliPoint for the software controlling the mouse. Official or not, we'll use IntelliMouse to refer to the whole enchilada throughout this section.)

The IntelliMouse looks just like the old dove bar mouse, except it has a wheel between the left and right buttons. When you roll the wheel "up" (generally with your middle finger), the Office "document" scrolls up. By document, we mean Word documents, Excel spreadsheets, PowerPoint presentations, all the scrollable windows in the various Office applications. Roll it down and the document scrolls down. But you can also click the wheel itself—and once it's been clicked, simply moving the mouse up and down controls the scrolling. The sensitivity has been finely calibrated (and can be adjusted): move the wheel or the mouse slowly and you scroll slowly; move it quickly and you jump across documents at lightning speed. It takes a while to "train" your fingers to use the wheel, but once you've realigned your synapses, you'll wonder how you ever lived without it.

Windows applications have to be written specifically to use the mouse; in addition to the Office 97 applications you'll find Win95's Explorer, Help, and Internet Explorer 3 all use it. (The fact that not all applications use it will make training your fingers all the more difficult.) Aside from the IntelliMouse wheel-scroll-zoom feature set (clearly its main draw), there are lots of bells and whistles that you'll definitely want to explore while calibrating the IntelliMouse to your liking. Of the features shown in Figure 6-18, two are our favorites:

- The Focus feature, that provides a clickless way to change the focus between title bars, icons, folders, menus, and dialog boxes. Just move your mouse pointer over the object, and it pops into focus automatically.

- The SnapTo feature. The IntelliPoint software looks at dialog and message boxes and tries to figure out which button is the default (meaning, the button that has the focus when the dialog is initially opened). For example, with SnapTo active, if you right-click a file in Explorer and choose Delete, the mouse pointer will land dead-center on the Yes button before you can say "Truth by the gleaming merciless truckload." It takes some getting used to, and occasionally the pointer ends up somewhere you don't expect it, particularly if you switch back and forth between a primary PC that has IntelliMouse on it and others that don't. There's a trick to reducing the unexpectedness of the pointer's SnapTo behavior. If IntelliPoint can't figure out what button is the default, it jumps to the physical center of the dialog box; however, you can set the pointer to instead simply stay put. Here's how (you'll be editing your Registry so proceed very carefully):

1. To edit the Registry select Start ➤ Run ➤ regedit ➤ OK.

2. Locate the key `HKEY_CURRENT_USER\Control Panel\ Microsoft Input Devices\Mouse`.

3. Change the setting of the `SnapToCenterOfWindow` value from ON to OFF.

4. Exit the Registry Editor.

5. Restart your PC and the change will be enforced.

Here are our favorite Office features that coordinate with IntelliMouse:

- Pan. Click the wheel button once anywhere inside a document's display space. This displays what the IntelliPoint literature calls the "origin mark" cursor. Now move the mouse pointer (it's a uni-directional pointer shaped like a triangular arrow with a round dot at its base) down to pan down, right to pan right, and so on. The panning speed

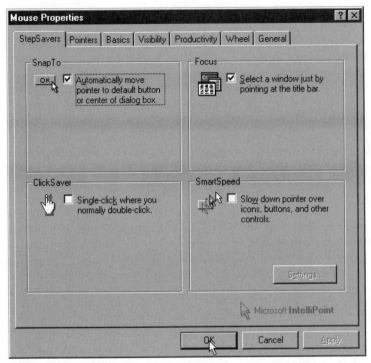

*Figure 6-18: The top-most tab in the IntelliPoint Mouse Properties dialog box
(notice the mouse pointer centered perfectly on the OK button)*

changes in direct proportion to how far away from the origin mark you move the mouse. Click any mouse button or the wheel to turn panning off. (Access and Excel support horizontal panning; Outlook, PowerPoint, and Word don't.)

- Zoom. In Excel simply press and hold Ctrl and move the wheel down to zoom out, and up to zoom in (each wheel click is 15%); annoyingly, the IntelliMouse only zooms up to 100%, whereas Excel itself zooms up to 400%, so for over 100% you'll have to use the Zoom control on the Standard toolbar (Excel's zoom range is 10% to 400%). No such problem elsewhere—in PowerPoint, the IntelliMouse can zoom you through the program's full range of 10-400%; ditto in Word where, the full range is 10-500%.

There are other IntelliMouse features you can explore on your own; just ask the Office Assistant "intellimouse" from inside the application you're interested in. For example, Outlook supports the IntelliMouse in several ways, depending on which facility you are using, and each is listed in the help file. Word supports AutoScroll (which starts your document scrolling up your display), and you can expand or collapse headings in Word or PowerPoint.

Office Art

Office Art is an evolutionary step in Microsoft's goal to give Word, Excel, and PowerPoint a uniform set of drawing tools (and mine the market carved out by the folks at Visio in the process).

Even if you're only an occasional user of the drawing capabilities in your Office applications, you'll find that Office Art levels the graphics playing field across most of the Office Suite. Earlier versions of the Office applications implemented different drawing features, whereas Office Art enables you to take advantage of the "learn it once" approach. Office Art (code name Escher) is a stunning collection of drawing tools that is—more or less—common to three members of the Office 97 family: Excel, Power-Point, and Word. Access and Outlook are different animals when it comes to creating a picture or doodle, although as we'll touch on later, you can actually get an Office Art object into either application by using Insert ➤ Object. These two Office siblings just don't have a native Office Art interface.

Office Art allows you to do the following:

- Choose from a large number of predrawn shapes (called AutoShapes,* of course) organized into various categories

- Draw Bezier curves (a curve is an AutoShape)

- Choose from a set of predefined smart connectors (a connector is an AutoShape specifically designed to intelligently connect two shapes, like an arrow-style connector between two sequential steps, A and B, in a flow chart)

- Add text and hyperlinks to drawing objects

- Position, align, and distribute drawing objects

- Group and ungroup drawing objects

- Apply shadow effects

- Apply 3-D effects

- Apply sophisticated shading, fill, texture, and transparency effects

We could write a book about the subtleties and permutations of Office Art, but instead we'll cover the highlights, have some fun, then leave it to you to fiddle and play to your heart's content.

---

* We'll often use "drawing object" as a synonym for the term AutoShape.

NOTE   You'll find that many of the Drawing toolbar commands
               are tear off submenus and can be quite useful in their float-
               ing state. For example, the AutoShapes submenu itself is
               nice to have floating when you're working with multiple
               shapes (as in a flowchart or process diagram). Another of
               our favorites is the Draw ➤ Nudge submenu for precisely
               aligning individual (or multiple-selected) objects once
               drawn.

AutoShapes are the Foundation

First things first. Office Art's communications, command, and control
center is the Drawing toolbar (see Figure 6-19), which is identical in
PowerPoint, Excel, and Word, with one notable exception—Word does
not support the use of connectors, one of the AutoShapes available from
the AutoShapes submenu. We'll discuss Word's shortcoming in this regard
and show you how to work around it shortly.

Figure 6-19: The Drawing toolbar, Office Art's central node

Table 6-1 lists the predefined AutoShape categories supported by the
three drawing-enabled components of the Office suite.

*Table 6-1: The AutoShapes Submenu and Accompanying Sub-Submenus (Shown
Here Floating)*

Category	Submenu
AutoShapes	Lines ▸ / Connectors ▸ / Basic Shapes ▸ / Block Arrows ▸ / Flowchart ▸ / Stars and Banners ▸ / Callouts ▸
Lines	Lines

Table 6-1: The AutoShapes Submenu and Accompanying Sub-Submenus (Shown Here Floating) (continued)

Category	Submenu
Connectors[1]	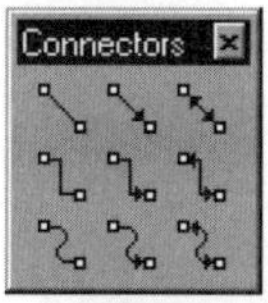
Basic Shapes	
Block Arrows	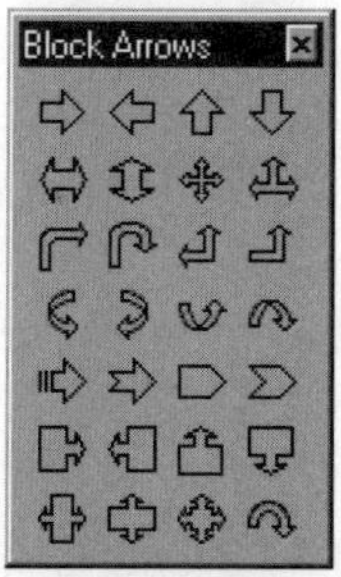
Flowchart	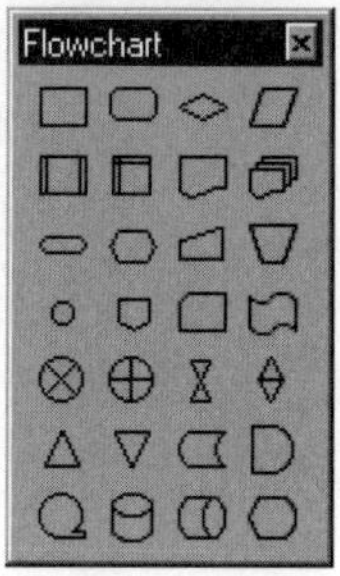

Table 6-1: The AutoShapes Submenu and Accompanying Sub-Submenus (Shown Here Floating) (continued)

Category	Submenu
Stars and Banners	
Callouts	

---

[1] Word does not support Connectors; you have to simulate them by using lines or arrows to connect your shapes or use the MS Draw 97 OLE Object to work around the problem.

AutoShapes Step by Step

Let's work our way through the various key capabilities of Office Art by adding a plain-vanilla Rectangle object (it may seem boring at first, but this simple shape lends itself to lots of playful 3-D effects, so bear with us). Use either PowerPoint or Excel for this exercise so you can work with connectors:

1. Turn on the Drawing toolbar if you haven't already—View ➤ Toolbars ➤ Drawing.

2. Click the Draw button, choose Snap, and make sure the submenu's To Grid option is selected (the button will look depressed). This forces your drawn objects to use PowerPoint's or Excel's underlying cell grid to position the AutoShapes.

3. Click the AutoShapes menu button, choose Basic Shapes, choose the Rectangle object (upper-left corner), left-click where you want the AutoShape's upper-left corner to go, then drag to the appropriate size and release the mouse. (Alternately, since Rectangle is a commonly used shape, it's already on the Drawing toolbar as an independent button just to the right of the arrow button.)

4. Your rectangle is now selected (it's framed by eight sizing handles). To see what formatting actions you can apply to it right now, right-click it and choose Format AutoShape to display the Format AutoShape dialog box. We leave it to you to explore the dialog box's

four property sheets: Colors and Lines, Size, Protection, and Properties (see Figure 6-20, which in this example shows the Format
AutoShape dialog from Excel.) (Note: different applications will
display different panels depending on the types of formatting options
they support.) For the time being, look but don't touch, and let's
click Cancel to dismiss the dialog box.

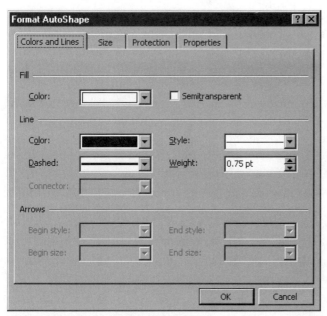

Figure 6-20: The Format AutoShape dialog box for a no-text AutoShape

To move an AutoShape, left-click and drag it to its new destination. To
resize it, select it (one left-click anywhere on the shape will do nicely),
then drag any of its sizing handles in the appropriate direction. More
complex AutoShapes may have one or more special sizing handles—
they're yellow and diamond-shaped (we call 'em tilt handles)—that allow
you to tilt the shape in a particular dimension. For a quick example,
insert a Can shape (AutoShapes ➤ Basic Shapes, select the shape in the
first column, fourth row). Drag the tilt handle down to give the can a
more down-angled appearance. (The trick here is to precisely touch the
tilt handle until you see the mouse pointer change to a tail-less traditional
pointer, then start tilting.)

Yes, Office Art provides all the rotate and flip operations you'd expect, including free rotation. For precise movements, you can use the Nudge submenu (Draw ➤ Nudge). Here are a couple of tips:

- Nudge operations will not move the object beyond the borders of the sheet's current display area (window); instead you have to manually scroll the display, then Nudge some more. Bug or feature? We're ambivalent, so send us your opinions on this.

- If Snap To Grid is on, then all movements are in grid increments (for example, in Excel, in one-cell increments), your keyboard arrow keys produce matching Nudge operations (grid increments), and Ctrl+arrow keys produce micro-Nudges (one-pixel increments). If neither Snap to Grid nor Snap to Shapes is on, then all movements are in one-pixel increments. In PowerPoint, with Snap to Grid on, you get approximately 0.1" grid increments (the default setting); same for the Nudge command. With Snap turned off you get approximately 0.02". We say approximately because with Snap on we've seen 0.1" then 0.09", then 0.08", all resulting from a series of movements both with the mouse and the Nudge command. Not what you'd call precise, but exactly what you'd call annoying. If you need precision, then right-click on the AutoShape, choose Format AutoShape to display the Format AutoShape dialog, and from the Position tab type in exact coordinates. This lack of precision applies to Word as well.

Word actually lets you set the grid increments. Don't you wish each application would work the same way? Hey, that's your incentive to upgrade! Ah, but we digress. You can set the grid increments in Word by clicking on the Draw button on the Drawing toolbar, then on Grid. In Figure 6-21 we've set the horizontal increment to one-half inch.

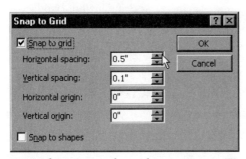

Figure 6-21: Setting the grid increments in Word

- Annoyingly, you can't press and hold any Nudge button and have it auto-repeat, but you can get the auto-repeat effect by using your arrow keys.

Watch out for this annoying pothole: Snap settings are not persistent across application sessions. If you have Snap to Grid set on, close Power-Point or Excel, then restart it, all Snap settings (to Grid and to Shapes) will be turned off. Since Word has no grid, the issue is moot with that particular Office application.

Adding Text and a Hyperlink to an AutoShape

Here's an annoyingly misleading quotation from the *Office 97 Resource Kit*, "Text can be added to any object without creating an additional text box, and any drawing object can have a hyperlink associated with it." We're here to tell you they just didn't properly qualify that statement. You can add text to any AutoShape *except* lines, connectors, and freeforms. For these three shape types, you'll have to hack it by adding a text box next to the shape in question.

Follow these steps to add text to your rectangle shape:

1. Right-click the shape and choose Add Text. The AutoShape is now hatch-bordered and you've got a flashing text cursor inside it, as shown in Figure 6-22. Type in your text. When you're done with your text simply press Esc. Note that the text can extend beyond the boundaries of the AutoShape object. In PowerPoint, you have to set the Text Box properties to wrap the text. (To do this, right click inside the AutoShape, select Format AutoShape, select the Text Box tab, then check the "Word wrap text in AutoShape" box.) In Excel and Word, the text wraps by default.

Figure 6-22: Adding text to an AutoShape

2. You can format the text by right-clicking the AutoShape's border then choosing Format AutoShape. (You'll know you missed clicking the

border and that you're still in text-editing mode if the pop-up menu includes the command Exit Edit Text, in which case choose this command and click carefully on the AutoShape's border.) And formatting is where the feature sets diverge most sharply between the three applications (Excel, Word, and PowerPoint). More on this in a moment. The Format AutoShape dialog box in Excel now includes three new file tabs (relative to its flavor when no text had been added to the shape): Font, Alignment, and Margins. (See Figure 6-23.) You can still selectively format smaller ranges of text within the AutoShape; just select the text, right-click on the selection, choose Format AutoShape, and now you'll see only one tab visible—Font.

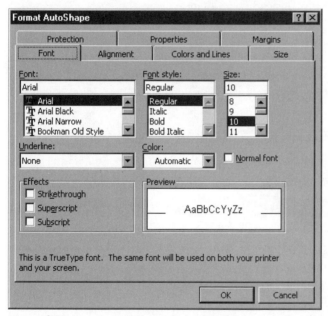

Figure 6-23: Format AutoShape dialog box for an AutoShape with text in Excel

In Word and PowerPoint, you select the text in the AutoShape object and just use the Format ➤ Font commands as you normally would in either of those applications. Neither Word nor PowerPoint bother with the disappearing/re-appearing dialog box tabs—the tabs not applicable in a given context are grayed out, as the PowerPoint Format AutoShape dialog in Figure 6-24 shows. There are some additional differences between the Word and PowerPoint dialogs as well, but they simply address the requirements of working within a particular application and are not all that annoying.

Here's how to add a hyperlink to an AutoShape (we'll apply the hyperlink to a new Oval AutoShape):

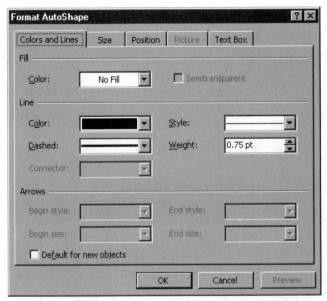

Figure 6-24: Format AutoShape dialog box for an AutoShape with text in PowerPoint

1. Insert an Oval AutoShape to the right of your rectangle, then add some text to it (we used "Visit http://www.ora.com").

2. Exit text-edit mode and, with only this one shape selected, click the Insert Hyperlink button on the application's Standard toolbar. Now type in the desired URL into the "Link to file or URL" edit box and click OK. Note that the shape will appear to not have changed, *but it has*. Prove this to yourself by right-clicking on it while it's still selected; notice the addition of the Hyperlink option at the bottom of the menu. (See Figure 6-25.)

Once an AutoShape with a hyperlink has been unselected, if you later want to edit the AutoShape in any way, you'll be faced with the conundrum of selecting it without triggering the hyperlink in Word or Excel (in PowerPoint the link is only active in Slide Show view). Here's how: *without clicking yet*, touch your mouse pointer to the shape until it turns into a Pointing Index Finger™, press and hold Ctrl (the pointer turns into a traditional mouse pointer with a plus sign affixed to it), then left-click to select the shape. Now you can right-click the shape without going off on a wild Web hunt.

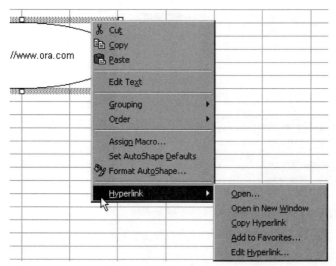

Figure 6-25: The pop-up menu for an AutoShape that includes a hyperlink, showing the Hyperlink submenu

Additional AutoShape Formatting Options

Even more AutoShape formatting options sing their siren song, hoping to lure you from your busy work day. (Warning: Office Art fiddling is highly addictive; the Surgeon General advises no more than 30 minutes of exposure per day!)

For example, exploring the Fill Effects dialog box has so much to offer (select an AutoShape, click the Fill Color downward arrow on the Drawing toolbar, then click Fill Effects), you'd better pack some lunch and water for a thorough trek here. See Figure 6-26 for a taste of the plethora of effects you can generate by tweaking gradients, textures, and patterns; and hey, you can even stuff a picture inside an AutoShape (in this example we chose a color—Sky Blue—and opted for the "One color" Colors option and the "From center" Shading styles option).

For shadow effects, click the Drawing toolbar's Shadow button, choose a shadow to your liking, click Shadow again and this time choose Shadow Settings to display a floating Shadow Settings toolbar.

Finally, for 3-D effects, you'll want to click the 3-D button on the Drawing toolbar and choose the 3-D Settings command. This tears off a floating 3-D Settings toolbar, and we guarantee you'll want to check out each of its ten commands. Especially cool are the Depth, Direction, Lighting, and Surface settings. (See Figure 6-27.) Go for it, and don't forget your spelunking helmet and a spare battery pack!

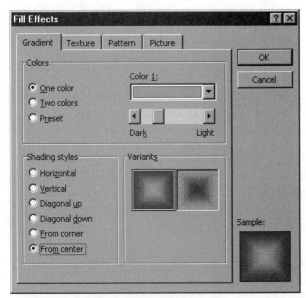

Figure 6-26: Fill Effects dialog box in a classy "From center" shading style

Figure 6-27: 3-D Settings tear off menu with its Lighting submenu displayed

Connector Coolness

Let's say you've created a rectangle and an oval in Excel and want to connect these shapes. Here's how you can do so:

1. Click AutoShapes, choose Connectors, then choose from among the nine available connectors. For our purposes, choose Curved Arrow Connector (you'll see why in a moment).

2. Touch the rectangle shape with the connector cross-hair (looks more like a HUD gun-sight, actually) and each of the shape's edges lights up with a small blue dot in the center of each edge. Land on the right edge's connector marker, drag over to the left-most connector

marker of the oval shape, land on it, then release the mouse button. So far so good: you see a right-pointing arrow connecting the two shapes.

3. Now the connecto-fun begins. Select and move the oval shape down six rows (remember, Snap to Grid should be on). Release the shape and the connector is nicely curved, as shown in Figure 6-28. Select it (the connector) and notice it's got a tilt handle. Drag the tilt handle about two column widths to the right and watch the connector bow out. Neat!

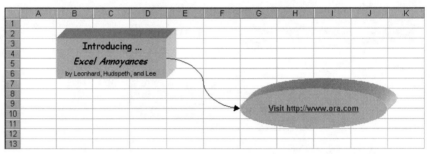

Figure 6-28: Two AutoShapes linked by a smart curved arrow connector

But wait, there's more. If you're moving connected shapes around like a shell game out on the boardwalk, you'll love the Reroute Connectors feature that optimizes the connection points for the connected objects and rethreads the connector's route to take the shortest path without crossing either shape. Try it: drag the oval shape down and around the rectangle shape until it (the oval) is to the left and below the rectangle. The connector has to follow a long, winding route to retain the bond, so right-click the connector and choose Reroute Connectors. The connector instantly finds the closest two points and, well, reroutes itself.

As we've said, there are no connectors in Word. Most annoying. If you want to connect two AutoShapes in Word, you'll have to fake it with a Line type of AutoShape (an arrow looks best in our opinion, but any line type will do). Unfortunately, this means you'll have to manually line up the pseudo-connector in Word; and whenever you move an object on either end of the pseudo-connector, the pseudo-connector won't follow along as it does in PowerPoint and Excel, and it can't reroute itself.

There is, however, an alternative. This workaround applies to any application inside or outside of Office that supports OLE objects. Microsoft has released a free OLE mini-app (Microsoft hates it when we call these things "mini-apps") that you can download from *http:// www.microsoft.com/OfficeFreeStuff/download/Draw97.exe*. Install it, and then from Word pull down the Insert menu and choose Object. You'll find a new Object type of Microsoft Draw 97 Drawing. (See Figure 6-29.)

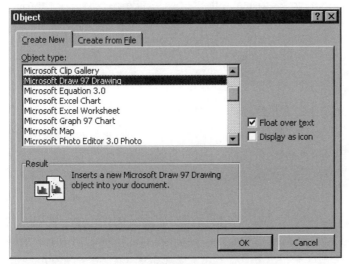

Figure 6-29: Using the Draw 97 (Office Art) mini-app

Clicking OK fires up a drawing object in your Word document (just like WordArt or MSGraph) and gives you a toolbar complete with connectors. (See Figure 6-30.)

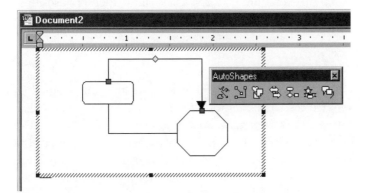

Figure 6-30: Using the Draw 97 drawing object

Overall, Draw 97 is not nearly as flexible as native support for Office Art directly inside Word. It does get you around Word's missing connector problem, but that's a bug to begin with. So Draw 97 is actually a kludge in sheep's clothing. You wind up with a single Draw 97 object in your Word document that contains all the AutoShapes and connectors, but you have to edit the object first to get at the AutoShape objects inside it. Blecch.

You have to use Draw 97 to get AutoShapes inside Access (set the data type to OLE Object) or in Outlook for, say, a map to a lake cabin you want to store in a Contact note field. Of course, you could always use Excel to create the Office Art drawing, group the various components, and then copy and paste the graphic to Access or Outlook. Your choice.

AutoShape Adjustment Nuances

To move shapes in unison, first select them all: click the Select Objects button, left-click and drag the mouse pointer to draw a selection frame that encloses them. To move them, either drag them around with the mouse or use Nudge. To group several objects together logically, select the objects to be grouped, click Draw, then click Group. (Hint about multiple selections: if the objects are positioned so that using the Select Objects selection frame won't work, use Shift+left-click to select the objects.) Grouped objects can be flipped, scaled, etc. as a group, and their properties can be set in unison. You'll see the outline of the grouped shapes marked by eight sizing handles (you won't see a border, though).

Once you have the desired group of shapes selected, you can also align and distribute them in several preset ways. Click Draw, then choose Align or Distribute.

Bookshelf Basics

The Microsoft Office 97 Professional Edition includes the following as an "in the box" reference resource: an on-disk version of the *Original Roget's Thesaurus*, the *American Heritage Dictionary*, and the *Columbia Book of Quotations*. These are collectively referred to as "Bookshelf Basics," an annoying MicroSpeak misnomer that means Office 97 Professional has been downgraded from the previous edition of Office that included the full-blown Bookshelf product.

What you *don't* get with Bookshelf Basics (that you *did* get in the Bookshelf version of Office 95) are:

- National Five-Digit ZIP Code and Post Office Directory
- The World Almanac and Book of Facts 1996
- Concise Encarta 96 World Atlas
- The People's Chronology

- Concise Columbia Encyclopedia, Third Edition

- Internet Directory 96

You can access Bookshelf from the Tools menu in Word, Excel, and PowerPoint by clicking on Look Up Reference. (See Figure 6-31.)

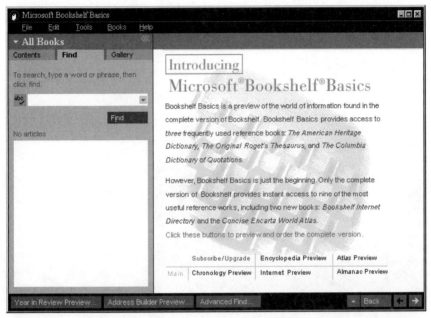

Figure 6-31: Bookshelf Basics

Note that you get a "preview" version of the Bookshelf components you don't get with the Basics edition. The Encyclopedia preview has all of four short examples to whet your appetite for the full version.

The "books" that make up Bookshelf reside on your Office 97 Professional CD-ROM, so you'll need to have your CD loaded in order to use Bookshelf Basics. You can select a word in Word or PowerPoint, right-click it, and choose Define from the pop-up menu to search the American Heritage Dictionary. If found in the dictionary, the result is displayed, as shown in Figure 6-32. What's more, you can click on the wave sound symbol (the speaker-like picture) to the right of the word at the top of the definition and actually hear the word pronounced. Is this great or what?

This works a bit differently in Excel. Select a cell and choose Look Up Reference from the Tools menu, and the contents of the cell (the result, if the cell contains a formula) appears in a dialog box that lets you search Bookshelf Basics. (See Figure 6-33.)

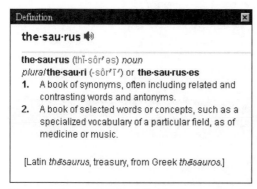

Figure 6-32: Getting the definition!

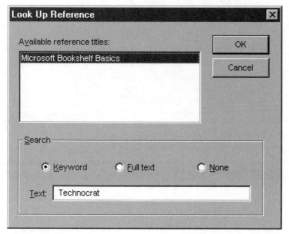

Figure 6-33: Searching the Bookshelf Basics reference from Excel

If you click on Look Up Reference without any text selected, you get the same dialog box with the Text control empty. In that case you'd just type in what you want to look up. Definitions, articles, synonyms, and quotations can all be copied directly from Bookshelf Basics into Excel, PowerPoint, or Word. In Bookshelf, just pull down the Edit menu (or highlight, then right-click the material to be copied) and you can choose the application the current information should be copied to. (See Figure 6-34.)

If the destination application is not running, it will be started and the data from Bookshelf Basics automatically inserted into a new document/ spreadsheet/slide. If the application is already running, you'll be asked for the precise destination you want. In Figure 6-35, you can see the message box you get when copying to Word.

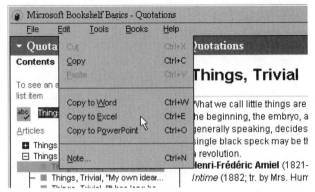

Figure 6-34: Copy data from Bookshelf Basics to your Office applications

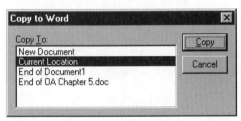

Figure 6-35: Picking the destination in Word

There's an OSB toolbar called Bookshelf for accessing Bookshelf Basics without having to go through a particular application. Overall the Bookshelf is a great addition to Office. However, it's very annoying that Microsoft saw fit to downgrade the Bookshelf features that come with Office 97 Professional.

The Age of the Macro Virus

The macro virus is a clear and present danger to Office users. As of the time of this writing, there are (depending on which industry list you last checked) between 300 and 500 known Word macro viruses. You can argue about how many are truly "in the wild" and how many have never been outside the labs of the anti-virus companies and the interested parties who track these things. But any way you slice it, that's a passel of nasty creepy-crawlies. Stop by some of the Web sites where anyone with a browser can download a hundred or so working versions of these little nightmares—to say nothing of a complete do-it-yourself virus creation engine—and you'll stop arguing and start reaching for the aspirin bottle.

There's good news and bad news as far as Word 97 is concerned. The good news is that very few of the Word 95 WordBasic macro viruses are capable of infecting Word 97 since it switched to VBA as its macro language. The bad news is that the first of the Word 97 specific VBA macro viruses have been identified. Epidemic to follow.

Excel users have to worry about a burgeoning crop of macro viruses. XM.Laroux, XM.Robocop, XM.Legend, XM.Sofa, and XM.Delta, just to name a few, are all running around waiting for you to open the wrong workbook.

We'll not get into a detailed discussion of which virus is worse than another. They are all bad; some can cripple your system, and every one of them is annoying as heck. Word is the most likely application to be hit by an infected document, followed by Excel. PowerPoint and Access are less likely to be infected by a virus, but are quite vulnerable to a Trojan Horse type attack. While a Trojan Horse (which is a macro included in a database application or presentation that causes damage without copying itself anywhere) does not replicate itself, that's small consolation if you get hit by one that reformats your hard disk. What does Office do to protect you from these VBA spawned threats?

Office 97 ships with a built-in "brick wall" virus protection feature. Many people hate this annoying "Warning" dialog—the one that pops up whenever you try to open a Word document, Excel spreadsheet, or PowerPoint presentation. In Figure 6-36 you see the warning you get in Excel when opening a workbook with macros in it.

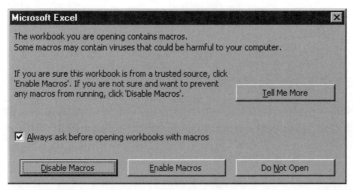

Figure 6-36: Your last line of defense; don't turn it off!

Don't think that this is anything more than a warning message, because it's not. It doesn't look for viruses, it doesn't identify viruses, it doesn't eliminate viruses, and it doesn't do a whole lot to protect you from virus infection. Still, when you get the "Warning" message, you need to sit up and pay attention. Nine times out of ten, the file you're trying to open won't be infected. But that other one time can ruin your whole day.

In PowerPoint you get a slightly modified version of the warning message, the significant difference being that PowerPoint doesn't give you a button to avoid opening the presentation altogether. (See Figure 6-37.)

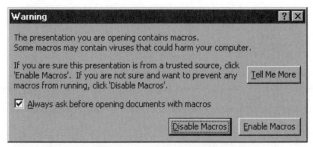

Figure 6-37: Macro virus warning in PowerPoint

All the warning dialogs in Office give you the check box "Always ask before opening documents with macros." Whatever you do, don't uncheck this check box or, equivalently, the "Macro virus protection" check box that you'll find on the Tools ➤ Options, General dialog in Word, Excel, and PowerPoint. Even if you think the Warnings are annoying, they could save your tail some day. Trust us. This "Warning" message is not an annoyance. It's a last line of defense in all your applications with the notable exception of Access, which does not warn you about macros at all.

Open an Outlook form that contains VBScript macros (Outlook 97 does not yet support VBA) and you'll get a warning similar to the PowerPoint message (see Figure 6-38). This warning talks about registering the form in the forms library. Like PowerPoint, you can't opt to not open the form. Another difference: with Outlook, there is no option to turn off the warning as there is in Word, Excel, and PowerPoint.

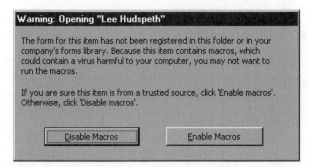

Figure 6-38: Outlook form macro warning

The biggest danger from Outlook at the moment is in getting an email message with an attached executable file or document/spreadsheet that's infected with a macro virus. Especially in the case of an executable, you double-click on the attachment and, without warning, you are in trouble. A lot of the patches and interim "service pack" fixes that you'll see for Outlook (which should be available by the time you read this) will be focused on this potential threat.

Access does not warn you at all when opening databases that contain macros that may autoexecute (or any other macros for that matter). Then again, macros have not been the threat to Access that they have to Word and Excel (at least so far). People exchange documents and spreadsheets more readily and frequently than they do databases.

As you might surmise, this brick wall type of warning is *not* the only Office virus defense you'll need. Not by a long shot! These dialogs basically let you open the file with macros enabled (something you should only do if you *know* the file is clear of potential viri), open the file with the macros disabled, or, in the case of Word and Excel, forget the whole thing and not open the file at all. The better option is to run a real virus checker on the suspect file.

For this you must buy, use, and frequently update a good anti-virus (AV) software package that's capable of dealing with the Office macro viruses. There are many to choose—from the biggies like Norton Anti-Virus from Symantec (*http://.symantec.com*) and McAfee's VirusScan (*http:// .mcafee.com*), to the smaller AV manufacturers like FRISK Software, who make F-PROT (*http://.datafellows.fi/vir-info/index.htm*).

Rather than recommend any one package, check the latest reviews from any of the major PC magazines, including *PC Computing* (*http://.pccom-puting.com*) and *Office Computing* (*http://.officecomputing.com*), and choose one that you fancy. Then use it.

The ValuPack

The ValuPack is a folder on the Office 97 CD-ROM that contains a number of very interesting tools and things that you should be aware of. Not all these components are installed even if you do a custom installation of Office and choose every option you can find.

There is a help file with additional information on the various goodies included with the ValuPack; see the *Valupak8.hlp* file in the CD-ROM's ValuPack folder. The help file includes installation instructions and can launch many of the setup programs to install the ValuPack items. The contents of the Office97 ValuePack is listed in Table 6-2.

Table 6-2: What's Included in the ValuPack

ValuPack Item	Description
\ValuPack\Access\Openbook.htm	Online version of the booklet *Building Applications with Microsoft Access 97* in HTML format. A developer's guide for building serious Access applications.
\ValuPack\Amovie\	ActiveMovie and Active Movie Stream add-ins. These are Internet gizmos that enable the streaming of ASF (ActiveMovie Streaming Format) files to your PC.
\ValuPack\Animgifs\	A collection of animated GIF files that you can use to jazz up your Web pages. Minimal eye-candy value.
\ValuPack\ASF\Asfppt.exe	Installs a utility that lets you publish to ASF (ActiveMovie Streaming Format).
\ValuPack\AveryWiz\	The Avery Labels Wizard. A Wizard that Avery-Dennison distributes that works with Word to print Avery label products.
\ValuPack\AXPlugin\	The NCompass ActiveX plugin. Allows Netscape to display and run ActiveX controls. If you are running the latest version of Netscape's browser, you might check on the NCompass web site (*http://www.ncompasslabs.com/scriptactive/index.htm*) for the latest version of this utility.
\ValuPack\Binders\	An Office Meeting and Proposal Binder template. Also in A4 paper format. Just copy these to the *C:\Program Files\Microsoft Office\Templates\Binders* folder.
\ValuPack\CCMail\	Outlook support for Lotus CCMail, this lets you use Outlook as a front-end client to a cc:Mail postoffice.
\ValuPack\Convert\	Additional Outlook import/export converters.
\ValuPack\Cursors\	Additional animated mouse cursors for Word, Excel, and Outlook. High cutesy factor, low functionality. (Do you really need the cursor to change into a printer icon while you print a document in Word?)
\ValuPack\Dataacc\	Microsoft DataAccess Pack, installs a number of ODBC drivers for accessing data external to your Access or Excel databases.

Table 6-2: What's Included in the ValuPack (continued)

ValuPack Item	Description
\ValuPack\Fareast\	Foreign language support for the Chinese, Japanese, and Korean languages.
\ValuPack\Iexplore\	Microsoft Internet Explorer Web browser. The version depends on how old your Office CD-ROM is; Microsoft is constantly updating IE. Check *http:// www.microsoft.com/ie/download/* for the latest version.
\ValuPack\Morehelp\	Additional and updated help files for using VBA with various Office applications. The help for Outlook is for the VBA language, which Outlook does not support—VBScript is all Outlook supports in its first release. We take this as an indication that VBA support is on the way in the next left-of-decimal version of Outlook.
\ValuPack\Mscam\	The Microsoft Camcorder program lets you record actions, procedures, and sounds as you work on your computer. Play back as a mini-movie.
\ValuPack\Msfonts\	150 additional TrueType fonts. There's a nifty preview file, *_preview.gif*, that you can review in Microsoft Photo Editor or in your browser that shows you a sample of each font.
\ValuPack\Musictrk\	Music Tracks is a PowerPoint 97 add-in that lets you add a custom soundtrack to your presentation.
\ValuPack\Offclean\	When you install Office 97, the setup program handles uninstalling previous versions of Office unless you opt to have multiple versions of Office installed on the same PC. This is a standalone version of the uninstaller for removing previous versions after Office 97 is installed.
\ValuPack\Patch\	A collection of patches for various bugs. It includes a patch for the Themes on the Microsoft Plus! product to let Themes use the newer *.JPG* graphics filter installed with Office 97.
\ValuPack\Ppt4view\	The PowerPoint viewer that lets you view presentations even without PowerPoint being installed. Mainly for distribution with your presentations to others who do not have PowerPoint installed. This utility is installable from the Office setup program.

Table 6-2: What's Included in the ValuPack (continued)

ValuPack Item	Description
\ValuPack\Pptanim\	The PowerPoint Animation Player lets you play presentations across the Internet.
\ValuPack\Pubtrial\	A 60-day trial version of Microsoft Publisher—the full Publisher program that stops working 60 days after installation.
\ValuPack\Realaud\	The RealAudio add-in for PowerPoint that lets you play RealAudio sound files in your presentations.
\ValuPack\Sounds\	A number of sounds that are installed as new default cues for various operations in Windows and Office. Despite its high cutesy factor, it is amazingly useful, and we highly recommend you install it. Once you turn Office Sounds off, or use a PC without them, you'll be longing to get these sound cues back.
\ValuPack\Template\	Additional templates for Word, Excel, PowerPoint and Outlook (forms). Some of these are very special interest sort of things (Business Planner in Excel, for example), but there are a number of items, and it's worth your time to look them over.
\ValuPack\Textures\	A number of *JPG* images suitable for backgrounds for HTML Web pages.
\ValuPack\Timex\	A utility that lets you export Outlook data directly to the Timex Data Link Watch.
\ValuPack\Tutorial\	A tutorial on creating slide presentations and using the new features in PowerPoint 97.
\ValuPack\Webpost\	Microsoft's FTP utility that lets you upload files to your Web site. Works with a number of services that used to force you to use their proprietary software to post your files, including CompuServe, Sprynet, America Online, and GNN.
\ValuPack\Wordview\	Like the PowerPoint viewer, this is a viewer program that lets someone read and print Word documents even if they don't have Word installed.
\ValuPack\Wrd97cnv\	This converter installs on previous versions of Word (Word 95/Word 6) and allows these versions of Word to open Word 97 documents.

The only real annoyance that we've encountered with the ValuPack is that the utilities offered may be outdated by the rapidly changing nature of software today. For things like converters and viewers, ActiveX add-ins and the like, your best bet is to check the appropriate Microsoft site (or third-party site for those utilities not provided directly by Microsoft) on the World Wide Web to see if a later version is available for downloading.

Various OLE Applets

Earlier in this chapter, we briefly talked about the Microsoft Draw 97 Drawing applet that you can download and install from the Microsoft Web site. Office 97 comes with a number of these OLE server* applets whose primary job is to let you create an object within another application's data file using a unique set of special purpose tools.

You can peruse these handy programs by selecting Object from the current Office application's Insert menu and inspecting the resulting Object dialog, as Figure 6-39 shows. Objects can be inserted into documents, workbooks, presentations, Outlook messages and note fields, and Access forms.

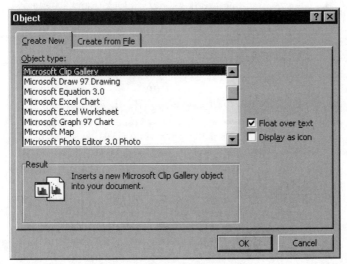

Figure 6-39: A plethora of OLE applications (shown here in Word)

You'll notice that Excel charts and sheets, Word documents, and Power-Point presentations and single slides are all considered OLE objects as displayed in this list. You can insert an Excel chart in a Word document,

---

* OLE is being replaced with the new buzzword "ActiveX." But we'll use the old term for clarity since ActiveX is usually heard in an Internet context these days. An OLE server is an application that embeds its data in a container application's data file. For example, an Excel chart is embedded in a Word document; here, Excel is the OLE server and Word is the OLE client (container) application.

a PowerPoint slide in Word document, a Word document in an Excel worksheet, an Excel workbook in an Outlook email message, etc., etc. This lets you use the best tool for the job at hand, depending on the type of data you're working with.

In theory, any OLE-compliant server application appears in this Object type list when you are in a container application. The annoying exception is Excel, which doesn't want you embedding workbooks within workbooks. So if you are in Excel and you select Insert ➤ Object, you won't see any Excel choices in the "Object type" list. Word lets you embed Word objects in Word documents, and PowerPoint is happy to let you insert a slide within a slide, but Excel balks.

When you insert an object, the local application displays the menu bar, toolbars, and commands unique to that mini-app. This is called *in-place editing*. For example, in Figure 6-40, you see an active Microsoft Map object embedded in a Word document. The Microsoft Map applet lets you create a map graphic that is tied to data in Excel or Access. Notice how the standard Word menu and toolbars are replaced with those that let you work with the Map object (in-place editing). Once you click back in your document (or chose the Return option from the File menu), you see the local command bars and an embedded object in your local Word document.

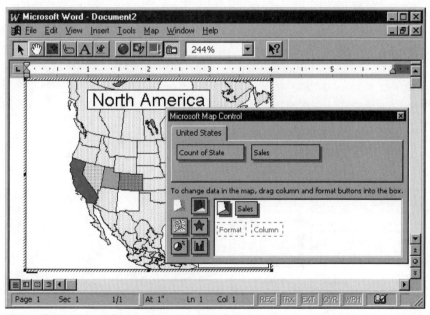

Figure 6-40: Microsoft Map object in a Word document

Other OLE server applications, like the Microsoft Org Chart applet, run in
their own windows and actually let you save out an Org Chart data file
(there is no facility to print the chart from within the server applet; for
that you'll have to embed the org chart in a client application like Word).
(See Figure 6-41.)

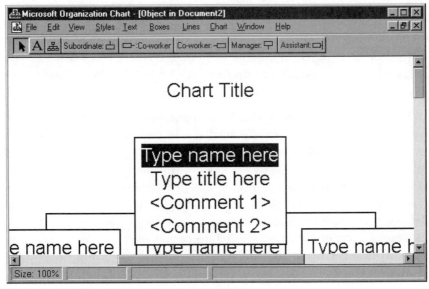

Figure 6-41: Using Microsoft Org Chart in Word

PowerPoint includes an Organization Chart as an AutoLayout choice when
creating a new presentation, as shown in Figure 6-42. This AutoLayout
gives you a slide with an embedded Microsoft Organizational Chart object
(the object displayed as an icon). You double-click on the icon and create
your chart using the Microsoft Org Chart OLE server application.

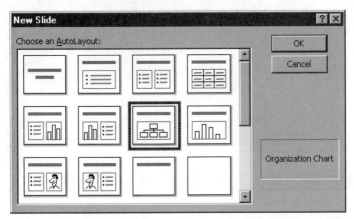

Figure 6-42: PowerPoint incorporates the Microsoft Org Chart object

When you create your embedded objects, you can select the "Display as Icon" check box (see Figure 6-39) to create an object that you activate by double-clicking just as in the PowerPoint example. This is particularly useful when you want to provide unobtrusive data in your container document that can be triggered for display when necessary.

Whereas the Object dialog in Word and Excel includes two separate tabs, one for creating a new object and one for embedding an object from an existing file, PowerPoint, Access, and Outlook provide a slightly different version of the Insert Object dialog box—two option buttons rather than separate tabs are provided for this purpose. (See Figure 6-43.) The "Create from file" option lets you create an embedded object using an existing file—an Org Chart *.OPX* file, a Word document, a PowerPoint presentation, etc.

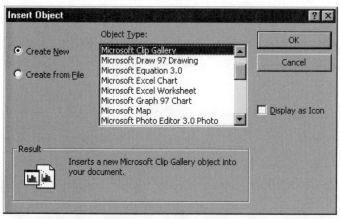

Figure 6-43: Inserting an object in Access, Outlook, or PowerPoint

Here are some annoyances to watch out for when working with OLE server applications and embedded objects: If you want a large object to span more than a single page (say an Excel sheet embedded in a Word document), you're going to be unhappy. Spanning pages (promised way back in the OLE 2.0 specification) is a feature that has just never materialized. Keep the table to a single page or change tactics and go with a Word table instead.

Also, watch your properties. When you embed objects, the properties set by the server application are isolated from the container application. This means that to format the text or change the shading of the object, you'll have to activate the server application and make your changes there. You can't just select an object in the local application and make it, say, bold using the local application's bold command.

There are more of these OLE applets that come with Office. Microsoft Graph 97, Microsoft Photo Editor (which is also a handy standalone application), and others, are all worthy of a few minutes of your time to explore. We recommend you set aside some time to experiment with each object type that's listed in your Insert ➤ Object dialog box.

7

Strategies

> **strategy** *n. a) skill in managing or planning, especially by using stratagems b) a stratagem or artful means to some end*
>
> **stratagem** *n. any trick or scheme for achieving some purpose*

Office is vast, and the plethora of new features in the 97 version create an interesting sea of possibilities for answering Microsoft's siren song, "Where do you want to go today?" Well, if you're like us, you just want to get your work done and go home.

With five major applications and a number of utilities, OLE applets, a Web browser, and assorted add-ins, we're obviously not going to cover all possible strategies that you can employ to get the best use out of Office. As we've gone along in the previous chapters, we've pointed out the most egregious annoyances and how to work around them, and highlighted Office's best features from the point of view of in-the-trenches productivity. Similarly, in this chapter we'll focus on strategic issues that involve some of the most heavily hyped features that Office offers.

First, we'll dig into the on-line help and resources that are a part of the Office application interface—have you really studied that help menu lately? This is the future; printed manuals have become rare collector's items, and the help files that come with your applications will soon be updated automatically across the Internet. As a first step down this path, Microsoft has moved its resources onto the Web and provided hooks to this information right in your applications. Several add-ins (Word's Web Page Wizard comes to mind) offer to update themselves automatically now, and this trend will continue. So like it or loathe it, the Internet is in your future.

Speaking of the Web, Office 97 provides everything you need to develop Web pages and to publish your content on the Internet/intranet. We'll give you the straight scoop on using Office to get published on the Web.

Tying all your documents/spreadsheets/presentations together with the new hyperlink feature that Office supports is a snap; that is, it's easy if you understand how to work around the annoying (read: broken) interface. Hyperlinks are not just for the Internet either. You can link documents on your local disk or network just as you do across cyberspace.

Last, we'll clasp hands and gird our loins as we step carefully through the minefield that is your Outlook Contacts list. With all your business and personal contacts in this module of Microsoft's super-PIM, you owe it to yourself to find out as much as you can about the beastie, particularly as it concerns contacts—your most important batch of data.

The World Wide Office

The most common action performed by Office users the world over is undoubtedly File ➤ Open. No big surprise there. The second most commonly performed act is to ask for some help, either by clicking on the Office Assistant button or selecting the Help command on the main menu bar. We've covered Robert extensively in earlier chapters, so now let's take a look at an often-overlooked gold mine of built-in help features: the Microsoft on the Web menu.

Whether you are a big-time Web surfer or hold the Internet in total disdain, this is the future publishing method of choice for software vendors. The latest bug fixes, patches, services releases, updates, FAQs, and related information hits the Web first. Microsoft is betting heavily on the Web and has actually built in a number of Internet hyperlinks into the Help menu of all your Office applications.

From any Office application—Access, Binder, Excel, Outlook, Power-Point, or Word—select Help, then choose Microsoft on the Web. You'll see the Microsoft on the Web cascading menu as shown in Figure 7-1. The various components of Office offer the following menu items:

- Free Stuff—If you're in Word, this launches Microsoft Internet Explorer—remember, you need Internet Explorer 3.01 or higher for Office 97 compatibility—and jumps to *http://www.microsoft.com/*

Figure 7-1: The Microsoft on the Web menu (shown here in Word)

OfficeFreeStuff/Word/. (If you're not currently connected to the Internet, you'll be prompted to do so first, of course.) Each individual application takes you to its own Free Stuff page, and in Figure 7-2 we swam upstream one level to show you the main Free Stuff page.

Figure 7-2: Microsoft's Free Stuff Web page

- Product News—This command links to the current application's News Headlines Web page. The address for Word is *http://www.microsoft.com/word/default.htm*. These pages typically contain a handful of newsy pieces (or links to them); some are stale, some are current, and some are pure pabulum.

- Frequently Asked Questions—This command takes you to a FAQ page for the current application. In the case of Word, it's *http://www.microsoft.com/MSWordSupport/content/faq/*.   These   pages include a plethora of options for searching and navigating through Microsoft's vast Web resources. Lots to do here.

- Online Support—Although this page can help you find answers to Office questions, when you first access it you may feel like you just stepped into a mine field. The page address for Word is *http://www.microsoft.com/MSWordSupport/*, and it uses an OCX (ActiveX) control that has been digitally signed by its publisher but whose signature doesn't match the component. *Kaboom!* If you have Internet Explorer set to High Security (View, Options, Security, click the Safety Level button, select the High option button) then the very first thing you'll see on this page is the "Potential safety violation avoided" message box (see Figure 7-3), and the offending component won't be downloaded to your system. If you have Internet Explorer set to Medium Security, then you'll see the alarming "Authenticode™ Security Technology" message box shown in Figure 7-4. If you click Yes, then *Survey.ocx* will be downloaded to your system. It appears to be used by the "How's Our Support" Feedback aspect of this page, so feel free to—we did so with great relish—delete this file from your system.

NOTE   You should always leave Internet Explorer set to Medium
              Security so you can see and deal with what's trying to land
              on your hard disk via the Web on a case-by-case basis.

- Microsoft Office Home Page—This page (*http://www.microsoft.com/office/default.htm*) is the root of all, well, Office information. But truthfully, it's hard to stifle a big yawn while perusing the items listed here.

- Send Feedback—Keep those cards, letters, and electrons comin', folks,   right   here   at   *http://www.microsoft.com/office/feedback/default.htm*! Here's where you can hit 'em right between the eyes with your personal diatribe (or kudos). You can submit ideas and sug-

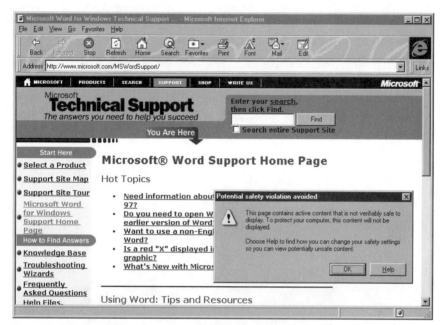

Figure 7-3: Online Support wants to install Survey.ocx on your system

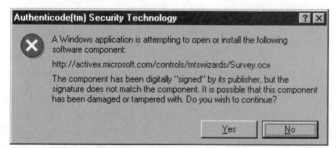

Figure 7-4: The Survey.ocx control's digital signature doesn't match

gestions for future products. Now, we didn't make this up; the following language actually appears on this page:

All product or service suggestions received become the sole property of Microsoft. Should a suggestion be implemented, Microsoft is under no obligation to provide compensation.

Ha ha ha! We laughed until we cried when we read that one. Too much! Anyway, you can also submit problem reports, find out how to buy Microsoft products, comment on the Microsoft Web site, and send in a story about your use of Office.

- Best of the Web—A hodge-podge of stuff. Whether it's the best stuff, well, that's an entirely personal judgment. This is all sizzle and fluff, so breeze on by this one.

- Search the Web—This URL (*http://home.microsoft.com/access/alli-none.asp*) is intended as a one-stop search umbrella. It includes scads of predefined categories like General Searching, International, Business & Finance, Computers, and so on. Interesting if you don't have your favorite sites already bookmarked.

- Web Tutorial—Don't bother with this one. It's a total sleeper. Zzzzzzz.

- Microsoft Home Page—This command goes straight to *http:// www.microsoft.com.*

- Developer Forum—This command appears only in Access, and takes you to *http://www.microsoft.com/accessdev/.* This is a tremendously useful page, and it makes us wonder why all the Office applications don't include one more Microsoft on the Web command entitled "Office Development" that links up to the Microsoft Office Developer Forum at *http://www.microsoft.com/OfficeDev/Default.htm* (separate and distinct from the Microsoft Access Developer Forum).

Web Development with Office

Microsoft has spared no PR resource in exalting Office 97's Internet features. Amazingly, some of these features actually measure up to the hype surrounding them. Using Office 97 alone, you can put together a very credible web site, be it on the Internet or an intranet.

You get everything you need in Office to create Web pages, post them directly to your Web site, and view them. Microsoft's Internet Explorer browser can be used to view not only standard HTML web pages but native Office 97 files as well. This can be either from your local drive via File ➤ Open ➤ Browse, or from a web site as shown in Figure 7-5.

About the only thing that Office does not provide you is actual Web server software—which you need to actually run a web site on your hardware. Not to worry though, you can get a copy of Microsoft's Personal Web Server (PWS) free. Download it from *http://www.microsoft.com/ msdownload/* under Server Software. The set up, care, and maintenance of a Web server is beyond the scope of this book, so we'll focus on using the Web features of the various Office components.Word and Excel as HTML Generators

Every Office 97 application, save for Outlook, lets you save data directly to an HTML format. We discussed how the Access Web Publishing

Wizard works back in Chapter 4, *VBA Fights Office Annoyances.* We'll treat PowerPoint as a separate animal later in this chapter, given some of its unique abilities. So in this section we'll look at Word and Excel as web page generators.

HTML is the native format of web pages. It is a straight ASCII text format and uses <TAGS>, or special instructions enclosed in angle brackets, that tell the browser how to display the text and graphics of the page.

NOTE   According to the Microsoft spin doctors, "Microsoft Office 97 integrates seamlessly with Microsoft Internet Explorer 3.0 or later to allow users to easily access, view, and edit information contained in Office documents regardless of where it resides. With ActiveX Document Technology, Internet Explorer users who link to or open an Office document will view this information *inside* Internet Explorer, providing full access to all the tools of the Office application. This highly integrated solution eliminates the need for user (sic) to have multiple windows open on the desktop at one time." The techno-babble phrase "ActiveX Document Technology" may have a nice ring to it, but there's a gaping crack in this bell.

We've found that Internet Explorer is not happy opening Office documents (like a Word document or an Excel workbook) from your local disk when you are *not* connected to the Internet. We try to open Excel workbooks and have to repeatedly click Back, Forward, and Refresh buttons to coerce the file to open. We have Office documents that just refuse to open at all, and sundry related problems. If we are connected to the Internet, opening Office documents on the local drive in Internet Explorer seems to work every time, at least in terms of opening the documents themselves. Go figure.

Oh, and don't you just hate the annoying File ➤ Open ➤ Browse interface and its clunky restrictions: no predefined Office file types in the "Files of type" list, no Favorites button, no memory of the prior folder or file type selection from one use of the Open dialog to the next, not even a simple File ➤ Open button on the browser's main interface.

Word and the Web

While you can generate HTML pages or portions of pages with different applications in Office, Word is the best all around editor for Web work. You create a Word document consisting of the text and graphics you want to have on your Web page, and use Word's excellent table feature

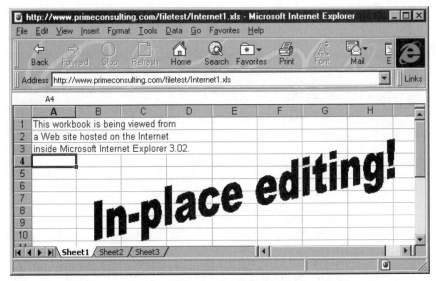

Figure 7-5: Viewing an Excel workbook using Internet Explorer 3.02

to position your content on the page. Don't forget you have to uncheck the "Float over text" check box to get a graphic into a table cell. (See Figure 7-6.)

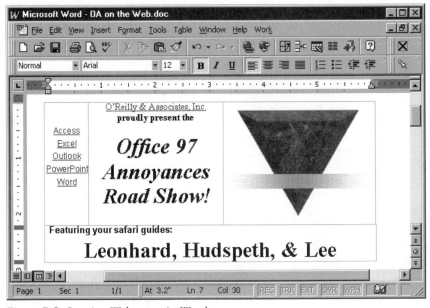

Figure 7-6: Creating Web pages in Word

Create hyperlinks to other pages by selecting the text you want to become a link, and clicking on the Insert Hyperlink button on the Standard toolbar (you've seen how to do this trick in previous examples).

You can jazz up your page by adding background colors or fill effects. Format ➤ Background ➤ Fill Effects lets you choose from a number of options for backgrounds, patterns, pictures, etc. (See Figure 7-7.)

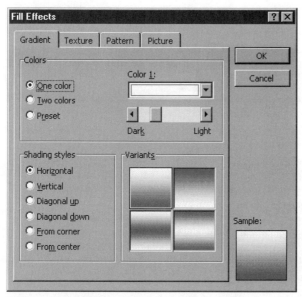

Figure 7-7: Adding special visual effects to a Word document destined to become an HTML page

Once you have completed your Word document, you simply save it in HTML format. (See Figure 7-8.)

When you save your document as HTML, save it to a separate folder. Any graphics you have inserted into the document are converted to the GIF or JPEG graphics format (so that they can be displayed in Web browsers) and saved with the Word/HTML document. Word uses the GIF format unless the graphic is already a JPEG image. Any background effects you have used are also saved as separate graphics files along with the Word/ HTML file. You'll lose some formatting in the translation, the most annoying of which are animated text, AutoShapes, WordArt, and related drawing items in your documents.

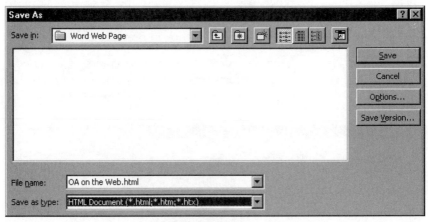

Figure 7-8: Saving a Word document as an HTML page

NOTE   Word converts images in your document to generically named graphics files like *Image7.gif.* The first character of the filename is capitalized and if you look at the converted HTML code, any references to the graphic file are capitalized the same way. Since many Web servers are hosted on UNIX operating systems, and since those systems are case sensitive, you must be careful not to change the capitalization of the filenames when uploading your files to your Web site.

Word also comes with a Web Page Wizard (see Figure 7-9) that walks you through the creation of several types of generic Web pages.

Just select File ➤ New, and choose the *Web Page Wizard.wiz* option (you'll find it in the Web Pages tab) and click OK. You can choose from a list of page designs, as shown in Figure 7-10.

In the next panel you choose from a list of eight styles (choices like Contemporary, Elegant, or Professional), and you wind up with a Word document, complete with hyperlinks, ready to save as an HTML Web page. This Wizard lets you quickly crank out very credible basic Web pages.

Excel for HTML tables

Since an Excel spreadsheet is essentially a large table, Excel comes with a nifty Internet Wizard that lets you take a selected portion of your worksheet and create an HTML table out of it. To use this Wizard, you have to

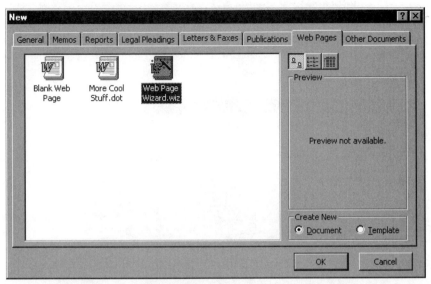

Figure 7-9: Using the Web Page Wizard

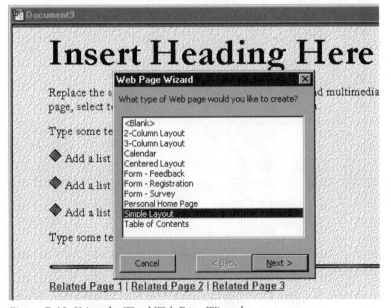

Figure 7-10: Using the Word Web Page Wizard

make sure you installed the Internet Assistant Wizard when you installed Excel or Office.

Open the workbook you want, and select a specific sheet to be converted to HTML code. Select Save as HTML from the File menu and the Wizard appears. (See Figure 7-11.) The Wizard automatically lists the current selection and any embedded charts in the "Ranges and charts to convert" list box. It's mildly annoying that named ranges don't appear in the list. Still, you can click the Add button, which rolls up the Wizard dialog and lets you select a range in the current sheet manually.

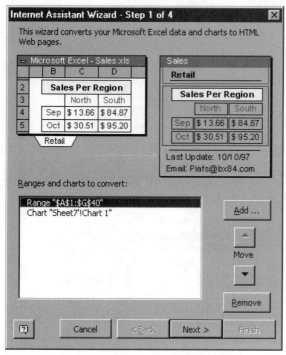

Figure 7-11: Excel's Internet Assistant Wizard

What you wind up with is a table (what else?) in HTML code. The Wizard lets you choose between creating a standalone HTML file, or to have the selected range or chart injected into an existing HTML document. For the latter, the trick is to first open the existing document and add `<!--##Table##-->` at the point in the code where you want the Excel information inserted. The Wizard replaces that string of text with the table data or chart graphic reference from Excel.

Charts are converted into GIF format images, which means, just like in Word, you have to deal with multiple files—the HTML page, and the GIF file that it references.

NOTE   As in Word, you have to mind that you don't change the
         capitalization of any of the files or your Web page will not
         display correctly. (We discuss this at length when we cover
         PowerPoint later in this chapter.) For example, if you save
         a chart in Excel as an HTML document and accept the de-
         faults, you wind up with a Web page named
         MyHTML1.htm. Notice the odd capitalization. The chart is
         saved as a separate file named *MyHTML1.gif.* Again you
         get mixed case in the filename. The Web page references
         the chart graphic using the exact same case. Unix Web
         servers are notoriously case sensitive, so if you rename any
         of the files when you upload them to your server, the page
         won't be able to find the referenced file, since
         MyHTML1.gif is not the same as *myhtml1.gif* as far as Unix
         is concerned.

The tables and charts, once converted, are not linked to the original
spreadsheet data, so don't expect anything like dynamic updating of information. Font formatting is preserved when a table is converted to HTML,
as are cell background color and merged cell layout. This makes Excel
one great table generator.

Generating PowerPoint Web Presentations

PowerPoint lets you take a slide presentation and save it as a series of
linked HTML pages, or as a "ready to run across the Internet/intranet"
presentation. This feature is so amazingly useful that we'll walk through
the steps necessary to create each type. All we assume is that you have
already created a slide show in PowerPoint.

A PowerPoint slide show

In Chapter 4 we discussed some of PowerPoint's Web features and
showed you presentations converted as either a series of linked pages or
as an actual PowerPoint slide show, playable across the Internet using the
ActiveX Animation Player. This ability to convert a slide show into ready-
to-go Web pages is an example of a feature that actually lives up to its
hype. In this section we'll walk through creating both types of
presentations.

What makes this work is PowerPoint's ability to save entire slides out as
graphic images. The Save as HTML Wizard generates a series of HTML
pages that display both the slide and a set of navigational controls to
view the various slides that make up the presentation. As an added
benefit, PowerPoint also generates a series of plain text (no graphics)

Web pages that contain the text of each slide. This lets people with non-graphical browsers view the text from your slides. This is all handled automatically by the Wizard.

Presentation to web page

Once you have created and saved your presentation, open it in Power-Point, and from the File menu click on the Save as HTML option. You'll see the first panel of the Wizard, as shown in Figure 7-12. The graphic on the left of this dialog gives you an at-a-glance view of where you are in the process. Click Next to proceed to the next step.

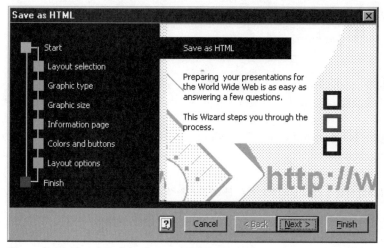

Figure 7-12: Panel 1 of the Save as HTML Wizard

In Figure 7-13, you can choose a layout for your slides. In this context, *layout* refers to the rest of the options you can select in the remaining Wizard panels. If you select the New layout option button, you get the default settings in the subsequent Wizard panels. You can then change each setting as you work through the Wizard. When you finally click on the Finish button, you can assign a name to your settings. When you subsequently run the Wizard, you'll see any saved layouts in the "Load existing layout" list box. A layout stores things like frames/no frames, graphic format, browser colors, button style and placement, all of the settings covered in the following Wizard panels. This lets you create your own default settings. You still have to move through the panels but you start off with the settings you want and you can change anything along the way if you need to.

Assuming this is the first time you've run the Wizard, go with the New layout option and click Next.

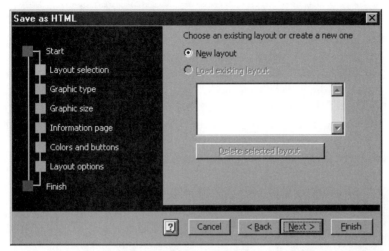

Figure 7-13: Selecting a layout for your Web pages

Next, PowerPoint offers you a choice of using what it calls "standard" page style (meaning *no* frames) or a style that does use frames. (If you aren't up on the latest developments in the HTML world, don't confuse PowerPoint's use of the term "style" with the styles feature being incorporated into the HTML specification—that's a whole 'nother animal entirely and beyond the pale of what we're talking about here.) If you don't have a good reason to use frames, go with the Standard setting as a page style, as shown in Figure 7-14. Frames allow different areas of the page to be scrolled independently of each other and is best left to advanced Web page developers familiar with this feature. Click on Next.

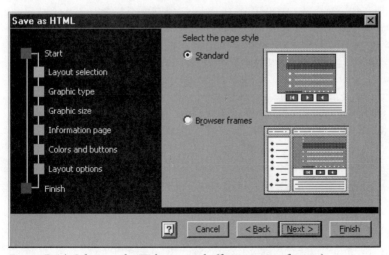

Figure 7-14: Selecting the Web page style (frames or no frames)

Each slide in your presentation is saved as a separate graphic file, which is then referenced by an HTML Web page. You can choose between two of the most common formats supported by the World Wide Web—GIF or JPEG (see Figure 7-15). The rule of thumb is to use the GIF format if you have clipart or line art images on your slides. If you have photographs or shaded art work, the JPEG format gives you better results. Both of these option buttons (GIF and JPEG) cause your slide show to be translated into a series of linked Web pages. This means you lose any animation effects and sound/video multimedia you may have included in your presentation. But there is a way around this, as you'll see in a moment.

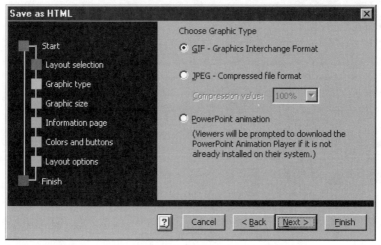

Figure 7-15: Choosing a graphics format

The third option button on this panel lets you create a playable slide show using the PowerPoint Animation Player. This is an ActiveX control that lets a browser play the slide show as if it was running in PowerPoint (even if the person viewing the Web page does not have PowerPoint or Office installed). The browser must have the Animation Player installed. If they don't have the Player, the ActiveX control is downloaded and installs itself automatically—you'll see the status bar message "Installing components" while it's being downloaded. The Player download transfers about 800KB to the local system, and the player itself (*C:\Program Files\Common Files\PowerPoint Animation Player\surge.exe*) is just a tad over 1.3MB installed. You can save yourself the downloading hassle by just installing the player from the *\Valupack\Pptanim\Axplayer.exe* file on the Office 97 CD-ROM. The Player actually comes in two flavors, the ActiveX version for Microsoft Internet Explorer and as a Netscape plug-in, if you're running Netscape as your browser. The installer is smart enough to give you the right one.

WARNING   Microsoft has had some problems with their ActiveX controls getting registered improperly according to their own
Certificate system. With security in Internet Explorer set to
High, we've endured the entire 800KB download only to
be told by our browser that the control we want does not
have the correct digital signature, that we've been rescued,
and that the 800KB PowerPoint Animation Player has been
deleted from our systems. So we change the security level
to Medium (View ➤ Options ➤ Security ➤ Safety Level ➤
Medium ➤ OK ➤ OK) and download the Player again, this
time telling Internet Explorer not to save us but to proceed
with installing the control. Hopefully Microsoft will have
this glitch fixed by the time you read this.

But with this ActiveX control, you get all the animations and special effects of the original slide show. The slides can be run in the browser window, advanced forward and back, or you can right click on the slide and run the presentation full screen. It's very impressive.

Once you've selected the way to have your slide show presented click the Next button.

To make a solid decision for monitor resolution (see Figure 7-16), you have to make some assumptions about your web site's audience. If you are loading your presentation on your company's intranet, you probably know the resolution used by most of the site's visitors. On the Internet, it is not so easy. Your best choice is either 640 by 480 or 800 by 600. You can also choose the width of your slide graphic. Start out with the default of Ω width of the screen and see how it looks. There's no real rule of thumb here—it depends on the look of your slides. If you want to change the width setting later, you'll have to run the Wizard against the original presentation again. Click Next to proceed.

In Figure 7-17, you can set options that control what appears on the *index.htm* file that is generated by the Wizard. The *index.htm* page serves as the presentation's home page. PowerPoint assumes that each slide show will be placed in its own folder on your Web site, and so generates an index page (also called a home page) automatically. You place the files that PowerPoint's Save as HTML Wizard creates, including the *index.htm* page, in a folder, and anyone who points their browser at that folder without indicating the name of an HTML file within the folder gets the index page displayed by default. From the index page, they can jump to a particular slide from the Table of Contents list of hyperlinks or

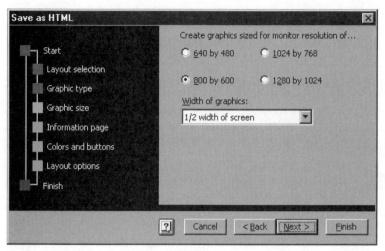

Figure 7-16: Choosing a screen resolution

start the presentation by clicking on the "Click here to Start" hyperlink. (See Figure 7-17.)

You can include your email address so that you can be contacted by people viewing your presentation; include the address of your site's main home page (a button appears on the pages that let users jump right to your main home page if you include the address here), and add a note in the "Other information" box—comments or instructions that'll appear on the index page.

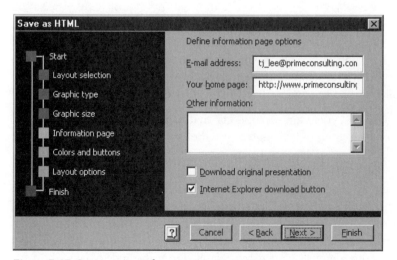

Figure 7-17: Setting your information page options

Checking the "Download original presentation" box puts a download link on the index page that lets someone download the original *filename.ppt*. This is the original PowerPoint slide show you started with. The last check box reads "Internet Explorer download button," but when checked it includes either the familiar Internet Explorer button (if you are creating a series of linked slide pages) or the PowerPoint Animation Player (if you are creating a Player presentation). (See Figure 7-18.) The Internet Explorer button is linked to the Microsoft site and downloads the latest version of Microsoft's browser. The Animation Player button gets the user the latest version of the Animation Player ActiveX control from Microsoft. Click Next to proceed.

Figure 7-18: Download buttons

You can tweak the colors used to display text and links—unvisited or visited. Unless you have a compelling reason to use custom colors, you should check the "Use browser colors" option button shown in Figure 7-19. Surfers on the Net grow accustomed to their default browser colors to indicate which links they have or have not visited, and when you change these colors, it's quite annoying. Click Next to proceed.

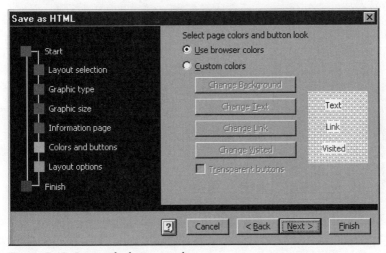

Figure 7-19: Setting the browser colors

A choice of three graphic button designs or a plain "Next slide" text link is shown in Figure 7-20. Choose a button or the Next slide option and click on Next to proceed.

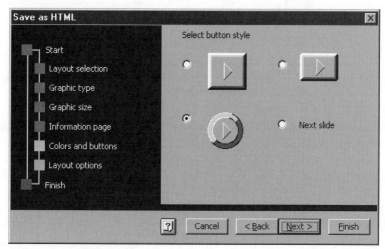

Figure 7-20: Choosing button styles

In the next panel (see Figure 7-21), you choose where you want your navigation buttons positioned in the various slide pages (top, bottom, left, or right). If you check the "Include slide notes in pages" check box, the notes for that slide (View ➤ Notes Page in PowerPoint) are included in the HTML. Pick a location and click on the Next button to proceed.

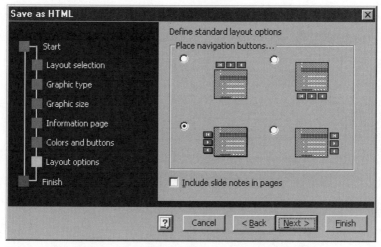

Figure 7-21: Choose a button location

Almost done. In Figure 7-22, you select the location where the generated files and graphics should be saved. PowerPoint wants a local folder. If you click on the Browse button, you might be tempted to go right to your web site. (See Figure 7-23.)

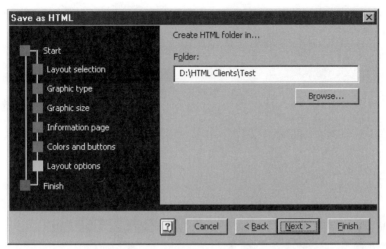

Figure 7-22: Saving the Web pages and related files to a folder

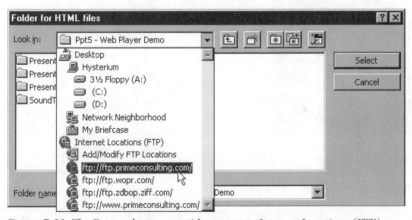

Figure 7-23: The Browse button provides access to Internet Locations (FTP)

The Internet Locations option is found at the bottom of the "Look in" drop-down list in the File ➤ Open and File ➤ Save As dialog boxes in Office. The "Folder for HTML files" dialog box should let you save your files right to your Web site. At least that's what we thought. Major annoyance! If you try to save to a web site, you'll get the message shown in Figure 7-24.

You'll have to save your Web presentation to a local folder and then transfer all the files in that folder to your web site in a separate operation. Be sure to save each presentation to a separate folder or you'll wind up overwriting and mangling your files, since files are just sequentially

Figure 7-24: Bzzzt! You can't do it!

numbered during naming—*img001.JPG*, *img002.JPG*, etc. Each presentation gets an *index.htm* file as the default home page.

Clicking on the Next button gets you to what appears to be the end of the line. (See Figure 7-25.)

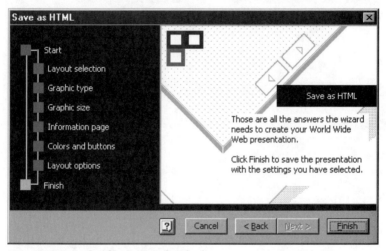

Figure 7-25: Looks like you are finished

Click on the Finish button and you'll see a series of messages informing you that PowerPoint is generating your Web presentation. But you are not quite done. Way back in Figure 7-13, you got a chance to choose a predefined layout (or you would have if there were any). Now you get the chance to save the settings you just selected as a layout for later use. Up pops the dialog box shown in Figure 7-26. Type in a name (if you want to reuse the current settings as a Layout for future slide shows that you convert to Web presentations) and click Save. If you don't want to save these settings, just click on Don't Save.

There you have it. A PowerPoint slide show repackaged as a set of Web pages, all ready to be uploaded to your Web site. Next we'll tell you how to get around the lurking annoyances that are waiting to pounce on you,

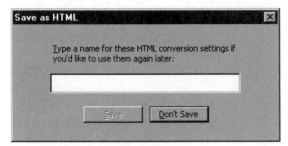

Figure 7-26: Save your current settings as a Layout

and then we'll discuss the features provided in Office for uploading your Web files.

The lurking annoyances

To understand how this PowerPoint to the Web process can trip you up, you need just a smattering of Unix vs. Windows NT knowledge. It won't hurt a bit.

Your Web server will more than likely be hosted by a web server on either a Unix or Windows NT operating system. The short version of the potential problem is this: Unix is case sensitive, Windows NT is not. So if you copy your converted presentation to a Windows NT machine, you're all set. No worries. But if you are going to a Unix computer, you may have a problem. Some administrators are quite harsh about capitalization and arbitrarily convert every filename to lowercase. Some FTP (file transfer protocol) software can be set to automatically do this type of conversion to lowercase as it uploads the files.

This is a problem due to PowerPoint's really annoying habit of using all uppercase letters for the filename extension for the original slideshow, as well as any graphics files it generates (i.e., for the graphical representa- tions of the slides themselves). For example, *img001.JPG* or *slideshow1.PPT.* The HTML pages reference these filenames *exactly*, and so if they get changed during uploading or by the administrator, you have a broken presentation. Most annoying, but forewarned is forearmed.

Updating a Web Site (FTPing) with Office

Office provides two methods for you to transfer files to Web and FTP server sites (such as HTML pages developed in Word, or PowerPoint slide shows that have been converted to Web presentations.)

The first is Microsoft's Web Publishing Wizard. This program can be found (as we discussed in the section "The ValuPack" in Chapter 6, *More*

Hard-Core Office) in the *ValuPack**Webpost*\ folder of the ValuPack that comes with Office 97 Professional. Simply double-click on the *Webpost.exe* file and the Wizard installs a shortcut to itself under your Start menu (Start ➤ Programs ➤ Accessories ➤ Internet Tools). The shortcut points to the actual executable file: *C:**Program Files**Web Publish**WPWIZ.EXE*. It's most annoying that you don't get any chance to influence the decision where the shortcut is installed, but you can manually clean up your Start menu if you so desire (as we demonstrated in Chapter 2).

The Web Publishing Wizard is strictly for uploading files to a Web site or FTP server. And it works with a number of services that used to force you to use their proprietary software to post your files—services like CompuServe, Sprynet, America Online, and GNN.

You tell the Wizard where the files that you want to upload—like the PowerPoint presentation that you have saved for publishing on the World Wide Web as discussed in the previous section—are located. (See Figure 7-27.) To transfer your web pages, you need to know the following:

- Your FTP server name (for example, *www.primeconsulting.com*)

- Your username and password (you must have access privileges to the server for posting files)

- The subfolder to which you want to install the files (if any)

Figure 7-27: Using the Web Publishing Wizard

The Wizard walks you through each step of the process and will validate all your information before attempting to upload any files to your site.

NOTE   Some people find the Wizard's step by step methodology—
              once they are comfortable with the basic process—to be
              annoying in the extreme. They want to use a more direct
              tool, and there are any number of FTP utilities available
              that give you more direct control over the process of up-
              loading and manipulating files on the Internet. WS_FTP is
              one we highly recommend (*http://www.ipswitch.com*).

The second method provided by Office 97 is built directly into the
common File ➤ Open and File ➤ Save As dialog boxes. As you saw in the
last section, this method failed miserably when it came to uploading a
PowerPoint presentation to a Web site. It is more suited to saving files—
created in an Office application like Excel or Word—to a site, or opening
files from a Web or FTP site directly into an Office application.

For example, in Word, click on File ➤ Open and pull down the "Look in"
drop-down list. There at the bottom of the list you'll find the FTP (file
transfer protocol) options. There is a resource called "Internet Locations
(FTP)." Below this resource is an option "Add/Modify FTP Locations" that
lets you add new sites or modify existing Web or FTP locations. Finally,
all the locations that have already been set up are listed. (See Figure
7-28.) Click on the Add/Modify option and you can enter the information
necessary to access a given site. (See Figure 7-29.)

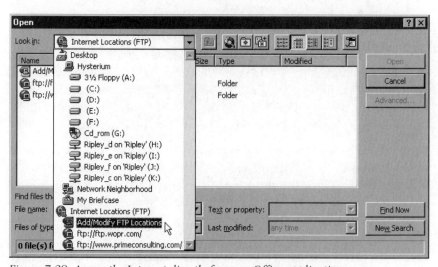

Figure 7-28: Access the Internet directly from an Office application

If you're in Word and want to try opening a file from a site on the
Internet, you can create a Location as shown in Figure 7-29. Use

Figure 7-29: Creating an Internet Location

ftp.microsoft.com as the Name of the FTP site and Anonymous as the "Log on as" option. Leave Password blank. Click on Add and then on the OK button. You can now select the Location you just added in the Open dialog. You'll need to be connected to the Internet, so if you are using a dial-up connection, you should log on to your service provider beforehand.

The files and folders that are located on the Microsoft FTP server appear in your Open dialog as though they were resources on your local network, and actually they are—you're just using the Internet as part of your network. In the root folder of the Microsoft site, you should find a file called *disclaimer.txt*. Select this file and click the Open button.

Next the file is transferred to the temporary folder on your local disk. A status box titled "Transferring File..." appears as the file is pulled down to your computer. Once the download is complete, Word opens the document. You won't be able to save files to this server, though, since you don't have the proper authorizations.

To transfer files to and from your own web site, you just need to create a Location entry using the proper username and password. Once you do, however, best keep your computer secure, as Office will remember your password the next time you want to access files at that location. Anyone gaining use of your computer will have access to your web site as well.

Another potential annoyance you'll encounter when using FTP from within Office applications: you are summarily dumped into the root folder of the server Location. When you set up your Location, you can only specify the domain name (like *http://www.primeconsulting.com*), and you can't use a URL like *http://www.primeconsulting.com/powerpoint* to drill down to a subfolder. This can force you to do quite a bit of navigating to get where you want to be depending on how many folders you have to navigate. And when you hit a folder that has a lot of files in it, you can wind up waiting quite a while until the file list can be displayed and you can drill down further.

The good news is that there is a workaround. Slog through the folders and select the folder that is your ultimate goal in the File Open or File Save As dialog box (select it but don't open it). Right-click on it and from the pop-up menu choose Create Shortcut. You'll get a message box telling you that you can't create the shortcut there (in the server folder), and suggesting that the shortcut be created on your Desktop. Click Yes, and a shortcut to your target folder is created. Move the shortcut from your Desktop to whatever folder you favor, and the next time you want to FTP to that folder, click on that shortcut in your dialog. This takes you straight to your target folder, bypassing all points in between.

Practically Hyperlinking

In Office documents, hyperlink destinations aren't limited to intranet or Internet Web pages, or even to whole Office documents. Indeed, a hyperlink can drill down below the file layer and take you to an Access database table, an Excel worksheet or a range—named or not—in an Excel worksheet, a slide in a PowerPoint presentation, a bookmark in a Word document, or a section in a Binder. This is a "handy as a pocket on a shirt" kind of feature. To be able to instantly drill down on spreadsheet data from a Word report on a local drive or half-way across the world via the Internet is very cool.

A word of caution about heavy use of hyperlinks, particularly when using Internet Explorer: Microsoft has posted a bug report about memory problems and hyperlinking. See the Microsoft Knowledge Base article *OFF97: Memory Problems When Hyperlinking Between Programs (Q157763).* The article describes the symptoms like so, "When you use hyperlinks to switch multiple times between your Web browser and Microsoft Office programs, your system slows down and begins to run low on available memory." There is no workaround. How, ahem, annoying. We offer a new ad campaign suggestion, "How low in memory do you want to go today?"

Word Hyperlink Strategies

Word provides several interesting non-web uses for hyperlinks. The harmonious blending of hyperlinks and cross-references is particularly clever and useful.

Cross-references as hyperlinks

In Word, cross-references are maintained via a set of hidden bookmarks. You can see these when you display a cross-reference in field code mode or when you check the "Hidden bookmarks" box in the Bookmarks dialog (Insert ➤ Bookmark). A cross-reference can refer to a numbered item, heading, bookmark, footnote, endnote, equation, figure, or table, as well as an internal sequence you create yourself, either in the current document or a subdocument that belongs to the same master document set. (For information about Word's master document features, ask Robert about "master document.")

When you insert a cross-reference (Insert ➤ Cross-reference), the Cross-reference dialog's "Insert as hyperlink" box is checked by default. This means that, when the user passes the mouse over such a cross-reference, the mouse pointer changes to the traditional hyperlink "pointing finger" pointer and a ToolTip displays information about the hyperlink's destination. Figure 7-30 shows that a hyperlinked cross-reference uses Word's {REF} field, not the {HYPERLINK} field. The \h switch in the {REF} field activates its hyperlinking features.

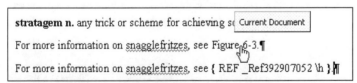

Figure 7-30: The same hyperlinked cross-reference shown in field result mode (top) and field code mode (bottom)

Although you could use Insert ➤ Hyperlink to create cross-references, we don't recommend it. It's much too clumsy, because:

1. You have to know the obscure hidden bookmark name of the destination figure caption ("_Ref392907052" in this example).

2. The hyperlink feature display text defaults to the hidden bookmark name, which isn't user-friendly, so you have to rekey the hyperlink display text.

3. You lose the power and flexibility of Word's built-in cross-reference feature.

Copy-and-paste hyperlinks and drag-and-drop hyperlinks

You can also create hyperlinks by using either copy-and-paste techniques or drag-and-drop techniques. Let's say you have a sales figure in an Excel worksheet (cell C42 of sheet Distributions). (See Figure 7-31.)

	B	C	
40	Wizelflingers	19	
41	Nertzholders	27	
42	Total units sold	628	
43			

SnagglefritzSales.xls

◄ ◄ ► ►◄ \Distributions / Sales / Expe

Figure 7-31: Linking to Excel data

NOTE   To get the hyperlink options in either the copy-and-paste or the drag-and-drop methods, the destination document must be saved to disk. You can't hyperlink to a file that has never been saved.

Follow these steps to create a hyperlink from this worksheet with copy-and-paste:

1. Open the hyperlink's destination Excel workbook (in this example, *SnagglefritzSales.xls*), select sheet Distributions, select cell C42.

2. Select Edit ➤ Copy.

3. Activate Word and select Edit, Paste as Hyperlink.

This sets up a hyperlink with display text equivalent to the cell's contents (see Figure 7-32), in the case of a single-cell destination. In the case of a range you get a graphic representation of the range. (See Figure 7-33.)

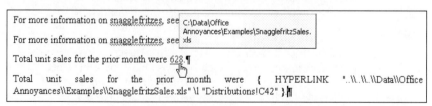

For more information on snagglefritzes, see C:\Data\Office Annoyances\Examples\SnagglefritzSales.xls

For more information on snagglefritzes, see

Total unit sales for the prior month were 628.¶

Total unit sales for the prior month were { HYPERLINK "..\\..\\..\\Data\\Office Annoyances\\Examples\\SnagglefritzSales.xls" \l "Distributions!C42" }¶

Figure 7-32: Looking under the hood of a hyperlink to a specific cell in an Excel worksheet

Wizelflingers	19
Nertzholders	27
Total units sold	628

Figure 7-33: Looking at a hyperlinked range

The steps for a drag-and-drop hyperlink are:

1. Arrange Excel and Word windows so both are visible.

2. Open the hyperlink's destination Excel workbook (in this example, *SnagglefritzSales.xls*), select sheet Distributions, select cell C42.

3. Right-click and drag the cell to the current Word document.

4. Release the mouse and select Create Hyperlink Here from the pop-up menu.

NOTE Copy-and-paste and drag-and-drop techniques work just as well with information located *inside* the current document as *outside* the current document. You can also use the Insert Hyperlink dialog (Insert ➤ Hyperlink) to hyperlink to an existing bookmark inside the current document.

Although you would expect the drag-and-drop equivalent of the above copy-and-paste operation to have the same end result, annoyingly, it ain't so. Instead of displaying the cell's value, "628," the hyperlink confusingly displays the relative path, in this case "..\..\..\Data*Office Annoyances**Examples**SnagglefritzSales.xls* - *Distributions!C42*." Go figure.

NOTE These hyperlink strategies are fine and good for navigating between bits and pieces of Office documents, but not for attempting to reflect current linked data from one document in another. There is a fundamental distinction between a hyperlink and an OLE link. In a hyperlink, if the location you're visiting (cell, named range, bookmark, etc.) changes, the hyperlink display doesn't change, ever. On the contrary, by using an OLE link, you have the option of forcing the information displayed in your document to automatically update whenever the source information—in this example, the value in cell C42—changes.

To see what we mean, you can create an OLE link by copying the cell in Excel and in Word choosing Paste Special from the Edit menu. Check the "Paste link" option button and click on OK. Change the value in Excel, and the new value is instantly reflected in the Word document.

Inside Office applications, we prefer using copy-and-paste techniques over drag-and-drop in general, simply because it's typically much faster to copy-and-paste than to try to resize the source and destination application windows so you can see what you're dragging and where you're dropping.

Here's another good tip that applies to all fields, not just hyperlinks.

TIP   Hot tip for unlinking: Word's Unlink Fields command comes in handy whenever you want to permanently convert a field—be it a hyperlink, date, ref, or any field—from its current display while discarding the underlying field code forever (thus the term "unlink"). The keyboard shortcut Ctrl+6 is the fastest way to go; you can apply this to the field the insertion point is in, the currently selected field, or all fields in the current selection (say, the entire document). Or you can create your own toolbar button to do the same: in the Customize dialog's Commands tab, select All Commands from the Categories list box, then scroll down the Commands list box until you find UnlinkFields. You may want to update some fields before unlinking them so they reflect the most current value: select the field and press F9 (the command name is UpdateFields), or right-click and choose Update Field.

There is another way to remove a hyperlink. Right-click on a hyperlink, select Hyperlink, select Edit Hyperlink, then click the Remove Link button. It works, but it's too much trouble. We much prefer the good ol' Ctrl+6 method ourselves, rather than this awkward three-click drill-down. Besides, Ctrl+6 works on any field, not just a hyperlink.

Excel Hyperlink Strategies

In Chapter 6 of *Excel 97 Annoyances*, we describe how important it is to maintain certain information about a model's development—author, purpose, date of origin, design notes, etc. If you routinely keep this information on a cover sheet or notes sheet, a practical application of hyperlinks would be to hyperlink directly to the author's email address as well as to Word documents containing the development specifications, design notes, maintenance documentation, etc. You could also provide a Table of Contents sheet that has hyperlinks to the model's various input and output ranges. (See Figure 7-34.)

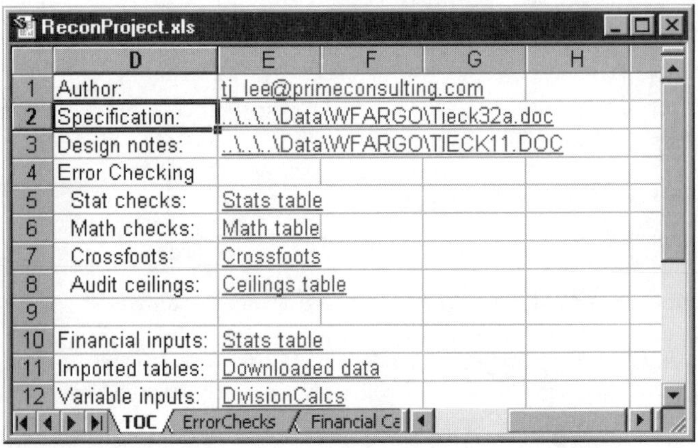

	D	E	F	G	H	
1	Author:	tj_lee@primeconsulting.com				
2	Specification:	..\..\..\Data\WFARGO\Tieck32a.doc				
3	Design notes:	..\..\..\Data\WFARGO\TIECK11.DOC				
4	Error Checking					
5	Stat checks:	Stats table				
6	Math checks:	Math table				
7	Crossfoots:	Crossfoots				
8	Audit ceilings:	Ceilings table				
9						
10	Financial inputs:	Stats table				
11	Imported tables:	Downloaded data				
12	Variable inputs:	DivisionCalcs				

Figure 7-34: Using hyperlinks within an Excel workbook

PowerPoint Hyperlink Strategies

Probably the most common use of hyperlinks in PowerPoint is quickly jumping to a supporting document; be it the details of an Annual Report in Word or a Cost of Goods Sold model in Excel. However, if the PC running the presentation isn't connected to the company's network or doesn't have all the ancillary hyperlink destination files on the local disk (in the case of a remote presentation), the hyperlinks dead-end and can turn your dream promotion into a nightmare tongue-lashing from The Big Kahuna.

PowerPoint's Action Settings feature provides a way to trigger hyperlinks that is unique, idiosyncratic, and under-powered. (Action Settings do provide the intriguing capability of triggering events other than hyperlinks, though—events like run a program, run a macro, act on an object, play a sound, or highlight upon receiving a click.) From Slide view, right-click an object, select Action Settings, and from there select either the Mouse Click tab or the Mouse Over tab (see Figure 7-35.) Why would someone go to the trouble to configure an Action Setting triggered by a mouse click (one result being to activate a hyperlink) instead of simply creating a traditional hyperlink? Go figure. If you do pursue this technique—an Action Setting—and choose "Other File..." in the "Hyperlink to" list, you can only select a filename (there's no support for deep hyperlinks, say to a particular range or bookmark). However, setting up an Action Setting of the "Mouse Over" variety might be worthwhile, since that way you can trigger a hyperlink when the user passes the mouse over that object. You can't do that with a typical hyperlink. The Office developers really missed a beat when they didn't have the Action Setting's "Other File..." option invoke the Insert Hyperlink dialog you see in PowerPoint's siblings. Instead you see a dialog entitled "Hyperlink to Other File" that looks more like a File Open dialog. This rough edge could have been more smoothly polished.

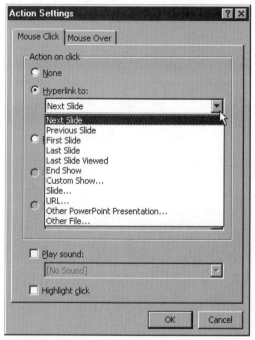

Figure 7-35: PowerPoint's Action Settings dialog gives you a "mouse over" as well as "mouse click" trigger for hyperlinks

---

NOTE   If you create a hyperlink in a PowerPoint slide, you can't activate the hyperlink while in Slide view by clicking on it. (You can activate it in Slide view by right-clicking it, selecting Hyperlink ➤ Open.) Instead, you need to be in Slide Show view. This is by design, because PowerPoint slides are comprised of AutoShapes, and the correct behavior for clicking once on an AutoShape is to select it; double-clicking behavior is to fire up the Format AutoShape dialog.

Deep Hyperlinking Hits Bottom

By "deep hyperlinking" we mean linking outside the current container's application—inter-application links—and below the document level to locations like Access database objects, Excel named ranges, PowerPoint slides, or Word bookmarks. Unfortunately, deep hyperlinking is half-broken, which is an annoying shame considering how useful this feature is. But you can usually work around the problem.

If you were planning on establishing inter-application hyperlinks using the Insert Hyperlink dialog box (Insert, Hyperlink) and then browsing for the destination file's data items using the "Named location in file (optional)" field's Browse button, forget it. This is true even in the simplest hyperlink scenario—your PC's local hard disk. The dialog's own text says, "If you want to jump to a specific location within the document, such as a bookmark, a named range, a database object, or a slide number, enter or locate that information above." But inter-application browsing for these named locations just doesn't work. Given the amount of hype—the saying "get out your hip boots" springs to mind—Microsoft has propagated regarding Office 97 and its Web-readiness, it's a shame this feature was left in such an incomplete and poorly documented state.

Instead you'll have to use the convenient copy-and-paste or drag-and-drop techniques described earlier. These techniques allow you to establish a deep hyperlink without having to know the official name of the destination data item. These techniques have another distinct advantage over the Insert Hyperlink dialog: the link's destination can be *any* location in the destination document, even if that location has no bookmark or range name. If you can't use the copy-and-paste or drag-and-drop techniques, you'll have to know the exact reference, bookmark, or range name of the destination, and you'll have to type it in manually.

We tested deep hyperlinking between the three Office 97 Standard applications—Excel, PowerPoint, and Word. Each application used a single document that tested hyperlinking to itself and its sibling applications; the results are shown in Table 7-1. You can conduct the same experiments yourself by creating the following three files:

- Excel—*Hyperlink.xls*—As a destination document, it contains two named ranges called `Range1` and `Range2`. Each range defines a single cell containing some junk text.

- PowerPoint—*Hyperlink.ppt*—As a destination document, it contains eight slides. Create the presentation using the AutoContent Wizard, select the type All (default), select Recommending a Strategy (default), then click Finish; you'll end up with eight slides; the eighth has the title "Recommendation."

- Word—*Hyperlink.doc*—As a destination document, it contains two bookmarks called `Bookmark1` and `Bookmark2`. Each bookmark defines a single short paragraph containing some junk text.

Table 7-1: Creating Deep Hyperlinks with the Standard Office Applications

Hyperlink Lives Here	Hyperlink Destination		
	Excel	PowerPoint	Word
Excel	Works as expected; range names are viewable (see Figure 7-36).	Named location Browse doesn't work (see Figure 7-38). **Solution:** manually type in a slide reference (for the last slide, either 8 or `Recommendation`) and the link works.	Named location Browse doesn't work (see Figure 7-38). **Solution:** manually type in `Bookmark1` and the link works.
PowerPoint	Named location Browse doesn't work (see Figure 7-37). **Solution:** manually type in `Range1` and the link works.	Works as expected; slide names are visible (see Figure 7-38). The following text appears in the "Named location…" text box: "262,8,Recommendation."	Named location Browse doesn't work (see Figure 7-37). **Solution:** Manually type in `Bookmark1` and the link works.
Word	Named location Browse doesn't work. First you see the dialog shown in Figure 7-39, but when you select Entire Workbook and click OK, you see Word's own Bookmark dialog (see Figure 7-40). And if you select Sheet1, Word does not reveal any known valid range names. **Solution:** Manually type in `Range1` and the link works.	Named location Browse doesn't work. When you click Browse, you immediately get Word's own Bookmark dialog (see Figure 7-40). **Solution:** Manually type in a slide reference (for the last slide either 8 or `Recommendation`) and the link works.	Works as expected; Word displays its own Bookmarks dialog.

Outlook: Jump Start Your Contacts

As discussed in Chapter 4, Outlook is Microsoft's tour de force PIM. It has excited users—and upset competitors—since you can look at Outlook as a "freebie" that comes with Office. Since it is in the Office box, sooner or

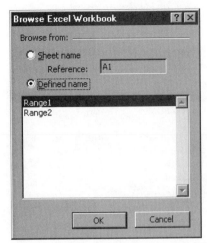

Figure 7-36: Excel's Browse Excel Workbook dialog appears when deep hyperlinking from Excel to Excel

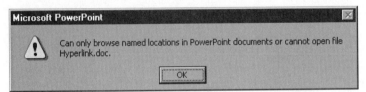

Figure 7-37: This message box appears in PowerPoint when you try to deep hyperlink to a named range in Excel or a bookmark in a Word document

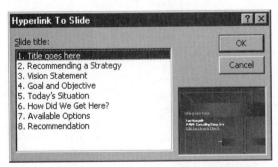

Figure 7-38: PowerPoint's Hyperlink To Slide dialog appears when deep hyperlinking from PowerPoint to PowerPoint

later you're probably going to try it. Personal Information Managers are pretty heavy on the *personal* when it comes to how you use them, so we're going to focus on the strategic issues you are likely to run afoul of.

The most fundamental thing everyone uses a PIM for is to store and organize all their business and personal contacts in one handy and accessible

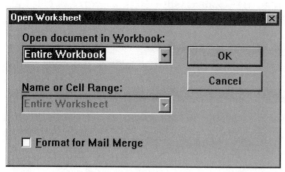

Figure 7-39: Word's Open Worksheet dialog appears when deep hyperlinking to a named range in Excel

Figure 7-40: Strangely, Word displays its own Bookmark dialog when trying to deep hyperlink to a named range in Excel

place. We're talking names, addresses, and phone numbers. If you don't use Outlook for anything else, we're betting you keep contact information in it.

A Cookbook for Conversion

If you've been using Windows 95 and Outlook's predecessor, Exchange, you probably already have all your names and addresses tucked in the personal address book—*mailbox.pab*—commonly referred to as the PAB. Outlook has its own address book known as the Contacts list (a.k.a. the Outlook Address Book).

For reasons we'll be discussing in the following sections, you should consider getting your PAB data into Outlook. The trick is getting your information from the PAB to the Contacts list. Not to worry, we'll walk you through the process.

The first thing to be aware of is that Outlook only recognizes one PAB at a time—the one that is referenced in the current profile. To check your profile in Outlook, click Tools ➤ Services. On the Services tab, you'll see a list of the current services for the profile you are using. (See Figure 7-41.) To see which *mailbox.pab* file the profile service is referencing (assuming you have more than one), select Personal Address Book and then click on the Properties button.

Figure 7-41: The PAB in the current profile services is the source for importing

The Personal Address Book dialog displays the path to the PAB file referenced in the profile (see Figure 7-42). If this is not the file you want to import to your Contacts list, click the Browse button and select the PAB file you want imported.

Once you have the proper PAB file referenced, just click on OK and then on OK in the Services dialog. You are now ready to import the PAB entries to an Outlook Contacts list.

Outlook has a Contacts folder for storing your contacts, but you can create multiple Contacts lists. This is useful if you want to keep your business contacts separated from your personal contacts. Or you may create a Contacts list for a special project and want to keep the people on that list separate from all other contacts.

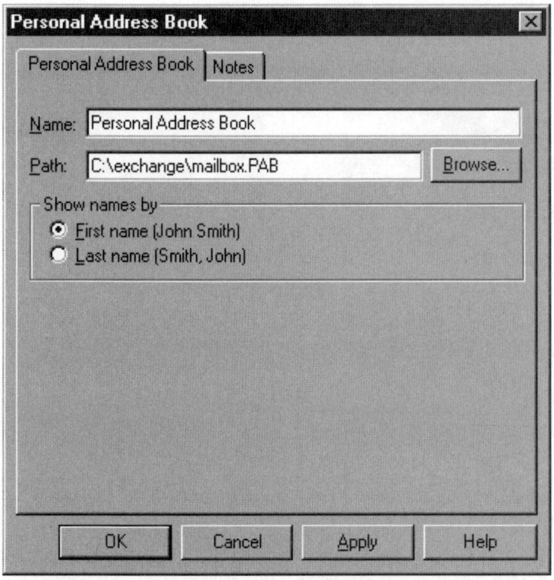

Figure 7-42: Check the path to the PAB file

To create a new folder for Contacts, click on File ➤ New ➤ Folder. This displays the Create New Folder dialog box (see Figure 7-43). In the folder tree, select the folder under which you want to create your subfolder. Type in a Name for your folder and be sure to tell Outlook what type of data this folder will contain. Under the label "Folder contains" is a drop-down list of the types of data your Outlook folders can contain. You must select Contact Items or you will not be able to import PAB data to it. Click on OK to return to Outlook.

Next, pull down the File menu and click on the Import and Export option. This starts the Import and Export Wizard. (See Figure 7-44.) Preposterous as it may seem, there is no specific choice for importing a personal address book. How obvious is it that when you want to import a PAB, you should choose the "Import from Schedule+ or another program or file"? Anyway, that's the option you want. Click on Next to proceed to the next step.

This next list is much less cryptic (see Figure 7-45). Scroll down the list and you'll find an option for Personal Address Book. Select this option and click on the Next button.

If you have created a new folder (and have set the folder type to Contacts Items, as shown in Figure 7-43), select it as the destination folder. To use the default folder, just click on Contacts in the list. (See Figure 7-46.) Click on Next to proceed.

Figure 7-43: Creating a new folder in Outlook

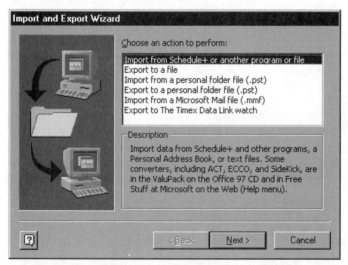

Figure 7-44: The PAB qualifies as "another program or file"

All that's left is to click on the Finish button (see Figure 7-47) and start the import process. Once you click on Finish you'll see the Import and Export Progress status box that lets you monitor the progress as the PAB is imported to Outlook.

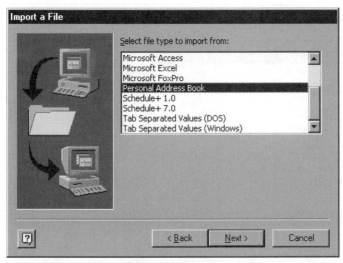

Figure 7-45: Selecting the type of data being imported

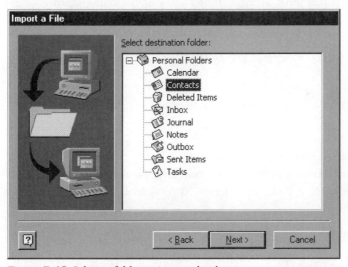

Figure 7-46: Select a folder to import the data to

When the import process is complete, the status box disappears and you can display your Contacts list in Outlook. You can't filter the PAB; it's an all or nothing proposition, but once you have the data translated as Contact Items, you can search the list and prune the records as needed.

Contacts lists provide you more flexibility in Outlook than trying to work with the PAB, but don't discard the Personal Address Book from your profile just yet. Outlook has no provision for email distribution lists at

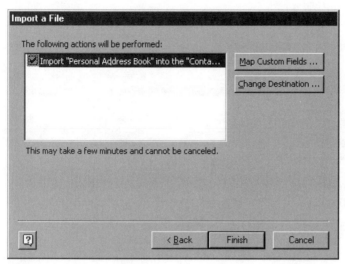

Figure 7-47: Ready to import!

present, so keep that PAB around until Microsoft fixes this glaring omission in Outlook.

Word and Outlook—A Strategic Alliance Gone Awry

Whether you decide to move all your name and address information into the Contacts list or leave it in the Personal Address Book, the first thing you'll probably want to do is access these names and addresses from inside some other program, like in a letter you're writing in Word, or perhaps a form letter to everyone in your PAB or Contacts list. You get the drift. Let's take a look at a letter to a single person from inside Outlook first.

Contacts to Word—take a letter

In Outlook, select one of your Contacts. Then pull down the Contacts menu and click on New Letter to Contact. Word starts. If Word is already running, it is ignored, and a new instance of Word is started. Geez, we just started and already we're annoyed.

Next, the Letter Wizard in Word kicks in. (See Figure 7-48.) This Wizard is a bit unique in that each of the four tabs shown in the Letter Wizard dialog box corresponds to a step in the Wizard. The Letter Format tab is Step 1, the Recipient Info tab is Step 2, the Other Elements tab is Step 3, and the Sender Info tab is Step 4. This Wizard helps you create a letter in Word and pops in the Contact's name and address in the appropriate spot. From the "Choose a page design" list, you can pick from several letter templates that ship with Word.

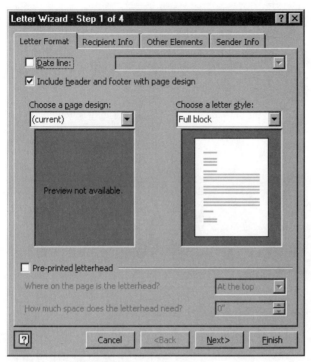

Figure 7-48: The Word Letter Wizard

You can click on the Next button or you can click on the individual tabs at the top of the dialog box to work your way through the Wizard. In Step 2, Recipient Info, you'll see the Contact information that will be plunked down in your Word letter. (See Figure 7-49.)

If this isn't the name and address you want, you can click on the "Click here to use Address Book" icon and search your address books for a different name. You'll notice that the Address Book icon has a drop-down arrow next to it. It saves the last 16 names you accessed in a drop-down list under the assumption that you'll use one of these names again soon.

Overall, this method is pretty brain-dead. First, there is the multiple instances of Word problem (if Word is already running when you start a new letter from within Outlook). Next, apparently it's impossible to tell the Wizard exactly where you want the name and address dropped into the document (if it's not impossible, it has completely eluded us). Instead, the Wizard is intent on putting the name and address starting with the

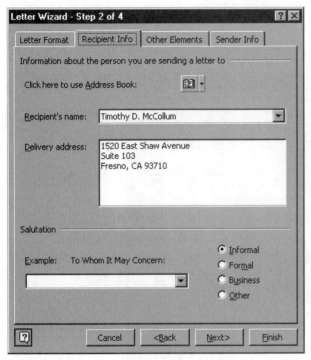

Figure 7-49: Your Contact item information

first line in the document. For a full discussion of Word's Letter Wizard see "Dealing with the Letter Wizard" in *Word 97 Annoyances*.

Word to Contacts—give me an address

If you ask the OA something like "Getting an address from Outlook," the closest topic you'll receive is "Insert an address from my personal address book." And if you follow the instructions there, you'll go to the Tools menu, then click Envelopes and Labels. This lets you find the Insert Address icon in Word, but the best you'll do with it is create a label or an envelope with a Contact address in it.

Not so good for the letter you want to create. To get the Insert Address icon out where you can actually use it to get a name and address into a document, you have to start jumping through some annoying hoops:

1. Pull down the Tools menu and click on Customize.

2. In the Customize dialog box, click on the Commands tab.

3. In the Categories list select Insert.

4. Scroll the Commands list until you find the Address Book entry.

5. Drag the Address Book icon to a suitable toolbar.

Now you can create a letter, and when you have the cursor where you want the name and address, just click on the Address Book icon. This displays the Select Names dialog box. (See Figure 7-50.)

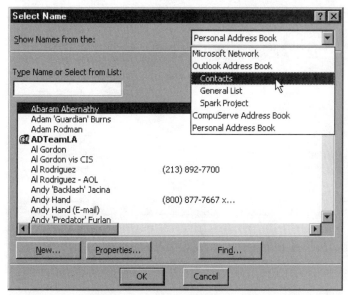

Figure 7-50: Selecting names from various names lists in Outlook

Notice that the various and sundry address lists that Windows/Office support are selectable in the "Show Names from the" drop-down list. You can select a Contact list from Outlook, the Personal Address Book, or other lists depending on which online service you may be using. Pick a name from the displayed list, and that name and address is inserted into the document like this:

> Timothy D. McCollum
> 1520 East Shaw Avenue
> Suite 103
> Fresno, CA 93710
> United States of America

Actually, you may get more and less than you want. In this example, we inserted a name from the Outlook Address Book's Contacts list and, while the Company name was omitted, the text "United States of America" was appended to the end of the address. When you add Contacts to Outlook, it likes to fill in the Country field for you. PAB entries that are imported into the Contact list only get a Country field value if the PAB record had one. The only way we've found to turn this off is to open the Contact item in Outlook, click on the General tab for the displayed contact, click

on the Address button, then delete the entry in the Country field and do a
Save and Close. (See Figure 7-51.)

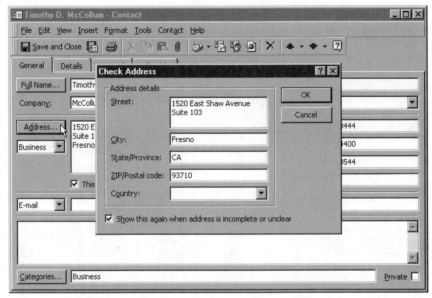

Figure 7-51: Clearing the Country field

You'll have to add the Company information manually if you want it.
Very annoying. But given that the Insert Address button in Word allows
you to control which address book to query and how contact information
is placed within the Word document, this is the recommended way to
bring in names and addresses for single documents.

Mail merge in Word

Doing any kind of mass mailing requires using the Mail Merge feature
built into Word (yes, even in this electronic age, many of us still need to
send form letters, invitations, notices, etc., from time to time). You can
use your Personal Address Book or your Contacts list as a data source for
a Word mail merge.

When Microsoft designed the Exchange PAB and later the Outlook
Contacts list, they adopted a, um, *unique* method for handling mail
merges. The way merges work can cause you some major annoyances, so
we'll discuss each step in depth so that you can understand what's
happening.

Let's see what happens using the PAB as your data source. To do a mail merge to generate labels in Word linked directly to your PAB do the following:

1. Create a new Word document.

2. Select Tools, Mail Merge, click the Create button, choose Mailing Labels (we'll use Mailing Labels for all the examples in this section, but this technique works equally well for any other type of mail merge), click the Active Window button, click the Get Data button, choose Use Address Book, select Personal Address Book in the Use Address Book dialog (see Figure 7-52), click OK.

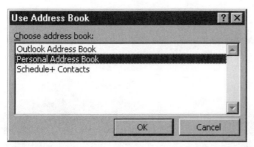

Figure 7-52: Word's Use Address Book dialog appears when mail merging with Outlook

3. Click the Set Up Main Document button, make your choices in the Label Options dialog (we selected Avery standard 5162), click OK.

4. In the Create Labels dialog, click the Insert Merge Field button and select the desired fields (one at a time) from the cascading menu. Click OK when done. See Figure 7-53 for the list of fields we chose.

5. To merge without any filtering (querying), click the Merge button, accept the Merge dialog's defaults (Merge to - New document, Records to be merged - All, Don't print blank lines...), click Merge. Word reports the record numbers on its status bar as it merges them. The time it takes for the merge depends, of course, on the number of records in your PAB.

6. You can save, print, or discard the mail merge output document at your discretion (see Figure 7-54). Currently it has a name like Labels1.

7. Save your mail merge main document now with the filename *PAB mail merge (postal info).doc*.

So far so good, right? Wrong. Something's about to hit the fan. Go ahead and close *PAB mail merge (postal info).doc*. Word (sometimes) prompts you, "PAB mail merge (postal info).doc is a mail merge main document

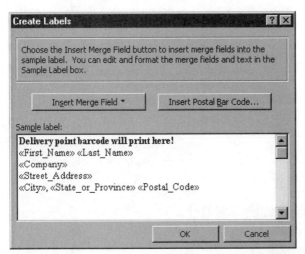

Figure 7-53: Word shows you a sample label in "merge field" format in its Create Labels dialog

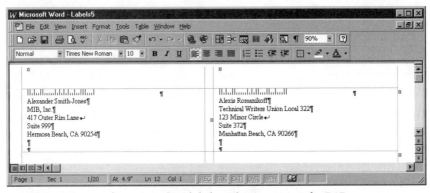

Figure 7-54: Output from a mailing label mail merge using the PAB

that is attached to a data source Personal Address Book that has not been saved. Do you want to save Personal Address Book?" Maddeningly, there's no Help button on this red herring message box.

If you choose Yes, you'll next see a message box, "This document will be saved in Word format. Do you want to continue?" Click Yes. The next message box has to be seen to be believed; it's shown in Figure 7-55 (note that the message box text is oddly truncated at the end). The first time we saw this message was on a PC with 230 MB free on a 1.2 GB drive and plenty of free system resources. Subsequent tests on this and other PCs yielded the same result, so this is not a case of a machine-specific glitch. Something's terribly wrong here.

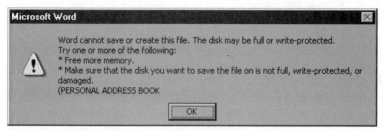

Figure 7-55: Clear evidence that Word has lost its way (and mind) while tidying up after a simple mail merge with a Personal Address Book

Word wants to create a background copy of the PAB, but mismanages the process horribly.

Without making any changes to your PAB, immediately open *PAB mail merge (postal info).doc*, then select Tools, Mail Merge (this invokes the Mail Merge Helper dialog), click the Data source section's Edit button, and notice the bizarre data filename: *C:\~~\~~~_virtual_file_~~~.pab.** (See Figure 7-56.)

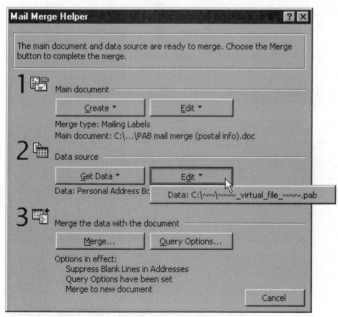

Figure 7-56: The Mail Merge Helper dialog reveals the existence of the ~~~_virtual_ file_~~~.pab virtual file

---

* You can actually view this file in Word like this: click the Mail Merge Helper button, click the Data source section's Edit button, choose the bizarre item entitled Data: C:\~~..., and click View Source in the Data Form dialog.

As bizarre as this is, you can still perform a successful merge using this main document. *However, if you subsequently edit your PAB, this main document will never see any changes to existing records or any new records.*

Here's the proof: close the main document, add a new record to your PAB—we used a name of `aaaFirst aaaLast` with bogus information in the appropriate data fields for easy identification—and run a new merge. *The new record is not in the new merge.* Update a record that was present in the previous merge and run a new merge. *Changes to the record are not reflected in the new merge.*

It gets even worse. Close Outlook and Word. Restart Outlook and then Word. Open *PAB mail merge (postal info).doc*, and you'll see the weird message shown in Figure 7-57. Click Yes to make a copy, and you'll see the dismaying message displayed in Figure 7-58.

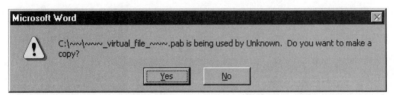

Figure 7-57: Word descends deeper into PAB mail merge hell

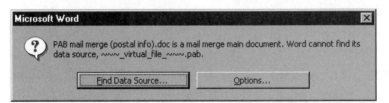

Figure 7-58: Word descends even deeper into PAB mail merge hell

Click Options (don't bother with the Find Data Source button—you'll never locate the non-existent file), then writhe in the agony of Microsoft's obfuscatory hell with the message shown in Figure 7-59. Note the unprofessional truncated text (looks like the developers didn't plan for long filenames in the message prompt).

Microsoft suggests this workaround: click Remove Data/Header Source, select Tools, choose Mail Merge, click Get Data, choose Use Address Book, select Personal Address Book, click OK; all in order to create a new virtual file based on the current PAB. We've found this technique doesn't work reliably. In some tests this caused the Merge button to be

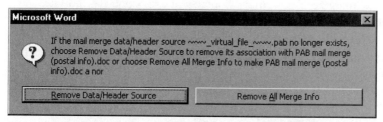

Figure 7-59: Nowhere left to go in the PAB mail merge inferno's inner circle

disabled in the Mail Merge Helper dialog. Ouch, there's a belly-up main document. In others, the technique worked. Go figure.

Could it possibly get any worse, you ask? Oh yes. Say you've just given up in disgust on this particular fubar* main document. With the same session of Word still running (the one in which Word's been misbehaving like a wolverine on amphetamines), add a new record to your PAB. Back in Word, create a new main document and work your way through all the normal merge steps. You'd think you'd be establishing a nice, clean link to your PAB—albeit a link that's going to be hosed as soon as you close the document, but we digress. Wrong. Do a merge and this new main document fails to see the new record. You have to exit and restart Word, and invoke the clumsy "Remove Data/Header Source" workaround to re-establish (sometimes) a direct PAB link.

Here's what the Microsoft Knowledge Base has to say about this, "This behavior is by design to prevent you from accidentally overwriting the original Outlook 97 (Schedule+) contact list with a format not recognized by Outlook 97 (Schedule+). Since this file [~~~_virtual_file_~~~.pab, .olk, or .scd] is a temporary file, it is deleted when you exit Word." By design? Well, what this really means is that Microsoft decided not to make the link simple, elegant, dynamic, and one-way (for safety's sake) and instead kludged this virtual file solution. Perhaps this is a MAPI limitation or perhaps there's a more deeply-rooted problem here. It's an inexcusable annoyance nonetheless.

Mail merge and the Contacts list

Mechanically, using a Contacts list as your data source for a mail merge works the same way as using the PAB. However, there's good news and bad news.

First, the bad news. All of the infuriating problems with a PAB-direct mail merge that we described in the previous section apply to a Contacts-

---

* Fouled up beyond all repair.

direct mail merge. (The terms "Contacts list," "Contacts module," and "Outlook Address Book" are all synonymous.) After you set up your Contacts-direct main document, run a mail merge, close Word, open Word, and open up the Contacts-direct main document, here comes that series of message boxes you love to hate (see Figure 7-60), only this time the virtual file has an extension of *.olk*.

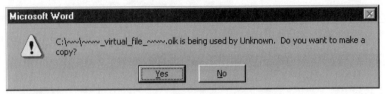

Figure 7-60: Déjà vu—a Contacts-direct mail merge has all the problems of a PAB-direct mail merge

Setting up a Contacts-direct link from your main document involves the same steps you used for a PAB-direct link. The only difference is that when you select Outlook Address Book in the Use Address Book dialog (see Figure 7-52), you then have an additional dialog box to contend with, as shown in Figure 7-61.

Figure 7-61: Word's Mail Merge from Contacts Folder dialog shows a list of all the available Outlook Address Book folders

In the Mail Merge from Contacts Folder dialog box, you can choose any Contacts folders that are set up in Outlook to display as resources in the Outlook Address Book. The default Contacts folder—named, not surprisingly, Contacts—is already set to appear in your Outlook Address Book. To prove this, right-click the Contacts icon in the Outlook Bar, choose Properties, click the Outlook Address Book tab, and you should see that the "Show this folder as an e-mail Address Book" box is checked (and the name is "Contacts"), as shown in Figure 7-62.

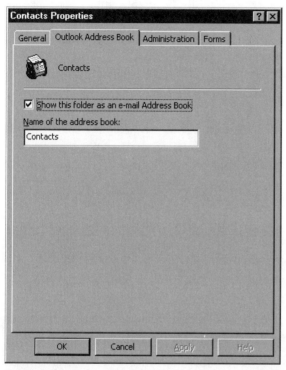

Figure 7-62: Look at the default Contacts folder's properties, then its Outlook Address Book tab settings, to verify that it will appear as an e-mail Address Book

This check box and name designation can be applied to any folder containing Contact items. This brings us to the good (sort of) news: with a Contacts-based mail merge, you don't have to use filtering on the Word side to narrow down the desired records. Instead, you can create a new temporary Contacts folder—say, Contacts Mail Merge—to store records for your mail merge, copy records from Contacts to it, then use it in the mail merge. Here are the steps:

1. To create a new folder, select File, New, Folder, enter **Contacts Mail Merge** in the Name field, select Contact Items in the "Folder contains" drop-down control, select Contacts in the "Make this a subfolder of" check box, make sure the "Create a shortcut to this folder in the Outlook Bar" box is checked, click OK.

2. Verify that the Contacts Mail Merge folder's properties designate it as "Show this folder as an e-mail Address Book."

3. When you set up a mail merge, point to this folder instead of Contacts.

This approach is still fraught with all the virtual file problems we discussed earlier. It introduces the new problem of duplicate records existing in multiple Contact items folders—a kludge is still a kludge—but it's a tad easier than dealing directly with the PAB.

Mail merge—conclusions and workarounds

We'd like to think that Microsoft has a crack team of programmers working on the fundamental issue of effortlessly shuffling and inserting names and addresses between Outlook and *any* other Office application. We'd like to think so, but it's hard to get worked up to that level of optimism.

First, we recommend you move all your names and addresses from your PAB to an Outlook Contacts list. Not that this solves the mail merge problems we've discussed, but it's one step towards consolidation of the diverse address books that Windows and Office has foisted on you.

Then you need to decide if working with the *virtual file* methodology is going to drive you nuts or not. If you can live with having to remove the Data/Header source every time you want to remerge a mail merge main document, then you're all set.

Well, almost all set. Outlook has another annoying flaw: you can't merge all of the Contact item fields. Of the 100+ Contact item fields, you can only merge 40 of them (the ones that appear in Word on the Insert Merge Field menu). How big an annoyance this is depends on what information you need to merge.

There is one other workaround that deals with the use of the virtual file and most of the problems concerning the limits on which Contact item fields you can merge (under no circumstances can you merge custom user-defined fields). You can export the Contacts list to another application—like Excel or Access—and merge from there.

Exporting a Contacts list is very easy:

1. In Outlook, select the Import and Export option from the File menu. This starts the Import and Export Wizard. Select the "Export to a file" option and click the Next button. (See Figure 7-63.)

2. In the next panel, select the Contact folder you want to export. (See Figure 7-64.)

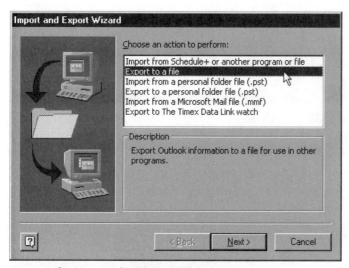

Figure 7-63: Starting the Import and Export Wizard

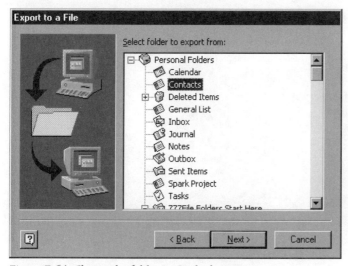

Figure 7-64: Choose the folder in Outlook to export

3. You have a fairly complete choice of file types to which you can export your Contacts list. Pick the file type you are most comfortable doing mail merges with and click on the Next button. (See Figure 7-65.)

4. Type a path and filename for the exported file. You can use the Browse button to choose a folder on your hard disk if you wish. Click on the Next button to proceed. (See Figure 7-66.)

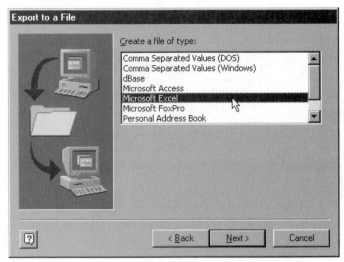

Figure 7-65: Choose the file type for the exported file

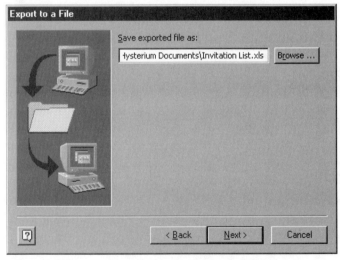

Figure 7-66: Designate a destination folder and filename

5. The last panel, which is shown in Figure 7-67, shows you what actions will be performed and admonishes you that this may take a while (depending on the number of contacts you have), and that you can't cancel the process once it starts. Click on Finish and you're done.

Is this the panacea for all your mail merge headaches? No. You have the annoying problems of subsequent updates to your Contacts list in Outlook, and the usual problems with line breaks included in text fields;

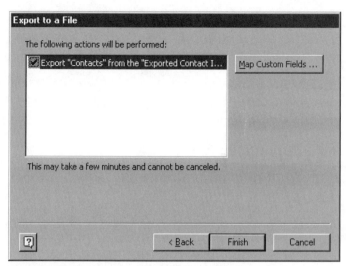

Figure 7-67: Ready to rock and roll, er, export!

on the up side, you have a great deal of control over your data once you get it in an exported format.

Maybe our hopes are not misplaced and Microsoft will address this rather obvious issue in the next release of Office.

8

Where and How to Get Help

Some of the individual component pieces of Office have been around for a long time, and there are a number of rich sources of information on them. Microsoft has done a crackerjack job of providing ancillary knowledge bases and the like for information on Office as a whole.

These are of a few of the places you should look at for more information on Office. Of course, some sources are better than others.

The Horse's Mouth

You might try Microsoft's Product Support people. In the U.S. the number is 425-635-7145. Be prepared with your registration number (click Help, About), and if at all possible be sitting in front of your PC when you call. Keep in mind that, like all the major software companies, Microsoft has started outsourcing its support services, and you might be talking with someone that knows less about Office than you do. We've heard a lot of horror stories about PSS over the years; they're good at the basic stuff, but getting answers to complex questions can take forever. Assuming you get an answer at all.

Microsoft maintains several Office-related newsgroups on the Net at *http://msnews.microsoft.com*. The names of the groups change from time to time, but as we went to press the important ones related to Office as a whole started at *microsoft.public.office* (a count of six). There are literally dozens of newsgroups for each of the individual Office applications: *microsoft.public.access* (36), *microsoft.public.excel* (15), *microsoft.public.outlook97* (10), *microsoft.public.powerpoint* (2), and *microsoft.public.*

word (20). You can easily access these newsgroups using the Internet Mail and News reader that comes with Internet Explorer 3.x.

NOTE   Microsoft doesn't support these newsgroups. They're "peer to peer," which means the people who provide answers are acting out of the goodness of their hearts. Many of them are quite knowledgeable and have developed large scale, industrial strength applications used by Fortune 500 companies. These folks are typically—though not always—designated as Microsoft MVPs (Microsoft Most Valued Professionals); others come across as well-meaning but not terribly well-informed. Keep that in mind as you struggle through your problems.

Surfing the Web

Microsoft puts a lot of effort into its Web site, and as long as you don't mind looking for your own answers, they can be very helpful. Microsoft's Office-related web pages include:

- *http://www.microsoft.com/office* contains the latest information on Office. Or, you can zero in on the specific application in Office on which you want information.

- *http://www.microsoft.com/msword* has the latest and greatest on Word.

- *http://www.microsoft.com/msexcel/* is as assemblage of current news headlines regarding Excel.

- *http://www.microsoft.com/msaccess/* contains all things database. The hot stuff for Access users and developers.

- *http://www.microsoft.com/mspowerpoint/* has news and information on PowerPoint.

- *http://www.microsoft.com/outlook/* is where you can pick up the latest utilities, Wizards, patches and fixes for Outlook.

- *http://www.microsoft.com/officedev* is the place to start for VBA FAQs.

- *http://www.microsoft.com/kb*, the Microsoft Knowledge Base, remains the indispensable source of information, albeit occasionally with a pro-Microsoft spin. This is where you can find information on known bugs and problems as well as the odd tip, and technique. Overall, quite useful.

- *http://www.microsoft.com/OfficeFreeStuff/* has the latest Wizards, templates, workbooks, sounds, tools, and Microsoft offered add-ons.

- *http://www.primeconsulting.com/faq13.shtml* is our compendium of *Where to Find Office 97 Official Public White Papers from Microsoft.*

Every serious Office user should have those on their browser's Favorites list.

NOTE   Also, as we discussed in Chapter 7, *Strategies*, make good use of each Office application's Help ➤ Microsoft on the Web cascading menu.

ORK and CBT

In addition to these sources, Microsoft offers some advanced products that can be of use to the dedicated Office user. *The Microsoft Office Resource Kit* (ORK)—billed as "The Professional's Companion to Microsoft Office 97"—is a fair source of technical data on Office and its components. However, it is written more for people who support Office in a network environment (Information Systems types) than for the "down in the trenches" users.

The ORK can be ordered through Microsoft Press at (800) 677-7377.

For the developer who's not afraid of computer based training (CBT), there is *Mastering Microsoft Office 97 Development*, a CD-ROM based tutorial (er, "in depth, interactive training," according to the box) for developers. It's not bad for a good overview of the VBA object models, using the DAO (data access objects), and the like. Get the *Mastering Microsoft Office 97 Development* from Microsoft's Internet Platform and Tools Division at (800) 621-7930. Ask for part number 087-00047_99.

MSDN and TechNet

For a fee, Microsoft will send CD-ROMs full of information (some actually quite useful, too) right to your door via U.S. Snail Mail.

The TechNet program delivers two (sometimes more) CDs once a month for $299/year. You get resource kits for various Microsoft operating systems and products, technical notes, reviewer's guides, white papers, drivers, bug reports, and the latest patches. Also included is the Microsoft Knowledge Base on disk as well as numerous case studies from and by companies implementing Office solutions.

Magazines

All three of us write for *PC Computing* and its sister publication, *Office Computing*. We naturally recommend both of these publications for their in-depth coverage of Windows and Microsoft Office. In particular, if you're interested in creating custom solutions in Office with VBA, templates, workbooks, forms, or just about any other technique, and appreciate a concise step-by-step approach, *Office Computing* can't be beat. Check *Office Computing*'s Web site at *http:// www.officecomputing.com.*

WOW

We strongly urge all Annoyances readers to subscribe to WOW, *Woody's Office Watch*, our free weekly electronic bulletin with up-to-the-nanosecond news about Office. From the latest rumors, to warnings about viruses, bugs and patches, to contrarian opinions by Office's most devoted (and knowledgeable!) detractors, to the famous ask.woody column, WOW keeps you abreast of the good, the bad, and the ugly sides of Microsoft Office. And the price sure is right.

To subscribe, send email to *wow@wopr.com.*l

Index

Symbols, Numbers

' (backtick) + Ctrl key (Excel), 145–146
= (equal sign) for Excel formulas, 208
3-D effects (AutoShapes), 286

A

About dialogs (Help menu), 16–17
absolute cell references, Excel, 146–148
Access
    Database Wizard, 185–188
    Developer Forum command, 310
    event handling, 142
    hyperlinks in, 189–192
    IntelliSense in, 273
    linking with Word, 181–185
    macro viruses, 296
    multi-level undo, 181
    object model, 127–128
    Outlook and, 185, 198–200
    Performance Analyzer, 196–198
    programming environment, 83
    Query Wizards, 188–189
    toolbar buttons for macros, 137
    Trojan Horse attacks, 294
    Web Wizard, 192–196
    where to store macros, 135
Access folder (templates), 37
Action Settings (PowerPoint), 336–337
ActiveMovie add-ins, 297

ActiveX controls
    NCompass ActiveX plugin, 297
    registering, 321
add-ins, 76
    (see also ValuPack folders)
address books, 2
alert messages (see dialog boxes)
alphabetizing (see order)
Always on Top option (OSB), 33
animation
    mouse cursors, 297
    Office Assistant, 259
    PowerPoint Animation Player, 299,
      320
    ValuPack's Animgifs files, 297
    (see also graphics)
annoyances, in general, 6–7
Answer Wizard (Office 95), 262
anti-virus (AV) software, 19–20, 296
API, Windows, 124
applets, OLE, 300–304
arranging (see order)
art (see graphics)
ASF (ActiveMovie Streaming
    Format), 297
Audio Compression component, 29
audio effects, 28–30
    Music Tracks add-in, 298
    by Office Assistant, 42
    RealAudio add-in, 299

About the Authors

Woody Leonhard's books include *Windows 3.1 Programming for Mere Mortals*, *The Underground Guide to Word for Windows*, *The Hacker's Guide to Word for Windows*, *The Mother of All PC Books*, *The Mother of All Windows 95 Books*, and several others. He was series editor for Addison-Wesley's *Underground Guides* (11 books) and A-W's *Hacker's Guides* (4 books). Along with T.J. Lee and Lee Hudspeth, he's editor-in-chief of PC Computing's *Undocumented Office*, a monthly hardcopy newsletter. He's a contributing editor at *PC Computing* (circulation 1,000,000+), and productivity editor for *Office Computing* (circulation 400,000), a new monthly magazine from the editors of *PC Computing*. He also publishes a free weekly electronic news bulletin on Microsoft Office called WOW ("Woody's Office Watch"), available by sending email to *wow@wopr.com*. Woody's software company makes WOPR, Woody's Office POWER Pack, the Number-One Enhancement to Microsoft Office. A self-described "grizzled computer hack, frustrated novelist, and Office victim," by day he's a Tibetan human rights activist and co-founder of the Tibetan Children's Fund. Woody lives on top of a mountain in Coal Creek Canyon, Colorado.

Lee Hudspeth is a co-founder of PRIME Consulting Group, Inc. in Hermosa Beach, CA, a Microsoft Solution Provider. His background is in operations research, financial analysis, and marketing analysis (formerly with Unocal Corp.). He has co-authored several books on Office, including *The Underground Guide to Microsoft Office, OLE, and VBA*, and *The Underground Guide to Excel 5.0 for Windows*. He is co-editor-in-chief of *Undocumented Office*, he's a Microsoft MVP (Most Valued Professional), co-author of the Microsoft course on application development using WordBasic, and a certified Microsoft trainer in Visual Basic and WordBasic. Along with other PRIME Consulting staff, Lee has developed innumerable lines of VB, VBA, and WordBasic code for the firm's numerous Office add-ins (PRIME for Excel and PRIME for Word), going way back to Word 2.0. Lee also writes and delivers Office usage and development custom courses to hordes of interested parties the world over.

T.J. Lee, also a co-founder of PRIME Consulting Group, has a background as a certified public accountant and has done computer and management consulting for years. He has co-authored several books on Office, including *The Underground Guide to Microsoft Excel 5* and *The Underground Guide to Microsoft Office, OLE, and VBA*. T.J. is co-editor-in-chief of *Undocumented Office* and a certified Microsoft trainer. He has written countless courseware packages and manuals, co-authored the Microsoft Education Services course on Developing Applications in Word, and taught and lectured for thousands of developers and end users.

Colophon

Our look is the result of reader comments, our own experimentation, and feedback from distribution channels. Distinctive covers complement our distinctive approach to technical topics, breathing personality and life into potentially dry subjects.

The bird on the cover of *Office 97 Annoyances* is a dodo. The dodo lived in the Mascarene islands in the Indian Ocean, primarily on Mauritius. These flightless birds are believed to have been related to pigeons, but scientists have found it difficult to categorize them.

Our knowledge of the dodo's appearance is based on descriptions from sailors and explorers who settled the Mascarene islands in the 16th and 17th centuries, and who were fascinated with these peculiar-looking birds. The dodos' plump bodies were covered with grey feathers, which ringed their bare faces like a hood. Because they were flightless, their wings had regressed to a tiny size, and their white tail feathers had become a small, curly tuft. Most remarkable was the beak, which was large, strong, hooked, and light green or pale yellow. The dodo used its powerful beak to open hard fruits and snail shells.

The dodo was extinct by the beginning of the 18th century. The Europeans who settled Mauritius and the other Mascarene islands hunted the dodo for food, sport, and as curiosities. Several attempts were made to bring live dodos back to Europe with them, with varying degrees of success. The European settlers also introduced animals such as cats, dogs, pigs, and rats to the islands. These animals hunted the dodo, trampled their nests, and ate their eggs. Prior to the arrival of these various foreigners, the dodo had no natural enemies, and so had no defense mechanisms.

Edie Freedman designed the cover of this book, using a 19th-century engraving from the Dover Pictorial Archive. The cover layout was produced with Quark XPress 3.3 using the ITC Garamond font. Whenever possible, our books use RepKover™, a durable and flexible lay-flat binding. If the page count exceeds RepKover's limit, perfect binding is used.

The inside layout was designed by Edie Freedman and Nancy Priest and implemented in FrameMaker 5.0 by Mike Sierra. The text and heading fonts are ITC Garamond Light and Garamond Book. The illustrations that appear in the book were created in Macromedia Freehand 7.0 by Robert Romano. This colophon was written by Clairemarie Fisher O'Leary.

More Titles from O'Reilly

Annoyances

Windows Annoyances

By David A. Karp
1st Edition June 1997
300 pages, ISBN 1-56592-266-2

Windows Annoyances, a comprehensive resource for intermediate to advanced users of Windows 95 and NT 4.0, details step-by-step how to customize your Win95/NT operating system through an extensive collection of tips, tricks, and workarounds. You'll learn how to customize every aspect of these systems, far beyond the intentions of Microsoft. This book shows you how to customize your PC through methods of backing up, repairing, compressing, and transferring portions of the Registry. Win95 users will discover how Plug and Play, the technology that makes Win95 so compatible, can save time and improve the way you interact with your computer. You'll also learn how to benefit from the new 32-bit software and hardware drivers that support such features as improved multitasking and long filenames.

Word 97 Annoyances

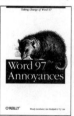

By Woody Leonhard, Lee Hudspeth & T.J. Lee
1st Edition August 1997
356 pages, ISBN 1-56592-308-1

Word 97 contains hundreds of annoying idiosyncrasies that can be either eliminated or worked around. Whether it's the Find Fast feature that takes over your machine every once in awhile, or the way Word automatically selects an entire word as you struggle to highlight only a portion of it, *Word 97 Annoyances* will show you how to solve the problem. It's filled with tips and customizations, and takes an in-depth look at what makes Word 97 tick—mainly character and paragraph formatting, styles, and templates.

This informative, yet humorous, book shows you how to use and modify Word 97 to meet your needs, transforming the software into a powerful tool customized to the way *you* use Word. You'll learn how to:

- Customize the toolbar so it works the way you want it to
- Reduce your stress level by understanding how Word defines sections or formats paragraphs and accepting some apparent annoyances that are built into Word
- Write simple VBA programs to eliminate your own personal annoyances

Excel 97 Annoyances

By Woody Leonhard, Lee Hudspeth & T.J. Lee
1st Edition September 1997
336 pages, ISBN 1-56592-309-X

Learn how to shape Excel 97 in a way that will not only make it most effective, but will give you a sense of enjoyment as you analyze data with ease. Excel 97, which ships with Office 97, has many new features that may be overwhelming. All of the various toolbars, packed with what seems to be an unending array of buttons, might seem a bit intimidating, not to mention annoying, to the average user. *Excel 97 Annoyances* is a guide that will help create some order among the available options by providing customizations that require only a few simple clicks of the mouse button.

This book uncovers Excel 97's hard-to-find features and tells how to eliminate the annoyances of data analysis. It shows how to easily retrieve data from the Web, details step-by-step construction of a perfect toolbar, includes tips for working around the most annoying gotchas of auditing, and shows how to use VBA to control Excel in powerful ways.

Office 97 Annoyances

By Woody Leonhard, Lee Hudspeth & T.J. Lee
1st Edition October 1997
396 pages, ISBN 1-56592-310-3

Despite marked improvements from version to version, much in Office 97 remains annoying. Two dozen shortcuts are scattered on the Start menu in no apparent order; the Shortcut Bar is filled with an overwhelming number of applications; and many hidden gems are tucked away in various places on the Office 97 CD. *Office 97 Annoyances* illustrates step-by-step how to get control over the chaotic settings of Office 97 and shows how to turn the vast array of applications into a simplified list of customized tools ready to execute whatever task they've been designed for.

This book shows you how to:

- Configure the Office Shortcut Bar to provide an effective tool for accessing Office applications and documents
- Customize the toolbar of each Office application except Outlook
- Use Visual Basic for Applications (VBA) as a macro language to control the behavior of the individual Office components
- Control pan-Office "sticky" settings

How to stay in touch with O'Reilly

1. Visit Our Award-Winning Site

http://www.oreilly.com/

★ "Top 100 Sites on the Web" —*PC Magazine*
★ "Top 5% Web sites" —*Point Communications*
★ "3-Star site" —*The McKinley Group*

Our web site contains a library of comprehensive product information (including book excerpts and tables of contents), downloadable software, background articles, interviews with technology leaders, links to relevant sites, book cover art, and more. File us in your Bookmarks or Hotlist!

2. Join Our Email Mailing Lists

New Product Releases

To receive automatic email with brief descriptions of all new O'Reilly products as they are released, send email to:
listproc@online.oreilly.com
Put the following information in the first line of your message (*not* in the Subject field):
subscribe oreilly-news

O'Reilly Events

If you'd also like us to send information about trade show events, special promotions, and other O'Reilly events, send email to:
listproc@online.oreilly.com
Put the following information in the first line of your message (*not* in the Subject field):
subscribe oreilly-events

3. Get Examples from Our Books via FTP

There are two ways to access an archive of example files from our books:

Regular FTP

- ftp to:
  ftp.oreilly.com
  (login: anonymous
  password: your email address)
- Point your web browser to:
  ftp://ftp.oreilly.com/

FTPMAIL

- Send an email message to:
  ftpmail@online.oreilly.com
  (Write "help" in the message body)

4. Contact Us via Email

order@oreilly.com
To place a book or software order online. Good for North American and international customers.

subscriptions@oreilly.com
To place an order for any of our newsletters or periodicals.

books@oreilly.com
General questions about any of our books.

software@oreilly.com
For general questions and product information about our software. Check out O'Reilly Software Online at **http://software.oreilly.com/** for software and technical support information. Registered O'Reilly software users send your questions to: **website-support@oreilly.com**

cs@oreilly.com
For answers to problems regarding your order or our products.

booktech@oreilly.com
For book content technical questions or corrections.

proposals@oreilly.com
To submit new book or software proposals to our editors and product managers.

international@oreilly.com
For information about our international distributors or translation queries. For a list of our distributors outside of North America check out:
http://www.oreilly.com/www/order/country.html

O'Reilly & Associates, Inc.
101 Morris Street, Sebastopol, CA 95472 USA
TEL   707-829-0515 or 800-998-9938
        (6am to 5pm PST)
FAX   707-829-0104

Titles from O'Reilly

Please note that upcoming titles are displayed in italic.

WEB PROGRAMMING
Apache: The Definitive Guide
Building Your Own Web
  Conferences
Building Your Own Website
Building Your Own Win-CGI
  Programs
CGI Programming for the World
  Wide Web
Designing for the Web
HTML: The Definitive Guide
JavaScript: The Definitive Guide,
  2nd Ed.
Learning Perl
Programming Perl, 2nd Ed.
Mastering Regular Expressions
WebMaster in a Nutshell
Web Security & Commerce
Web Client Programming with
  Perl
World Wide Web Journal

USING THE INTERNET
Smileys
The Future Does Not Compute
The Whole Internet User's Guide
  & Catalog
The Whole Internet for Win 95
Using Email Effectively
Bandits on the Information
  Superhighway

JAVA SERIES
Exploring Java
Java AWT Reference
Java Fundamental Classes
  Reference
Java in a Nutshell
Java Language Reference
Java Network Programming
Java Threads
Java Virtual Machine

SOFTWARE
WebSite™ 1.1
WebSite Professional™
Building Your Own Web
  Conferences
WebBoard™
PolyForm™
Statisphere™

SONGLINE GUIDES
NetActivism   NetResearch
Net Law   NetSuccess
NetLearning   NetTravel
Net Lessons

SYSTEM ADMINISTRATION
Building Internet Firewalls
Computer Crime: A Crimefighter's
  Handbook
Computer Security Basics
DNS and BIND, 2nd Ed.
Essential System Administration,
  2nd Ed.
Getting Connected: The Internet
  at 56K and Up
*Internet Server Administration
  with Windows NT*
Linux Network Administrator's
  Guide
Managing Internet Information
  Services
Managing NFS and NIS
Networking Personal Computers
  with TCP/IP
Practical UNIX & Internet
  Security. 2nd Ed.
PGP: Pretty Good Privacy
sendmail, 2nd Ed.
sendmail Desktop Reference
System Performance Tuning
TCP/IP Network Administration
termcap & terminfo
Using & Managing UUCP
Volume 8: X Window System
  Administrator's Guide
Web Security & Commerce

UNIX
Exploring Expect
Learning VBScript
Learning GNU Emacs, 2nd Ed.
Learning the bash Shell
Learning the Korn Shell
Learning the UNIX Operating
  System
Learning the vi Editor
Linux in a Nutshell
Making TeX Work
Linux Multimedia Guide
Running Linux, 2nd Ed.
SCO UNIX in a Nutshell
sed & awk, 2nd Edition
Tcl/Tk Tools
UNIX in a Nutshell: System V
  Edition
UNIX Power Tools
Using csh & tsch
When You Can't Find Your UNIX
  System Administrator
Writing GNU Emacs Extensions

WEB REVIEW STUDIO SERIES
Gif Animation Studio
Shockwave Studio

WINDOWS
Dictionary of PC Hardware and
  Data Communications Terms
Inside the Windows 95 Registry
Inside the Windows 95 File
  System
Windows Annoyances
Windows NT File System Internals
Windows NT in a Nutshell

PROGRAMMING
Advanced Oracle PL/SQL
  Programming
Applying RCS and SCCS
C++: The Core Language
Checking C Programs with lint
DCE Security Programming
Distributing Applications Across
  DCE & Windows NT
Encyclopedia of Graphics File
  Formats, 2nd Ed.
Guide to Writing DCE
  Applications
lex & yacc
Managing Projects with make
Mastering Oracle Power Objects
Oracle Design: The Definitive
  Guide
Oracle Performance Tuning, 2nd
  Ed.
Oracle PL/SQL Programming
Porting UNIX Software
POSIX Programmer's Guide
POSIX.4: Programming for the
  Real World
Power Programming with RPC
Practical C Programming
Practical C++ Programming
Programming Python
Programming with curses
Programming with GNU Software
Pthreads Programming
Software Portability with imake,
  2nd Ed.
Understanding DCE
Understanding Japanese
  Information Processing
UNIX Systems Programming for
  SVR4

BERKELEY 4.4 SOFTWARE DISTRIBUTION
4.4BSD System Manager's Manual
4.4BSD User's Reference Manual
4.4BSD User's Supplementary
  Documents
4.4BSD Programmer's Reference
  Manual
4.4BSD Programmer's
  Supplementary Documents
X Programming
Vol. 0: X Protocol Reference
  Manual
Vol. 1: Xlib Programming Manual
Vol. 2: Xlib Reference Manual
Vol. 3M: X Window System User's
  Guide, Motif Edition
Vol. 4M: X Toolkit Intrinsics
  Programming Manual, Motif
  Edition
Vol. 5: X Toolkit Intrinsics
  Reference Manual
Vol. 6A: Motif Programming
  Manual
Vol. 6B: Motif Reference Manual
Vol. 6C: Motif Tools
Vol. 8 : X Window System
  Administrator's Guide
Programmer's Supplement for
  Release 6
X User Tools
The X Window System in a
  Nutshell

CAREER & BUSINESS
Building a Successful Software
  Business
The Computer User's Survival
  Guide
Love Your Job!
Electronic Publishing on CD-ROM

TRAVEL
Travelers' Tales: Brazil
Travelers' Tales: Food
Travelers' Tales: France
Travelers' Tales: Gutsy Women
Travelers' Tales: India
Travelers' Tales: Mexico
Travelers' Tales: Paris
Travelers' Tales: San Francisco
Travelers' Tales: Spain
Travelers' Tales: Thailand
Travelers' Tales: A Woman's
  World

O'REILLY™

TO ORDER: **800-998-9938** • order@oreilly.com • http://www.oreilly.com/
OUR PRODUCTS ARE AVAILABLE AT A BOOKSTORE OR SOFTWARE STORE NEAR YOU.
FOR INFORMATION: **800-998-9938** • **707-829-0515** • info@oreilly.com

International Distributors

UK, EUROPE, MIDDLE EAST AND NORTHERN AFRICA (except France, Germany, Switzerland, & Austria)

INQUIRIES
International Thomson Publishing Europe
Berkshire House
168-173 High Holborn
London WC1V 7AA, UK
Telephone: 44-171-497-1422
Fax: 44-171-497-1426
Email: itpint@itps.co.uk

ORDERS
International Thomson Publishing
Services, Ltd.
Cheriton House, North Way
Andover, Hampshire SP10 5BE,
United Kingdom
Telephone: 44-264-342-832 (UK)
Telephone: 44-264-342-806 (outside UK)
Fax: 44-264-364418 (UK)
Fax: 44-264-342761 (outside UK)
UK & Eire orders: itpuk@itps.co.uk
International orders: itpint@itps.co.uk

FRANCE

Editions Eyrolles
61 bd Saint-Germain
75240 Paris Cedex 05
France
Fax: 33-01-44-41-11-44

FRENCH LANGUAGE BOOKS
All countries except Canada
Telephone: 33-01-44-41-46-16
Email: geodif@eyrolles.com

ENGLISH LANGUAGE BOOKS
Telephone: 33-01-44-41-11-87
Email: distribution@eyrolles.com

GERMANY, SWITZERLAND, AND AUSTRIA

INQUIRIES
O'Reilly Verlag
Balthasarstr. 81
D-50670 Köln
Germany
Telephone: 49-221-97-31-60-0
Fax: 49-221-97-31-60-8
Email: anfragen@oreilly.de

ORDERS
International Thomson Publishing
Königswinterer Straße 418
53227 Bonn, Germany
Telephone: 49-228-97024 0
Fax: 49-228-441342
Email: order@oreilly.de

JAPAN

O'Reilly Japan, Inc.
Kiyoshige Building 2F
12-Banchi, Sanei-cho
Shinjuku-ku
Tokyo 160 Japan
Tel: 81-3-3356-5227
Fax: 81-3-3356-5261
Email: kenji@oreilly.com

INDIA

Computer Bookshop (India) PVT. LTD.
190 Dr. D.N. Road, Fort
Bombay 400 001 India
Tel: 91-22-207-0989
Fax: 91-22-262-3551
Email: cbsbom@giasbm01.vsnl.net.in

HONG KONG

City Discount Subscription Service Ltd.
Unit D, 3rd Floor, Yan's Tower
27 Wong Chuk Hang Road
Aberdeen, Hong Kong
Telephone: 852-2580-3539
Fax: 852-2580-6463
Email: citydis@ppn.com.hk

KOREA

Hanbit Publishing, Inc.
Sonyoung Bldg. 202
Yeksam-dong 736-36
Kangnam-ku
Seoul, Korea
Telephone: 822-554-9610
Fax: 822-556-0363
Email: hant93@chollian.dacom.co.kr

TAIWAN

ImageArt Publishing, Inc.
4/fl. No. 65 Shinyi Road Sec. 4
Taipei, Taiwan, R.O.C.
Telephone: 886-2708-5770
Fax: 886-2705-6690
Email: marie@ms1.hinet.net

SINGAPORE, MALAYSIA, THAILAND

Longman Singapore
25 First Lok Yan Road
Singapore 2262
Telephone: 65-268-2666
Fax: 65-268-7023
Email: db@longman.com.sg

PHILIPPINES

Mutual Books, Inc.
429-D Shaw Boulevard
Mandaluyong City, Metro
Manila, Philippines
Telephone: 632-725-7538
Fax: 632-721-3056
Email: mbikikog@mnl.sequel.net

CHINA

Ron's DataCom Co., Ltd.
79 Dongwu Avenue
Dongxihu District
Wuhan 430040
China
Telephone: 86-27-3892568
Fax: 86-27-3222108
Email: hongfeng@public.wh.hb.cn

AUSTRALIA

WoodsLane Pty. Ltd.
7/5 Vuko Place, Warriewood NSW 2102
P.O. Box 935,
Mona Vale NSW 2103
Australia
Telephone: 61-2-9970-5111
Fax: 61-2-9970-5002
Email: info@woodslane.com.au

ALL OTHER ASIA COUNTRIES

O'Reilly & Associates, Inc.
101 Morris Street
Sebastopol, CA 95472 USA
Telephone: 707-829-0515
Fax: 707-829-0104
Email: order@oreilly.com

THE AMERICAS

McGraw-Hill Interamericana Editores,
S.A. de C.V.
Cedro No. 512
Col. Atlampa 06450
Mexico, D.F.
Telephone: 52-5-541-3155
Fax: 52-5-541-4913
Email: mcgraw-hill@infosel.net.mx

SOUTHERN AFRICA

International Thomson Publishing
Southern Africa
Building 18, Constantia Park
138 Sixteenth Road
P.O. Box 2459
Halfway House, 1685 South Africa
Tel: 27-11-805-4819
Fax: 27-11-805-3648

O'REILLY™